Parties, Political Finance,

A major challenge for the advancement of democratic governance in Africa is the extraction of money by ruling parties from the state to fund their electoral campaigns and gain political advantage over opponents. Drawing upon in-depth case studies of Benin and Ghana, Rachel Sigman considers how, and with what consequences, party leaders control and access public funds to finance their political operations. Weaving together biographical data on government ministers, surveys of civil servants, elite interviews, and archival research, Sigman explains leaders' extraction strategies and connects these strategies to how politicians manage state personnel. In so doing, she challenges the perception of African states as uniformly weak and argues that effective government is possible even in contexts of widespread state politicization, corruption, and clientelism. Demonstrating the profound impact that extractive financing practices have on democratic institutions, Sigman illuminates and develops our understanding of "good governance" across the African continent.

Rachel Sigman is Assistant Professor of Democratic Governance at the Josef Korbel School of International Studies at the University of Denver and Project Manager with the Varieties of Democracy (V-Dem) Institute at the University of Gothenburg. She previously served as Assistant Professor at the Naval Postgraduate School.

Parties, Political Finance, and Governance in Africa

Extracting Money and Shaping States in Benin and Ghana

Rachel Sigman

Josef Korbel School of International Studies, University of Denver

Shaftesbury Road, Cambridge CB2 8EA, United Kingdom

One Liberty Plaza, 20th Floor, New York, NY 10006, USA

477 Williamstown Road, Port Melbourne, VIC 3207, Australia

314–321, 3rd Floor, Plot 3, Splendor Forum, Jasola District Centre, New Delhi – 110025, India

103 Penang Road, #05–06/07, Visioncrest Commercial, Singapore 238467

Cambridge University Press is part of Cambridge University Press & Assessment, a department of the University of Cambridge.

We share the University's mission to contribute to society through the pursuit of education, learning and research at the highest international levels of excellence.

www.cambridge.org
Information on this title: www.cambridge.org/9781009262828

DOI: 10.1017/9781009262798

First published 2023
First paperback edition 2024

A catalogue record for this publication is available from the British Library

ISBN   978-1-009-26283-5   Hardback
ISBN   978-1-009-26282-8   Paperback

Contents

Figures

Tables

Acknowledgments

I am deeply grateful to the many individuals and institutions that supported me during the many years (!) in which I was developing this book. First and foremost, I offer my deepest gratitude to the thousands of bureaucrats and politicians in Benin and Ghana who participated in the interviews, surveys, and focus groups that I conducted throughout the course of the project. The book is made possible by their generosity, insight, and honesty.

It was only with the support of wonderful colleagues and friends that I was able to overcome the many challenges I encountered in the field. In Ghana, I am greatly indebted to Professor E. K. Sakyi who welcomed me as a visiting researcher in the Department of Public Administration at the University of Ghana Business School (UGBS) in 2013–2014. My time there was greatly enriched by the department's faculty, especially Daniel Appiah and Abdul-Gafaru Abdulai, with whom I spent many hours discussing research, politics, academic careers, family, and much more. At UGBS, I also benefited from Portia Twerefoo's research assistance. Without her diligence, the Classroom survey that forms a large basis of the empirical material in the book would not have been possible. In George Bob-Milliar, I found a wonderful colleague and friend whose research on Ghanaian political parties exerts much influence on the argument I develop throughout the book. The silver lining of Air Cote d'Ivoire's terrible service was meeting Paul Opoku-Mensah, who shared wonderful insights about Ghanaian politics and connected me with his many accomplished colleagues and friends. Anita Daniels, Innocent Fiagbe, Akosua Kuranchie, and Ernest Opoku also provided excellent research assistance at various points during the project. Last but not least, the Otu family and Bertha Asabiya always made sure I had a roof over my head and a hot meal to eat.

In Benin, I am most grateful to Kassim Assouma, Agnes Badou, and Cyriaque Edon who were always willing to spend time with me to provide guidance on my research, help with translation, or share their insights into Beninese politics and governance. Two talented and dedicated research assistants – Monel Sakponou and Charif Zimé – traipsed all over the country with me to collect biographical data on ministers and administer the Classroom survey. Hyacinthe Koudhorot not only welcomed me into the meticulously kept archives at La Nation but also provided wonderful guidance for much of my research in Benin. Thanks to Stephanie Rochatte and the welcoming team at Guesthouse Cocotiers, I always had a comfortable and convenient place to stay in Cotonou. I was lucky to have met Eric Degila in Mozambique in 2014. Eric has been instrumental in helping me to better understand life and politics in Benin.

The second survey of bureaucrats that I conducted in Ghana was made possible by the vision and dedication of Jan Meyer-Sahling, Christian Schuster, and Kim Sass Mikkelsen. I am extremely grateful for their willingness to include me in the project. Not only did this survey enable me to greatly enrich the empirical evidence in the book, but I learned a lot about survey research from working with their team of collaborators, which also included Adam Harris and Brigitte Seim. Of course, the survey would not have been possible without funding from the UK's Department for International Development (DFID) and the British Academy, support from Ghana's Public Services Commission, as well as a team of talented Ghanaian enumerators led by Leonard Anaman, Abdul-Gafaru Abdulai, and Daniel Appiah. Special thanks to Valeriya Mechkova for traveling with me to Ghana and helping to manage the early stages of the survey.

This book began as my dissertation project at Syracuse University where I was fortunate to have a tremendously supportive dissertation committee. Hans Peter Schmitz stuck with me even as the project kept deviating further and further away from his own interests and expertise. His astute guidance and responsiveness throughout the process helped to propel me past each successive hurdle. Three classes with Matt Cleary early in the graduate program helped me to anticipate any possible challenge to my research, making me a stronger thinker, writer, and presenter. Jon Hanson has always showed confidence in my abilities and encouraged me to build up my methodological skills in ways that have made me a more proficient and confident researcher. I am grateful to Brian Taylor for his honesty and attention to detail in reviewing my work and for always ensuring that I have the relevant literature covered. I am delighted that Dominika Koter was able to join the committee. Her insights into party mobilization and financing in Benin were extremely useful in the development of the project.

From my initial recruitment trip to Syracuse, I always felt well supported by the Political Science community at the Maxwell School. Thanks to Candy Brooks, Jacquie Meyer, and Sally Greenfield for making the department an efficient and welcoming place to pursue a PhD. I am especially grateful to Tom Keck and Kristi Andersen for the interest they took in my progress and their willingness to offer support and guidance throughout. Many faculty members in the department have read and offered useful comments on my work, among them are Seth Jolly, Dimitar Gueorguiev, Chris Faricy, and Spencer Piston. I am equally grateful for the support and fellowship from the community of political science graduate students. Mike Beckstrand, Keneshia Grant, and Sean Miskell were particularly apt at helping to make light of the peculiar trials and tribulations of what Keneshia affectionately called "PhD School."

I conducted part of my research for this book while serving as a postdoctoral fellow at the Varieties of Democracy (V-Dem) Institute in the Department of Political Science at the University of Gothenburg. I am extremely grateful to Staffan Lindberg for the tremendous support he provided during my time there, helping me to hone my research skills and connect with many colleagues across the discipline. It was also such a treat to work alongside someone with such rich knowledge of Ghanaian politics. At the University of Gothenburg, I benefited tremendously from feedback I received from fellow postdocs including Ruth Carlitz, Adam Harris, Kristen Kao, Anna Lührmann, Kyle Marquardt, Constanza Sanhueza, and Steven Wilson; and from the wonderful community of scholars associated with the Quality of Government Institute, who welcomed me to their seminars and workshops, including Monika Bauhr, Carl Dählstrom, Marcia Grimes, Victor Lapuente, and Marina Nistotskaya.

At the Naval Postgraduate School (NPS), I was lucky to have yet another group of wonderful colleagues. Much to my benefit, Naazneen Barma, Mariana Giusti-Rodríguez, and Jessica Piombo engaged substantively with the manuscript. Many others, including Anne Marie Baylouny, Chris Darnton, Ryan Gingeras, Mohammed Hafez, Michael Malley, Alex Matovski, Emily Meierding, Covell Meyskens, Clay Moltz, Afshon Ostovar, Maria Rasmussen, and Chris Twomey, provided guidance and motivation (or both) in navigating the research, writing, and publishing processes. Thanks also to Jason Altwies, Cat Grant, Eric Hovey, and Chris Ketponglard for various types of administrative and research support along the way. I am also lucky to have taught such smart and dedicated students in the 681-Africa curriculum at NPS, which enabled me to deepen my knowledge of, and reflect on, many of the issues that lie at the core of this book.

I received valuable feedback on parts of the manuscript from audiences at various venues including the American Political Science Association (APSA) Africa Workshop in Maputo, Mozambique, the University of Florida, the University of Gothenburg, the University of North Carolina (Chapel Hill), Syracuse University, the NPS and the APSA and Midwest Political Science Association (MPSA) annual meetings. I owe special thanks to Leo Arriola, Naazneen Barma, George Bob-Milliar, Mariana Giusti-Rodríguez, Anna Grzymała-Busse, and Martha Johnson for the incredibly helpful direction they provided at my book workshop. The manuscript really began to take shape after their extremely thoughtful and constructive engagement with it. I am especially indebted to Martha and Mariana, whose continued engagement led (in my opinion) to some of the book's most important insights. I also thank Sarah Brierley, Barry Driscoll, Sebastian Elischer, Nicholas Kerr, Mai Hassan, Amanda Pinkston, and Anne Pitcher, and Rachel Riedl for providing feedback and ideas at various stages of the project. Finally, I am grateful to the two Cambridge reviewers. Their detailed comments enabled me to greatly improve the manuscript.

None of this would have been possible without my family and friends, whose support over many years has enabled me to pursue an academic and research-focused career in the first place. Shawn Butler has not only held down the fort during the many months that I have spent away from home in pursuit of my career, but was always prepared with an amazing meal or something fun in the works when it was time for a break. Many friends have been there for me with shelter, food, airport transportation, or whatever I needed at any particular moment. Dave and Debbie Kladney, Belinda Morris, Tony Brunello, Sudeep Chandra, Scott Attinger, and Debra-Ellen Glickstein have been especially supportive in my times of need. I owe much to my sister Laura, who has always served as a role model and inspiration for me and who, during one memorable visit sometime after I graduated from college, effectively told me to stop f-ing around and go to graduate school! I am most grateful to my parents, David and Diane, who always prioritized my education above all else and have always supported the (sometimes unconventional) paths that I have taken.

List of Abbreviations

ADB African Development Bank
ANC African National Congress
AU African Union
AU African Union
BCEAO *Banque Centrale des Etats de l'Afrique de l'Ouest*
BDP Botswana Democratic Party
CCM *Chama Cha Mapinduzi*
CHRAJ Commission on Human Rights and Administrative Justice
CPP Convention People's Party
CSO Civil Society Organization
DFP Democratic Freedom Party
DPP Democratic Progress Party
DWM 31st December Women's Movement
ENAM *Ecole Nationale d'Administration et Magistrature*
EPRDF Ethiopian People's Revolutionary Democratic Front
FAO Food and Agriculture Organization
FARD-Alafia *Front d'Action pour le Renouveau, la Démocratie et le Développement*
FCBE *Force cauris pour un Bénin émergent*
FCPA Foreign Corrupt Practices Act
GNPC Ghana National Petroleum Company
HHI Herfindahl–Hirschman Index
IFAD International Fund for Agricultural Development
IMF International Monetary Fund
IRT item response theory
KANU Kenya African National Union
MADEP *Mouvement africain pour la développement et le progrés*
MDAs ministries, departments, and agencies
MMDCE Metropolitan, Municipal, District Chief Executive
MP member of parliament
MPLA *Movimento Popular de Libertação de Angola*

NDC National Democratic Congress
NDI National Democratic Institute
NHIP National Health Insurance Program
NLM National Liberation Movement
NPP National Patriotic Party
NRM National Resistance Movement
PDS *Parti Démocratique Sénégalais*
PNDC People's National Democratic Congress
PP Progress Party
PPA Public Procurement Authority
PR proportional representation
PRD *Parti du renouveau démocratique*
PRPB *Parti de la Révolution Populaire du Bénin*
PS Parti Socialiste
PSI party system institutionalization
PSM Public Service Motivation
RB *Renaissance du Bénin*
RPF Rwandan Patriotic Front
TANU Tanganyika African National Union
TI Transparency International
UDF United Democratic Front
UGCC United Gold Coast Convention
UPD *Union Progressiste Dahoméenne*
YEF Young Executive Forum

1   The Politics of Extraction

One of the major challenges for the advancement of democratic governance in Africa and throughout the world is that political leaders regularly extract resources from the state to gain political advantages over their opponents. This practice undermines democratic competition, threatens the rule of law, and weakens the capacity of state institutions. It is a common challenge across different political contexts: in authoritarian regimes where incumbents use state resources to maintain hegemonic power over their opponents, in newer democracies struggling to eliminate earlier authoritarian abuses of power, and, to a growing extent, in established democracies experiencing an erosion of their democratic institutions.[1] The question of how to constrain leaders from using state resources to entrench their political power is what at least one observer has called "*the* core democratic dilemma of the early twenty-first century."[2]

Perhaps nowhere is the extraction of state resources more central to existing models of politics than in Africa. Political competition across African countries is widely viewed as a contest over access to the state and its resources.[3] Once in power, incumbent leaders make good on their political promises by using state power to distribute patronage to their political networks.[4] They survive in office by co-opting those that threaten their political survival: granting opponents positions from which they too can extract resources from the state,[5] so long as these practices do not seriously undermine the incumbent's grip on power.[6]

---

[1] On authoritarian regimes, see Magaloni (2006); Greene (2007). On incumbent exploitation of the state in new democracies, see Geddes (1994); O'Dwyer (2006); Grzymała-Busse (2007), and in established democracies, see Levitsky and Ziblatt (2018: 79).

[2] Gingerich (2013: 1).

[3] Bayart (1993); Bratton and van de Walle (1997).

[4] Joseph (1987); Chabal and Daloz (1999).

[5] Widner (1992); Arriola (2009).

[6] Roessler (2016); Arriola et al. (2021*a*).

Whether in Africa or elsewhere, this extraction-based model of politics is associated with persistent and uniform state weakness. In "robbing the state of its revenues and developmental effectiveness," politically driven extraction erodes the human and material capacities of the state's executive and bureaucratic institutions.[7] Widespread political extraction undermines the ability of governments to commit credibly to public policies,[8] to meaningfully resolve distributional conflicts that arise in the face of political reform,[9] and to manage the state apparatus in ways that advance longer-term economic growth and welfare provision.[10] From this perspective, governing successes, if and when they do occur, are attributed largely to anomalous "pockets of effectiveness," where bureaucrats are granted the professional autonomy necessary to effectively implement public policies.[11]

What this model of political extraction tends to overlook, however, is that the processes of extraction are themselves varied, contentious, and constrained. In Indonesia, political parties compete with bureaucrats and military personnel to secure extractable state funds.[12] In Nigeria, politicians seeking office compete for funds from political brokers, widely known as "godfathers," many of whom have profited from past or present positions in government or parastatal organizations.[13] In India, politicians at different levels of government extract political funds in ways that depend on the rents available to them and the broader power structures in which they operate.[14] In Argentina, politicians depend on bureaucrats to collect bribes, especially in the weeks leading up to an election.[15] And, similarly, in the United States in the nineteenth and early twentieth centuries, party bosses widely sought to place supporters in government jobs where they could extract material and political benefits for the party in power.[16]

As these examples make clear, leaders do not simply and freely steal money from the state to finance their political operations, though that certainly does occur. Instead, they use a variety of strategies to access and control state money. These strategies involve different sets of state

[7] van de Walle (2001: 123).
[8] Pitcher (2012).
[9] Acemoglu and Robinson (2006).
[10] Bates (1981); Rose-Ackerman (1999); Guardado et al. (2018).
[11] On "pockets of effectiveness" or similar phenomena, see, for example, Roll (2014); Whitfield et al. (2015); McDonnell (2020).
[12] Mietzner (2007).
[13] Olarinmoye (2008: 67).
[14] Bussell (2012).
[15] Figueroa (2021).
[16] Skowronek (1982).

personnel, public organizations, and networks of extraction; all of which reflect an array of problems and choices that politicians face in the course of extraction. In short, the "politician's dilemma" for many leaders is not *whether* to exploit the state for their political advantage, but *how* to do so.[17]

This book is about how and with what consequences leaders extract money from the state for political financing. Through the course of the book, I explain why incumbent political leaders devise different strategies of extraction. I further document how leaders manage state institutions in ways that advance their favored political extraction strategies, illuminating why there is such varied performance in the implementation of public policies in contexts of extensive political extraction. The book contributes new insight into why political competition does not always produce more capable, effective, and responsive states.

1.1   The Concept of Political Extraction

The practice of political extraction has generated significant attention in studies of politics and development both in Africa and around the world. Many scholars have focused on the extent of political extraction and its implications for outcomes such as economic growth, democracy, and citizen well-being. I pursue a different approach in this book: I focus on variation in *how* leaders extract political money from the state. Because competitive and social pressures to extract are widespread in many African countries, and because institutional constraints on extraction are often weak, I assume that extraction is prevalent and focus instead on the methods of extraction that leaders employ.

I conceive of extraction as part of a broad set of practices in which politicians use state power and resources to advance their political interests. Such practices range in scope, legality, and normative acceptance. They include widely accepted practices such as the creation of laws and policies designed to generate an electoral benefit for those in power. They also include illicit acts such as the diversion of state resources to a politician's political purse, as well as government officials generating and collecting rents through their interactions with private actors, for example in the form of bribes or campaign donations. I view the exercise of state power for political gain as extractive when it involves the *removal* of resources from public or private domains and redirects them for private political benefit.

---

[17] The "politician's dilemma" is a reference to Barbara Geddes' (1994) book bearing that title.

Because I aim to explain variation in how politicians finance their parties and political campaigns, this study excludes leaders' efforts to extract for their own personal enrichment. Although the lines between political finance and personal enrichment are sometimes blurred, extraction for political finance often involves actors and political dynamics that are distinct from extraction that is motivated by personal gain. By narrowing the scope of this study to extraction for political finance, I eliminate analytical noise associated with politicians' personal proclivities for self-enrichment.

Moreover, I do not treat extraction as fundamentally corrupt. Corruption, commonly understood as the use of public resources for private benefit, implies behavior that deviates from established public interest norms and seeks to subvert existing rules.[18] The core theoretical concern of the literature on corruption is whether officials have incentives to break with established rules and norms. This concern with rule-breaking is often moot in contexts where leaders experience strong pressures to extract and where they face few immediate costs of doing so.[19] In such environments, leaders' concerns are less likely to focus on *whether* to engage in extraction, but rather on questions about *how* to extract in ways that mitigate the political risks involved. It is these questions about the politics of extraction that form the central focus of this book, guiding both the development of my theoretical argument and the empirical approaches I employ.

1.2   The Argument in Brief

Since the early 1990s, politics in many developing and postcommunist countries have become both more competitive and more expensive. Incumbents are considerably more likely to lose power through elections than they were in earlier decades. They must also spend increasingly large sums of money to compete.[20] Even in nonelection years, politicians often require vast sums of money to sustain their coalitions and political party organizations.[21] Although politicians across the world face challenges in raising money, those in African countries are especially disadvantaged in this regard. One major obstacle to fundraising is the

---

[18] Scott (1972); Mbaku (2000: 5). See Rose-Ackerman (1999: 7) and Kurer (2014) for reviews of this definition.
[19] Scott (1969); Olivier de Sardan (1999).
[20] For example: Weyland (1998); Norris and Van Es (2016); Wardle (2017); Kapur and Vaishnav (2018).
[21] Greene (2007); Arriola (2012).

clientelistic structure of politics: voters typically expect to receive material inducements from politicians rather than to provide any monetary or in-kind support to them.[22] Even where there are growing incomes and middle-class urban populations, clientelistic linkages in which voters expect to receive material benefits from politicians remain prevalent.[23]

In the absence of widespread supporter contributions, parties and candidates rely on a mix of other sources of financing. In Africa, public financing is formally available in around 70 percent of countries but, in practice, this support tends to be insufficient to cover campaign expenses.[24] Domestic business communities have historically comprised an important source of political finance in African countries, but high levels of informality in the private sector and weak financial institutions mean that they, too, have serious limitations in their reservoirs of potential funding.[25] Foreign multinational corporations looking to do business in African countries are also known to supply politicians with cash for their political operations.[26] Although potentially very lucrative, this source of funding is, at least to some extent, constrained by domestic laws that prohibit foreign political contributions, by international laws such as the US Foreign Corrupt Practices Act (FCPA) or by citizens and opposition parties who view foreign sources of money with great suspicion.[27]

Thus, in the face of both rising costs and limited fundraising opportunities outside of the state, politicians face serious obstacles in financing their political activities. Incumbents undoubtedly use the state and its resources to overcome these challenges. They do so by "extensively dipping into the state treasury for their own political needs," and by distributing state positions, services, and economic opportunities in exchange for material support for their political campaigns.[28] Incumbents further secure their own financial advantages by employing "financial reprisal regimes" – restricting opponents' access to state-controlled resources, finance, or other economic opportunities.[29]

Most scholarly accounts of extraction assume that incumbent leaders in Africa face few, if any, constraints in their efforts to extract political

---

[22] Kitschelt and Wilkinson (2007); Hicken (2011); Bussell (2019); Stokes et al. (N.d.).
[23] Nathan (2019).
[24] International IDEA (2019).
[25] For an overview of historical and contemporary business financing of politics, see Arriola (2012).
[26] Reno (1999).
[27] Molomo (2000).
[28] Bratton and van de Walle (1997: 66).
[29] Arriola (2012).

money from the state. Anecdotal accounts of repeated, egregious patterns of extraction by authoritarian leaders such as Mobutu Sese Seko in (then) Zaire and Teodoro Obiang in Equatorial Guinea have helped to perpetuate this view, as have major episodes of fraud and embezzlement that continue apace in many of Africa's more democratic countries, such as in South Africa under Jacob Zuma or in Kenya under Daniel Arap Moi. Although *institutional* constraints on political extraction remain weak in many countries, leaders face a range of *political* constraints in the course of extraction. First, leaders must keep extracted resources away from current or future opponents. Empowering opponents with access to state money undermines the advantages that leaders derive from incumbency and risks depleting the resources available for their policy or political agendas. Second, leaders must protect themselves from the risk of prosecution. In the increasingly likely event that they lose power, leaders and their families become vulnerable to prosecution, often politically motivated, for causing financial loss to the state. These quests for (political) justice have often involved newly installed leaders seeking to paralyze former leaders (or their close affiliates) by subjecting them to legal action, exile, or imprisonment.[30]

Incumbents therefore face a dilemma. They can mitigate the potential for future prosecution by delegating extraction to party agents and channeling extracted resources through more diffuse political networks, thus making extraction less visibly attributable to themselves. Delegation, however, magnifies the risk that extracted monies fall into the hands of political opponents, thereby jeopardizing their more immediate reelection prospects.

To understand how incumbent leaders navigate these politics of extraction, I focus on three specific challenges they face. First, leaders must consider *to whom* they can safely delegate extraction. Delegation to unreliable extraction agents can result in extracted resources falling into the hands of the opposition. Second, leaders must decide *how* they or their agents can best access state money and channel it to political coffers. Some channels of extraction may contain higher risks of leakage to the opposition as well as greater potential for future attribution to the incumbent leader. Third, political leaders must determine *which instruments of control* are available to ensure that extracted resources benefit their party.

How leaders address these challenges, I argue, is closely connected to the institutionalization of their political party. Institutionalized political parties are those with durability beyond a founding leader; coherent

---

[30] Tangri and Mwenda (2006); Lawson (2009).

internal rules and procedures; established roots in society; and collective identities, brands, and values.[31] Despite common conceptions of highly personalized forms of political organization in Africa, often with a "big man" at the center,[32] there is considerable variation in party institutions across African countries.[33]

1.2.1 *Party Institutions and Extraction*

The first part of my argument is that party institutionalization shapes leaders' responses to the three extraction problems: who to select as extraction agents, how to channel extractable resources, and which monitoring and discipline instruments can be used to control extracted monies. Leaders embedded in more institutionalized political parties can, with greater confidence, delegate extraction to party agents, channel resources through diffuse party networks, and rely on the party's internal instruments of monitoring and discipline. Party institutionalization therefore leads to more *collusive* strategies of extraction in which party agents work collectively to channel state money through supporter networks, enabling the incumbent leader to remain distant from extraction and evade attribution. A typical example of collusive extraction is when elite party agents, such as politically appointed ministers, award procurement contracts to party-affiliated businesses in exchange for kickbacks or material support for the party.

Leaders of parties with low levels of institutionalization, by contrast, rely on *coercive* extraction strategies. Fearing the defection of elites from the party, leaders eschew delegation of extraction to elite political agents. Instead they either manage extraction deals themselves, or co-opt or coerce more vulnerable actors, such as rank-and-file bureaucrats, whose compliance is more easily bought or coerced due to the attractiveness of their public sector jobs. Lacking stable party networks through which to channel resources, leaders concentrate their extraction efforts more intensely within state organizations, for example, by pressuring bureaucrats to collect rents or divert state revenues for the party. Leaders also

---

[31] Described in greater length in Chapter 2, this definition of party institutionalization draws on approaches developed by Mainwaring and Scully (1995); Randall and Svåsand (2002); Levitsky (2003); and Lupu (2016). Party institutionalization is related to, but not synonymous with, party system institutionalization (PSI). One principal difference between the two concepts is the unit of analysis. Whereas party institutionalization focuses on the characteristics of individual parties, PSI focuses on strategic interactions between parties.

[32] Jackson and Rosberg (1982).

[33] See Chapter 2 for a detailed discussion of this variation.

rely on more coercive means of control, such as threats of dismissal or transfer, to ensure that agents extract in service of the incumbent.

Why does the level of party institutionalization lead incumbents to pursue these different strategies of extraction? First, the durability and organization of institutionalized parties help leaders to identify and select loyal and competent extraction agents. Through repeated election cycles and internal party competition, leaders learn about the competencies and loyalties of party officers, especially elite members who have worked their way up the party hierarchy. Leaders in institutionalized political parties can, with relatively low levels of risk, delegate extraction to reliable agents. Absent durable and rule-bound party institutions that facilitate these learning processes, leaders of parties with low levels of institutionalization are unable to identify and select competent and loyal extraction agents, choosing instead to extract rents themselves or delegate extraction to more coercible agents, such as rank-and-file bureaucrats.

Thanks to their party's stronger roots in society, leaders of institutionalized parties are also better positioned to engage their party networks in extraction. They can channel money through partisan-aligned businesses or civil society organizations without fear that those organizations will use the extracted money to support opposition candidates or expose the party's extraction efforts. In the absence of robust partisan networks, leaders have a more limited set of choices about how to access and channel state money, thus generating stronger incentives to concentrate extraction within state organizations.

Finally, by shaping the incentives of agents to act in service of the incumbent, party institutions also condition which instruments leaders can use to maintain control over extracted resources. Party durability lengthens the time horizons for agents, generating incentives to serve the party's pecuniary and electoral interests. Strong internal organizations and collective values also incentivize agents to act in service of the party, as an agent's failure to do so may jeopardize their opportunities for advancement in the party. Absent durable, organized, and value-infused party institutions, agents are more likely to defect from the party or manage resources in ways that do not align with the incumbent's interests, driving incumbent leaders to use more coercive instruments to monitor and discipline agents.

This argument linking party institutions to extraction strategies, summarized under the heading "Extraction type" in Figure 1.1, implies that collusive and coercive modes of extraction emanate from two poles on a linear spectrum of party institutionalization. These two poles, however, do not exhaust the potential range of party institutionalization and extraction strategies. Instead, they are designed to build a framework to understand how party institutions shape leaders' choices about extraction. As I elaborate at greater length in Chapters 2 and 8, extraction in contexts of intermediate levels of party institutionalization may combine elements of collusive and coercive extraction. In other words, the argument can (and should) be adapted to alternative settings where party structures deviate from either the high or low levels of party institutionalization described here.

1.2.2   Extraction and State Politicization

The pursuit of these different extraction strategies implies important variation in the ways that governing party leaders strategically manage the state's personnel and organizations. More specifically, extraction methods shape how – and how much – leaders politicize the recruitment of state staff, the rotation of executive personnel, and the day-to-day business of bureaucratic organizations.[34] Although politicization occurs in *both* collusive and coercive systems, I argue that coercive extraction involves more intrusive forms of politicization that are, ultimately, more detrimental to the state's pursuit of public policy goals.

Since leaders in collusive systems rely to a greater extent on elite party agents, they are likely to place their party loyalists into high-level executive positions, particularly those that oversee major extraction opportunities. In relying on elite extraction agents who they have come to know through repeated cycles of both internal and external party competition, leaders in collusive systems encounter fewer agency problems, leading to relatively stable and cohesive executive cabinets. Collusive extraction also requires less intrusive forms of political monitoring and interference in the day-to-day workings of bureaucratic personnel, since bureaucrats remain largely marginal to the collusive extraction system.

The patterns of politicization in coercive extraction systems are quite different. Fearing defection by political elites, leaders in coercive systems of extraction are unlikely to place elite party or coalition members into executive positions with access to extraction, favoring instead the appointment of technocrats or personal loyalists. However, these technocrats and personal affiliates often lack the political know-how necessary to navigate a highly challenging and fluid political environment.

---

[34] Throughout the book, I distinguish between executive and bureaucratic levels of the state apparatus. The executive level includes the presidency, government ministers, and other elite-level positions. Bureaucratic institutions are organizations that employ career bureaucrats, that is, those that are neither political appointees nor temporary hires.

As such, leaders of coercive extraction systems frequently encounter agency problems that generate instability and undermine both their political and governing agendas.

Coercive extraction also politicizes and impairs bureaucratic institutions. In their efforts to co-opt rank-and-file bureaucrats as extraction agents, leaders in coercive systems more frequently apply political criteria in the recruitment of career bureaucrats, particularly to positions with access to rents and revenues. To effectively monitor and discipline their bureaucratic extraction agents, leaders are considerably more likely to interfere in the day-to-day work of bureaucratic agencies, threatening dismissal and other forms of reprisal for those who do not extract in service of the incumbent. These dynamics result in rather unproductive bureaucratic working environments.

Throughout the book, I explain how these patterns of politicization, summarized under the heading of "State politicization" in Figure 1.1, contribute to divergence in state institutional performance. Collusive extraction generates more cohesive, stable, and productive institutional environments where the simultaneous pursuit of both political and policy agendas is possible. The tactics involved in coercive extraction, by contrast, generate instability and mistrust within the executive in ways that undermine elites' commitment to policy agendas. Coercive extraction also leads to greater levels of politicization and interference in bureaucratic organizations, generating a work environment characterized by paralysis and low levels of employee motivation. Even if leaders using

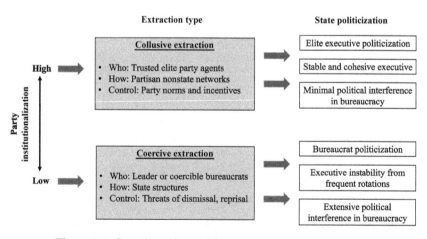

Figure 1.1 Overview of argument

coercive extraction strategies are serious about implementing their policy agendas, the dynamics involved in their extraction operations are likely to prove detrimental to that pursuit.

1.3   Alternative Explanations

Why, other than their party institutions, might incumbents pursue different extraction strategies? Existing literature in the areas of political economy, institutions, patronage, and corruption offer some potential alternative explanations for understanding why leaders adopt different strategies of extraction. In this section, I discuss five possible alternative or complementary hypotheses: opposition strength, economic structure, bureaucratic institutions, ethnic politics, and electoral systems. Ultimately, each of these hypotheses has important limitations in its ability to explain leaders' varied responses to the political risks involved in extraction.

1.3.1   Opposition Strength

A number of studies posit that more robust forms of competition involving strong opposition actors constrain politicians' efforts to exploit the state and its resources for political advantage. A stronger opposition party or coalition can force the ruling party into embracing more meritocratic forms of government[35] or raise the costs and lower the benefits for incumbents seeking to exploit the state for their political advantage.[36] Additionally, stronger opposition parties can better monitor their opponents, further constraining incumbents' efforts to extract.[37]

Applied to the question of *how* leaders extract from the state, it would be reasonable to expect that incumbents who are more secure in their power – those who face weaker oppositions – would extract in less circumspect (delegated) ways. One issue with this perspective is that, even among strong authoritarian leaders who face relatively weak oppositions, there is considerable uncertainty about the circumstances that might drive leaders from power or subject them to risks of prosecution once departed from office. Recent cases such as the prosecutions of Omar al-Bashir in Sudan, Jacob Zuma in South Africa, and Isabel dos Santos in Angola underscore these risks. Despite the very weak electoral opposition that their parties faced for much of their time in

---

[35] Geddes (1994).
[36] Grzymała-Busse (2007).
[37] O'Dwyer (2006).

office, these former leaders have been subject to legal charges, raising serious questions about whether dominant party leaders are as
unconstrained in their extraction practices as much of the literature
assumes.

Additionally, in contexts where most (or all) parties depend on state
resources for political survival, opposition parties are considerably less
likely to engage in efforts to limit opportunities for extraction. In these
contexts, high levels of political competition often generate considerable
pressure for both incumbent and opposition parties to exploit the state[38]
and voters are unlikely to punish extracting politicians at the polls.[39]
Whether the opposition is strong enough to defeat the ruling party in
elections – or monitor their behavior in office – would therefore have
little bearing on the specific extraction strategies that leaders employ,
particularly in the highly extractive contexts I study in this book (see
Chapter 3).

1.3.2   Economic Structure

Literature in political economy suggests that leaders would select their
extraction strategies based on the economic resources and opportunities available to them. From this perspective, if economic production
is more abundant, more diverse, or more dispersed throughout society, leaders will pursue extraction strategies that, for example, involve
larger networks of individuals and private sector channels of extraction. By contrast, if the economy is smaller, less diverse, and centrally
managed by the state, leaders will opt for extraction strategies that are
concentrated among a smaller group.[40] According to this body of work,
leaders devise their extraction strategies in accordance with the structure
of revenue-generating economic sectors and select extraction tactics that
are conditioned by sector-specific governing structures.[41]

Economic structure alone, however, is unlikely to fully account for
leaders' decisions about how they delegate, channel, and control extraction. Consider, for instance, oil-rich countries such as Angola, Gabon,
and Nigeria, all of which have much of their country's economic power
concentrated among a small number of public and private oil sector
actors. Ruling parties in all three countries are known to rely on extracted

---

[38] Kopecký (2011); Asunka (2016); Driscoll (2018); Pierskalla and Sacks (2020).
[39] Bauhr and Charron (2018); Pavão (2018).
[40] David Kang's (2002) account of cronyism in the Philippines and South Korea
embodies this approach.
[41] For example: Krueger (1974); Keefer and Knack (2007); Caselli and Cunningham
(2009); Ross (2012).

oil rents to sustain their power, yet leaders have devised very different institutional frameworks and tactics for extraction. In Angola, the ruling *Movimento Popular de Libertação de Angola* (MPLA) has largely used Sonangol, the massive state oil company, to manage oil revenue in ways that collectively benefit the party and the ruling family.[42] In Gabon, the ruling Bongo family and their *Partie Démocratique Gabonais* have channeled money through the supranational Bank of Central African States to supply money to their own political coffers as well as to those of French politicians who, in turn, help to prop up the regime.[43] In Nigeria, extraction occurs at multiple steps in the oil production and management process,[44] with especially large diversions of funds occurring at the stage where oil revenues are transferred from the Nigerian National Petroleum Company to the central government budget.[45] As illustrated by these examples, economic conditions alone cannot easily foretell the more granular decisions involved in the practice of extraction.

More generally, explanations based on economic opportunities are likely to be limited in contexts where leaders possess considerable power to fashion economic production and institutions for their political benefit. Political leaders in African countries have proven themselves adept at managing the economy in ways that secure opportunities for political extraction and exploitation. For example, politicians have favored spending in urban areas where state agents can more easily access rents,[46] they have adapted structural adjustment and privatization reforms to serve their extractive political needs,[47] and they have often managed key economic sectors in ways that attract and maintain political support by allowing key coalition members to extract revenues for their own benefit.[48] These widely documented practices suggest that economic structures are, more often than not, endogenous to elite political interest.

1.3.3 Bureaucratic Institutions

Central to institutional theories of corruption, bureaucratic institutions require careful consideration as a potential explanation of incumbent extraction strategies. Like economic structure, the structure and rules of

[42] De Oliveira (2015); Croese (2017).
[43] Yasmine Ryan, "Gabon 'Siphoned Funds' to France," Aljazeera, December 29, 2010.
[44] Barma et al. (2012).
[45] See, for example, Nshira Turkson, "The Nigerian Oil Company's Missing Billions," The Atlantic, March 18, 2016.
[46] Bates (1981).
[47] Mbaku (1994); Tangri (1999); van de Walle (2001); Pitcher (2012).
[48] Bayart (1993); Lewis (2007); Whitfield et al. (2015).

the state's bureaucracy could shape bureaucrats' incentives to participate in extraction as well as politicians' incentives to collude with or coerce bureaucrats.

There are a number of channels through which bureaucratic institutions could shape incumbents' extraction strategies. First, professional bureaucracies – those characterized by meritocratic selection and promotion, job security, adequate salaries, and norms of political neutrality – are more likely to be staffed by bureaucrats committed to professional principles and public service, making them less willing to participate in extraction.[49] This constraint implies that, in the presence of more professional bureaucratic institutions, leaders would need to expend more resources – or use more coercive tactics – to compel bureaucrats to participate in extraction.

Discretion is another important feature of bureaucratic institutions. High levels of discretion may incentivize bureaucrats to engage in extraction, either for themselves or on behalf of a political principal.[50] If bureaucratic institutions characterized by high levels of discretion permit widespread extraction, leaders would presumably have strong incentives to capture the rents collected by bureaucrats – and to employ coercive strategies to do so.[51]

This leads the discussion to a third potentially important institutional feature of bureaucracies: the existence of effective monitoring and sanction mechanisms that enable politicians to control bureaucrats. Depending on the political principal's motivation, monitoring and sanctions could be used to deter bureaucrats from engaging in extraction at all[52] or to ensure that extracted rents accrue to the principal.[53] These institutional mechanisms of control can take different forms: power over personnel management decisions, formal audits, partisan political appointees placed in bureaucratic agencies, or the use of legislative or judicial powers to oversee the bureaucracy. These control mechanisms would enable politicians to pursue more coercive strategies of extraction at lower costs.

Taken together, these perspectives imply that bureaucratic institutions characterized by low levels of professionalism, widespread bureaucratic discretion, and high levels of political control would drive leaders to adopt more coercive strategies of extraction. The strength of this

---

[49] See, for example, Rose-Ackerman (1999: 69–70).
[50] Klitgaard (1988).
[51] Shleifer and Vishny (1993).
[52] Olken (2007); Avis, Ferraz, and Finan (2018).
[53] Shleifer and Vishny (1993).

explanation hinges on two questions. First, does this configuration of bureaucratic institutions also discourage leaders from engaging in more collusive forms of extraction? It is plausible that the same institutional instruments of control that political leaders employ to capture rents from bureaucrats could be used to pursue collusive extraction strategies, such as by hiring and placing trusted agents (assuming they exist) into positions with extraction opportunities. The presence of these bureaucratic institutions alone is therefore insufficient to know whether principals would pursue *either* collusive or coercive strategies.

The second question concerns the broader strength of bureaucratic institutions. In many contexts around the world, political principals have significant power to shape bureaucratic institutions in ways that serve their political and extractive needs. Leaders often mold bureaucratic procedures to align with their political motivations.[54] They grant autonomy and independence to bureaucrats and agencies when it is politically safe for them to do so,[55] and, when necessary, they flout existing rules, norms, and procedures to secure their political survival.[56] It is for these reasons that, in many countries around the world, bureaucratic institutions are more likely to be a consequence, rather than a cause, of specific extraction practices.

1.3.4   Ethnic Politics

The extraction strategies chosen by incumbent leaders could also be attributed to the politicized ethnic divisions that are prevalent in many African countries. Indeed, much of the literature on African politics emphasizes ethnicity as a major organizing principle for party politics and political behavior.[57] Leaders base their political and governing decisions on ethno-political interests such as rewarding politically supportive ethnic groups and restricting rival groups from such rewards.[58] These practices of ethnic governance could easily extend to extraction, whereby leaders arrange and delegate extraction using similar ethnicity-based calculations. For example, leaders who are members of larger ethnic groups might have greater opportunities to collude with co-ethnics in extraction. Leaders that come from small ethnic groups, by contrast, might

---

[54] Olowu (2001); Gingerich (2013).
[55] Whitfield et al. (2015); Teodoro and Pitcher (2017).
[56] van de Walle (2001); Holland (2017).
[57] For example: Horowitz (1985); Posner (2005); Habyarimana et al. (2007); Ferree (2010).
[58] Arriola and Johnson (2014); Kramon and Posner (2016).

have incentives to extract more coercively because of lacking availability of co-ethnic agents, lack of trust in non-coethnics, or both.

Increasingly, however, scholarship on African politics also recognizes the complexities and limitations of identity-based explanations of political party formation and elite decision-making. Recent studies affirm that high levels of ethnic fragmentation do not necessarily produce highly fragmented party systems[59] and that seemingly identity-driven behaviors may actually better reflect economic divisions.[60] There is also mounting evidence that leaders manage the state apparatus in ways that are *not* demonstrably consistent with ethno-political motivations.[61] In short, even where parties or political groupings have clear ethnic undertones, ethnicity may still be insufficient to explain leaders' extraction decisions. As I demonstrate with comparative analysis of Benin and Ghana throughout the book, countries with similar patterns of ethno-political division can produce very different patterns of extraction.

1.3.5   Electoral Institutions

Finally, leaders' extraction strategies could be shaped by a country's electoral institutions. Like ethnic politics, electoral institutions serve as a potential driver of political organization, thus shaping decisions about who leaders trust to extract. A large body of work concentrated primarily in Western contexts links electoral institutions to outcomes such as party system development and intra-elite competition (or cooperation).[62] Some research has also posited a more direct relationship between electoral institutions and extraction,[63] but the evidence from these studies remains largely inconsistent on questions about which types of electoral systems generate stronger incentives for rent-extraction and why.[64]

If electoral systems structure party institutions, they may indeed represent a more fundamental explanation of extraction strategies, rendering party institutions a more proximate variable. The evidence linking electoral institutions to party institutions in Africa is, however, quite mixed. Some studies have found that African party systems align with

---

[59] Erdmann and Engel (2007); Weghorst and Bernhard (2014).
[60] Kim (2018).
[61] Francois et al. (2015); Buckles (2017); Kroeger (2018); Simson (2018).
[62] For example, Duverger (1959); Lijphart (1968); Shugart and Taagepera (1989); Cox and McCubbins (1994).
[63] For example, Kunicová and Rose-Ackerman (2005); Chang and Golden (2007); Gingerich (2013).
[64] For an overview, see Golden and Mahdavi (2015).

the theoretical expectations of the broader literature, namely that first-past-the-post systems combined with low district magnitudes tend to produce more concentrated party systems[65] and that patterns of coalition formation generally conform with those of other regions of the world.[66]

There is also a considerable body of research arguing that the impacts of electoral systems on political parties in Africa do not follow the theoretical expectations developed in other contexts.[67] In cross-national analysis, Rachel Riedl finds that plurality electoral systems in Africa are associated with lower levels of party-system institutionalization as subnational voting patterns can generate high levels of electoral volatility, even where plurality systems reduce the number of competitors in particular districts.[68] Joel Barkan and Andrew Reynolds further explain that, in agrarian societies, electoral rules do not serve as a meaningful predictor of partisan alignment.[69] In Senegal, Catherine Kelly has shown that fragmentation of the party system is driven less by Senegal's mixed plurality and proportional representation (PR) system than by the uneven playing field on which incumbents and opposition parties compete.[70] That leaders in Africa and elsewhere often fashion electoral institutions in ways that serve their political interests also casts doubt on the extent to which electoral rules meaningfully structure party alignments.[71] Thus, although electoral rules to some degree shape the institutionalization of partisan alignments that, in turn, condition extraction practices, their influence is not sufficiently consistent to form a powerful explanation.

To summarize, alternative explanations provide a number of potential insights into leaders' strategies of extraction. Some of these approaches, including those focused on opposition strength, economic structure, and bureaucratic institutions, highlight the potential constraints faced by leaders in their decisions to pursue one extraction method versus another. At times, these constraints undoubtedly shape incumbents' extraction decisions, such as decisions about from which sectors of the economy to extract. In general, however, incumbent leaders in many countries operate with significant power to overcome these constraints,

---

[65] Mozaffar (1997); Lindberg (2005).
[66] Ariotti and Golder (2018).
[67] For an overview, see Ferree, Powell and Scheiner (2014).
[68] Riedl (2014: 69).
[69] Barkan (1995); Reynolds (1995).
[70] Kelly (2018). See also Chhibber and Kollman (2009), who make a more general argument that party institutions vary widely in countries with similar electoral institutions.
[71] Robinson and Torvik (2016); Driscoll (2020).

adapting or evading institutional designs and economic organization to pursue their own political interests. Other approaches, including those focused on ethnic politics and electoral systems, help account for the organizing principles of politics that shape the formation and durability of political alliances and parties. Despite their potential relevance to party institutionalization – and leaders' selection of extraction agents – these explanations often fall short in their ability to account for changing political alignments and patterns of agent loyalty, both of which, I argue, form the basis of extraction decisions. A focus on party institutions is, as I have outlined in Section 1.2 and as I elaborate further in Chapter 2, better suited to understanding the roles of *both* constraint and organization in leaders' strategies of extraction.

1.4   Research Approach

I examine the relationship between party institutions, extraction, and state politicization through in-depth case studies of two African countries, Benin and Ghana. The period of investigation begins at their transitions to democracy in the early 1990s and continues through the late 2010s.[72] I develop and assess the argument with nested comparisons between and within the two countries. I also provide four additional brief case studies to show that the theory of extraction developed in this book can apply more broadly to a range of ruling party institutions and electoral regimes.

1.4.1   The Country Cases: Benin and Ghana

The book's core empirical focus on Benin and Ghana reflects a dual case selection strategy. First, Benin and Ghana represent "extreme" cases of the independent variable – party institutionalization. Extreme cases are those that lie distant from the mean, making them particularly valuable for exploratory, theory-building purposes.[73] Ghana contains some of Africa's most highly institutionalized political parties, whereas Benin's parties are among the least institutionalized in Africa.[74] Throughout the

---

[72] Benin held the first multiparty presidential elections of the current democratic era in 1991. Ghana's were held in 1992. The scope of the inquiry does not involve the events in Benin, which, since 2019, have undermined electoral competition. I do, however, briefly address these events in the conclusion.

[73] Seawright and Gerring (2008).

[74] In Chapter 3, I provide detailed information on party institutionalization in Benin and Ghana.

book, I connect Ghana's strong party institutions to its system of collusive extraction and I show how weak party institutions in Benin generate coercive forms of extraction.

I also treat Benin and Ghana as plausibly most-similar cases. As I describe in detail in Chapter 3, their regime trajectories and extraction environments are similar in ways that generate a common set of political risks that leaders are likely to confront in the course of extraction. Although the two countries differ to some extent in their economic structures, bureaucratic institutions, colonial legacies, and electoral institutions, these variables are unlikely to match the explanatory power of party institutions for understanding the countries' different systems of extraction (see Section 1.3 and Chapter 3). To the extent that Benin and Ghana embody most-similar cases, their selection helps to confirm that party institutions, rather than competing factors, have driven leaders to adopt their respective extraction practices.[75]

Despite the book's potential relevance to a broad range of electoral regimes (see Chapter 8), I situate the study in democratic countries for both theoretical and practical reasons. Theoretically, the competitive political environments in the two countries ensure similarity in the scope and nature of leaders' concerns about political survival and political financing. Practically speaking, the selection of countries with more open political environments was important to obtain reliable information on sensitive topics without putting survey and interview respondents at risk.

Benin and Ghana diverge not only in their party institutions but also in the governing successes and challenges they have experienced in recent decades. Although it is not my goal to offer an exhaustive account of governing performance in the two countries, it is useful to briefly consider the two countries' divergent governing records, which highlight the significance of varying patterns of extraction and state politicization that I discuss throughout the book.

Although both countries entered the democratic era amidst severe economic crises that, like in many other African countries, wrought serious havoc on state institutions, Ghana's longer-term recovery has, compared to Benin's, been accompanied by a more ambitious set of national social and economic programs. For example, Ghana is one of the few African countries to have introduced and implemented a national health insurance program. They have greatly expanded, among other public services,

---

[75] Mill (1872); George and Bennett (2005).

national transportation networks and tertiary education. The government has also overseen the successful development of a growing oil and gas industry. These programs are by no means perfect. In many cases, they are unevenly distributed[76] or unfinished.[77] Nonetheless, Ghana's record in these and other sectors has impressed observers across Africa and the world.

Benin's policy and developmental record since the early 1990s is less impressive. Although there have been some positive developments in access to education, citizens in Benin, on average, complete only four years of schooling, compared to seven years in Ghana.[78] Long-standing plans to implement national or community health insurance schemes have never come to fruition. Repeated efforts to reform the economically vital Port of Cotonou and the cotton-producing sector have largely failed to move forward.

These governing differences are visible in cross-national governance indicators. In Figure 1.2, I show that Ghana's scores on measures of state capacity and public goods provision increased modestly between 1995 and 2015 and remain on the high end of the spectrum for African countries, while Benin's scores have stagnated during this time period.

1.4.2 Data and Analysis

For each component of the argument, I piece together quantitative and qualitative data to compare the two countries while also providing insight into the causal processes and relationships within each case. Cross-national comparisons, which are largely descriptive, illuminate broad differences in extraction strategies and patterns of state politicization. Within-case analyses, including process tracing and quantitative analysis of variation across ministries and individual bureaucrats, assess the theorized causal linkages. Together, the data and analyses comprise an empirical strategy that combines multiple sources of data from across different levels and sectors of the state apparatus to provide a holistic view of the relationships between party institutions, extraction, and state politicization.

I investigate the extraction-based argument in three main steps. First, I use data from elite interviews and secondary accounts to describe how party structures produce different modes of extraction in the two countries: collusive extraction in Ghana and coercive extraction in Benin.

[76] Abdulai (2017); Briggs (2021).
[77] Williams (2017).
[78] This statistic is from the 2019 Human Development Index.

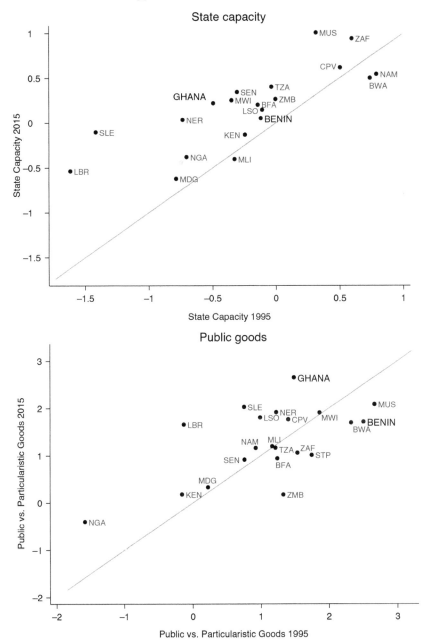

Figure 1.2 State capacity and public goods provision in Africa, 1995–2015
Source: State capacity data from Hanson and Sigman (2021), public goods data from V-Dem v9 (Coppedge et al. 2019).

Interviews with current and former ministers, party officials, bureaucrats, journalists, and civil society experts provide insight into specific extraction practices. Given the sensitive nature of the interview content, respondents are kept anonymous, using only vague references to titles and organizational affiliations. I corroborate the qualitative narratives of collusive and coercive extraction with data from bureaucratic surveys (described in Section 1.4.3).

Second, I analyze whether and how the different systems of extraction produce variation in the politicized distribution of jobs at different levels of the state apparatus. To analyze executive job distribution, I draw on an original database containing detailed biographical data for all minister appointees ($n = 586$) spanning twelve different presidential terms across the two countries. Minister data come from a variety of sources including government communiqués, newspapers, legislative archives, and interviews with political historians. The database includes information on each appointee's educational, professional, and political backgrounds. Using these data, I construct a novel, latent measure of politicization for each minister appointment using a Bayesian item response theory (IRT) model. I pool this measure with ministry-level data on procurement contracts, personnel, and budgets to analyze the role of extraction in patterns of executive job distribution. To analyze the relationship between extraction and the distribution of public service jobs, I draw principally on data from surveys of bureaucrats.

The third analytical step is to understand how incumbents in the two countries, given their different extraction strategies, manage the day-to-day business of the state's executive and bureaucratic institutions. Combining data on minister appointments, interviews, secondary accounts, and surveys of bureaucrats, I show divergent patterns of political management of the state apparatus and connect these management practices to leaders' collusive and coercive extraction strategies.

In each of the main empirical chapters (4–7), I provide additional detail on the specific data and analytical methods that I employ. It is important to note, however, that the political behaviors I study are not always easily observable. Parties in Benin and Ghana do not regularly or reliably report their financing sources. Interviews sometimes generated opposing responses about particular phenomena, for example in perceptions about the scope or nature of state politicization. To some extent, the systems and processes I study endure precisely because reliable information is limited. These challenges mean that the empirical work does not always yield direct observation of the theorized behavior, forcing instead the use of proxies or triangulation.

1.4.3   Surveys of Bureaucrats

Throughout the book, I use data obtained from two different surveys of bureaucrats that I conducted in the two countries. Surveys of public service personnel are increasingly common in political science and public administration because they provide granular empirical information about attitudes and capabilities of public servants, as well as information about the constraints that employees face in the course of their work.[79] Although the surveys capture only attitudes and not actual behaviors, bureaucrats' perceptions are potentially useful insofar as they, unlike expert observers or citizens, are closely involved in the day-to-day business of the state and are thus likely to have knowledge about the extraction, politicization, and management practices that form the focus of this book. I use the survey results to aid in the comparison of patterns of extraction and politicization across the two countries and to analyze the relationship between extraction and politicization within each country.

Both surveys were comprised primarily of public service personnel employed by central government ministries, departments, and agencies (MDAs). The first survey, which I conducted from October 2013 through June 2014, was carried out with a total 1,096 public service employees in the two countries (581 in Benin and 515 in Ghana). To administer this survey, I distributed questionnaires in public service educational and training programs at multiple sites in each country. In Benin, the survey was conducted in Cotonou, Abomey-Calavi, and Parakou. In Ghana, the survey was conducted in Accra, Kumasi, Navrongo, and Wa. The survey, which was identical in both countries except for the language in which it was administered (French in Benin and English in Ghana), captures a diversity of public servants across different agencies and experience levels. The survey was conducted in classroom settings in which public servants regularly speak candidly about the challenges they face at work, including those related to politics and political pressures.[80] Throughout the book, I refer to this survey as the *Classroom* survey.

A second, somewhat larger survey of public service employees was conducted in March 2017, only in Ghana. The survey was part of a broader cross-national survey project.[81] This survey included 1,641

---

[79] Schuster et al. (2020).

[80] Prior to fielding the survey, I visited and observed a number of these courses to assess the survey's viability.

[81] See Meyer-Sahling et al. (2018) and Sigman et al. (2018) for an overview of this project.

public service employees from 49 different MDAs in Ghana's public service.[82] The survey was limited to central government employees and excluded street-level bureaucrats such as teachers, nurses, and police officers, whose primary work location is in the capital of Accra. The survey sample is based primarily on access and convenience, with an effort to stratify the sample across public service institutions and employee grades. This survey was conducted face-to-face by a talented group of Ghanaian enumerators. The surveys lasted, on average, about one hour for each respondent and included a mix of both standard and experimental questions. Throughout the book, I refer to this survey as the *Workplace* survey.

Although complete and reliable demographic statistics for the populations of public service employees in the two countries are not fully available, I compile statistics from government reporting and other researchers' surveys to show that the survey samples, despite having been based primarily on access and convenience, are largely in line with what is known about the relevant populations (see Appendix A.2). Where the survey samples do diverge from known or estimated parameters of the population, I apply survey weights to ensure that key findings throughout the book are not biased by the samples (presented in Appendix B). Using official data contained in Benin's annual *Tableau de bord des agents de l'etat*, I estimate that Benin's Classroom survey sample represents 1 percent of the relevant population of public service employees. In Ghana, I use the Ministry of Finance and Economic Planning's 2014 annual budget statement appendices, which list the number of personnel for each organization, to estimate that, in Ghana, the Classroom survey sample represents 0.5 percent of the relevant population and the Workplace survey represents 1.6 percent of the population.

When possible, I compare responses across the Classroom and Workplace surveys for Ghana, where both surveys were conducted. Although we might expect that the different survey designs – their settings (classroom vs. workplace), procedures (written vs. face-to-face), timing (after an incumbent party election victory in Ghana in 2013 vs. after an opposition party election victory in 2017), survey samples (greater vs. lesser organizational diversity) and, in some cases, differences in the wording of survey questions[83] – would produce divergent results, I often find considerable consistency across the Classroom and Workplace surveys.

---

[82] The list of organizations is provided in Appendix A.1.

[83] The differences in the wording of questions across the two surveys are primarily a function of having had different partners in survey implementation with different analytical plans and interests.

This consistency instills confidence in the reported results and in the survey procedures used.

1.5   Contributions

This book makes several important theoretical and empirical contributions to the study of political parties, governance, and democracy. First, the book articulates an important mechanism linking party institutions to governing outcomes. There is a growing volume of work theorizing the effects of party institutionalization on outcomes such as political stability, democracy, policy reform, and economic governance.[84] This body of work has not, however, fully incorporated the role that party finance plays in mediating these relationships. By centering parties' financial imperatives and (extractive) fundraising practices, I demonstrate how the intersection of pecuniary and agency problems faced by party leaders explains divergence in the governing practices of party elites.

Second, the book broadens knowledge about the politics of state institutional performance. It emphasizes the necessity of studying state capacity and performance as a function of political institutions, processes, and interactions. Although this perspective is already well-advocated among political scientists, there are still many international organizations that see the state's institutional performance as a technical problem to be solved by development practitioners. In explaining how political leaders strategically manage their state personnel and organizations to more or less productive ends, the book pinpoints particular dimensions of contemporary politics – party institutions and political finance – on which scholars and practitioners ought to focus to better understand the political correlates of state performance.

This focus on party institutions as a locus of state performance is important because it bridges structural and strategic theories of the state. Structural explanations, such as those that focus on geography,[85] colonial history,[86] conflict,[87] or social coalitions[88] are useful for understanding the broad limits and opportunities for state action. Whether and how state capacity is (or is not) deployed in contemporary states, however, also requires an understanding of political elites' strategic

---

[84] Pitcher (2012); Cruz and Keefer (2015); Bizzarro et al. (2018); Bleck and Van de Walle (2018); Geddes et al. (2018); Kroeger (2018); Bernhard et al. (2020).
[85] Herbst (2000).
[86] Migdal (1988); Kohli (2004).
[87] Tilly (1990); Centeno (2002); Besley and Persson (2009).
[88] Boone (2003); Saylor (2014).

interests.[89] I argue in this book that leaders make strategic choices about how to manage state organizations and personnel not only within the confines of the broader state structures they have inherited but also according to the varied party structures in which they have come to operate.

The book goes further to highlight that neither the extraction of state resources by politicians nor the politicization of state personnel are, as many assume, universally and uniformly detrimental to state capacity and performance. This finding builds on studies that recognize considerable variation in governing outcomes that result from institutional weaknesses and high levels of corruption.[90] It also speaks to growing concerns about the usefulness of concepts like neopatrimonialism that cloud tremendous diversity in governance across African states.[91] Although widespread extraction of state resources undoubtedly causes serious financial loss to the state and permits unethical accumulations of personal wealth, my study explains how some forms of extraction are much less disruptive to the pursuit of public policy than others. Specifically, when extraction involves trusted party agents and partisan networks outside the state, it is considerably less likely to undermine the day-to-day workings of the state. By contrast, when incumbents fear elite defection and delegate to agents with weaker partisan links, extraction is more likely to wreak havoc on the functioning of executive and bureaucratic institutions. Different extraction strategies therefore illuminate how, even in the presence of widespread state exploitation by political elites, more effective states may emerge.

Third, this book adds to a growing literature that studies the inner workings of executive and bureaucratic institutions in Africa and across the developing world. Despite longstanding assertions in the Africanist literature about the executive and bureaucracy as important sites of politics and distribution,[92] there had, until recently, been surprisingly little systematic work on the way these institutions operate.[93] Recent studies of executive institutions have greatly advanced knowledge about the composition and rotation of minister personnel in Africa.[94] Much of

---

[89] Slater (2010).

[90] For example, both Kang (2002) and Ang (2020) argue that government-driven economic growth is possible even in the presence of high levels of cronyism.

[91] Pitcher et al. (2009); Mkandawire (2015).

[92] For example, Hyden (1983); Callaghy (1987); Berman (1998).

[93] Exceptions include Price (1975); Montgomery (1987); Widner (1992).

[94] Arriola and Johnson (2014); Osei (2018); Woldense (2018); Ricart-Huguet (2020); Nwankwor (2021); Arriola et al. (2021b).

this literature, however, has glossed over the financial and agency problems that leaders face when they must share power and resources with opponents or potential defectors. As my research demonstrates, leaders' responses to these problems are critical for understanding why executive institutions vary in their composition, stability, and cohesion. In this book, I develop a set of theoretical and empirical tools to study these problems, including novel ways to measure politicization across different levels of the state apparatus.

Turning to literature on bureaucracy, this book helps to answer the call for "additional research that carefully considers the specific administrative and political context in which bureaucrats operate."[95] A growing body of research highlights considerable *sub-national* variation in the politics of the bureaucracy in the developing world.[96] An important subset of this literature focuses specifically on Ghana.[97] This book complements these works by highlighting the national party-based conditions that drive politicians' strategic management of the bureaucracy, providing specific insights into questions about when and why bureaucrats are allowed more or less autonomy to complete tasks[98] or to respond to citizen demands for accountability.[99] For example, knowing that the ruling National Resistance Movement (NRM) in Uganda relies on extraction by party members at the local level (see Chapter 8) helps to explain why political oversight of bureaucrats is particularly challenging in ruling party strongholds, as Pia Raffler's field experiment finds.[100]

Finally, the argument I develop in the book sheds important light on democratic survival across Africa and the world. The question of whether and how democracy "delivers" is central to understanding a range of democratic regime threats including the rise of populist movements, the growing frequency of military coups, and leaders' intensifying efforts to subvert democratic institutions. The book highlights a troubling paradox regarding government performance and democratic politics: in helping leaders to solve their extraction problems, strong party institutions also create better-governing environments. Unless there are significant changes in leaders' incentives to extract from the state for political finance, the best-case political context for effective democratic governance is one in which members of institutionalized

---

95 Pepinsky et al. (2017: 250).
96 Gulzar and Pasquale (2017); Pierskalla and Sacks (2020); Xiao and Zhu (2022).
97 Asunka (2016); Williams (2017); Driscoll (2018); Luna (2019); Brass et al. (2020); Brierley (2020).
98 Rasul and Rogger (2018); McDonnell (2020).
99 Asunka (2017); Martin and Raffler (2021).
100 Raffler (2020).

parties collude in extraction. The rapid undoing of Benin's democracy during the time I was writing this book (2019–2021) forms a portentous example of how the combination of weak party institutions and money politics can threaten democratic institutions.

1.6   Organization of the Book

I develop the book's arguments over the following six chapters. In Chapter 2, I describe the political financing landscape faced by many leaders in Africa and develop a theoretical account of how and why leaders extract from the state in differing ways. Chapter 3 provides background and additional case selection rationale for the two main country cases, Benin and Ghana. In Chapters 4–7, I sequentially investigate each part of the argument depicted in Figure 1.1 with an analytical focus on Benin and Ghana. Chapter 4 describes the collusive and coercive systems of extraction in the two countries. In Chapter 5, "Staffing the State for Extraction," I show how collusive and coercive extraction lead to different patterns of politicization in the recruitment and selection of state personnel. I turn to dynamics within the executive in Chapter 6, showing how differences in elite agency problems in the two extraction systems lead to divergent patterns of stability and cohesion within executive cabinets. Moving further downstream in the state apparatus, Chapter 7 investigates how collusive and coercive modes of extraction play out for bureaucratic personnel and organizations in Benin and Ghana.

The concluding chapter, Chapter 8 addresses two issues not yet resolved in the book. First, I discuss the potential application of the book's argument to other countries. I do so with attention to two shadow cases – Botswana and Malawi – that help to reinforce how variation in ruling party institutionalization leads to either collusive or coercive forms of extraction. I then move to consider an "intermediate" case of party institutionalization in Uganda, followed by a case of party de-institutionalization in Senegal. The Uganda and Senegal cases illustrate how the argument can be adapted to other party and regime contexts. In the second half of the chapter, I discuss in more detail the theoretical and practical implications of the book, focusing in particular on how to better incorporate party institutions and party financing into studies of state performance in Africa and throughout the world.

2   A Theory of Extraction

Political competition in Africa, like in many other places across the world, has become extremely expensive. Candidates engage in an ever-expanding array of campaign activities that require large sums of money. The growing use of helicopters at campaign rallies points to one visible manifestation of this trend.[1] Extensive advertising on billboards and in media outlets constitutes another major expense for parties and candidates.[2] Somewhat less visible, though certainly no less expensive, is the widespread practice of distributing money or goods to voters as a way for candidates to convey their credibility as effective providers.[3] Even when not directly campaigning, political elites and party officials frequently require resources to meet their communities' expectations of financial support.[4] Politicians also require money to form and maintain elite coalitions, both among opposition members and incumbent parliamentarians.[5]

Exact costs of political campaigns are difficult to discern since few, if any, African countries enforce regulations on reporting of campaign expenses.[6] In South Africa's 2019 elections, an estimated total of 2 billion rand ($120 million) was spent by all forty-eight parties competing, half of which was expended by the ruling African National Congress (ANC).[7] In the run-up to the 2017 elections in Kenya, party officials estimated that total presidential campaign spending would exceed

---

[1] Eme and Anyadike (2014); Paget (2019).

[2] Olorunmola (2016); Mensah (2017).

[3] Kramon (2018).

[4] This is a recurring theme in the Westminster Foundation for Democracy's series on "The Cost of Politics" (Wardle, 2017). Also, Paller (2019) documents how residents of urban neighborhoods in Accra look for, and depend on, sustenance from politicians.

[5] Arriola (2012); Bwalya and Sichone (2016); Gueye et al. (2017).

[6] Check et al. (2019). I provide additional analysis on political finance regulations later in this chapter.

[7] Tom Head, "Estimates reveal how much political parties spent on their election campaigns," The South African, May 19, 2019.

$50 million for each of the main parties.[8] In terms of parliamentary seats, average spending by candidates appears to range from around $20,000 in Malawi[9] to $700,000 in Nigeria.[10] In many countries, parliamentary candidates must pay handsomely – both to the party and to the state's electoral authority – just to get one's name on the ballot.[11]

There is also mounting evidence that costs of election campaigns in Africa have been rising rapidly. In Uganda, estimates suggest that spending by the ruling NRM party increased from around $13 million in the 1996 election to around $30 million in 2011, but that additional election-related activities financed by the president himself brought total campaign spending to around $200–$350 million that year. In the 2016 elections, total spending by the NRM is estimated to have jumped to $655.6 million.[12] In Ghana, the winning NPP reportedly spent an estimated $30 million in its successful bid for the presidency and control of parliament in 2004, followed by a sum of around $100 million in 2008.[13] Spending in individual parliamentary elections in Ghana grew by approximately 60 percent between the 2012 and 2016.[14] In Benin, costs per voter in parliamentary races are estimated to have risen from $1–2 per voter in 2011 to around $10 per voter in 2015.[15]

Amidst these accounts of rapidly inflating costs, there remains a common assumption about political money in African politics: that incumbents enjoy largely unfettered access to state resources, including money, to finance their political parties and election campaigns. This chapter challenges this longstanding assumption, not by denying the centrality of state money in politics or by questioning the idea that incumbents typically have greater financing opportunities than their opponents, but rather by highlighting the political constraints that incumbent leaders face in extracting money from the state. Sitting leaders in competitive political regimes confront an array of risks – especially political risks – in their efforts to appropriate state finances to their political projects.

---

[8] Reported in local and international media. See, for example, "Millions of dollars at play as Kenyans go into their most expensive election yet," The East African, May 22, 2017.

[9] Wahman (2019).

[10] Olorunmola (2016).

[11] Wardle (2017).

[12] Estimates for 1996 and 2011 from Tangri and Mwenda (2013: 107). For 2016 estimates, see Fred Ojambo, "Uganda May be Headed for Highest-Ever Level of Campaign Spending," Bloomberg News, December 27, 2019.

[13] Daddieh and Bob-Milliar (2012).

[14] Asante and Kunnath (2017).

[15] Koter (2017).

In the pages that follow, I outline these risks and develop a theoretical account of how leaders respond to them. The central argument is that leaders manage the political risks of extracting money from the state in ways that depend on the party institutions in which they operate. Incumbents who lead highly institutionalized political parties have an array of tools – trusted party agents, robust networks through which to access and channel extracted monies, and party instruments of control – to manage the risks of extraction. They engage in what I call *collusive* extraction: working collectively for the financial benefit of the party and without significant involvement by the incumbent leader. In collusive extraction, leaders delegate extraction broadly to their trusted and reliable party members, who, in turn, extract financial resources for the benefit of the party.

Leaders whose parties are less institutionalized pursue different extraction strategies. Facing high probabilities of elite defection, leaders have difficulty finding reliable extraction agents, and agents themselves have little incentive to serve incumbent interests if the party's prospects for survival are low. In response, incumbent leaders either administer extraction deals themselves or engage in more *coercive* forms of dele-gated extraction: co-opting and coercing more vulnerable rank-and-file bureaucratic actors. Since leaders of parties with weaker institutions lack broader partisan networks to help facilitate extraction, they concen-trate their extractive efforts more intensely within the state apparatus, where they can use their executive authorities to compel participation and maintain control over extracted resources.

An important insight emerging from this chapter is that the extraction of money from the state is itself a contested process that requires greater analytical attention. Leaders' extraction strategies impact not only state finances. As I elucidate in this chapter and throughout the remain-der of the book, specific extraction practices hold important implica-tions for the politicization and ultimately the performance of the state apparatus.

I begin the chapter with a discussion of political financing in Africa, including the strong tendency of incumbent political leaders to finance their political operations with extracted state money. In the second sec-tion, I discuss the growing political challenges that incumbent leaders in electoral regimes face in extracting money from the state. The third section outlines a specific set of problems leaders must overcome to nav-igate the politics of extraction and theorizes the role of party institutions in structuring leaders' responses to these problems. I then introduce the main contours of collusive and coercive strategies of extraction, followed

by a discussion of why and how these two extraction strategies produce variation in the ways that leaders politicize the state's executive and
bureaucratic institutions.

2.1   Political Financing in Africa: What We Know

Although there is little question about the need for politicians to raise
increasingly large sums of money to compete effectively in political contests in many African countries, there is far less systematic knowledge
about the sources from which politicians raise that money. A growing
number of case studies suggest that politicians draw from a multitude
of funding sources including, but not limited to, mandated public funding, party membership dues, party-owned enterprises, donations from
wealthy individuals or businesses, and the extraction of state money.[16]
These accounts of party funding are accompanied by increasing attention to an upsurge in candidates who self-finance their parties and
campaigns, either with their own funds or through loans they obtain from
banks or wealthy individuals.[17]

One reason why it is difficult to study political financing practices
is because, in many African countries, legal provisions that mandate
reporting on party and campaign finances are either nonexistent or
only weakly enforced. Only around half of African countries formally
require candidates running in elections to file reports on their campaign finances, whereas 79 percent of countries outside of Africa have
candidate reporting mandates.[18] Among the twenty-two African countries that do require candidates to file reports, only half (eleven) require
itemized documentation of funding sources and expense categories.
By contrast, outside of Africa, 80 percent of countries with reporting
requirements require itemized accounts of funding sources or spending.
According to expert survey data from the Varieties of Democracy (V-
Dem) project, African countries score, on average, lowest in the world in
terms of de facto disclosures of campaign donations. In 2018, all but two
African countries – Seychelles and Rwanda – were rated as having either
nonexistent or "ambiguous" disclosures of donations to national election

---

[16] For example, Bryan and Baer (2005); Wardle (2017).

[17] Koter (2017).

[18] Data on political finance regulations come from International IDEA's 2020 Political
Finance Database. The database includes data on countries' legal provisions in four
areas: private sources of funding; public campaign funding; campaign spending; and
reporting, oversight, and sanctions. The 2020 version includes data for 51 African
countries, and 180 countries in the world. It is current through December 2019.

campaigns, meaning that there are some disclosure requirements in place but it is unclear to what extent they are observed or enforced.

Despite the many difficulties in obtaining accurate financing records from parties and candidates, existing research based on interviews, surveys, and participant observation has generated substantial insight. In general, they have identified four main sources of political finance: public funding, party funding, private funding (from business or individuals), and the extraction of money from the state. As the following discussion makes clear, however, the extraction of state money remains central to many politicians' fundraising and campaign efforts, in part because such access also shapes the supply of funding that is sourced from private and party actors.

2.1.1   Public Financing

Public financing for election campaigns or political parties is formally mandated in thirty African countries.[19] Among these thirty countries, however, there is widespread variation in the regularity of funding, the types of expenses covered, the amounts that are distributed to parties and candidates, and the allocation criteria. Additionally, at least thirty-seven countries, including some that do not provide direct public financing, provide some free or subsidized media access.

The amounts provided through public funding programs vary considerably but, in general, public funds are far from sufficient to cover actual party and campaign costs. In Tanzania, the amount of money available to distribute among political parties falls below the legal limit of 2 percent of the annual budget, meaning that funding is insufficient, particularly for opposition parties.[20] In Benin, prior to the passage of a new political parties law in 2019, parties received around 5 million CFA francs ($10,000) per year which, even if added up over multiple years, constitutes only a small fraction of the amounts that parties spend in elections.[21] Even in Kenya, where significant sums of money are provided to the country's larger political parties, the public disbursements represent but a small proportion of total party spending. The Office of the Registrar of Political Parties reports that, in 2018/2019, the ruling Jubilee party received 240,374,734 Kenyan shillings ($2,359,038) and the Orange Democratic Movement, the second largest party in

---

[19] Unless otherwise cited, the information on public financing of parties and campaigns comes from International International IDEA (2019).

[20] Bértoa and Sanches (2019).

[21] Author interview, Cotonou, June 24, 2019. Since 2019, the amounts disbursed have become significantly larger but fewer parties have qualified for funding.

parliament, received 112,255,766.17 shillings ($1,101,678).[22] Since major parties in Kenya's 2017 elections are estimated to have spent upwards of $50 million during the campaign alone, these sums constitute a relatively small share of the funds needed to compete effectively. It is telling that, in their multicountry research, the WFD concludes that public funding is, on the whole, "relatively insignificant" as a source of political finance for candidates and parties in Africa.[23] According to V-Dem's expert survey data, which assesses the de facto availability of public financing for parties and election campaigns, only Cape Verde, South Africa, and Namibia provide significant sums of public funding; with Botswana and Zambia providing the least.[24]

Where public funding is available to parties, incumbents often manipulate the allocation rules and the timing of disbursements to disadvantage opposition parties. In South Africa (and elsewhere), systems that allocate funds based on a party's previous electoral performance tend to disadvantage newer parties, even if there is a shift in public support in their favor.[25] In Zimbabwe, the ruling ZANU-PF party has manipulated the rules to disadvantage opponents' receipt of public funding.[26] In Mozambique's 1999 elections, significant amounts of government and aid funding – around $3 million – were made available to parties but the opposition party Renamo (Mozambican National Resistance) complained that the electoral commission delayed the release of these funds.[27] In short, the availability of public funding is no guarantee of sufficiency for either incumbent or opposition parties.

2.1.2   Party Fees and Profits

Some political parties in Africa raise money from their members and candidates or, in several cases, from party-owned enterprises. Party membership fees have, at times, served as an important source of party funding. In Botswana, for example, the ruling Botswana Democratic Party (BDP) recorded as many as 471,000 paying members in 2009,

---

[22] Data obtained from the website of the Kenya Office of the Registrar of Political Parties, www.orpp.or.ke/index.php/en/services/funding-and-political-parties, accessed September 14, 2020.

[23] Wardle (2017: 7).

[24] These assessments are based on a question asking "Is significant public financing available for parties' and/or candidates' campaigns for national office? A score of 0 represents "none" and 4 represents "Yes, public financing funds a significant share of expenditures for nearly all parties."

[25] See Friedman (2010: 167) and Bértoa and Sanches (2019).

[26] Dendere (2021).

[27] Pottie (2003).

thus providing a significant source of funds.[28] The National Democratic Institute (NDI) reports that, in the early 2000s, around 20 percent of survey respondents in African countries named membership dues and other party-generated revenue as an important source of political financing.[29] Additionally, Muna Ndulo notes that membership dues have served as an important source of party funds in Zambia.[30] Many parties, however, encounter problems collecting and sustaining payments from members. As George Bob-Milliar has elaborately detailed in the case of Ghana's two main parties, individuals often join political parties out of a need or desire for material support, and they are rarely in positions to make any financial contributions, even in the form of small payments, to the party.[31] Likewise, in South Africa, the ANC had planned to collect fees from its mass membership to ensure financial solvency, but "the impoverishment of most ANC members meant that a membership fee of only R12 a year was charged."[32] ANC membership dropped drastically under President Jacob Zuma, and some accounts suggest that fee payments by remaining members have diminished.[33] In Nigeria, it is the "godfathers" – influential political financiers, some of whom occupy legislative seats or governorships – who purchase party membership cards en masse and distribute them to citizens as a way to garner support for the party.[34] In cases like these, membership fees are more aptly categorized as donations from wealthy financiers than revenue generated through membership payments by party members.

Many parties in Africa raise funds by charging large fees to individuals who want to run for office on the party's ticket or who want to compete in a party's primary election. In Nigeria, candidates pay parties anywhere from 2.2 million naira ($6,000) to run for a seat in the house of representatives to 27.5 million ($75,000) to run for president.[35] In Ghana, those wishing to run for president in one of the two main parties must pay 200,000–300,000 Ghanaian cedis ($35,000–$53,000) to their party. For the NPP, presidential candidates seeking to run in the 2020 election had to pay 200,000 Ghanaian cedis ($35,000) to the party. In the same

---

[28] Good (2010: 89).
[29] Bryan and Baer (2005).
[30] Ndulo (2000).
[31] Bob-Milliar (2012b).
[32] Friedman (2010: 159).
[33] Marianne Tham, "Payment of membership fees shows just how moribund the ANC has become," The Daily Maverick, August 27, 2019.
[34] Kura (2014: 135).
[35] These figures, reported by Olorunmola (2016), include both an "expression of interest" fee and a nomination fee.

election year, the NDC had initially charged 400,000 cedis, but reduced the amount after receiving complaints.[36] In Uganda, the funds necessary for parliamentary candidates to get their name on the ballot can be "exorbitant," especially considering that many are recent university graduates, unemployed, or earn only modest incomes.[37]

Some political parties in Africa raise funds through the operation of enterprises. One well-known case is the Rwandan Patriotic Front's (RPF) Crystal Ventures Investments. The holding company, as one recent article describes, "has investments in everything from furniture to finance...owns the country's biggest milk processor, its finest coffee shops, and some of its priciest real estate."[38] Party-linked companies have also been established in Ethiopia, where the Ethiopian People's Revolutionary Democratic Front (EPRDF) was known to have four large umbrella holding endowments linking together a network of for-profit entities operated by party officials.[39] Tanzania's ruling *Chama Cha Mapinduzi* (CCM) also operates a range of enterprises, and its affiliated organizations own valuable real estate in Dar es Salaam and other cities.[40] In Angola, the state oil company, Sonangol, is staffed with party-affiliated "oligarchs" who have ensured that the company's investments accrue to the benefit of the MPLA and its leaders.[41]

2.1.3   Private Contributions

Contributions from wealthy donors constitute a major source of political financing in many African countries. The example of "godfatherism" in Nigeria is perhaps the most vivid, but wealthy contributors play an outsize role in political financing elsewhere. In Leonardo Arriola's account of business financing in Kenya, for instance, he explains that President Jomo Kenyatta relied heavily on the entrepreneurial base of the Kikuyu, who profited heavily from early coffee and tea production.[42] However, as Arriola also explains, similar business sources of financing have not been readily available in many countries, particularly for opposition parties, where regimes have maintained tight control over the financial sector and heavily restricted access to capital.

---

[36] "NDC filing fee slashed to GH/¢300,000, aspirants have up to December 8 to pick forms," Ghanaweb, December 5, 2018.

[37] Golooba-Mutebi (2016: 9).

[38] "The Rwandan Patriotic Front's business empire," The Economist, March 7, 2017.

[39] Abegaz (2013).

[40] Ewald (2013: 347).

[41] De Oliveira (2015).

[42] Arriola (2012: 42–43).

African countries tend to have permissive regulations on private political contributions. Figure 2.1 shows the proportion of countries in Africa compared to those outside of Africa that possess various types of formal restrictions on private funding. In nearly every category, the proportion of African countries with the relevant restriction is considerably lower than the proportion for the rest of the world. The figure also shows that African countries tend to put more restrictions on parties than they do on candidates, and that only a very small proportion of countries place limits on the amounts of contributions.

Although some African countries have banned corporate contributions to political parties or candidates, and approximately 60 percent prohibit foreign contributions to parties, there are often loopholes through which such donations can occur.[43] For example, party leaders seek donations from members of their countries' diasporas who own or

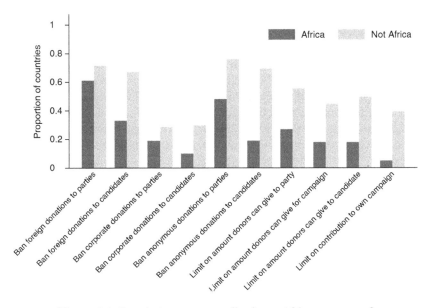

Figure 2.1 Restrictions on contributions, Africa vs. rest of world
Proportion of countries that ban donations from different sources or place limits on contributions. The database includes 51 African countries and 129 countries not in Africa. Source: International IDEA (2019)

[43] See Sokomani (2005); Wardle (2017).

operate businesses abroad.[44] Moreover, with lax reporting requirements and enforcement, bans and limitations are often easily ignored.

Parties and candidates raise funds from private donors in different ways, with some focusing on the collection of modest amounts from friends and supporters and others seeking to secure large financial or in-kind donations from wealthy supporters and sympathizers. In Uganda, for example, candidates tend to reach out to friends and associates to garner a series of small donations while also searching for larger donations from wealthy contributors and businesses.[45]

Despite their formal legality, private donations are often dependent on illicit access to state funds or power. Political leaders award state jobs, contracts, or regulatory favors to wealthy donors in exchange for their financial support. These practices, of course, are widespread both in Africa and throughout the world. In Kenya, for example, party financing has been linked to several major government corruption scandals.[46] In the infamous "Goldenberg Affair," party-affiliated individuals were supposedly importing gold and other precious minerals through a company called Goldenberg International Ltd. Goldenberg was paid huge sums of money by the Central Bank of Kenya (CBK) for what were eventually found to be imaginary imports. Another well-known example comes from South Africa, where President Jacob Zuma had offered the wealthy Gupta brothers significant control over government decision-making in exchange for large sums of financial support for himself and the ANC.[47]

Additionally, wealthy individuals are themselves running for office more frequently and self-financing their campaigns. In Nigeria, Sulaiman Kura notes that even younger members of parliament (MPs) in Nigeria tend to be wealthy individuals who can provide much of the money necessary to win their seats.[48] In Benin, individuals with business backgrounds have displaced politicians with public service backgrounds, due in large part to the rising costs of elections.[49] While in some countries, such as Ghana, wealthy business-people have been active in politics for some time,[50] their prominence does seem to be expanding elsewhere. In Zambia, parties look for wealthy parliamentary candidates to join their

[44] Beck (2008) describes this practice in detail in the case of Senegal.
[45] Golooba-Mutebi (2016: 10).
[46] Mwangi (2008: 237).
[47] See, for example, Norimitsu Onishi and Selam Gebrekidan, "In Gupta Brothers' Rise and Fall, the Tale of a Sullied A.N.C." *The New York Times* December 22, 2018.
[48] Kura (2014).
[49] Pinkston (2016); Koter (2017).
[50] Austin (1964).

tickets.[51] In many cases, however, the continued accumulation of wealth and power by politicians often depends on their past ability to benefit from state contracts, privatization concessions, or other state resources and business opportunities. Thus, the upsurge of private wealth into politics is not always as private as it may appear.

2.1.4   Money Extracted from the State

Perhaps equally important as private contributions, particularly for incumbents, is the extraction of state funding. Those in positions of power can extract rents and divert revenues to political parties and candidates, despite most countries having laws against these practices.[52] Although it is impossible to know the full extent of these practices across countries, they are commonly invoked in studies of political financing and political corruption in Africa and across many other parts of the world.

Politicians extract from the state in many different ways. They do so through deals with businesses, extracting rents from administrative processes, or by directly diverting state money to political coffers. Describing the intricate systems of extraction of political money in Kenya, Oscar Gakuo Mwangi writes:

Political banks were created to channel stolen monies from public enterprises. The embezzlement of such monies was facilitated by the patronage appointees, and the money was used to campaign for Moi's re-election and to bribe his political opponents. Political corruption was used to acquire and retain political power by the elite, when KANU was facing stiff competition from other parties. Those who used political corruption to acquire finances were in turn elected to Parliament, and some among them were later appointed to cabinet positions that ensured that they protected the wealth acquired by corruption. Those who were not interested in party politics, but had economic interests to be protected, contributed to the KANU campaign funds directly or indirectly. Large-scale projects of questionable viability were also initiated as conduits for raising funds to be used for political activities.[53]

Leaders in Uganda have relied on a somewhat different strategy: using the classified military budget and the inclusion of "ghost soldiers" on military payrolls to fund candidates on the ruling NRM's ticket.[54]

---

[51] Arriola et al. (2021a).
[52] According to International IDEA, 86 percent of African countries ban state resources from being used in favor of, or against, a political party and 63 percent prohibit any parties from receiving state money or resources.
[53] Mwangi (2008: 270–271).
[54] Tangri and Mwenda (2013: 109).

A probe into the Nigerian Office of the National Security Adviser to former President Goodluck Jonathan similarly revealed that public funds of $2.1 billion meant for equipping the Nigerian military were diverted to finance party activities for the 2015 general elections.[55] In South Africa, ANC leaders in government have designed and targeted programs, such as the Black Economic Empowerment program, to cultivate and support party donors.[56]

No matter what the specific channel of extraction, it is clear that extracted money plays an important role in political financing in many African countries. Parties and candidates depend to a large extent on access to state power and resources in some form or another. Few governments provide meaningful public funding to parties and election campaigns. Truly private donations or party membership fees are limited both by the ways in which parties recruit members and the many well-documented ways in which private donors require access to the state in order to sustain their businesses.[57] These conditions perpetuate both the large and growing influence of moneyed interests in politics, as well as the strong and perpetual pressure for politicians to extract money from the state to finance their increasingly expensive political operations.

2.2   Easy Extraction?

When it comes to parties and politicians extracting money from the state, there is a widespread assumption that incumbents enjoy "easy" and "unfettered" access to state money. This assumption is hard-wired into theoretical accounts of authoritarian regimes in particular, where incumbents "routinely abuse state resources" to embed their power.[58] Hegemonic parties can continue to attract votes as long as the state has sufficient resources to sustain them,[59] and leaders distribute these resources in ways that appease both the selectorate and winning coalitions.[60]

Indeed, studies of electoral authoritarian countries in Africa have emphasized to a large extent how resource and organizational advantages sustain both dominant party and personalistic forms of authoritarian rule. Yonaton Morse, for example, explains how resource advantages allow incumbent parties to continually convey their credibility to a large

[55] Falodi (2016), cited in Olorunmola (2016).
[56] Lodge (1998).
[57] For example, Bayart (1993).
[58] Levitsky and Way (2002: 53).
[59] Magaloni (2006); Greene (2007); Reuter and Gandhi (2011).
[60] De Mesquita et al. (2005).

base of the population. In Tanzania, he documents how the dominant Tanganyika African National Union (TANU) party has in recent decades been successful in using their control over state resources to redistribute widely across the countryside, thereby fueling support for the regime and reducing perceptions of bias in resource allocation.[61] In contexts of weaker parties, incumbents often share power (and resources) to stave off coup attempts or to fragment the opposition.[62]

The narrative of unencumbered access to state money also pervades accounts of more competitive political environments in Africa. Jennifer Widner, for example, explains the advantages enjoyed by incumbent parties "with both easy access to public resources and enormous capacity to intimidate the private sector, preventing it from financing the opposition."[63] Leonardo Arriola notes that incumbents can "easily" pay for cross-ethnic endorsements with public resources.[64] Amidst growing electoral competition in 2006, the NRM in Uganda evaded legal restrictions on access to state funding by calling itself a "movement" rather than a "party."[65] This view is reinforced by many accounts of incumbent party strength in Africa, which is widely seen as a function of their use of state power and their advantages in extracting state money to build national bases of support.[66]

The idea that incumbents are free to divert money from the state to their political coffers is reinforced by observations of weak institutional constraints on rulers. Leaders in many African countries often manage to neutralize horizontal constraints, such as legislative oversight, by limiting either the resources allocated to the legislature or the number of parliamentary sittings.[67] Judicial constraints are also often very weak. If political corruption cases reach the courts at all, they are rarely free of political influence, which leads to either harsher treatment of regime opponents[68] or lighter consequences for political allies.[69] Even in South Africa, where both legislative and judicial institutions are strong and independent relative to other African countries, these institutions did not deter ANC leaders such as Jacob Zuma from engaging in political extraction on a mass scale. Thus, even if formal institutions are

---

[61] Morse (2018: 12).
[62] Arriola (2009); Roessler (2016); Arriola, DeVaro and Meng (2021).
[63] Widner (1997: 79). Cited also by Manning (2005).
[64] Arriola (2012: 28).
[65] Rakner and van de Walle (2009: 114–115).
[66] For example, van de Walle (2003); Wahman (2017); Dendere (2021).
[67] Opalo (2019).
[68] Lawson (2009).
[69] Adebanwi and Obadare (2011).

now more likely to shape incumbent behavior than was the case in earlier decades,[70] most of these institutions remain weak in their ability to
constrain elite extractive behavior.

The perception of "easy" extraction is also supported by prevailing
accounts of vertical accountability in many African countries. Because
citizens look to political patrons for access to jobs, security, or other
benefits, they are unlikely to punish leaders at the polls for engaging in
extractive actions, which ultimately bring citizens some benefit. Citizens
or party activists may even reward extracting leaders for their subsequent
distribution.[71] Local leaders often help to reinforce these dynamics, capturing and distributing public resources, goods, and services to establish
or maintain their authority or to advance their political career aspirations.[72] Additionally, citizens in African countries widely perceive risks
of retaliation or loss of benefits if they report extractive acts by politicians
or public officials. In the 2016–2018 round of Afrobarometer surveys,
an average of 67.1 percent of respondents across all thirty-four countries surveyed said that ordinary people risk retaliation if they report
corruption.[73]

2.2.1   Political Constraints on Extraction

Despite weak horizontal and vertical institutional constraints, incumbents are not completely unconstrained in their extractive pursuits.
Leaders face an array of *political* constraints in their efforts to extract
money from the state for political financing. These political constraints
emanate largely from the competitiveness of elections and the heightened probability of an incumbent leaving office, both of which have
grown considerably since the early 1990s. Multiparty electoral competition is now commonplace across African countries. Among sub-Saharan
African countries, there were roughly twice as many presidential elections held from 1990 to 2018 (217) as there were from 1960 through
1989 (108). Additionally, elections are now more competitive than they
were in previous decades. The average vote share for winning presidential candidates has dropped from close to 90 percent in the 1970s and
1980s, to 57 percent in the 2010s.[74] Even if incumbents are able to retain
power through elections, the days of overwhelming incumbent victories
are largely in the past.

[70] Cheeseman (2018).
[71] Driscoll (2018).
[72] Baldwin (2013); Koter (2016).
[73] Afrobarometer (2018).
[74] Cruz et al. (2020).

Heightened electoral competition, along with the growing institution-alization of term limits, has led to significant increases in the rate of leader turnover. Whereas, in the 1970s and 1980s, incumbents retained power in nearly 80 percent of electoral contests (if elections were held at all), that statistic has dropped to around 60 percent since the early 1990s. Elections since 2010 are nearly three times as likely to result in a new party assuming power than was the case in the 1980s. From 2015–2019 alone, more than one-quarter of elections held in African countries resulted in an inter-party transfer of power, including in some rather unexpected cases, such as The Gambia and the Democratic Republic of Congo. Leaders are also now considerably more likely to leave power through term limits than they were in previous decades.[75]

These trends of rising levels of political competition and increasing likelihoods of incumbents leaving power pose (at least) two important challenges for incumbents in their efforts to extract political money from the state. First, the increasing competitiveness of elections raises the value of resource capture: leaders seeking to preserve incumbent advan-tage must ensure that large sums of state money do not fall into the hands of opponents or potential defectors. There are potentially serious costs to an incumbent if members of their party or coalition defect with extracted political funds. With access to such funds, opposition politicians can buy support from other elites or build their own parties or bases of support. In Senegal, for example, President Macky Sall, who served as prime min-ister from 2004 to 2007 in the government of then-President Abdoulaye Wade, used his position to amass valuable real estate holdings to the tune of $1.3 billion. He subsequently used that fortune to build his own political operation, eventually leading him to defeat Wade in the 2012 election.[76]

Incumbents therefore need to ensure that the money they extract for political financing does not wind up in the hands of potential oppo-nents. One way to address this challenge is for leaders to minimize the number of people involved in extraction. Doing so, however, creates an alternative risk: that, once departed from office, leaders (and their fam-ilies or other close associates) will be vulnerable to prosecution, often politically driven, for causing financial loss to the state. The Senegalese case is once again instructive. Suspicious of Sall's political ambitions, President Wade dismissed Sall as prime minister in 2007, after which Wade allocated a number of key government portfolios to his son Karim

---

[75] Posner and Young (2018).
[76] "Sénégal: Macky Sall, président équilibriste," Jeune Afrique, June 4, 2012.

Wade who, by many accounts, extracted handsomely from these positions. Despite the Wade family's ability to gain financially from this arrangement, this move was not without political and personal costs. After Sall won the 2012 election, he used his influence over the judiciary to force Abdoulaye Wade into exile to avoid potential prosecution. Karim Wade, who remained in Senegal, was prosecuted, imprisoned, and eventually barred from running against President Sall in the 2019 election. Similar types of cases in Malawi, Zambia, Burkina Faso, and elsewhere further illustrate the risks of political prosecution once leaders have departed office.

These political constraints imply that leaders face a principal-agent problem in the course of extraction. In seeking to keep extracted resources away from opponents and potential defectors, they will prefer to manage extraction themselves. Doing so, however, raises the risk of prosecution after leaving office. To mitigate this longer-term risk of prosecution, leaders (principals) will delegate extraction to agents, but only if agents are reliable in the sense that they will extract in service of the incumbent.

2.2.2   Leaders' Responses to Political Constraints

Incumbent leaders have responded to the political risks of extraction in a variety of ways. In some cases, they have sought to manage extraction themselves or involve only very close personal associates. This type of response is evident in the aforementioned examples of the Kenyan Goldenberg Affair and President Wade's 2007 move to place his son Karim in charge of key, extraction-rich portfolios in Senegal. Despite real possibilities of power turnover and eventual political prosecutions in both countries at the time, leaders in these cases opted to manage extraction themselves or in conjunction with their families, eschewing efforts to delegate extraction more broadly to party or state agents.

In other cases, leaders have sought to distance themselves from extraction by delegating extraction responsibilities more broadly to agents. This strategy minimizes the risk that leaders become targets of political prosecution after leaving office. Delegation, however, raises the risk that extracted monies fall into the hands of opponents or party defectors. In some cases, leaders have delegated extraction to a diffuse array of party officials. Accounts of extraction in places like Angola (before Isabel dos Santos was appointed head of Sonangol in 2016), Ghana, and Tanzania reflect this approach. Leaders rely broadly on party agents, often placed into key government positions, who in turn extract state money, often through deals between state and business. By removing themselves from direct involvement in these deals, political principals lower the longer-term risk of becoming a target of politically driven prosecution.

An alternative delegation tactic is to enlist rank-and-file bureaucrats who, in the course of their jobs, extract rents or divert revenues to support the ruling party. Leaders capture rents by placing co-partisans into extraction-rich positions in the public service or by co-opting or coercing bureaucrats who might not otherwise extract for the principal. In these cases, extraction is concentrated more deeply in state organizations, involving not just political appointees but also those hired into career positions. Examples include the 2013 Cashgate scandal in Malawi, President Museveni's use of the Ugandan military for extraction, and the ministerial "rackets" largely administered by civil servants in Sierra Leone.[77] In these cases, leaders seek to remain distant from extraction by enlisting agents from the state, rather than from the party, in their extractive pursuits.

To summarize, politicians in Africa face considerable pressure to extract money from the state to finance their increasingly expensive political operations. Despite widespread perceptions that incumbent leaders can freely extract whatever state money they desire, leaders' efforts to extract are constrained by (1) the need to protect extracted resources from current opponents and potential defectors, and (2) to minimize risks of political prosecution should they leave office. Leaders have responded to these political risks in varied ways, thus raising questions about why and how leaders navigate the politics of extraction.

2.3   Extraction Problems and Party Solutions

In their efforts to manage the political risks of extraction, incumbent leaders confront a number of specific problems: who they can (or cannot) trust to manage extraction, how to access and channel extracted resources, and which instruments they can use to maintain control over those extracted resources. How leaders respond to these problems is consequential for their ability to preserve incumbent resource advantage, to avoid the risk of prosecution and imprisonment after leaving office, or both. As I discuss later in this chapter, their responses also have implications for the broader politicization and performance of the state apparatus. In this section, I explain how the political risks and agency dilemmas described in the previous section translate into three core problems that leaders seek to address in the course of extraction. I then

[77] See Anders (2017) on Malawi, Khisa (2019) on Uganda, and Kpundeh (1994) on Sierra Leone.

explain how incumbents' party institutions are key for understanding how leaders respond to these challenges.

For the purposes of the theoretical discussion, I make several simplifying assumptions. First, I assume that leaders are concerned about the efficiency of extraction meaning that, all else equal, leaders will prefer extraction methods that enable them to extract greater volumes of money at lower costs. The costs of extraction could be monetary, such as payments to agents who extract on behalf of the incumbent. They can also take less tangible forms such as efforts that leaders must expend to monitor and coerce extraction agents or the opportunity costs involved in using state personnel for extraction rather than for the advancement of the incumbent's policy agenda. No matter what the specific nature of the costs, I assume that leaders will seek to minimize them.

I also assume that neither political leaders nor their agents – individuals to whom leaders delegate extraction – are meaningfully constrained by the state's bureaucratic institutions. This assumption incorporates two underlying principles: (1) that politicians can shape bureaucratic institutions to serve their political interests and (2) that bureaucrats can be compelled by politicians to partake in extraction, even if doing so goes against bureaucratic rules, professional norms, or the bureaucrat's own political preferences. As discussed in the preceding chapter, political leaders in Africa enjoy considerable power to fashion bureaucratic institutions to their liking: they can reshape or violate bureaucratic norms and rules to advance their political interests, or apply rules arbitrarily to compel bureaucrats to partake in their extractive projects. Even if agents possess high levels of professionalism and public service commitment, or have political interests that do not align with political principals, incumbent political leaders have significant power to co-opt and coerce their participation using administrative levers such as dismissals, transfers, promotions, performance evaluations, pay raises, and so on.[78]

Finally, I assume that a leader's risk of political prosecution after leaving office is constant across cases. Given a large degree of uncertainty in when or how leaders will depart office, and about what their post-tenure political fortunes will entail, it seems reasonable that most (if not all) leaders possess some moderate level of concern about the possibility of being (politically) prosecuted once out of office. This assumption of constancy in leaders' concerns about future prosecution implies that variation in extraction decisions is driven primarily by concerns about agent

---

[78] A number of recent studies affirm both that bureaucrats' interests are often unaligned with those of their political principals (Brass et al. 2020; Hassan 2020; Harris et al. 2020) and that there are potentially negative consequences if bureaucrats do not comply with political directives from above (Hassan and O'Mealia 2018; Brierley 2020).

defection and opposition access to extracted resources. Thus, in theorizing the extraction decisions that leaders make, I focus principally on variation in risks associated with loyalty, the associated loss of resources to opponents and defectors, and the options available to leaders to avoid or overcome such risks.

2.3.1 Three Extraction Problems

To effectively manage the politics of extraction, leaders must first address the problem of unreliable extraction agents. Seeking to avoid the risk of future prosecution, an incumbent wants to remove herself or himself from the extraction process by delegating extraction to agents. Delegation, however, comes with the potential problem of unreliable agents: individuals who will keep the extracted resources for themselves or channel them to an alternative political principal. To avoid the selection of an unreliable agent, leaders select agents with known loyalties. They also seek agents they know to be competent in managing extraction. Loyal and competent agents, however, may be in short supply or difficult for leaders to identify, thus complicating their decisions about who to select as extraction agents.

The second problem that leaders confront is that of limited networks to facilitate extraction. Leaders need more than reliable individual agents, they need robust networks of actors across different parts of state and society that can help extract and protect resources. Robust networks of supportive actors help to facilitate more flexible and diffuse strategies of extraction and further lower leaders' risks of future prosecution. Extraction networks may include a range of possible actors that serve in a variety of accessory roles that help to insulate the incumbent from the risks of extraction. For example, leaders may rely on networks of bureaucrats who facilitate the diversion of public funds to the party; businesses or civil society groups who provide financial support to the party in exchange for kickbacks or favors; or judges, auditors, or investigators who are willing to absolve extractors of legal responsibility if needed. If the incumbent's potential extraction networks are limited they will incur greater costs in the course of extraction. For example, they may have to co-opt numerous individuals through side payments or they may have to use coercion to compel individuals to support their extraction activities. Additionally, whereas well-established and tested networks decrease the likelihood that extracted monies will make their way into opposition hands, newer and untried networks generate higher monitoring costs for leaders.

This leads to a third problem for incumbent leaders: how to monitor and discipline extraction agents and network actors. Political leaders must ensure that, once extracted, the resources are used in ways that are consistent with the principal's interest. As described earlier, both agents and network actors may prefer to channel extracted money to an alternative political principal or to use the money for their own political or personal enrichment. In the course of deciding how to maintain control over extracted resources, leaders must address the problem of how to best monitor individuals involved in extraction and, when necessary, how to sanction those who do not use the extracted resources in service of the principal. The selection of reliable extraction agents helps to mitigate issues of monitoring and discipline. Nonetheless, these instruments of control are necessary for incumbents as a safeguard against the uncertainties and risks involved in the management of the extraction enterprise.

These three problems – unreliable agents, limited networks, and the costs of monitoring and discipline – represent a core set of challenges that leaders must confront in the course of extraction, particularly if they are to extract in ways that minimize the previously described political risks. The main argument of the book is that leaders' responses to these three problems are conditioned by the party institutions in which they operate. More specifically, I argue that institutionalized parties help political principals to solve these three types of problems. Where leaders are embedded in parties with higher levels of institutionalization, they are able to (1) select reliable extraction agents, (2) activate partisan networks to help facilitate extraction, and (3) effectively use party instruments of control in the management of extracted monies. By contrast, leaders of weakly institutionalized parties struggle to find reliable extraction agents, lack networks through which to channel extracted resources, and have fewer instruments available to monitor and discipline extraction agents.

2.3.2   Understanding Party Institutionalization and Its Variation in Africa

Before fleshing out these links between party institutionalization and extraction, it is useful to reflect on what it means for a political party to be more or less institutionalized. I adopt a definition that focuses on four key dimensions of party institutionalization, all of which figure prominently in extant literature on political parties.[79] The first dimension relates to a party's *durability* and can be described simply as whether the

---

[79] For an overview of different approaches to defining party institutionalization, see Randall and Svåsand (2002).

Table 2.1 *Party institutionalization dimensions*

Dimension	Description
Durability	Party endures beyond the founding leader or central figure
Organization	Internal consensus on boundaries, rules, and procedures
Social Roots	Party has identifiable social bases of support or partisan attachments
Identity	Party actors have shared identity, brands, and values

party persists beyond the political or physical life of its founding leader. The second dimension relates to what Samuel Huntington calls coherence in *organizational structure*, including whether the party has clear organizational boundaries, internal structures, and rules and procedures for resolving disputes within the organization.[80] Third, institutionalized parties are those that have stable *roots in society*, meaning that they have at least some defined and predictable constituencies of support.[81] Finally, institutionalized parties have collective *identities*, brands, or values.[82] While these shared identities or values are often associated with ideological or programmatic platforms, they may also be centered on particular social identities such as ethnicity or religion, or reflect shared values surrounding collective material benefits for party members, as in machine parties that exist in many places throughout the world. The four dimensions are summarized in Table 2.1. When parties rate higher (lower) on all dimensions, they are more (less) institutionalized. If parties rate highly on some, but not all, of these dimensions, I conceive of them as having intermediate levels of institutionalization.

There is considerable variation in party institutionalization across African countries.[83] In countries such as the Democratic Republic of Congo and Benin, parties serve largely as vehicles of personalistic, often ethnic, intra-elite accommodation with minimal coalitional stability or grass-roots organization.[84] In other cases, such as in Tanzania and Ghana, parties have developed much more elaborate and durable elite alliances

[80] Huntington (1968).
[81] Mainwaring and Scully (1995).
[82] See, for example, Levitsky (2003); Lupu (2016).
[83] Elischer (2013); Riedl (2014).
[84] Manning (2005); van de Walle (2007); Rakner and van de Walle (2009).

and organizations.[85] Many African parties fall somewhere between these two poles, with either relatively stable (ethnic) elite alliances or some degree of grassroots party organization.

In terms of durability, although some parties in Africa have shown tremendous staying power and enduring strength, many others have struggled to survive past a single election or term in office. Figure 2.2 shows the age of the executive ruling parties in Africa that held power in 2018. The median age of African ruling parties is twenty-eight years with a standard deviation of 22.2 years.

According to Anne Meng's study of party durability, African parties have survived, on average, 9.06 years following the death or departure of the party's first leader. Of the sixty-six African parties in Meng's dataset, forty-one survived less than one year after the founding leader's departure and the remaining twenty-five parties survived, on average,

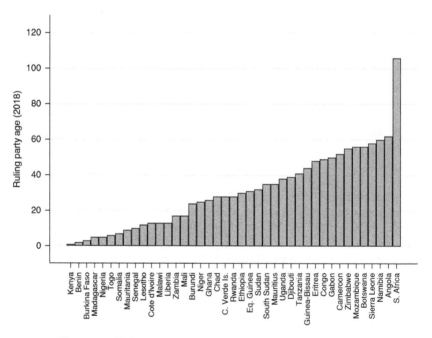

Figure 2.2 Ruling party age
The plot displays the age (in years) of ruling parties in Africa that held power in 2018. Source: Database of Political Institutions (2020).

[85] Osei (2013); Morse (2018).

23.9 years.[86] Additionally, measures of electoral volatility, which measure changes in a party's performance from one election to the next, show considerable variation, with some highly durable parties that generate consistent vote shares in successive elections and some highly volatile ones whose vote shares rise and fall across elections.[87]

Parties in Africa also vary in terms of the coherence of their organizations. In both democratic and authoritarian political regimes, there exist parties with highly organized structures as well as ones with very loose organizations comprised mainly of one main leader surrounded by a small and often fluid group of elite brokers. Those in the former category tend to have rules and procedures that govern membership in the party, clear systems for selecting party candidates and leaders, and party branches across multiple regions of the country. Although party-level data on these types of indicators are not widely available, Nahomi Ichino and Noah Nathan have documented that twenty-seven parties across fifteen African countries hold primary elections to select legislative candidates,[88] serving as a good indication that these twenty-seven parties have considerably higher levels of coherence in their organizations than the many African parties that do not hold primary elections to select candidates. Figure 2.3 presents another indicator of party organization: the extent to which a country's parties have permanent, professionally staffed organizations. Once again, there is considerable variation among African countries on this indicator.

Political parties in Africa also vary in terms of their roots in society and their resulting strength of partisan attachments. Figure 2.4 shows the proportion of respondents in Afrobarometer's Round 7 (2016–2018) surveys said they felt close to a political party. Proportions range from around 20 percent in Sudan and Togo to around 60 percent in a number of countries including Ghana, Botswana, and Uganda. Another indicator of the breadth of a party's social roots is its ability to win larger numbers of seats in the legislature, which demonstrates reliable support across different districts or regions. In legislative elections in Africa held between 1990 and 2016, the president's party won anywhere from 14 percent to 100 percent of seats in the legislature, with a mean of 65.6 percent

---

[86] Based on author calculations using replication data for Meng (2021), https://doi.org/10.7910/DVN/7H6XQO.

[87] Electoral volatility is measured as the Pedersen Index, which adds the differences between the vote shares for all parties in the last two elections and then divides by two.

[88] Ichino and Nathan (2018).

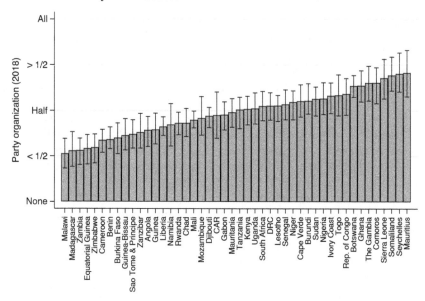

Figure 2.3 Party organization
The plot displays point estimates and confidence intervals for V-Dem's
Party Organization indicator. The indicator asks "How many political
parties for national-level office have permanent organizations?" The
responses range from no parties (0) to all parties (4). Source:
V-Dem v9.

of seats and a standard deviation of 20.2 percent.[89] Although many
incumbent parties have enjoyed the strength necessary to win significant
majorities in the legislature, there are a number of countries, including
the Democratic Republic of Congo, Benin, Liberia, Malawi, and Mada-
gascar, in which incumbent parties or coalitions have repeatedly failed
to win even one-third of legislative seats. Thus, whereas some parties
might reliably maintain support from, for example, a single ethnic group
comprising a smaller but significant proportion of the population, others
have managed to build enduring attachments to larger or more diverse
socio-economic or ethno-regional groups.

Finally, political parties in Africa are often seen as lacking strong ideologies or programmatic platforms, suggesting the absence of shared
identities and values among party members. This assessment is mis-
leading. Not only do some countries in Africa contain parties with

[89] I am grateful to Jaimie Bleck and Nicolas van de Walle for sharing their data on
legislative elections.

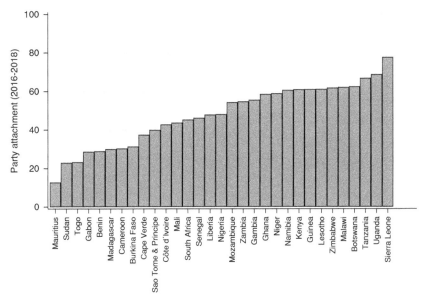

Figure 2.4 Feeling close to a political party
The graph displays the proportion of survey respondents in each
country who indicated that they feel close to a party.
Source: Afrobarometer Round 7 (2016–2018).

distinguishable platforms (See Figure 2.5), many parties in Africa possess alternative sources of shared values such as social identities or
historical legacies that shape party brands and cultivate shared interests among members. As I describe in more detail in the next chapter,
parties in Ghana form a compelling case of parties that lack clear programmatic content in their manifestos,[90] but contain historical legacies,
shared material interests, and ethnic identities that shape each party's
brand.[91] Even in Kenya and South Africa, where ethnic or racial identities are highly salient in party politics, shared economic interests or
social experiences serve as important signaling devices that can reinforce
voters' commitment to a party.[92]

Looking across the four dimensions of party institutionalization, parties in African countries demonstrate considerable variation in their

[90] Ayee (2011); Nathan (2019).
[91] Whitfield (2009); Riedl (2014); Kim (2018).
[92] Harris (2020); Kim (2020).

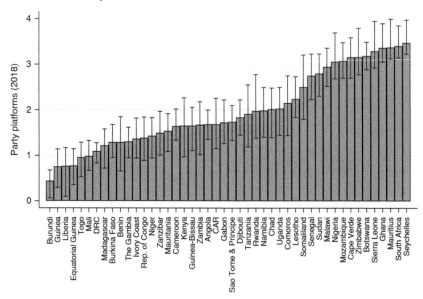

Figure 2.5 Distinct party platforms
The graph displays point estimates and confidence intervals for
V-Dem's Distinct Party Platforms indicator. The indicator asks "How
many political parties with representation in the national legislature or
presidency have publicly available party platforms (manifestos) that
are publicized and relatively distinct from one another?" The
responses range from no parties (0) to all parties (4).
Source: V-Dem v9.

levels of institutionalization. This variation is evident even among parties whose attachments to voters and collective identities are primarily
ethnic in nature. Although there is no single party-level measure that
neatly aggregates durability, organization, social roots, and party identity, country-level variation is nonetheless estimable with expert survey
data. Figure 2.6 shows African country scores on V-Dem's Party Institutionalization index, which aggregates indicators measuring organization,
values and identity, and social roots, as well as party cohesion in legisla-
tures. A considerable body of qualitative research reinforces the existence
of variation in institutional strength among African parties.[93]

Although party institutions in Africa are not immutable, they do display a large degree of historical continuity. Recent scholarship debates

[93] Elischer (2013); Resnick (2014); Riedl (2014); Morse (2018); Sanches (2018).

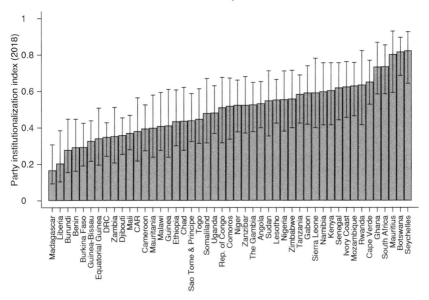

Figure 2.6 Party institutionalization
The plot displays point estimates and confidence intervals for V-Dem's
Party Institutionalization index. The index aggregates five variables:
party organizations, party branches, party linkages, distinct party
platforms, and legislative party cohesion. Note that the underlying
indicators are *not* specific to the ruling party, they measure
institutionalization among all parties in the country. Source:
V-Dem v9.

the precise historical origins of African party institutions, with some
arguing that key moments of institutional formation occurred during
processes of decolonization in the middle of the twentieth century,[94] and
others asserting that periods of authoritarian rule in the 1970s and 1980s
represent the most critical periods of party formation.[95] In either case,
scholars tend to agree that party institutions pre-date, and have largely
survived, transitions to the more open and competitive political regimes
that exist across the continent today.[96]

[94] See Bleck and Van de Walle (2018: 104) for an overview of this perspective.
[95] LeBas (2011); Riedl (2014).
[96] Lindberg (2007). The main exceptions are ruling parties, such as the *Parti
Démocratique Sénégalais* (PDS) in Senegal, that have undergone processes of de-
institutionalization following a loss of power (Kelly 2020). I discuss this case at greater
length in Chapter 8.

2.3.3   Party Institutionalization and Extraction Incentives

Strong party institutions help incumbents to solve the three extraction problems – unreliable agents, limited networks, and monitoring
and control. Parties' durability, organizational structure, extensive social
roots, and shared identities and values shape opportunities and incentives for incumbents to select reliable extraction agents, activate partisan
networks to facilitate extraction, and utilize less costly, party-based
instruments to maintain control over extracted resources. Stronger party
institutions therefore allow incumbents to extract in ways that more
efficiently manage the political risks of extraction.

Endowed with durable and coherent organizations, leaders in more
institutionalized political parties are better able to overcome the problem of selecting (un)reliable extraction agents. When party organizations
persist over time, political principals learn about potential extraction
agents, including their loyalties and competencies. The attributes of
party members as potential extraction agents become especially apparent over repeated election cycles in which members either remain in or
defect from the party. The longer that individuals remain in the party, the
more likely it is that they have proven themselves as loyal and competent
agents who will serve the principal's interest.

Strong party organizations also contribute to a leader's ability to overcome the problem of unreliable extract agents. With organizations that
clearly specify membership, leadership hierarchies, and procedures such
as internal elections through which members can advance in the party
hierarchy, political principals can more easily learn about the loyalties
and competencies of potential extraction agents as they watch these processes play out. Internal selection processes such as primary elections
and leadership contests are particularly useful for the identification of
reliable extraction agents because they reveal party members' abilities to
raise money and perform politically. In short, durable and well-organized
party institutions incentivize leaders to select elite party agents to oversee
extraction.

Weakly institutionalized political parties, by contrast frequently dis-
band or reform with new alliances and members, making it difficult
for party leaders to gain useful information about the preferences of
potential agents. Likewise, in parties lacking in organizational coherence,
frequent shifts in party boundaries and structures further complicate
leaders' abilities to learn about the loyalties and competencies of members. Internal contests often fail to materialize in weakly institutionalized
parties, as personalistic leaders unilaterally determine leadership succession and candidate slates. The absence of these contests denies party

leaders important information-gathering opportunities that could help them to overcome problems related to unreliable extraction agents. As such, leaders of weakly institutionalized parties have incentives to either manage extraction themselves or delegate to less powerful individuals whose compliance can be bought or coerced.

With their party's stronger and more extensive roots in society, leaders in more highly institutionalized parties are also better positioned to engage robust networks in extraction. Party networks provide extractors with partisan-affiliated organizations and individuals that offer both flexibility and efficiency in the extraction process. For example, party members who own or operate businesses may participate in extraction by financing party operations in exchange for licenses and procurement or privatization contracts. A well-institutionalized party may also possess networks within the government that can assist with or, when necessary, turn a blind eye toward, extraction activities. Such networks provide party leaders and their extraction agents with flexibility in choosing how to access and channel extracted resources, enabling them to reduce both the potential costs and political risks involved in extractive activities. Importantly, robust networks incentivize leaders to extract in more diffuse ways and to rely less intensively and extensively on state personnel and structures.

Lacking clear and stable roots in society, leaders in less institutionalized parties are unlikely to have robust networks on which to depend for extraction support. They rely, instead, on a more narrow group of personal affiliates, or those they can co-opt or coerce to participate and act in the party's interest. As with the selection of extraction agents, activating network actors with unknown loyalties or incentives could pose both immediate and future risks to the incumbent. Unlike their counterparts in institutionalized parties, leaders are not able to efficiently engage broader networks to "grease the wheels" of extraction. The absence of robust networks therefore limits leaders' options in how to access and channel political money and incentivizes them to concentrate extraction within the state.

Finally, party institutions shape the potential costs incurred by the political principal to monitor and discipline extraction agents and networks. In delegating extraction to agents, leaders take on a risk that agents will use the extracted money to benefit an alternative political principal, to advance their own political career, or to personally enrich themselves. A party's durability, organizational coherence, and identity all shape agents' incentives to act in service of the incumbent. Agent behavior, in turn, shapes the extent to which political principals invest in instruments to monitor and discipline agents.

Party durability lengthens the time horizons for agents and network actors. Knowing that the party is likely to survive – and hold power – in the future, agents are not only less likely to defect from the party, but they will also have incentives to act in ways that would advance the party's interests, as well as their own standing in the party. Organizational coherence also reduces the principals' costs of monitoring and discipline by incentivizing agents to act in service of the incumbent and the party. Well-organized parties set guidelines about how members advance within the party. If party agents act in ways that undermine the party's interest, for example by mismanaging extracted resources, they may become ineligible for advancement or lose internal elections.

Collective identities and values infused into the party have a similar effect: they incentivize agents to act in the interest of the party and reduce the need for leaders to invest in monitoring and discipline. In institutionalized parties, agents are conditioned to act in accordance with party values and/or sanctioned by the party when they do not do so. To the extent that party values reflect a drive for redistribution and accumulation in favor of party members – common among the clientelistic and machine-type parties found in Africa and elsewhere – agents' participation in extraction may be expected as part of their duty to the party.[97]

Together, a durable, organized, and value-infused party generates strong incentives for agents to act in service of the incumbent and the party and reduces incentives for political leaders to use more coercive methods of control. Absent these party institutions, agents are more likely to defect from the party and/or handle extracted resources in ways that do not align with the incumbent's interests, thereby generating incentives for principals to use more coercive instruments to monitor and discipline agents, and to maintain control over extraction.

Table 2.2 summarizes how strong and weak party institutions generate different incentives for leaders in their extraction decisions. Whereas leaders embedded in well-institutionalized political parties can more easily overcome (or avoid) problems of unreliable agents, limited networks, and the costs of monitoring and discipline; those in parties with weaker institutions have fewer and more costly options. The differing incentive structures generated by the incumbent's party institutions shape subsequent decisions about *to whom* to delegate extraction, *how* they access and channel extracted monies, and *which* instruments of control they employ to ensure that extracted monies serve their political benefit.

---

[97] Bayart (1993) and Zolberg (1966), for example, describe many African parties as valuing accumulation for their members. This is not to say that they do not also

Table 2.2 *Extraction problems and party institution incentives*

Extraction Problem	Institutionalized Party Incentives	Noninstitutionalized Party Incentives
Unreliable Agents	Delegation to elite party agents with known loyalty and competence	Unknown loyalty of elite party agents: no delegation or delegate to coercible agents
Limited Networks	Activate partisan networks to support diffuse, flexible extraction	Few network actors available: concentrate extraction in state apparatus
Monitoring & Discipline	Minimal investments in monitoring and discipline	Significant investments in monitoring and discipline

2.4   Strategies of Extraction: Collusive and Coercive

Based on the incentives outlined in Table 2.2, leaders of institutional-ized political parties are considerably more likely to delegate extraction to trusted party agents, activate robust partisan networks to facilitate extraction, and rely on internal party incentives to promote agent disci-pline. These practices form the basis of what I call *collusive* strategies of extraction. In collusive extraction, incumbent leaders engage loyal and supportive constituencies to extract money for collective benefit. In doing so, leaders remain distant from extraction, thus reducing their vulnerability to future political prosecution.

Leaders of weakly institutionalized (or nonexistent) parties have dif-ferent incentives because they face greater likelihoods of elite defection from the party and because they have fewer organizational tools available to them. As such, their extraction strategies are likely to be more *coercive* in form. In systems of coercive extraction, leaders limit delegation to elite party actors and they pursue more aggressive efforts to keep current or potential opponents away from extraction. This section introduces these two models of extraction, explains their basic differences, and further establishes their links to party institutions.

2.4.1   Collusive Extraction

Prevalent in political parties with higher levels of institutionalization, col-lusive extraction involves party agents working collectively toward the common goal of raising money for the party. Leaders trust elite party

have ideological values, but rather that many parties in Africa act as mechanisms of economic redistribution or accumulation for their members.

agents – many of whom have worked their way up the party hierarchy over time – to extract through deals and arrangements involving partisan networks spread across business, government, and civil society. Because it is largely in the longer-term interests of elite agents to support the party, collusive extraction does not require significant incumbent involvement, nor does it require their investment in either monitoring or coercive mechanisms of control.

In collusive systems of extraction, extraction agents are primarily drawn from the elite ranks of the party, since it is these individuals who have worked their way up in the party hierarchy by demonstrating their loyalty, commitment, and competence within the party's organization. Party leaders are well aware of the strengths, weaknesses and potential risks associated with elite party members as potential extraction agents. This knowledge, accumulated over time through interactions with elite members, helps them to manage risks associated with the problem of unreliable agents. In other words, leaders are likely to have the information they need to select trusted and competent extraction agents, particularly those with long histories in the party.

In collusive extraction, extraction agents engage partisan affiliates in government, business, and civil society to help facilitate extraction. The involvement of network actors can take any number of forms and is likely to depend on the social roots of the party. If the party is well supported by business interests, extraction is likely to involve government favors to businesses, such as procurement contracts, licenses, or regulatory privilege in exchange for their financial support to the party. If the party has a social base of support in the military or government bureaucracy, the party may engage these actors to help facilitate the diversion of resources, budget manipulation such as ghost workers, or provision of favors to financiers. In short, if the parties' social bases of support are well defined, incumbent party leaders and their agents can engage these constituencies in ways that make extraction less risky and more efficient. To the extent that the party's social roots extend across regions and economic sectors, leaders will be in a stronger position to activate robust networks.

Because institutionalized parties have members with longer time horizons and mechanisms that promote agent discipline, collusive extraction does not require incumbent leaders to invest significantly in monitoring their agents, nor do they require significant coercion to ensure their compliance. Elite agents are not only socialized into behaving in ways that support the party, but their future success in the party is likely to depend on shows of loyalty and support. Whether their aspirations are to receive prestigious appointments, ascend to leadership positions within the party, or win primary elections, members (agents) of well-institutionalized parties are likely to have party-based incentives to serve as faithful extraction agents. Thanks to these internal party incentives, incumbent party leaders can trust the party elite to serve as extraction agents and to use extracted resources in the interest of the party without significant effort to monitor or discipline agents. In the event that agents do not act in service of the party, the party itself can impose sanctions by denying the agent an opportunity to advance in the party or access to party spoils in the future.

In practice, collusive extraction involves party elites placed broadly into high-level government positions where they can coordinate extraction with partisan network actors in government or society. The specific types of exchanges of that these elite party agents oversee, however, may vary from one context to the next. In Ghana, ministers or other officials award procurement contracts to partisan-aligned business financiers in exchange for their financial or in-kind support of the party.[98] In South Africa, earlier ANC leaders in government designed and targeted programs, such as the Black Economic Empowerment program, to cultivate and support party donors.[99] In Tanzania, party officials in government give affiliates of the ruling CCM advantageous access to valuable real estate or private enterprises to generate income for the party.[100] Although the specific types of fundraising exchanges look different in these examples, they are similar in the sense that the ruling party's strong institutions provide incentives for elite agents to exercise government power in ways that engage partisan networks to advance the collective material benefit of the part, and do not require serious investments in instruments of control. In all of these manifestations of collusive extraction, incumbent leaders are able to remain distant from extraction, relying on agents who themselves are incentivized to act in the interest of the party.

2.4.2   Coercive Extraction

Leaders of parties with low levels of institutionalization face greater challenges in selecting and controlling extraction agents. They lack knowledge about the loyalties and competencies of potential extraction agents, they are unlikely to possess well-defined and robust partisan networks, and they cannot rely on any internal party mechanisms of control.

[98] I describe this extraction practice in detail in Chapter 4.
[99] Lodge (1998).
[100] Ewald (2013: 346–347).

They are therefore compelled to engage in more *coercive* modes of extraction that involve more serious efforts to co-opt, monitor, and coercively control extraction agents and processes. Due to the inability to control extraction agents through party structures, coercive extraction also relies to a greater extent on levers of control within the state. In coercive extraction, incumbent leaders cannot easily distance themselves from extraction, thus complicating their efforts to manage the longer-term risks of political prosecution.

In the absence of durable and organized party institutions, incumbents cannot discern the loyalties of party or coalition members. With the party's shorter time horizons and a more fluid political landscape, members have incentives to defect from the incumbent's party, particularly if they perceive incumbent vulnerability in the form of either waning political support or resource deficiencies.[101] Incumbents may be especially reluctant to delegate extraction to elite politicians, who can defect with the extracted resources to form their own parties and challenge the incumbent. This reluctance has two important implications. First, incumbents will seek to manage elite extraction deals themselves, keeping potential elite defectors away from extraction opportunities. Second, leaders in noninstitutionalized parties will seek to overcome the problem of unreliable extraction agents by co-opting or coercing more vulnerable actors, such as rank-and-file bureaucratic agents. Bureaucrats are more easily bought or coerced than elites because, whereas elites typically have other resources such as wealth or professional skills by which they can sustain themselves outside of office, rank-and-file bureaucrats are unlikely to have attractive job prospects outside the state.

In coercive extraction, the party's limited social bases of support means that there are few existing partisan actors available to facilitate extraction. Leaders therefore concentrate their extraction efforts within the state apparatus where they can co-opt or coerce participation from state employees under their authority. Leaders are inclined to focus such efforts in agencies with abundant opportunities to access revenue or seek rents such as in state-owned enterprises, service delivery organizations, tax collection, and so on.

In contrast to collusive extraction, there are no clear party procedures or norms in coercive systems to govern agent behavior. Incumbents must identify and cultivate mechanisms through which to monitor and, when necessary, discipline agents. To overcome this problem, leaders use the

---

[101] See Reuter and Gandhi (2011) and Andrews and Honig (2019) for accounts of defection in weak parties.

state apparatus more intensely; they reward loyal agents with desirable assignments or promotions and they punish disloyal agents with dismissal, transfers, or other undesirable career outcomes. These state administrative instruments of control require greater effort on the part of the leader themselves, and come at a greater cost in terms of efficient extraction.

What does coercive extraction look like in practice? It involves, first, incumbents' reluctance to delegate extraction to elite party agents. This reluctance implies that the political principal may become more directly engaged in extraction and relationships with those that form part of the extraction network. Intensive efforts by Nigeria's presidents to service relationships with key "godfathers" is a manifestation of this practice, as was Senegalese President Wade's delegation of key, extraction-rich portfolios to his son, Karim Wade. By maintaining close, personal control over these relationships, leaders can avoid problems related to unreliable agents. Even if political principals could control elites to some extent by threatening their dismissal, the lucrative nature of elite-level deals means that incumbents still risk serious political or financial loss if their elite agents extract, then defect.

Second, leaders are likely to co-opt and coerce lower-level extraction agents, such as rank-and-file bureaucrats, to engage in the diversion of state money, or in the collection of rents from their positions in the public sector. Malawi's "Cashgate" scandal is a particularly vivid example: civil service employees made vast payments for items that were never supplied, and which audit reports suggest made their way to party coffers.[102] The coercive nature of this arrangement was plainly evident from the fact that Paul Mphwiyo, the budget director in the finance ministry who had threatened to expose the corruption ring, was shot and seriously wounded in September 2013. Perhaps more common, however, is that leaders can threaten rotations and dismissals for public servants who do not extract in the party's interest.[103] Figure 2.7 summarizes the two strategies of extraction.

Several clarifying comments about these two extraction strategies are in order. First, the two models of extraction are conceptualized as ideal types associated with two poles on a linear spectrum of party institutionalization. They are designed to convey the idea that a leader's choice of extraction strategy is conditioned by the internal structures and organization of the party. However, these polar models of collusive and coercive

---

[102] "Money from Malawi 'Cashgate' scandal allegedly funded electoral campaigns," *The Guardian*, February 13, 2015.
[103] Iyer and Mani (2012); Bricrley (2020).

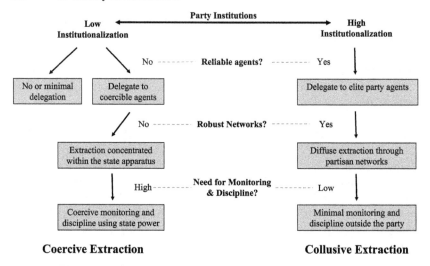

Figure 2.7 Collusive and coercive extraction

extraction are not the only possible responses to extraction problems. In Chapter 8, I discuss how this approach can be adapted to understand extraction practices in parties that do not fit neatly into the institutionalized or noninstitutionalized categories, including the NRM in Uganda and the PDS in Senegal.

Second, collusive and coercive extraction are not necessarily mutually exclusive, but there are important reasons why we would expect leaders to prefer collusive strategies, if available, over coercive ones. Whereas collusive strategies do not require high levels of involvement from the party leader, coercive strategies require leaders (or their close associates) to become more involved in either extraction deals themselves, or in the monitoring and discipline of agents. This involvement potentially raises the longer-term risk of prosecution after leaving office. Additionally, coercive forms of extraction are likely to be more costly in terms of co-optation payments, investments in coercive tools of monitoring and discipline, and the use of state personnel for extractive (rather than governing) tasks. In short, assuming that leaders trust their party elite, and that agents have incentives to act in service of the incumbent, broad delegation to party elites can generate potentially large sums of money with comparatively little risk and cost to the incumbent. Even if leaders have both strategies available to them, as leaders of institutionalized parties do, they are likely to prefer a collusive strategy.

Third, I do not intend for the models to predict how much money parties extract from the state. Although leaders of institutionalized parties may be able to extract with greater efficiency,[104] both systems have the potential to cause major financial losses to the state.

2.5   Extraction and State Politicization

Collusive and coercive strategies of extraction imply differences not only in how money is extracted but also in how and with what governing consequences leaders use the state to advance their extractive pursuits. In that the two strategies involve different sets of actors, different channels of extraction, and different instruments of control, they result in varied patterns of state politicization as leaders in each system are likely to politicize the positions, agencies, and functions that are more central to the extraction system. Because coercive extraction is concentrated to a greater extent within state networks, and depends to a greater extent on executive levers of control, it results in more extensive and more disruptive forms of politicization of the state's executive and bureaucratic institutions.

2.5.1   What Is State Politicization?

State politicization involves an array of practices in which the state is fashioned to advance political goals. One common approach sees politicization as the discretionary application of political criteria in the management of state personnel, including recruitment, selection, promotion, rewards, and discipline.[105] Politicians engage in this type of personnel politicization for a multitude of reasons, with much of the contemporary literature focusing on the use of jobs in exchange for political support.[106]

Another approach conceptualizes politicization as political pressure applied to state agents and organizations to act in the interest of politicians. These political pressures often impair the ability of state personnel to act in accordance with formally specified roles and directives in the implementation of public policy. The inability of agency personnel to

---

[104] This principle is consistent with Susan Rose-Ackerman's observation that strong party organizations may increase the volume of money changing hands in corrupt exchanges (1978: 46).

[105] Peters and Pierre (2004: 2). In a recent empirical application of this approach, Bersch et al. (2017) study politicization in Brazil's government agencies by measuring the percentage of political appointees and career civil servants who are members of political parties.

[106] Shefter (1977); Geddes (1994); Golden (2003); O'Dwyer (2006).

act autonomously from political pressure can therefore undermine state performance. As Barbara Geddes writes, "even if bureaucrats want to implement public policies supported by the citizenry, they may find it costly to do so if politicians reward other behavior."[107] Politicians often have a number of tools at their disposal to influence the behavior of bureaucrats. They may write more or less specific laws and statutes,[108] eschew the adoption of rules and practices, such as meritocratic recruitment, that insulate bureaucrats from political pressure,[109] or seek to sanction bureaucrats who do not comply with their desired behavior.[110]

Combining these two approaches, I conceptualize politicization as a broader effort by politicians to exercise state power for their own political benefit. Indeed, the selection, rotation, and dismissal of personnel are themselves potential mechanisms of broader political control and preservation – sending signals about acceptable and unacceptable bureaucratic behavior. These efforts involve not only the interest of political leaders in providing jobs to their supporters but also various efforts to compel certain behaviors on the part of state agents. In other words, state politicization can serve a variety of political needs, reflecting politicians' core efforts to use the power of the state apparatus to advance their political interests. Viewed this way, state politicization is neither an anomaly nor a pathology of modern states. Instead, this approach recognizes that politicization exists on a spectrum and comes in many forms.

2.5.2   *Politicizing the State for Extraction*

The second part of the argument focuses on how collusive and coercive modes of extraction shape state politicization in three areas: (1) the recruitment and selection of state personnel across the state apparatus; (2) politicians' efforts to manage and control executive actors, namely ministers and other high-ranking state officials; and (3) political control over the day-to-day business of bureaucratic organizations. I argue that collusive and coercive extraction strategies lead to important and consequential differences in politicization across these three areas.

First, in the course of their efforts to select reliable extraction agents, leaders of collusive and coercive extraction regimes have incentives to politicize the recruitment and selection of the state personnel who are most likely to serve as extraction agents. If leaders rely primarily on elite

---

[107] Geddes (1994: 48–49).
[108] Huber and Shipan (2002).
[109] Wood and Waterman (1991); Geddes (1994); Grzymała-Busse (2007).
[110] Hassan and O'Mealia (2018); Brierley (2020).

party agents to administer extraction, as is the case in collusive systems, they are especially likely to politicize executive appointment decisions by favoring party loyalists for high-level government posts that involve more significant opportunities for extraction. In more coercive systems, however, leaders risk empowering elite political rivals or future defectors if they place them in positions with access to extraction opportunities. As such, leaders in coercive extraction minimize the placement of political elites into executive posts, preferring instead to appoint technocrats and personal loyalists to these positions. Additionally, in coercive extraction, leaders are more likely to politicize the recruitment and selection of rank-and-file bureaucrats to serve as extraction agents within the public service, particularly into positions that are rife with extraction opportunities. Although leaders may be able to coerce non-supporting bureaucrats to participate in extraction, hiring based on political criteria reduces the costs of coercion because supporters are more likely to act as willing participants and less likely to require intensive monitoring.[111]

Second, different extraction strategies imply differences in leaders' efforts to control the workings of the state's executive apparatus – the president's office, cabinet positions, and other high-level ministerial posts. Collusive delegation means that, at the executive cabinet level, a more or less cohesive and stable group of party elites can, with relative ease, advance the party's policy and political agendas simultaneously. By contrast, leaders employing more coercive forms of extraction must control access to money and continually incentivize loyalty, often by dismissing and rotating ministers more frequently. These rotations and dismissals prevent coordination and the formation of trust among executive actors. Whereas the collusive dynamic is compatible with sustained and relatively effective implementation of public policies, the coercive system of executive management tends to undermine any serious policy implementation progress.[112]

Third, collusive and coercive extraction imply differences in the politicization of the day-to-day work of bureaucrats. In delegating extraction to high-level officials and activating partisan social networks outside the state to facilitate extraction, collusive extraction is less intrusive into

---

[111] Oliveros (2021).

[112] In her study of party institutions and economic policy in Mozambique and Zambia, Anne Pitcher observes similar patterns. Mozambique's well-institutionalized party system enables them to "anticipate and manage possible partisan effects" of particular investments, thereby sustaining momentum for reforms. By contrast, in Zambia, reforms often "clashed with the informal pursuit of opportunistic goals by party notables who frequently cycled in and out of their positions, usually at the whim of the President" (2017: 7–8). I add to this perspective by emphasizing how leaders' interests in extraction may condition these responses.

functions of the state's bureaucratic organizations. Extraction activities in collusive systems are unlikely to permeate an entire agency, or fundamentally alter the material resources available to an agency's employees. In short, the bureaucratic work environment is minimally disrupted by collusive types of extraction. By contrast, coercive modes of extraction are potentially much more disruptive to the workings of state bureaucratic agencies. With extraction agents embedded in the bureaucratic ranks, and limited networks with whom leaders can collude, leaders rely to a greater extent on bureaucrats to divert money directly from state coffers and/or to extract rents from the population. Bureaucratic extraction agents are drawn away from carrying out their duties and the resources of the organization are depleted in more visible and more impactful ways. Concerned about extracted resources making their way to opponents, leaders are more likely to interfere in day-to-day bureaucratic business, posing more sever threats to bureaucratic productivity.[113]

The combination of an unstable executive and politicized civil service that characterizes coercive extraction systems is particularly detrimental to state performance. Instability and low levels of cohesion in the executive not only undermine policy commitment but also disrupt the work of rank-and-file bureaucrats, further eroding morale and productivity in state institutions. In short, the specific patterns of politicization associated with coercive extraction are pernicious in the ways they impact state organizations: undermining elite commitment to governing agendas, paralyzing bureaucratic action, and demotivating personnel.

The idea that leaders' extraction efforts shape institutional forms and functions is by no means new. Even in classic theories of state formation, opportunistic rulers seek to cement their power by administering extractive protection rackets[114] or by acting as "stationary bandits,"[115] both of which imply the extractive origins of state institutions. More recently, Anna Grzymała-Busse explains that "state seizure does not simply corrode the state" as many studies of clientelism suggest. Instead, she argues that, whereas some extractive rulers "seek to maximize their discretion by weakening regulation and oversight," others "construct rules and durable practices of redistribution, budgeting, and authority," leading to divergent state institutions and capacities.[116] I build on these perspectives by centering leaders' financial imperatives and associated

---

[113] A growing body of research finds that, in African contexts, more autonomy for bureaucrats and less political interference are generally associated with better governing outcomes. See, for example, Teodoro and Pitcher (2017); McDonnell (2020).

[114] Tilly (1985).

[115] Olson (1993).

[116] Grzymała-Busse (2008: 639).

agency problems to advance our understanding of the varying patterns of politicization that are evident within clientelistic contexts. This approach illuminates why some forms of politicization are ultimately more harmful to state performance than others.

2.6 Conclusion

Whereas incumbent political leaders in Africa (or elsewhere) may have once enjoyed virtually unfettered access to state money, the growing competitiveness of elections and increasingly frequent turnovers of power complicate leaders' abilities to extract from the state at will. Instead, leaders must confront both immediate and longer-term political risks involved in their efforts to extract political money from the state. One possible solution – the delegation of extraction to agents – helps incumbent leaders to avoid risks associated with future political prosecution. Delegation, however, raises the probability that extracted resources wind up in the hands of the opposition.

This chapter has argued that leaders' responses to these problems hinge on the types of party institutions in which they operate. In contexts of high party institutionalization, leaders engage in more collusive forms of extraction: delegating extraction widely to trusted party elite who coordinate with networks outside of government to extract state funds for the party. Although this system certainly results in significant financial losses to the state, it largely avoids more disruptive forms of political interference in the day-to-day workings of the executive and bureaucratic apparatuses. In collusive systems of extraction, political leaders can, with some success, simultaneously pursue both their public policy and political agendas.

Leaders' responses to extraction dilemmas are much different in contexts of low party institutionalization. In these contexts, incumbents face elevated risks of elite defection and must overcome the problem of agents who are not incentivized to extract in service of the party leadership. Leaders of weakly institutionalized parties therefore prefer to manage elite extraction deals themselves or to co-opt and coerce more vulnerable individuals, such as rank-and-file bureaucrats, to participate in their extraction projects. In so doing, they not only concentrate extraction within bureaucratic institutions, for example by coercively engaging bureaucrats to divert rents and revenues to the party, but they also seek to retain tighter control over extraction up and down the ranks of the state apparatus. This strategy of extraction is characterized by executive instability and high levels of politicization in the bureaucracy, leading to a less productive state institutional environment.

3 Politics and Party Institutions in Benin and Ghana

When Patrice Talon assumed office as President of Benin in 2016, he became Benin's third consecutive head of state to have come to power as an independent candidate. Since the country's transition to democracy in 1990–1991, only Nicephore Soglo, who served as the first president of the new regime from 1991 to 1996, had won power for the first time as a party-affiliated candidate. Even Mathieu Kérékou, who led Benin's single-party regime of the *Parti de la Révolution Populaire du Bénin* (PRPB) from 1975 to 1990, contested his first two multiparty elections in 1991 and 1996 without any official party affiliation.

The virtual absence of parties in Benin's presidential elections stands in stark contrast to elections in Ghana, where the country's two major parties – the National Democratic Congress (NDC) and the National Patriotic Party (NPP) – have, over the course of seven national elections (as of the time of writing), consolidated their abilities to compete and win in both presidential and parliamentary elections. Not only have prospects of electoral victories for third-party candidates in Ghana's elections deteriorated over this time,[1] but as I document throughout this chapter, the major parties themselves have grown in terms of their size, their organizational infrastructure, their levels of internal competition, and their professionalization.

In this chapter, I focus on this divergence in party institutionalization. These differing party trajectories are integral to the book's core argument: that political leaders extract political money from the state in ways that are conditioned by the party structures in which they operate. Despite facing similar political and extraction environments, leaders in the two countries are embedded in parties with highly differentiated levels of institutionalization. The differences in party institutional strength have, in turn, conditioned their leaders to pursue different extraction strategies: collusive extraction in Ghana and coercive extraction in Benin.

---

[1] Bob-Milliar (2019).

In addition to establishing the divergent trajectories of party institutionalization across the two countries, this chapter elaborates on the
dual case selection strategy that I introduced in Chapter 1. In detailing
the major differences in the strength of party institutions across the two
countries, I establish the two countries as "extreme" cases of low (Benin)
and high (Ghana) party institutionalization. The selection of extreme
cases is designed to *build* the party-based theory of extraction that I
described in the previous chapter. I also use this chapter to establish the
plausibility of Benin and Ghana as most similar cases, first by detailing
how the two countries' similar democratic landscapes produce a common set of political constraints on incumbent extraction and, second, by
ruling out competing explanations derived from potentially confounding differences between the two countries. When viewed as most-similar
cases, the comparative analysis of Benin and Ghana that I conduct in
Chapters 4–7 can serve as confirmatory of the book's principal causal
argument: that party institutions, rather than competing factors, have
driven leaders to adopt their respective extraction and state politicization
practices.

This chapter is divided into three parts. In the first section, I discuss
the political environments in Benin and Ghana since their transitions to
multiparty politics in the early 1990s, establishing their similar democratic trajectories and the common ways in which electoral competition
has – and has not – shaped each country's extraction environment.
In the second section, I turn to the principal explanatory variable of
the book: party institutionalization. I document divergent trajectories of
party institutionalization in the two countries: the consolidation of highly
institutionalized parties in Ghana and the perpetuation of very weakly
institutionalized parties in Benin. In the third section, I address potential
confounding variables – differences in economic structures, bureaucratic
institutions (and their colonial origins), and electoral systems. I explain
why these factors are unlikely to match the explanatory power of party
institutions for understanding how and why leaders extract from the state
in collusive or coercive ways.

3.1 Electoral Competition and the Extraction Environment

Both Benin and Ghana have served as oft-cited examples of democratic
success in Africa. Since their adoption of democratic constitutions in the
early 1990s (1990 in Benin and 1992 in Ghana), both countries had
maintained a consecutive string of presidential and parliamentary elections. As of 2020, there had been three inter-party transfers of power in

Table 3.1 *Democracy indicators for Benin, Ghana, and Africa (1992–2018)*

Indicator	Ghana	Benin	Africa	Scale
Consecutive Presidential Elections (DPI)	7	6	3.33	–
Inter-party Electoral Turnovers of Power (V-Dem)	3	3	0.19	–
V-Dem Electoral Democracy Index	0.65	0.66	0.41	0 to 1
V-Dem Liberal Democracy Index	0.81	0.79	0.51	0 to 1
V-Dem Free Fair Elections	0.75	0.65	−0.32	−3.2 to 2.3
Polity2 Score	5.23	6.46	1.32	−10 to 10
Polity Political Competition	8.23	9.00	6.09	1 to 10
Freedom House Civil Liberties	2.65	2.15	4.32	7 to 1
Freedom House Political Rights	2.08	2.08	4.50	7 to 1

Scores reflect averages over the 1992–2018 period. For V-Dem and Polity, higher scores indicate higher levels of electoral competition, participation, or protection of rights and freedoms. For Freedom House, higher scores reflect lower levels of freedom.

each country.[2] Up until 2019, when Benin's government adopted a series of laws that undermined the ability of opposition parties and candidates to compete on equal ground, Benin and Ghana had continually rated among the most democratic countries in Africa, scoring above the African averages on indicators of electoral competition, participation, and protection of basic rights and freedoms. Table 3.1 shows ratings from V-Dem, Polity, and Freedom House, averaged across the 1992–2018 period, for Benin, Ghana, and the sub-Saharan Africa average. During this time frame, Benin and Ghana rated similarly on all indicators and their scores are, in most cases, significantly above the sub-Saharan African average.

As I explained in Chapter 1, selecting countries with similarly high levels of competition and considerable probability of electoral turnovers of power ensures that the political risks of extraction will be similarly present across cases. As I detail in this section, the political landscapes in Benin and Ghana not only are similar in terms of their high levels of electoral competition, but they are also broadly similar in their trajectories of democratic advancement, in the risks that leaders face after leaving office, and in their generally permissive environments for extraction.

---

[2] This turnover count does not include the immediate post-transition 1991 elections in Benin, in which the pre-transition president, Mathieu Kérékou, lost to Nicephore Soglo.

3.1.1   *Electoral Competition and Democratic Advancement*

Benin and Ghana both experienced periods of extreme political instability in the 1960s and 1970s followed by more stable but also more
repressive periods of military dictatorship in the 1980s. For both countries, this trajectory meant that, at the time of their regime transitions in
the early 1990s, there was little reason to believe that democratic institutions would survive in either country. By the 2000s, however, it was
clear that democratic institutions had not only survived in the two countries but, in many respects, had actually grown stronger over the course
of the previous two decades.[3] Although it is beyond the scope of this
book to offer an exhaustive account of democratic advancement in the
two countries, several important factors are worth highlighting as they
underscore similarities in the two countries' competitive political environments and the types of political risks that leaders have faced in the
course of extraction.

First, in both countries, the acceptance of electoral loss by previous
military dictators – Mathieu Kérékou in Benin following his defeat in
the 1991 elections and Jerry John (J. J.) Rawlings in Ghana, who opted
not to run in the 2000 elections after having served two terms in office –
was critical for solidifying each country's transitions to democracy. In
addition to setting the precedent of elites accepting constitutional rules
and seeing democratic alternation as "the only game in town,"[4] these
watershed events also set the expectation that soldiers would stay in the
barracks, declining to intervene to protect the political fortunes of past
military leaders.[5] Although this acceptance of defeat occurred much earlier in Benin than it did in Ghana, the symbolism of both events was
significant for the survival of democracy in both countries.

These important events also helped to establish norms that presidents
adhere to constitutional term limits. Constitutional provisions in both
countries allow presidents to serve for only two terms, and these provisions have been largely respected by presidents in both countries.[6]
Term limits have also shaped electoral dynamics to some extent: voters in
both countries have typically favored the reelection of incumbents after
their first term, but have frequently voted in favor of party alternation

---

[3] Mainwaring and Bizzarro (2019: 112).

[4] See Abdulai and Crawford (2010) on elite support for democracy in Ghana and
    Banégas (1998*a*) on Benin.

[5] On the military's role in Benin, see Akindes (2015) and Bierschenk (2009: 355). On
    Ghana, see Brenya et al. (2015).

[6] There are accounts that Thomas Boni Yayi, who served as Benin's president from
    2006 to 2016, had tried to engineer an effort to amend the constitution to allow him
    to run for a third term. This effort, however, did not progress beyond initial planning
    stages.

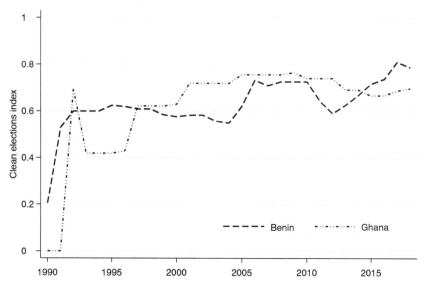

Figure 3.1 Election quality in Benin and Ghana
The graph depicts scores on V-Dem's Clean Elections index, which
aggregates the following expert-coded indicators: absence of
registration fraud, systematic irregularities, government intimidation of
the opposition, vote buying, and election violence. Source: V-Dem v9.

following a president's second term. In Benin, Soglo, the first demo-
cratically elected president of the current multiparty era, was the only
president not to have won a second term. In Ghana, the same is true for
the country's fourth president, John Mahama, but upon his defeat in the
2016 election, his party, the NDC, had at that point already served two
consecutive terms in office.[7]

Both countries have also seen improvements in election quality over
repeated cycles. The two countries figure prominently as supportive
cases for Staffan Lindberg's democratization-by-elections hypothesis,
suggesting that repeated elections serve as important drivers of democratic institutionalization.[8] In Figure 3.1, I show trends in the two
countries' elections using V-Dem's Clean Elections index, which measures the extent to which a country's elections are free, fair, and peaceful.

[7] Mahama served as vice president to John Atta Mills, who passed away while in office
in August 2012. Mahama assumed the presidency, won the 2012 election, and served
a four-year term from 2013 to 2017.
[8] Lindberg (2006).

Although progress in election quality has not always been consistent, there is an overall upward trend in both countries between their founding elections in 1991/1992 and 2018.

Adding to the democratization-by-elections perspective, George Bob-Milliar and Jeffrey Paller emphasize the important role of "democratic rupture" in the institutionalization of Ghana's democracy. Defined as "infractions in the democratisation process during competitive elections that has the potential to cause a constitutional crisis,"[9] ruptures are events that focus productive attention on weaknesses in the democratic system. Analyzing the contested results and the subsequent High Court case surrounding Ghana's 2012 elections, Bob-Milliar and Paller show how this controversy ultimately led to a series of electoral reforms, civil society mobilization, and party realignments that all contributed to Ghana's democratic advancement.

Similar events surrounding Benin's 2001 elections might qualify as a rupture of this kind. In the run-up to the 2001 election, the principal opposition candidates boycotted the second round polls because they believed that incumbent president, Mathieu Kérékou, had rigged the first round in his own favor. Opposition candidate Bruno Amoussou eventually stepped in to "save the election," keeping Benin's electoral streak more or less intact, but not without highlighting the fragility of Benin's electoral system. After the contentious election, opposition and civil society groups mobilized in support of decentralization reforms, including the long-awaited introduction of local elections. They also mobilized for reform of the country's voter registration system including the creation of a more reliable voter list.[10] These events suggest that the controversial 2001 election might have acted as a similar type of "democratic rupture," as occurred surrounding the 2012 events in Ghana.[11]

A third feature of democratic advancement in the two countries relates to the important role of civil society organizations (CSO) in the two countries. Civil society actors often act as important safeguards against a range of activities that undermine democracy including anti-democratic movements, the rolling back of democratic rules, the distortion of free and fair election results by incumbents, or the organization of coups and

---

[9] Bob-Milliar and Paller (2018: 8).

[10] Piccolino (2015: 278).

[11] Additional potential "ruptures" have occurred in Benin during President Boni Yayi's second term in office (Banégas 2014; Laebens and Lührmann 2021) and surrounding the 2019 legislative elections in Benin (Roberts 2019), but it is highly uncertain whether these episodes will have ultimately helped to advance or undermine democracy.

putsches.[12] In Ghana, domestic civil society groups have played crucial pro-democratic roles by stimulating political participation, protecting pro-democratic values, reporting on political activities, providing election observation, and supplementing efforts by political parties to engage Ghanaians in electoral and voting processes.[13] In Benin, too, civil society groups, especially labor unions and commercial associations, have often acted as pro-democratic forces, a legacy of the important role they played in the 1990 National Conference.[14]

These advancements in electoral democracy have proceeded amidst the persistence of political contestation that often centers on ethnic identity. In Benin, ethnic identity is a major predictor of vote choice, with politicians often making very direct appeals to voters based on ethnicity.[15] In Ghana, partisan attachments and voting patterns also break down to a large extent along ethnic lines, particularly among the populous Akan and Ewe groups.[16] Although direct ethnic appeals are less overt in Ghana than in Benin, the overall patterns of ethnic political division are remarkably similar across the two countries. In both countries, there are longstanding political rivalries between larger southern groups, such as the Fon, Adja, and Yoruba groups in southern Benin and the Akan and Ewe groups in southern Ghana, as well as a more diverse but less divided mosaic of northern groups. Although northern groups in Benin have historically amassed greater political power than their counterparts in Ghana, more recent elections in Benin have seen a resurgence of southern-dominated politics.

To summarize, there are a common set of factors that, from the early 1990s through (at least) the late 2010s, have propelled the institutionalization of competitive electoral democracy in Benin and Ghana. The parallel actions of reformed military dictators, the improvements in election quality resulting from electoral repetition and rupture, and the presence of strong pro-democratic civil societies represent key underpinnings of democratic advancement in the two countries. Even though their democratic experiences have often occurred in "fits and starts,"[17] the two countries have, to a considerable degree, tread similar paths. These similar paths are significant in the ways they shape the potential political risks of extraction, which I address in the next section.

---

[12] See Bernhard et al. (2020) for a theoretical overview.
[13] Abdulai and Crawford (2010: 37-38); Arthur (2010: 211).
[14] Heilbrunn (1993); Nwajiaku (1994); Gisselquist (2008).
[15] Koter (2016); Adida et al. (2017).
[16] Nathan (2019: 80).
[17] Fomunyoh (2001).

3.1.2   The Political Extraction Environments

Common trajectories of democratic advancement in Benin and Ghana have generated similar environments for political extraction. In both countries, there are strong pressures on politicians to extract, but also significant political risks for leaders in the course of extraction. In this section I highlight similarities in three important features of the extraction environments in Benin and Ghana. First, the real prospect of power turnover in both countries underscores the high stakes involved in ensuring that extracted resources benefit the incumbent party. Second, there are palpable threats of political prosecution of former leaders for various crimes – including those related to political extraction – after they leave office. Third, despite the presence of these political risks, the extraction environments in both countries remain largely permissive, with little chance of *immediate* legal or electoral punishment for politicians who extract money for their political operations.

The processes of democratic advancement described in the previous section underscore the growing risk that incumbent presidents and their parties will lose power through elections, thus raising the stakes of political fundraising. This electoral uncertainty is evident in incumbent parties' vote shares, which have dropped as low as 34 percent in Benin (2016) and 43 percent in Ghana (2000) and can fluctuate from 5 to 20 points from one election cycle to the next.

These high levels of electoral uncertainty are accompanied by increasingly monetized and expensive elections. In both countries, wealthy individuals are competing in elections with greater frequency,[18] bringing larger and larger sums of money to election campaigns. At the same time, particularistic demands from voters or party activists persist and grow more expensive.[19] As such, candidates must expend larger and larger amounts of money in order to demonstrate their credibility to voters, secure endorsements from influential elites, and execute common campaign activities such as rallies and meetings. It is therefore not surprising that overall spending in elections has increased considerably in both countries over the past several decades,[20] generating ever stronger pressures on leaders to raise political funds through extraction and to ensure that those funds do not wind up with opponents or potential defectors.

---

[18] See, especially, Asante and Kunnath (2017) on this trend in Ghana and Koter (2017) on Benin.

[19] Banégas (1998*b*, 2003); Lindberg (2010); Koter (2017); Nathan (2019); Driscoll (2020).

[20] See Chapter 4.

Turnovers of power in the two countries have also given rise to the prospect of (political) prosecution of former officeholders. These cases are often bolstered by civil society groups supporting or opposing what they see as (un)just actions of the departing leaders. The prospects of prosecution loomed especially large for former dictators Mathieu Kérékou (Benin) and Jerry John Rawlings (Ghana). Following his defeat in the 1991 election, Kérékou pledged his commitment to support the new government, citing his "deep, sincere, and irreversible desire to change."[21] The transitional government subsequently passed a law granting Kérékou judicial immunity. This act was met with large demonstrations by students who pressed (unsuccessfully) for judicial action against Kérékou.[22] In Ghana, the government of NPP leader John Kufuor, elected in 2000, established the National Reconciliation Commission to investigate abuses committed by Rawlings' military-led People's National Defence Council (PNDC) regime. Although Kufuor had previously announced that he would not pursue charges against Rawlings himself, he did allow for individuals to bring suits against the former regime.[23]

Debates surrounding the prosecution of former leaders have continued to occupy political space in both countries. The risks of political prosecution in Benin were on full display in June 2019 when President Patrice Talon put former president Thomas Boni Yayi under house arrest for having participated in public demonstrations against Talon's effort to disqualify opposition candidates from competing in the 2019 legislative elections. Talon also targeted second- and third-place finishers in the 2016 election – former Prime Minister Lionel Zinsou and business magnate Sebastien Adjavon – for violations of campaign finance laws and drug trafficking, respectively, resulting in prison sentences and their ineligibility for the 2021 elections.[24] In Ghana, major debates and divisions within the NDC emerged in the wake of their 2008 election victory surrounding the question of whether or not to prosecute former NPP political leaders. These issues became so divisive that those advocating for more harsh treatment of former officials mounted a primary election challenge against incumbent president John Atta Mills in his 2012

---

[21] Africa Research Bulletin, March 1–31, 1991, cited in Bratton and van de Walle (1997: 2).

[22] Africa Research Bulletin, April 1–30, 1991.

[23] "Ghana Swears in a New President," Reuters, January 8, 2001.

[24] Mathieu Millicamps, "Bénin: Lionel Zinsou condamné à 5 ans d'inéligibilité et 6 mois de prison avec sursis," Jeune Afrique, August 2, 2019.

reelection bid, citing Mills' refusal to pursue prosecutorial action against the NPP.[25]

Despite the risks of electoral loss and political prosecution after leaving office, the extraction environments in both countries remain largely permissive. In neither country are public officials likely to experience any immediate legal or electoral punishments for engaging in illicit extraction. The two countries' scores on Transparency International's (TI) Corruptions Perceptions Index (2018) are nearly identical: 41 for Benin and 40 for Ghana, measured on a scale from 0 to 100 where 0 represents the highest frequency of corruption and 100 represents the lowest. These scores indicate a medium-high level of corruption and significant impunity for violators. Across the two countries, there are abundant examples of corrupt acts by politicians and bureaucrats, most of which go unpunished in the short term.[26]

Additionally, in neither country are voters likely to punish politicians at the polls for engaging in extraction. In Benin, Richard Banégas observed that voters expect monetary handouts at the time of elections because they seek to recuperate money that they know has been extracted from the public purse.[27] Even if they denounce politicians who become rich through extraction, there is considerable ambiguity in that voters strongly expect politicians to possess large volumes of resources that they distribute during electoral campaigns.[28] Alongside the direct distribution of money for votes, politicians in Benin frequently make clientelistic appeals to voters by promising to direct state power and resources toward particular voters or communities that support them.[29] The effectiveness of these appeals[30] implies that voters are unlikely to base their vote choice on politicians' extractive behavior.

Pure vote buying in which money is distributed in advance of elections may be somewhat less common in Ghana,[31] but politicians widely base their campaign promises and their constituency services on the particularistic distribution of money, goods, and services to voters and

---

[25] For an overview of these events, see Bob-Milliar (2012a).
[26] TI's Country Reports for Benin and Ghana provide numerous examples, available at www.transparency.org/en/countries/benin and www.transparency.org/en/countries/ghana.
[27] Banégas (1998b: 79).
[28] Banégas (1998a).
[29] Banégas (2003); Koter (2016).
[30] Wantchekon (2003).
[31] Driscoll (2020).

communities.[32] They also "buy turnout" from party supporters by chan-neling patronage to party members and financially supporting party members' personal expenses.[33] Within Ghana, higher levels of polit-ical competition and polarization are associated with greater levels of patronage and financial mismanagement, suggesting that rising levels of political competition may actually *raise* voters' or party activists' expecta-tions of receiving some material benefit in exchange for their support.[34] In short, as long as voters and communities are able to derive some mate-rial benefits from political extraction, they are unlikely to vote against extracting politicians.[35]

In sum, the rise of highly competitive elections in Benin and Ghana have raised the costs – and stakes – of extractive political fundraising. Political turnovers have likewise generated significant debates among the public and civil society groups over the legal fates of former leaders. At the same time, the entrenched clientelistic structures of politics in both countries give rise to environments in which politicians are unlikely to suffer immediate legal or electoral consequences of extraction. As such, leaders in Benin and Ghana have operated in extraction environ-ments that closely resemble each other. Any differences in the political extraction strategies pursued by leaders are not easily attributable to one country having a more or less permissive environment for illicit behavior.

3.2   Party Institution Divergence

Despite their similar democratic trajectories and extraction environ-ments, Benin and Ghana differ considerably in terms of party institution-alization, which I argue is the basis for their equally divergent extraction systems. In Ghana, the two main political parties – the NDC and the NPP – are among the most institutionalized in Africa. Parties in Benin, by contrast, even those that have held power for a full two presidential terms (ten years), have not succeeded in building party institutions to any meaningful degree.

In this section, I describe Benin's and Ghana's party institutions in greater detail, highlighting contemporary variation across the four dimensions of party institutionalization that I introduced in Chapter 2: durability, organization, social roots, and identity. In the course of this discussion, I also describe the historical roots of party institutions in

---

[32] Nugent (2007); Lindberg (2010); Harding (2015); Klaus and Paller (2017); Nathan (2019); Paller (2019); Brierley and Kramon (2020).

[33] Bob-Milliar (2012*b*); Driscoll (2020).

[34] Asunka (2016); Driscoll (2018).

[35] Bleck and Van de Walle (2013); Weghorst and Lindberg (2013).

Table 3.2 *Party institutionalization indicators, Benin, Ghana, and Africa (1992–2018)*

Indicator	Ghana	Benin	Africa	Range
Party Institutionalization Index (V-Dem)	0.62	0.29	0.50	0.14–0.89
Electoral Volatility[a]	14	52	30	11–78
Age of Ruling Party (DPI)[b]	13.5	2	25.4	2–93
Party Organization (V-Dem)	0.45	0.24	0.32	−2.8 to 2.3
% Feel Close to Party (Afrobarometer)[c]	58.6	29.0	47.9	12.8–77.7
Ruling Party % of Legislative Seats[d]	61.6	37.7	62.9	18–98
Distinct Party Platforms (V-Dem)	1.19	−1.25	0.13	−2.8 to 1.7

Unless otherwise noted, scores are averaged over the 1992–2018 period.
[a] Pedersen index based on legislative elections from regime transition through 2016, from Sanches (2018).
[b] Average age of parties that held power each year.
[c] Afrobarometer data covers Round 7 (2016–2018) only.
[d] Data shared by Jaimie Bleck and Nicolas van de Walle, used Bleck and Van de Walle (2018).

both countries. This historical background helps to frame a discussion of potential endogeneity of my argument – whether early extraction systems shaped the party institutions we see today – that I include at the end of this section.

Before proceeding with a discussion of each country's party institutions, I provide in Table 3.2 a summary of scores for Benin and Ghana on the indicators of party institutionalization that were presented in the Africa-wide descriptive analysis in Chapter 2. On every measure, Ghana's scores indicate levels of party institutionalization that are considerably higher than those of Benin's. Additionally, on most of the indicators presented, Ghana's scores reflect a level of party institutionalization well above the average for sub-Saharan Africa. Benin's scores are, in all cases, well below the regional average.

3.2.1 Ghana's Institutionalized Parties

In Ghana, both the NDC and the NPP are exceptionally well institutionalized compared to most African parties. They have both endured well beyond their founding leaders. They both have robust organizations with coherent boundaries and structures including internally democratic procedures for selecting candidates and party officers. They have clear social bases of support, often historically rooted, including defined economic and ethno-regional groupings. They are "infused" with identities and ideological principles, even if those principles do not always guide their policies and platforms. Both parties also display a strong commitment to serving their party members' material interests.

In terms of their durability, both the NDC and NPP have continued to compete and win beyond the tenure of their founding leaders. The NDC is the successor party to the military-led PNDC regime, which held power following then-Flt. Lt. Jerry J. Rawlings' seizure of power in 1981. Rawlings was able to manage the transition from military dictatorship to a republican constitution in 1992 and the NDC, with Rawlings as its flagbearer, won elections in 1992 and 1996. As Rachel Riedl and others have described, consolidation of the NDC's political organization, in terms of both its structure, incorporation of social groups, and identity during the PNDC era, helped to ensure its successful transition to a civilian political party through the transition to a more democratic form of rule.[36] When Rawlings stepped down from power in 2001, there was some uncertainty about the future of the NDC, but with the subsequent election of NDC presidents Mills and Mahama in 2008 and 2012 respectively, both of whom had defeated Jerry Rawlings' wife, Nana Konadu Agyeman Rawlings, in the party's primary elections, it became clear that the party had taken on an existence autonomous from its founding leader.

The NPP had less personalistic origins than the NDC. According to Riedl, the NPP officially began as an umbrella for pro-democracy interests under the PNDC regime. Its primary groupings included those affiliated with the Danquah and Busia movements of the late colonial and post-colonial eras. In this sense, unlike the NDC, the NPP had not been forged in the image of one particular founding leader. The party's survival has nonetheless been threatened by factional rivalries, which tend to escalate around contests for party leadership positions.[37] John Kufuor, associated with the Busia legacy, triumphed in early contests within the NPP and was eventually elected president in 2000. After Kufuor left power in 2009, Nana Akufo-Addo, who is closely affiliated with the Danquah legacy, gained power over the party. In short, despite its fractious origins, the NPP has managed to resolve intra-party conflicts to persist beyond the tenure of its founding leaders.

The durability of Ghana's two parties is in many ways a product of their coherent organizations, strong partisan attachments, and infused values. Both parties possess organizations with clear boundaries and procedures for gaining membership. As Kwame Ninsin explains, the

[36] Riedl (2014). See, also, Whitfield (2009).

[37] For details of factional contests within the NPP, see Kennedy (2009); Bob-Milliar (2012b); Riedl (2014).

parties have devised flexible membership models to accommodate broad segments of the population, combining card-bearing or fee-paying membership with informal or floating membership. For some Ghanaians, Ninsin notes, membership is "an act of political faith and commitment," while for others, it is less formal, "spring[ing] to life only during general elections."[38] To join, individuals typically visit party offices and are issued membership cards. Membership provides both formal and informal benefits. Formally, members gain the ability to vote in internal party contests, which select the party's officers and candidates for parliamentary and presidential elections. In terms of benefits, members widely seek and gain access to material benefits, particularly if they become active in campaigning for the party.[39]

The NDC and NPP both maintain chapters and physical offices in most localities throughout the country, though chapters may be less numerous or less active in areas where the party does not enjoy as much support. In addition to serving as sites of membership recruitment and maintenance, local and regional offices recruit for party positions – from polling station managers to constituency executives. They maintain the physical offices, organize party activities, and serve as a hub in communication channels between the grassroots and the party leadership.[40] They also play significant social roles in their communities, representing the party at local events including festivals, weddings, and funerals. Staff and members at local party offices regularly help to organize internal elections including candidate primaries and contests to elect party leadership. Local offices also serve as centers of recruitment and management for party activists – often called foot soldiers – who play important and sometimes controversial roles in election campaigns.[41]

Both the NDC and the NPP have deep social roots originating in liberation-oriented political movements that gained strength during the late colonial period. Describing these anti-colonial movements in Ghana, David Apter writes that "two forms of nationalism reflected a very different set of social and traditional patterns," with one form based on the advancement of authority for the chiefs and their councils and the other rooted in the political aspirations of the newly educated elites.[42] The two approaches also had different views about how best to advance the cause of independence.[43] These divergent approaches to liberation produced

---

[38] Ninsin (2006: 11–12).
[39] Bob-Milliar (2012a).
[40] Osei (2016).
[41] Bob-Milliar (2012b, 2014); Bjarnesen (2020).
[42] Apter (1966: 263).
[43] Austin (1964).

two distinct political groupings. The Convention People's Party (CPP), led by Kwame Nkrumah, embodied the perspectives of the chiefs and mobilized youth. The educated elite were primarily represented by the United Gold Coast Convention (UGCC), led principally by J. B. Danquah.[44] Although, these movements went through many subsequent incarnations during Ghana's First, Second, and Third Republics, today's parties in many ways maintain these basic social legacies, with the NPP reflecting the social perspectives of the educated and business elite that were at the heart of the UGCC, and the NDC more closely affiliated with the traditional and more populist views of the chiefs.[45] According to Riedl, Rawlings deliberately sought to incorporate populations partial to Nkrumahist and CPP traditions as part of his party-building strategy. Moreover, socio-economic interests continue to shape party-voter attachment in Ghana: voters who do not share either of the party's economic interests are most likely to switch party preferences from one election to the next.[46]

In addition to their roots in different socioeconomic groups, the two parties have distinct attachments to particular ethnic groups, with the NDC possessing strong connections to the Ewes in eastern Ghana and the NPP having closer ties to Akan populations, especially to members of the Ashanti and Akyem subgroups. These attachments are well-documented throughout the literature on Ghana's parties and there is no shortage of election data to show that the NDC consistently performs very well in the Ewe-dominated Volta Region and that the NPP performs well in the Ashanti-dominated Ashanti region and the Akyem-dominated Eastern Region. There are, however, important limits to the ethnicity-based social roots of Ghana's parties. First, beyond the Ashanti, Akyem, and Ewe, there are a number of ethno-regional groups that are less strongly attached to either of the main political parties. The regions in the north of Ghana, for example, have some historical ties to the Progress Party (PP) – one of the predecessor parties to the NPP – but have, in some elections, shown up more strongly for the NDC. In the Western and Central Regions, Fanti groups have also been known to switch allegiances, most notably in the 2008 election when they helped to propel the NDC back to power. A second limitation has to do with the geographical distribution of members of different ethnic groups. If voters do not live in areas dominated by their ethnic groups, they may prefer to

---

[44] Nkrumah served briefly as Secretary General of the UGCC, but broke away to form the CPP shortly after its inception.

[45] Whitfield (2009).

[46] Kim (2018).

vote for the party that is most likely to deliver goods and services to the dominant ethnic groups in their communities.[47]

Irregardless of whether the social roots of Ghana's parties are primarily socioeconomic or ethnic in nature, there is an abundance of evidence that partisan attachments are both strong and durable. According to Afrobarometer polling, over 60 percent of citizens in Ghana report feeling close to a political party[48] and only about 23 percent of voters in Ghana are likely to change their vote from one election to the next, suggesting that the two parties' base voters comprise a large proportion of the voting population.[49] As Cadman Atta Mills explains, even if party support is not always neatly aligned with ethnic identity or economic interest, it is often like "the fan base of football or sports clubs" whereby fans remain unwaveringly loyal to one team.[50] The strength of these attachments has potential implications for parties' campaign activities. For example, Ghanaian parties may be more likely to focus on bolstering turnout in stronghold areas than on activities that seek to persuade swing or opposition voters,[51] or they might pursue different types of campaign activities in stronghold, swing, or opposition areas.[52]

Finally, the NDC and the NPP also have clear political identities and brands that promote shared values among members. Their party identities relate closely to the specific economic and social roots described in the preceding paragraphs, but they also embrace the distinct political ideas advanced by their predecessor parties and leaders. Riedl notes, of the PNDC in particular, that the socialists of Nkrumah's tradition (the CPP) "felt a direct link to the grassroots participation and revolutionary rhetoric," which still pervades the NDC's brand today. The NPP's political identity centers on the aforementioned Danquah–Busia tradition of Ghanaian politics, which has been associated with a number of different political parties since the 1950s. One portion of this group descends from the part of the UGCC that remained intact, led by J. B. Danquah, following the split with Nkrumah and the CPP. The other portion – the Busia tradition – was formed in support of Dr. Kofi Busia, who led opposition movements in the 1950s and served as prime minister of Ghana's Second Republic under the banner of the PP. These traditions

---

[47] Ichino and Nathan (2013).
[48] Afrobarometer (2018). See also Section 2.4 in the previous chapter.
[49] Adams et al. (2017).
[50] Atta Mills (2018).
[51] Driscoll (2020).
[52] Specifically, Rauschenbach (2017) and Brierley and Kramon (2020) argue that the parties are more likely to hold rallies in their strongholds and engage in canvassing and vote-buying in areas dominated by swing and opposition voters.

were resurrected in the 1980s under the banner of pro-democracy inter-ests and, over time, have fused together to consolidate common values and identity.[53]

Today, the NDC remains a left-leaning party that invokes socialist rhetoric, such as support for the poor and the importance of provid-ing material supplies to the poorer segments of Ghanaian society. As one Western Region NDC official explained, "We are committed to making sure the fishermen have fishing nets and the farmers have the fertilizers. If we don't do this, no one will."[54] By contrast, the NPP is largely asso-ciated with right-leaning business interests supporting liberal economic ideals. As Lindsay Whitfield explains, the two parties' distinct political traditions provide them with "founding mythologies, ideological images, and distinct political styles, around which elites gravitate and voters are mobilized."[55] Sebastian Elischer notes that Ghana is one of the few countries in Africa where parties take on programmatic platforms and "visible ideological predilections,"[56] even if the content of their cam-paign promises and the policies their governments have enacted when in power do not align neatly with such ideals.[57] Both parties, though especially the NDC, have evolved into strong party machines where it is clearly understood that membership and active support for the party come with access to various types of material benefit.[58]

In sum, Ghana's two main parties, the NDC and the NPP, clearly embody all four dimensions of party institutionalization. They have endured well beyond their founding leaders and they possess strong orga-nizations that administer membership, establish rules for advancement and leadership selection, and coordinate local campaign activities. Their social roots go beyond specific ethnic groups – though ethnic attach-ments are also important – to include distinct socioeconomic bases of support. Moreover, both parties have identifiable political legacies and ideological traditions that form the basis for distinct party brands and identities. Not only is this level of institutionalization relatively uncom-mon in Africa, but, as I will discuss in the next chapter, it forms the basis of a highly collusive extraction system in which party elites and their net-works work together to ensure the financial solvency of the party and the electoral viability of its candidates.

---

[53] Riedl (2014: 87).
[54] Author interview, Takoradi, December 10, 2013.
[55] Whitfield (2009: 627).
[56] Elischer (2013: 140).
[57] Nathan (2019).
[58] Bob-Milliar (2012b).

3.2.2   Low Party Institutionalization in Benin

In contrast to Ghana's parties, Benin's political parties are among the least institutionalized in Africa. Characterized by a large number of small parties centered around individuals who represent specific ethno-regional groups and highly mutable elite coalitions, Benin's party landscape is both fluid and unpredictable. This frequently changing party landscape has effectively prevented the formation or sustenance of parties that contain coherent organizational structures, strong or extensive social roots, or identifiable party brands or values.

Parties in Benin rarely survive beyond the tenure of the founding leader. If they do survive, they tend to encounter significant challenges in winning elections or maintaining power. The *Renaissance du Bénin* (RB) party of President Nicephore Soglo (1991–1996), for example, did survive for a period after Soglo's defeat in the 1996 presidential election, but only as long as he or his son Lehady remained in elected office, both having served as mayors of Benin's commercial capital and largest city of Cotonou.[59] When Lehady Soglo ran for president in 2006 under the RB label, he garnered only 8.44 percent of the vote. The RB did not field a candidate in either the 2011 or the 2016 presidential elections.

Similar fates have met the parties supporting Matthieu Kérékou. The PRPB, which Kérékou formed in the wake of his 1972 coup, "essentially imploded" during Benin's democratic transition in 1990–1991, despite Kérékou's earlier efforts to incorporate some particular groups, especially women and student movements, into the PRPB.[60] Kérékou subsequently ran as an independent candidate in the 1991 and 1996 elections. It was not until his 2001 reelection campaign that he formally ran under the banner of the *Front d'Action pour le Renouveau, la Démocratie et le Développement* (FARD-Alafia), which had supported his candidacies in 1991 and 1996. The electoral viability of FARD-Alafia decreased considerably during Kérékou's second term in office (2001–2006). Its electoral coalition won only thirty-one of eighty-three seats in the 2003 parliamentary elections. Then, in the 2006 presidential election, Kérékou's FARD-Alafia successor, Daniel Tawema, garnered less than 1 percent of the popular vote.

The short lifespans of Benin's parties mean that leaders tend not to invest significantly in building party organizations. Parties lack

---

[59] Nicephore Soglo served as mayor from 2003 through 2015, and his son, Lehady Soglo, served as mayor from 2015 through 2018.

[60] Dickovick (2008: 1129) describes this implosion as well as Kérékou's efforts, especially in the 1970s, to incorporate groups that were not ethnically based.

coherence in terms of both clear boundaries and internal structures. Party representatives are "hesitant to draw too sharp a line...given that the future may necessitate their coming together in a new strategic alliance."[61] Observers have used the concept of "*transhumance*," which translates as "movement" or "nomadism," to describe Benin's party landscape characterized by "episodes of denials, reversals and rallies of former opponents by national or local elected officials, who, having received the nomination of their parties, resigned to join the government movement with the hope of receiving some benefit."[62] Riedl notes that the destabilization of the party system toward the end of President Nicephore Soglo's term in office (1991–1996) led to patterns in which parties and candidates would regroup both in advance of, and following, each legislative and presidential election in order to improve their ability to "make their own personal mark."[63] Until a 2018 rule change that effectively disqualified opposition parties from running in national elections, no single party had ever won a majority of seats in Benin's legislative elections. The number of candidates competing in presidential elections with no incumbent (1991, 2006, 2016) has grown consistently since 2001, as has the number of independent candidates (Table 3.3).[64] As of 2018, there were reportedly 236 political parties and 17 alliances officially registered with the Ministry of Interior.[65] Even where clear political rivalries have emerged, such as between former presidents Soglo and Kerekou (and now Presidents Boni Yayi and Talon), voters do not

Table 3.3 *Party and candidate proliferation in presidential elections in Benin*

Election	Incumbent Running?	Candidates	Independents	Largest Vote Share[a]
1991	No	13	5	36.2
1996	Yes	7	3	35.7
2001	Yes	17	5	45.4
2006	No	26	11	35.8
2011	Yes	14	9	53.1
2016	No	33	15	28.4

[a]Largest percentage of votes won by a single candidate in the first round of the election.
Source: Data compiled by author.

[61] Riedl (2014: 202–203).
[62] Houngnikpo and Decalo (2013: 345).
[63] Riedl (2014: 200). See also Magnusson and Clark (2005: 83–84).
[64] By comparison, the maximum number of candidates that have ever competed in an election in Ghana is eight.
[65] Hounkpe (2018).

necessarily perceive clear distinctions between the parties or movements of these candidates beyond their specific ethno-regional identities.[66]

In addition to their fuzzy boundaries and fluid elite alliances, Benin's parties are largely devoid of organizational infrastructure outside of their campaign operations. Riedl notes that Benin's parties rarely have national headquarters, that the scope of party activity is very limited to regional or *commune* strongholds, and that there is at most one contact person who connects local and national party structures.[67] Benin has scored well below the African average in V-Dem's measure of party branches, which measures how many of the country's parties have permanent local branches.[68] Additionally, Benin's parties do not typically hold primary elections to select presidential candidates. In the 2015 legislative elections, the ruling *Force cauris pour un Bénin émergent* (FCBE) was the only party to have held a primary election to select its slate of candidates.[69]

To the extent that parties in Benin possess any clear and stable roots in society, they revolve around narrow ethno-regional groupings. Parties are "ethnicized" in the sense that voters tend to evaluate candidates on the basis of the ethno-regional origin of the party leader and, for parliamentary elections, on the ethnic identities of the specific candidates on the party list. The ethnicization of parties leads politicians to use what Dominika Koter describes as a "double ethnic strategy" – assembling candidate lists and key supporters in ways that heighten interest among coethnics and maximize their chances to reach beyond the ethnic group of the party leader.[70] So important is ethnic appeal that parties tend not to campaign in areas where they do not have a personal connection.[71] Instead, candidates tend to make direct appeals to voters in targeted ethnic groups, holding frequent rallies and meetings to interact directly with voters.[72]

Although many Beninese voters tend to vote for co-ethnic candidates, there is little evidence to suggest that parties become strongly attached to ethno-regional voting groups in ways that endure beyond particular candidates. For example, Soglo's RB party had traditionally enjoyed strong

---

[66] Riedl (2014: 203–204).

[67] Riedl (2014: 213).

[68] As expected, Ghana scores well above the African average.

[69] Ichino and Nathan (2018).

[70] Koter (2016: 85).

[71] Koter (2016: 88–89); Adida et al. (2017).

[72] In a study of citizen interactions with parties using Afrobarometer data, Lockwood et al. (2022) find that, relative to other African countries, a large proportion of Beninese citizens report having attended a party's or candidate's rally or meeting, a finding that speaks to this strategy of direct appeals.

support from the Fon community in and around the *commune* of Abomey. When the RB threw their support to the coalition behind Lionel Zinsou in 2016, however, the Abomey population did not follow suit, voting instead in large numbers for Patrice Talon who also originates from the area. In short, while parties may appear to draw regular support from particular ethnic groups, this support does not take the form of stable party attachments.

Although labor unions, professional associations, and other civil society groups are very active in Benin's political landscape, and were instrumental in bringing about the transition to democracy in the late 1980s and early 1990s,[73] there is little evidence to suggest that these groups align clearly with any particular parties. As Thomas Bierschenk and Olivier de Sardan note, "Leaders of many so-called [civil society organizations] have multiple identities and straddle the world of politics and the private sector."[74] These "multiple identities" imply that, like other political actors, CSO leaders are prone to act opportunistically in supporting particular parties or candidates. For example, in the 2016 election there were big questions as to which candidate the association of *zemidjan* (motorcycle taxi) drivers, some 300,000 strong, would lend their support.[75] Unlike in Ghana, there are no particular political legacies, ideologies, or social network structures that bind these types of (non-ethnic) groups with parties or candidates.

Benin's parties also tend to lack core identities, norms, and values. The fragmentation of the party system even suppresses shared interests in pursuit of election victory. One report on the status of the party system in Benin describes "a deprivation of political mores" that generates excessive "informality and personalization of the parties."[76] Rather than commit to a set of principles that guide strategic engagement or bind members together, parties are "constantly under threat by internal quarrels and splits" and "respond to the cyclical conditions of the country's 'big voters'."[77] Coordinated action, particularly in opposition, is highly tenuous. Within the FCBE, for example, one report notes that a debate among members about the party's opposition strategy devolved into accusations that members were "traitors," "opportunists," and "profiteers."[78]

[73] Allen (1992); Banégas (1995); Magnusson (1996); Seely (2009).
[74] Bierschenk and de Sardan (2003: 163-164).
[75] See Vincent Duham, "Bénin: Lionel Zinsou reçoit le soutien des zémidjans et se dit l'homme du 'consensus,'" Jeune Afrique, March 16, 2016.
[76] Aivo (2008: 147).
[77] Hounkpe (2018).
[78] Matthieu Millecamps, "Benin: guerre de tranchées au sein des FCBE, le parti de Thomas Boni Yayi," Jeune Afrique, September 25, 2019.

Overall, Benin's parties possess few, if any, of the institutional qualities that enable Ghana's party leaders to overcome the agency problems that they encounter in the course of extracting political money from the state (see Chapter 2). As such, collusive extraction is not available to Beninese political leaders. Instead, as I describe in the next chapter, incumbents in Benin have typically engaged in more *coercive* forms of extraction that seek to limit elite access to extraction, co-opt and coerce more vulnerable rank-and-file actors, and concentrate extraction within the state where incumbent leaders can better maintain control.

3.2.3   Is Party Institutionalization Endogenous to Extraction?

It would be logical to assume that stronger party institutions, such as those that exist in Ghana, emerge among political actors that have developed more successful systems of extraction. This possibility raises important questions about the potential endogeneity of this book's argument: do certain extraction systems generate stronger party institutions? A brief and dedicated discussion of the historical record of party formation in Africa, including in Ghana and Benin, helps to address this question.

Many of Africa's well-institutionalized parties, including the NDC and NPP in Ghana, have roots in the late colonial period, a period in which African leaders did not typically hold sufficient power over the state to devise effective extraction operations. In Ghana (then Gold Coast), for example, the predecessors of the NPP and the NDC – the UGCC and the CPP – emerged during colonial rule in the late 1940s. Both parties were borne out of nationalist ambitions, but with different views about how to achieve them. In June 1949, a youth-led faction within the UGCC who opposed their proposed constitutional reforms broke off to form the party, forming the CPP.[79] According to Dennis Austin's detailed political history of this era, citizen alignments with these early parties did break down to some extent along class lines, but there was no obvious financial or extractive element involved in these movements' activities. Prior to the 1951 elections, parties raised money primarily through membership dues. The CPP's resources grew more plentiful in the 1954 election, since a number of their members had been earning salaries as National Assembly members, but they still relied primarily on liberation-oriented messaging to mobilize voters.[80] In the period after the 1954 election, the CPP fended off serious political threats from the

[79] Austin (1964: 86–87).
[80] Austin (1964).

Ashanti-dominated National Liberation Movement (NLM), not through
resource-intensive methods but rather by reinforcing its broad nationalist
message and politically exploiting divisions among Ashanti chiefs.[81]

Unlike in Ghana, where parties developed distinct brands of nationalism during the late colonial period whose legacies persist to this day,
politics during the late colonial period in Benin (then Dahomey) took on
a more regional and personalist character. What had been the "golden
days" of elite nationalist unity, embodied in the existence of the single *Union Progressiste Dahoméenne* (UPD) party, dissipated when Hubert
Maga, a school teacher from the northern town of Nattitingou and candidate for the French National Assembly in 1941, deliberately exploited
northern grievances against southern populations, successfully forging
an alliance of northern groups to win the Assembly seat.[82] This development led to the "prompt collapse" of the UPD alliance as its three
dominant leaders broke apart, establishing separate regional bases of
support – two in the south and one in the north. By the time of independence in 1960, these divisions had become firmly entrenched and
were highly evident in results of Benin's first national election that same
year.[83] Thus, in neither country were the foundational political alliances
reliant on any kind of significant extraction operations.

The party-building strategies pursued by leaders in the postcolonial
period (1960s–1980s) are also not easily attributed to any financial or
extraction-related conditions. This period has gained significant attention in the historical institutionalist literature on party institutions in
Africa, as newly independent leaders pursued different strategies to manage elite political rivalries and establish control across territories and
social groups. Yonatan Morse, for example, emphasizes the importance
of the early independence period for understanding different party trajectories in Tanzania, Cameroon, and Kenya. In Tanzania, despite a lack
of finances and declining membership after independence, TANU was
able to survive and grow because of Julius Nyerere's "tough and risky
decisions that alienated [rather than co-opted] several political rivals."[84]
In Cameroon, Ahmadou Ahidjo relied primarily on the state's coercive capacity to "cajole and intimidate" other northern leaders into a
broader base that eventually became the Cameroonian Union.[85] Kenya's
weak-party trajectory was shaped by stark ethnicized political divisions

[81] Austin (1964: 285–286).
[82] Decalo (1973: 453).
[83] Decalo (1973: 454).
[84] Morse (2018: 96).
[85] Morse (2018: 100).

and Jomo Kenyatta's personal aversion to building a stronger party.[86] According to Morse's account, in none of these cases was extraction, or even incumbent financial advantage, key to understanding leaders' varied investments in party building during this period. In Kenya, for example, Kenya African National Union (KANU) leaders were tied to significant private wealth, but did not seem interested in using this wealth for party-building purposes.

Moving the focus back to Ghana and Benin, the 1960s and early 1970s were marked by high levels of political instability and praetorianism, meaning that few leaders stayed long enough in power to embark on any meaningful party-building initiatives. More stable polities emerged beginning in the mid-1970s in Benin and the early 1980s in Ghana, during which time military leaders – Kérékou in Benin and Rawlings in Ghana – pursued different party-based strategies of rule. In Ghana, Rawlings devised a strategy of incorporation for the PNDC and later, the NDC, that sought to build support among traditional leaders and existing grassroots social groups, particularly among those who had previously identified with the Nkrumahist/CPP tradition.[87] For those who identified more closely with the Danquah-Busia tradition, Rawlings was open to their incorporation,[88] but also willing to use his firm control over the coercive apparatus to intimidate and repress those who remained in staunch opposition.[89] In Benin, Kérékou pursued a different strategy: he used the PRPB to undermine existing political, economic, and social structures, subverting them to the revolutionary party's control.[90] But, despite the PRPB's extensive control of state resources, social divisions persisted in ways that made the PRPB more like a "private club" than a true mass party.[91] In short, despite both leaders having enjoyed strong authoritarian control over state money and resources during this period, they pursued different strategies of party-building and party-based rule that, as Riedl has explained, were a function of unpredictable and "highly personalistic" decisions.[92]

Since the transitions to multiparty politics in the early 1990s, most parties have not changed significantly in their levels of institutionalization. Riedl attributes this continuity to leaders' pre-transition incorporation strategies. Leaders like Rawlings who pursued strategies of

[86] Morse (2018: 100–101).
[87] Riedl (2014: 110–111).
[88] For example, eventual NPP rival John Kufuor served as Secretary of Local Government in Rawlings' PNDC government in 1982.
[89] Gyimah-Boadi (1994).
[90] Banégas (2003).
[91] Riedl (2014: 114).
[92] Riedl (2014: 102).

incorporation were able to steer transition processes and adapt their political organizations for the multiparty era, embodied for example in the political dominance of the NDC throughout the 1990s. By contrast, the "state substitution" party-building tactic pursued by Kérékou in Benin did not successfully mitigate the political threats posed by social and political opposition that arose in the midst of the regime transition in 1989–1990. As such, Kérékou lost control of the 1990 national conference and was unable to pull together a victorious coalition for the 1991 presidential elections, leading to the complete collapse of the PRPB apparatus.

These institutional trajectories have been largely sustained in the multiparty era for reasons that appear to have little to do with extraction. In a continent-wide analysis of party competition, Staffan Lindberg found considerable consistency within countries in the share of seats held by the largest and second-largest parties from one election to the next.[93] Although some observers have noted recent party de-institutionalization,[94] such assessments may be based to some extent on perceptions of earlier authoritarian parties having been more institutionalized than they actually were.[95] In Ghana, in particular, parties that were more highly institutionalized in the early 1990s, namely the NDC and NPP, have grown institutionally stronger in the democratic era while most others have either deteriorated in strength or have disappeared.[96]

This brief historical account conveys that divergence in party institutions in Benin and Ghana, as well as across other African countries, is not easily attributable to any financial or extraction-related conditions that were in place during key moments of party formation. Instead, the political alignments and party-building strategies pursued by leaders in the late colonial and post-independence periods have been influenced by a high degree of personal proclivity of leaders. These stochastic decisions have shaped the trajectories of party institutionalization, which have remained largely consistent in the face of regime changes that have taken place since the early 1990s. Though access to financial resources may explain why parties have at times formed successful opposition coalitions,[97] pecuniary accounts are considerably less helpful for

---

[93] Lindberg (2007).
[94] For example, Kelly (2020).
[95] Meng (2021).
[96] For example, Ichino and Nathan (2021) document how the growing institutionalization of Ghana's parties (i.e., in terms of the expansion of the primary electorate) has forced parties to abandon vote-buying and diversify partisan activity to incorporate previously inactive groups.
[97] Arriola (2012).

understanding why incumbent leaders have – or have not – pursued various party-building strategies during critical junctures.

3.3 Most-Similar Cases?

Thus far in this chapter, I have demonstrated similarities in the electoral and extraction environments in Benin and Ghana, I have established Benin and Ghana as "extreme" cases of party institutionalization, and I have shown that levels of party institutionalization are unlikely to have been meaningfully shaped by extraction. I now turn to the final element of my case selection strategy: examining whether and to what extent we can treat Benin and Ghana as plausibly most-similar cases and whether confounding variables undermine this approach.

In Chapter 1, I introduced five main competing explanations. As the foregoing discussion has previewed, two of those explanations – opposition strength and ethnic politics – are effectively controlled for in the comparison of Benin and Ghana. Regarding opposition strength, the prevalence of closely contested elections and multiple inter-party electoral transfers of power suggests that incumbents in both countries routinely encounter strong and viable oppositions. Regarding ethnic politics, I have discussed that dynamics are also similar across the two countries, particularly in terms of the major ethnic fault lines involving the presence of north-south divisions as well as intense rivalries among southern groups. In this section, I now revisit the remaining three alternative explanations – economic structure, bureaucratic institutions, and electoral systems – to assess their potential relevance for understanding differences in extraction strategies pursued by leaders in Benin and Ghana.

3.3.1 *Economic Structure*

One potential explanation for the prevalence of collusive extraction in Ghana is that Ghanaian officials may simply have more opportunities to pursue different types of extraction because they operate in a larger economy. Since 2000, Ghana's per capita GDP has been consistently about 30 percent higher than Benin's.[98] Although the sizes of their economies have diverged in recent decades, their levels of wealth and overall conditions were quite similar at the outset of the period I study in this book. From the late 1970s through the late 1990s – periods widely

[98] World Bank (2021). In 2018, Benin's GDP per capita was $1,211 and Ghana's was $1,808, both expressed in 2010 constant US dollars.

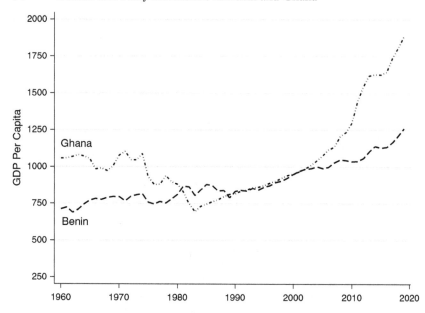

Figure 3.2 Per Capita GDP in Benin and Ghana, 1960–2018
The graph depicts per capita GDP expressed in constant 2010 US dollars.
Source: World Bank (2021).

associated with economic decline and "permanent crisis" in Africa[99] – per capita wealth, export revenue, and dependence on foreign aid were nearly identical in the two countries. It was only around the turn of the century – after the different systems of extraction had taken hold in the two countries – that significant divergence in economic performance became evident (see Figure 3.2). Additionally, the two countries have had similar levels of reliance on foreign aid: between 1990 and 2018, Benin received, on average, official development assistance totaling 7.8 percent of GNI compared to 7.6 percent of GNI in Ghana for the same period.[100] Aid dependence has declined considerably in both countries during the period of study.[101]

Ghana's economy is also more diverse than Benin's. Whereas Ghana relies on a number of key exports including gold, cocoa, oil, timber, and electricity, Benin's economy is reliant primarily on cotton as its key

[99] van de Walle (2001).
[100] World Bank (2021).
[101] Organisation for Economic Co-operation and Development (2021).

export as well as revenue from its transport sector, especially the Port of Cotonou and associated overland transport of goods to other countries including Nigeria, Niger, and Burkina Faso. It is indeed possible that Ghana's more diverse economy means that procurement opportunities and private actors are simply more widely available for collusive extraction. There is, however, little convincing evidence of major differences in these areas. A study of procurement markets conducted in 1998 estimated that Benin's and Ghana's procurement markets were sized similarly: around 13 percent of GDP in Benin and 12 percent of GDP in Ghana. It is also unclear as to whether Ghana's private sector is proportionally larger than Benin's. Benin and Ghana have rated similarly on measures of private investment, private consumption, and private credit.[102] In Ghana, a smaller proportion of employed individuals work in the informal sector than in Benin, which could contribute to the difference.[103] It is not clear, however, to what extent these differences are driven by Ghana's larger public sector workforce, which is about 5 times larger than Benin's despite having only about 2.5 times its population size.[104] In short, while Ghana's larger and more diverse economy could help to sustain opportunities for incumbents to pursue collusive strategies of extraction, the timing of economic growth and lack of evidence of any major differences in procurement markets and private sector size suggest serious limits to this explanation.

3.3.2   Bureaucratic Institutions and Colonial Legacies

In Chapter 1, I discussed how variation in institutional features of the bureaucracy, including meritocracy, discretion, and political control, could influence leaders' choices about extraction. Are there enduring differences in these bureaucratic institutions in Benin and Ghana that require consideration as potential explanations for their different extraction systems? Are there differences in bureaucratic institutions that would drive political leaders in one country to have stronger incentives to delegate extraction to bureaucratic agents, and would agents in that country have stronger incentives to engage in extraction? I consider these questions with particular reference to Benin's and Ghana's differing

[102] Stampini et al. (2011).
[103] According to statistics from the International Labor Organization (2021), 92 percent of Benin's workforce was employed in the informal sector in 2011, compared to 86.3 percent in Ghana in 2013. These were the only years for which comparable data from these two countries are available.
[104] Public sector size is based on author calculations from statistics described in Chapter 1 and Appendix A.2. According to United Nations statistics, Ghana's overall population was 29.8 million in 2018 and Benin's was 11.5 million.

colonial histories as well as their postcolonial trajectories of bureaucratic institutional development.

Colonial experiences in African countries varied in terms of the legal and administrative institutions that colonial powers introduced, leading to potential differences in bureaucratic meritocracy, discretion, and political control. That Ghana was subject to the British common law legal system means that its legal-administrative traditions are rooted to some extent in pluralistic and procedural principles that seek to limit, divide, and fragment governing power; and its Whitehall administrative system advocates the separation of politics from a politically neutral administration. Additionally, British colonial governments were known to use indirect rule to control and administer their colonial territories, which vested power in local chiefs – often appointed by colonial rulers – to collect taxes, organize economic activities, and enforce colonial laws.[105]

Whether the British colonial legacy would promote Ghana's collusive extraction system is, however, unclear. On the one hand, its norms of political neutrality in the public service might dissuade political principals from seeking to engage bureaucratic agents in extraction, and agents who select or are socialized into these norms may resist political pressures to extract. On the other hand, the deconcentration of power that is a hallmark of both the British legal-administrative and colonial systems implies potentially higher levels of power and discretion among bureaucratic agents across the state apparatus. This higher level of discretion could incentivize bureaucratic extraction, making it more attractive for political principals to engage bureaucratic agents, which I argue is *not* typically integral to the collusive extraction system.

Benin's experience as a French colony produces equally unclear expectations vis-á-vis leaders' choice of extraction strategy. The French system sees both the law and administrative corps as instruments for using, rather than limiting, state power. It also involves a more robust and complex hierarchy of formal laws, codes, and judicial review, all of which serve to limit (or at least define more formally) administrative discretion.[106] In their colonies, the French were also more likely to employ direct forms of rule that incorporated colonial administrative hierarchy into the metropole's broader governing apparatus, thereby reducing discretion for local administrators. The French system's active embrace of state power and its lesser emphasis on political neutrality, particularly at

---

[105] Young (1994); Mamdani (1996).
[106] Painter and Peters (2010: 20–22).

the upper echelons of the public service,[107] might generate incentives for political leaders to employ the state and its personnel for their extractive pursuits. The French system's more rigid hierarchies and more restrictive approaches to bureaucratic discretion, however, suggest that leaders seeking to employ the bureaucracy for their extractive purposes may encounter more stringent formal barriers to these efforts.

It is therefore not immediately clear that either of these bureaucratic systems, even in their ideal-type forms, would generate strong or weak incentives for leaders to engage bureaucrats in their extractive pursuits. The potential relevance of differing colonial bureaucratic legacies is further undermined by reforms that took place in the post-colonial era. Political instability and aggressive Africanization programs throughout the 1960s and 1970s reshaped colonial civil service systems and modified the colonial legal structures. Seen by leaders as a way to advance nationalist agendas and replace out-of-date colonial institutional vestiges, these programs deconstructed many of the legal-administrative norms and rules that colonial powers had established in Africa.[108] Even in countries with similar colonial histories, such as Ghana and Tanzania, independence-era leaders such as Kwame Nkrumah and Julius Nyerere re-purposed colonial bureaucracies and legal institutions to fit their own unique economic and political visions.[109]

These trends were evident in the two countries' postcolonial political and institutional trajectories. Postcolonial leaders in both Benin and Ghana inherited well-reputed administrative apparatuses. Ghana's administration was regarded as "the finest, most relevant and performance-oriented institution in Africa."[110] In Ghana's immediate post-independence era, however, political insecurity led to cycles of bureaucratic politicization. In the 1960s, Nkrumah's CPP government purged university and civil service employees who were suspected of disloyalty[111] and public officials who questioned the CPP damaged their prospects of promotion.[112] In the 1980s the PNDC government further undermined bureaucratic principles, "asserting that the very principle of bureaucracy was at odds with effective administration" because it stifled

---

[107] Rouban (2007).
[108] As Goran Hyden has noted, these changes did not reflect a lack of understanding on the part of those African managers, but rather the proclivities of political leaders, "for whom the reversal of the norms associated with colonial rule [was] a priority."(2010: 74).
[109] See, especially, Pinkney (1997).
[110] Ayee (2001: 2).
[111] Mwakikagile (2014: 438).
[112] Pinkney (1972: 52).

the initiative of employees.[113] In a 1982 policy document, the PNDC wrote that "the huge and parasitic Public Services...[which] continue to service the existing neo-colonial arrangements...must be dismantled, pruned, or abolished."[114]

In French West Africa, Dahomey (Benin) served as an intellectual center, supplying a large number of administrators, professionals, and teachers to other parts of France's African empire.[115] After independence in Benin, although the civil service was "left largely untouched"[116] by Kérékou's efforts to subvert state and society to the PRPB, the regime's policies designed to absorb oppositional groups into the state apparatus, such as automatic hiring of all university graduates into the public service, greatly expanded and reshaped the administrative apparatus from what it had been during the colonial period.[117]

Thus, on the eve of democratization in the late 1980s, not only were bureaucratic institutions depleted from years of fiscal crises, but they had also been molded in ways that fit the political agendas of their post-colonial leaders. These conditions meant that there would be considerable space for leaders in both countries, especially in the midst of political and economic reforms, to adapt or remake bureaucratic institutions in their interests.[118] The existence of variation in bureaucratic institutions *within* each country further suggests that leaders can find and exploit bureaucratic organizations and arrangements in ways that will serve their extractive pursuits.[119]

3.3.3   Electoral Systems

Ghana and Benin also have different electoral institutions, which, as explained in Chapter 1, are potentially important drivers of political organization and, in turn, extraction. Ghana has a plurality single-member district system with parliamentary and presidential elections occurring simultaneously every four years. Benin uses a closed-list PR system with low district magnitude in which parliamentary elections are held every four years, but presidential terms are five years in length. For presidential elections, both countries have two-round systems in which a run-off is held if no candidate receives the majority of the popular vote in

---

[113] Nugent (1995: 52).

[114] (Gyimah-Boadi and Rothchild, 1990: 229).

[115] Ronen (1975: 198) quoted in Magnusson and Clark (2005: 556–557).

[116] Allen (1992: 44).

[117] Bierschenk (2009).

[118] van de Walle (2001).

[119] Boone (2003); Whitfield et al. (2015); Kovo (2018); McDonnell (2020).

the first round. These differing electoral rules can impact the formation and institutionalization of political parties, especially whether politicians cultivate personal or party votes. In one study by Daniel Gingerich, closed-list systems are associated with more centralized and politically controlled extraction practices.[120] What remains less clear, however, is whether political control in the closed-list system is collusive or coercive in nature. Nonetheless, as the next chapter makes very clear, Benin's closed-list system, despite empowering party leaders, has failed to produce any kind of highly coordinated machine-like extraction system of the kind that Gingerich's theory would expect.

More broadly, the electoral institution argument lacks power because the selection and retention of electoral institutions in each country are not necessarily exogenous to the party institutions themselves. In Ghana, Rawlings, who laid the groundwork for a strong NDC party in the 1980s, retained significant power throughout the transition to shape the design of the 1992 constitution, devising an electoral system that would make it difficult for small parties to succeed.[121] As discussed earlier, the constitutional development process was much less controlled in Benin. It occurred in a context in which the ruling PRPB had been effectively stripped of its power and no clear or unified opposition had emerged. Instead, the design of the new constitution – including the closed list PR system – occurred with participation from a multitude of actors who favored political pluralism and opportunities for broad participation.[122] Although different electoral rules have likely served to reinforce and institutionalize the party frameworks that existed (or did not exist) during the periods of transition, the counterfactual argument lacks strength. Given their differing party histories and modes of transitions, it is highly plausible that Ghana would have continued on a path toward more institutionalized parties, and Benin on a path of less institutionalized parties, had the two countries selected different electoral systems.

3.4   Conclusion

In many ways, Benin and Ghana have tread similar paths since their transitions to multiparty democracy in the early 1990s. Over nearly three decades of democratic rule, both countries saw improvements in the election quality and frequent mobilization of civil society actors to protect democratic institutions. At the same time, the extraction

---

[120] Gingerich (2013).
[121] Riedl (2014); Rabinowitz (2018); Driscoll (2020).
[122] Riedl (2014: 166–167).

environments in both countries have remained largely permissive, allowing incumbent leaders to extract from the state to support their political endeavors with few immediate legal or electoral consequences. Despite their similar democratic trajectories, however, the two countries' political parties have highly differentiated levels of party institutionalization, which, as I argue in the next chapter, leads to divergence in the extraction strategies that their leaders have pursued.

In this chapter, I have also demonstrated the plausibility of viewing Benin and Ghana as most-similar cases. Not only do the two countries have similar political and extraction environments, but the different extraction strategies that I observe in the two countries are not easily attributable to other potential causal factors such as economic structures, colonial institutional legacies, or electoral systems.

4   Extraction Strategies in Benin and Ghana

In early January 2001, just as it became clear that John Kufuor had won Ghana's presidential election and would succeed President J. J. Rawlings in the country's first electoral transfer of power, Kufuor took a phone call from his biographer and close associate Ivor Agyeman-Duah. According to Agyeman-Duah's account, Kufuor began the call not by acknowledging the most notable members of his NPP party, but rather by giving thanks to some of his key business partners including Tommy Amematekpor and Gabriel (Gabby) Nketia:

> I should give credit to my associates. They may not be described as mainstream politicians but I tell you, they were thorough in their support...Tommy Amematekpor is more a businessman who declared faith in me from 1991 and he stuck with me through and through. Then there was Gabriel (Gabby) Nketia, another businessman who stayed with me from the 1980s as well.[1]

That these are the individuals who came to Kufuor's mind at this truly historic moment is revealing not only of the prominent role that money was likely to have played in this election victory but also of the importance of the NPP's long-standing ties to private business. These party–business ties are integral to understanding the collusive strategies Ghanaian leaders have used to extract political money from the state. Importantly, these ties stand in stark contrast to the much more contentious relationships between political and business leaders that are on repeated display in Benin.

This chapter provides an overview of how incumbent political leaders in Benin and Ghana extract state money to finance their political operations. In Chapter 2, I established that parties and candidates across African countries often rely on the extraction of state resources to fund their political operations, but the threat of losing political power complicates their efforts to do so. Specifically, leaders seek to overcome

---

[1] Agyeman-Duah (2003: 119) quoting Kufuor. Tommy Amematekpor is commonly known as "Efo Tommy" in Ghana.

the political risks of extraction by ensuring that extracted resources do not wind up in the hands of the opposition while also keeping themselves distant from extraction to reduce the longer-term risks of prosecution once they have departed from office. These predicaments generate three types of problems that extracting leaders seek to overcome – unreliable agents, limited networks, and monitoring and discipline. In this chapter I show how leaders in Ghana and Benin have responded to these problems in very different ways. I trace these differing responses to the specific incentives generated by the significant differences in their party institutions, which were detailed in the previous chapter.

In the first part of the chapter, I outline how Ghana's strongly institutionalized parties enable incumbent leaders to overcome the three extraction problems by delegating to reliable agents, channeling extracted monies through partisan networks outside the state, and relying primarily on party-based instruments of control. The discussion conveys how incumbent leaders in Ghana are able to effectively collude with a wide variety of partisan actors to extract money from the state, typically by awarding procurement contracts to partisan-aligned businesses in exchange for their financial support to the party.

Leaders of Benin's weakly institutionalized political parties, as I discuss in this chapter's second section, have encountered considerable difficulty overcoming the three extraction problems. Facing frequent elite defections from their ruling party or coalition, leaders struggle to identify reliable elite extraction agents, driving them to administer elite extraction deals themselves and, in some cases, delegate to lower-level, more coercible agents. The absence of robust party organizations and networks incentivizes leaders to concentrate extraction within the state apparatus, where they can use executive powers over personnel issues to control agents. I therefore show how incumbent leaders in Benin have typically engaged in more coercive forms of extraction: guarding extraction opportunities from rival elites and co-opting public servants to collect rents and revenues directly from state coffers.

The first two sections rely principally on qualitative data – interviews, journalistic accounts, and existing case research – to describe the systems of extraction in Ghana and Benin, respectively. In the final section of the chapter, I use data from two bureaucratic surveys – the Classroom survey and the Workplace survey – to corroborate the existence of these different extraction systems. The Classroom survey, which was conducted in educational and training programs for public service employees in both countries, provides evidence of cross-country differences in bureaucrats' perceptions of the methods of extraction that are prevalent in their organizations. The Workplace survey, which was conducted in forty-nine different MDAs in Ghana, serves to reinforce findings from Ghana and to provide finer-grained insight into collusive extraction practices across the Ghanaian state apparatus.

In outlining leaders' extraction strategies in the two countries, the chapter demonstrates considerable variation in the types of actors, networks, and channels of extraction that exist in two similarly competitive African countries. This variation underscores the importance of going beyond questions about *whether* politicians extract to also consider the specific forms and strategies of extraction that they employ. The chapter further demonstrates the utility of combining elite interviews, secondary sources, and survey data to study elite extraction strategies. By capturing perspectives from extraction agents themselves as well as outside observers operating from different vantage points, it is possible to gain valuable insight into practices that can be difficult to observe directly.

4.1   Collusive Extraction in Ghana

I begin my discussion of extraction in Ghana by providing background information on the costs and sources involved in financing Ghana's two main parties, the NDC and the NPP, including the well-established centrality of procurement-based exchanges in Ghana's party financing landscape. This practice is *collusive* in the sense that elite party members serving in high-level government positions collude in awarding contracts to private businesses who, in anticipation of or in exchange for such awards, provide financial or in-kind support to the party. Following this descriptive overview of the system, I explain how the NDC's and NPP's strong party institutions enable leaders to delegate extraction broadly to elite party agents, to channel extraction through the parties' networks, and to rely principally on internal party instruments of control.

4.1.1   Party Financing in Ghana: Costs and Sources

As large membership organizations, Ghana's two major parties, the NDC and NPP require vast financial resources for party infrastructure and campaign functions. It is estimated that the NPP spent at least $100 million in the 2008 presidential and parliamentary elections,[2] while a long-serving member of parliament, Alban Bagbin, estimated the cost of winning a parliamentary seat to be around 2 million Ghanaian cedis, the equivalent of about $450,000. This estimate is somewhat higher than a recent study, which estimated that the average expenditure of successful

---

[2] Daddieh and Bob-Milliar (2012).

parliamentary candidates across both at around 390,000 Ghanaian cedis ($150,000) in the 2016 elections.[3] In either case, there is a substantial investment of money involved.

Although official figures on campaign spending are not publicly available, and likely do not exist in any meaningful form, there is widespread speculation that campaign spending has increased substantially in recent years, a trend that is well documented, at least for parliamentary elections. For example, Kojo Asante and George Kunnath estimate that the cost of running for a parliamentary seat rose 59 percent between 2012 and 2016.[4] As one Electoral Commission employee explained, "the monetization of elections has become a bigger problem since the 2004 elections…money is much more important in elections than it used to be."[5]

In national campaigns, the bulk of costs cover expenses for high-profile party leaders and political celebrities to engage in mass media, political advertisements, and hold large-scale rallies. The national parties also have recurrent and capital expenditures for party administration, the procurement of technical and consulting services, and the administration of internal party elections.[6] With strong party organizations, including party chapters throughout the country and ongoing engagement in the community, Ghana's parties have a very consistent need for funds to keep the party viable and to remain "active and visible during non-elections periods."[7] The national party also supports parliamentary candidates in general elections: intraparty transfers comprise around 14 percent of parliamentary candidates' campaign funds.[8]

At the local level, candidates engage in retail politics in local communities including door-to-door canvassing, community meetings, and engagements at local events. Parliamentary candidates regularly make cash payments to party workers, commonly known as "foot soldiers," as well as to poor members of the candidates' constituencies.[9] In that politicians and local party organizations also play a support role to their communities, funds are required to help party members, or prospective

---

[3] Asante and Kunnath (2017: 13).

[4] Asante and Kunnath (2017). Lindberg and Zhou (2009) and International IDEA and Center for Democratic Development (2004) also reported rising costs of parliamentary elections.

[5] Author interview, Western Region Electoral Commission, Takoradi, December 6, 2013.

[6] Gyimah-Boadi (2009).

[7] Sakyi et al. (2015: 7).

[8] Asante and Kunnath (2017: 30).

[9] Asante and Kunnath (2017).

party members, in need of school or hospital fees or by making a customary contribution when attending events such as weddings and funerals. According to one detailed study of party membership in Ghana, individuals often choose to become active in political parties based on the expectation of receiving some form of financial benefit or employment from the party.[10] Indeed, one constituency party chairman emphatically noted that "you can't say no" when asked by community members for support.[11] Thus, rather than relying on members for financial support, local party chapters must often gain access to funds to support their party members.

The precise sources of party financing are somewhat difficult to ascertain. While parties are supposed to file reports with the Electoral Commission, these reports have not usually been made available to the public. According to one report, it is common for "the commission to turn a blind eye to obviously inaccurate returns from the parties."[12] It was also clear that some party officials I interviewed became uncomfortable when I posed questions about sources of funds beyond party membership dues and filing fees.

Although the state provides some in-kind support for parties, for example the provision of free airtime on Ghana's government-owned TV and radio stations, this support is minimal. Parties, in turn, generally raise funds in a "free-wheeling manner."[13] The sources of party funds are to some extent diverse. As Alban Bagbin has described, "major political parties in Ghana are funded privately either through donations made by institutions, kickbacks and corruption, fund-raising or membership dues, and nomination fees paid by aspirants of executive positions in political parties as well as parliamentary and presidential aspirants during party primaries and congress."[14] Recent surveys suggest that parties often rely on a mix of these different funding sources.[15]

Officials in both parties spoke openly about the challenges involved in collecting membership fees and the fact that the fees are collected from only a very small percentage of members. Said one regional NPP official, "even if every member paid his dues, it would not be nearly enough for the elections."[16] Since most party members expect to *receive* financial benefits from the party, the idea of collecting fees from many

---

[10] Bob-Milliar (2012*b*).
[11] Author interview, Western Region NDC, December 2, 2013.
[12] Ayee et al. (2007: 6).
[13] Gyimah-Boadi (2009).
[14] Bagbin and Ahenkan (2017: 111–112).
[15] Sakyi et al. (2015); Asante and Kunnath (2017).
[16] Ashanti Region NPP, December 4, 2013.

rank-and-file members is essentially counter-intuitive.[17] Instead, as far as individual contributions go, parties rely primarily on elite party members, businesses seeking contracts from the government (discussed in more detail later in this section) and those from the diaspora to make contributions to political parties.[18]

Parties also raise funds from candidates who pay filing fees to the party to run on the party ticket. As Lindsay Whitfield has explained, the NDC opened the party to moneyed individuals specifically to attract wealthy candidates who could fund their own campaigns and contribute to the party.[19] As a more economically liberal party with roots in the Akan business community, the NPP more naturally attracted wealthy individuals who could pay such filing fees. It is reported, for example, that for the 2016 elections, NPP presidential candidate Nana Akufo-Addo paid a filing fee of 80,000 Ghanaian cedis, the equivalent of $23,000 at the time of payment while the NPP's nonincumbent parliamentary candidates were required to pay a fee of 30,000 Ghanaian cedis, the equivalent of approximately $8,600.[20] In the lead-up to the 2012 elections, NDC presidential candidate John Mahama reportedly paid a 5,000 Ghanaian cedis filing fee. The fee for parliamentary candidates in the NDC for the same period was reported as 2,000 Ghanaian cedis.[21]

There is also a strong expectation that party elites occupying state offices, including elected and appointed officials, support their party with whatever means are available. Pressure to do so comes from both above and below. For example, Metropolitan, Municipal, District Chief Executive (MMDCE)s, who are appointed by the President, may be given directives to use their district funds to support party efforts during campaigns.[22] They are also under pressure from grassroots party members, especially foot soldiers, who have been known to riot or protest if they feel that leaders have not done enough to serve the party.[23] Accounts of party financing in Ghana widely support this perspective, asserting that contributions from wealthy party members and their associates comprise important sources of funds.[24] The practice of

---

[17] Bob-Milliar (2012b).

[18] Asante and Kunnath (2017).

[19] Whitfield (2018).

[20] "NPP's new filing fees angers party members," Citifmonline, March 24, 2015.

[21] Author interview, Accra, July 7, 2014. See also Bagbin and Ahenkan (2017) for information on amounts received by parties from candidate filing fees.

[22] Author interview, Kumasi, December 12, 2013.

[23] Driscoll (2015).

[24] Bryan and Baer (2003); Gyimah-Boadi (2009); Sakyi et al. (2015); Asante and Kunnath (2017).

wealthy individuals contributing to political parties in Ghana dates back to at least the 1960s when, as Dennis Austin described, wealthy members of parties regularly made voluntary contributions to the nationalist parties of the era.[25]

Private donations are supplemented by – and intertwined with – parties' efforts to extract money from the state. In particular, private donations to political parties are often closely tied to state business deals. Party officials solicit donations from businesspeople with the promise to provide access to contracts or other benefits once in office. Private donations to parties frequently come with expectations of returns on these "investments," often in the form of public procurement contracts.[26] This practice has been especially prevalent in public works and construction services,[27] with construction contractors described as "the single most important source of business funding to the NDC."[28] One prominent example involves the Construction Pioneers, a large German-owned road construction contractor based in Accra. One former NDC Minister acknowledged that they paid money to the NDC over multiple elections, beginning as early as 1992, and that "one imagines that they were not the only one to do so."[29] Further evidence of this extractive practice is detectable in official party reports, when they have been made available. For example, between 1992 and 1996, both major parties listed "founding members" as their chief benefactors but, despite the NPP's close ties to private business, the incumbent NDC raised double the amount of funds as the NPP in 1992 and quadrupled it in 1996.[30] More recent research on Ghana's local governments also emphasizes the role of procurement based exchanges in local party financing.[31]

As one former NPP minister explained, the practice of awarding contracts to political donors has now extended to many sectors, including even small contracts to, for example, provide stationery and printing to ministries. The system has become so widespread that, when a new party takes office, affiliates of key party officials create businesses in hopes of earning contracts.[32] Specific examples of this practice in Ghana are widely available in the media and increasingly in published

---

[25] Austin (1964).
[26] Whitfield (2018: 118).
[27] Luna (2019).
[28] Opoku (2010: 179).
[29] Nugent (2007: 284–265).
[30] Morrison (2004: 436).
[31] Driscoll (2015); Luna (2019); Brierley (2020).
[32] Author interview, Accra, December 12, 2013.

research.[33] They were also regularly cited in interviews. One noteworthy case involves a former head of the Public Procurement Authority (PPA), a longtime NPP affiliate, who was found to have created and run businesses that were subsequently awarded lucrative contracts under restricted (noncompetitive) tendering. The companies that received these contracts, rather than fulfilling the terms of the contracts themselves, sold the contracts to other companies, raising profits used both for the party and for their personal enrichment.[34] One official at Ghana's PPA estimated that around 30 percent of contracts are used for major party finance deals while many others provide smaller-scale benefits to politicians and their networks.[35]

Although most extraction in Ghana appears to involve procurement-based exchanges, direct embezzlement of public funds does also, at times, serve as a source of party financing.[36] According to Lindsay Whitfield, for example, money from the Ghana National Petroleum Company (GNPC) has regularly been siphoned to party accounts and similar reports have surfaced about the Ghana Educational Trust Fund.[37] The direct diversion of money to political coffers is, however, comparatively rare.[38]

In the remainder of this section, I describe how Ghana's strong party institutions incentivize actors to engage in these collusive procurement-based extraction practices. Following the contours of the theoretical discussion in Chapter 2, I highlight how Ghana's leaders have typically delegated extraction widely to elite party agents, how extraction agents engage with broader partisan networks, and how the system is supported by strong agent incentives to collude in service of the party.

4.1.2   Party Elites as Extraction Agents

As the preceding discussion suggests, Ghana's major parties have often raised funds by extracting kickbacks from the award of state procurement contracts to businesses owned or operated by party financiers. This practice is common in central government MDAs as well as across local governments. The diffuse nature of this extraction strategy is made possible by the broad availability of reliable party agents, the most loyal

---

[33] Opoku (2010); Whitfield (2018).

[34] The case was exposed in a documentary by investigative journalist Manasseh Azure Awuni, available at www.youtube.com/watch?v=TFhYPuRdg8s.

[35] Author interview, Accra, June 23, 2017.

[36] Bagbin and Ahenkan (2017).

[37] Author interview, Accra, October 30, 2013.

[38] Ayee et al. (2007); Sakyi et al. (2015).

of whom are appointed by the incumbent president into positions from which they can administer extraction.

Ghana's strong party institutions allow presidents to learn about potential extraction agents, many of whom have worked their way up party hierarchies by serving in local, regional, or national party positions. In many cases, the political agents being considered for appointments to positions with access to extraction opportunities have already proven themselves as effective fundraisers, either through their party positions or their past "gifts" to the party.[39] As one NDC official noted, "We know when someone is serious when they sacrifice some of their wealth for the party. They might provide money...some office space, some vehicles, some printing."[40] The practice of "purchasing" appointments, where those interested in a ministerial post make large financial contributions to the party, came up in several interviews. One NDC official noted that this practice had become more common, particularly among those who become deputy ministers, explaining that it "helps to give something to the party."[41] The expectation that prospective political appointees provide funds to the party came to light in a recording, leaked to the press in 2013, in which then-Deputy Minister of Communications Victoria Hammah, an NDC member whose family has a long history in the party, proclaimed that her "appointment was solid way back," interpreted to mean that she had made a contribution to the party that would ensure that she receive an appointment.[42] Likewise, one national-level executive of the NPP explained that it has become increasingly common for those seeking appointments in government to offer significant material support to the party.[43]

Internal party contests, including primary elections and elections for party officers, also help leaders to minimize the adverse selection of extraction agents. Structured contests within the party offer party leaders the opportunity to establish a corps of loyalists and, perhaps more importantly, to learn whose support is not as strong. This phenomenon was particularly evident within the NPP in the run-up to President John Kufuor's victory in the 2000 election. A heated primary contest between Kufuor and Nana Akuffo Addo resulted in the formation of well-defined party factions within the NPP. When Kufuor eventually

[39] Author interview, Takoradi, December 9, 2013.
[40] Author interview, Accra, April 8, 2014.
[41] Author interview, Accra, March 10, 2017.
[42] The tape recording was widely reported in the Ghanaian and international media. A transcription of the recording is available at www.modernghana.com/news/502582/full-transcribed-text-of-leaked-victoria-hammah.html.
[43] Author interview, Accra, October 11, 2013.

became president in 2001, "the Kufuor faction...consolidated its power base by monopolising all the key sectors of the state apparatus. In the two administrations of President Kufuor (2001–2008), members of his faction received the lion's share in the allocation of ministerial portfolios."[44] Following these events, quite a number of key supporters of the "Kufuor faction" were appointed to ministerial positions in the administration, including Jake Obetesey Lamptey (Minister of Presidential Affairs), Richard Anane (Minister of Health), Patricia Appiagyei (Minister, Ashanti Region), Alan Kyerematen (Minister of Trade), and Papa Owusu Ankomah (Attorney General).

Though succession in the NDC has generally involved less intense competition, the contests that do exist have also enabled party leaders to learn about the loyalties of their members. For example, shortly after John Atta Mills assumed the presidency, a group of NDC elite, including former President Rawlings and some of his loyalists, grew frustrated with Mills' unwillingness to aggressively prosecute members of the outgoing NPP government for corrupt practices and as revenge for the NPP's prosecution of Nana Konadu Agyemang–Rawlings, the former president's wife, and her business associates. In 2010, this group mounted an effort to undermine Mills' influence by supporting candidates for executive positions in the party's leadership contest,[45] thus exposing the extent and depth of fault lines within the party. In the end, Mills survived these challenges, winning the 2011 presidential primary with 96.9 percent of votes and even retaining support from longtime party members who had been closely associated with Rawlings. As I explain in the next chapter, some of these individuals were, in early 2012, appointed by Mills to key extraction posts.

Internal party contests not only help leaders to learn about agent loyalties but also about their competence as potential fundraisers and financial managers. Running in internal party elections, whether they are primary elections or party leadership contests, can cost considerable amounts of money. Several delegates at the NPP's 2014 Party Congress, held in the Northern Region capital of Tamale, noted that they received payments as high as $100 to cast their votes for a particular candidate for party chair.[46] These payments, noted one attendee, not only signal to party delegates that the aspiring national party chair will, if victorious, "take good care" of the party and its members, but also demonstrate their ability to "play a major role in getting the party to

[44] Bob-Milliar (2012a: 581).
[45] Bob-Milliar (2012a: 592).
[46] Author communication with delegates, Tamale, April 12, 2014.

the polls and to deliver power in the next election." The same logic was invoked in one former minister's explanation of why Ghanaian presidents have appointed so many MPs to minister posts: "Winning parliamentary elections is a big, big challenge. First, you have to contest the primary. Then you have to contest the general election. When you win, you know that the party respects you, the constituency respects you, and that they see you as someone who can help the party."[47]

By delegating extraction broadly to party agents, presidents in Ghana have remained largely distant from extraction. Decisions about procurement contracts have, over time since the passage of the 2003 Public Procurement Act, been decentralized to 550 procurement entities housed in ministries, agencies, and local governments.[48] Each procurement entity appoints a tendering committee to review bids and award contracts. The tendering committee is chaired by the minister, agency head, or the chief executive of the local government – all of whom are appointed by the president. The remainder of the committee comprises politicians and bureaucrats, including two members of parliament.[49] In practice, the political appointee serving as chairperson of the committee has significant discretion over the committee membership. According to one procurement officer, the minister "chooses his men for the [tendering] committee" and "gets the outcome he wants."[50] Recent studies support this perspective, asserting that "the organisational structures of public procurement are packed with government political appointees to favour the distribution of public contracts to party financiers, loyalists and clients."[51]

In short, Ghana's extraction system is primarily executed by trusted party elites who occupy executive-level positions from which they can facilitate the extraction of rents through public procurement processes.[52] If lower-level party agents or career bureaucrats participate in extraction, for example through their roles on tendering committees, they serve largely as accessories to the extraction system.[53] The broad delegation of extraction to elite party agents is made possible by the NDC's and

---

[47] Author interview, Accra, October 18, 2013.
[48] The entities are listed on the website of Ghana's PPA, www.ppa.gov.gh.
[49] These provisions are outlined in Ghana's Public Procurement Act of 2003.
[50] Author interview, Accra, June 17, 2017.
[51] Appiah and Abdulai (2017a: 26).
[52] In the next chapter, I analyze in detail the placement of Ghanaian party elites into the state's executive apparatus.
[53] As Driscoll (2015), Luna (2019), and Brierley (2020) explain, bureaucrats who are involved in procurement may face some pressure to go along with decisions of politicians, but the decisions mostly lie firmly in the hands of the politicians.

NPP's strong party institutions, including their durability and their internal organizations and competitions, which enable presidents to identify loyal and competent party agents and, as I explain in the next chapter, appoint them to positions with access to extraction.

4.1.3   Channeling Extraction through Party Networks

Both the NDC and the NPP have developed extensive networks that help to facilitate the extraction of money for the party. These networks include individual business financiers and party-affiliated civic groups. The robustness and diversity of these networks afford party leaders flexibility in *how* to channel extracted resources, allowing them to pursue extraction in ways that keep themselves distant from extraction, minimizing the potential for attribution and future prosecution.

The parties' links to business communities, many of which pre-date the 1992 transition to a republican constitution,[54] provide avenues through which politicians can extract and manage money while minimizing the political risks of opposition access and attribution that often come with such activities. Whereas the NPP has enjoyed close and long-standing ties to business communities for some time, the NDC has, until relatively recently, a much more tumultuous relationship with Ghanaian business communities.[55] In the 1990s, in particular, the NDC was forced to "rethink its attitude toward business" because, with the rise of private media after adoption of a new constitution in 1992, business leaders had a venue through which to call for investigations, embarrass the regime, and exert pressure for more favorable governing practices.[56] Despite a number of initial missteps in President Rawlings' efforts to improve the NDC's relationship with business communities, including a failed attempt to introduce a value-added tax in 1995, the NDC has, in more recent years, come to possess its own robust network of business affiliates.

Today, each of the major parties has a number of particularly well-known business financiers who are widely believed to donate huge sums of money. These have included, for example, such figures as Ken Ofori-Atta and Akenten Appiah-Menkah for the NPP and Yusuf Ibrahim and Alfred Woyome for the NDC. These financiers have either served as party officials or have maintained close, even familial, links to party leaders. Parties have managed to retain the loyalty of these big financiers,

[54] Chazan (1991); Handley (2008).
[55] See Handley (2008), especially chapters 4 and 5, for detailed accounts of these relationships.
[56] Opoku (2010: 120–121).

even in the face of electoral loss, in part through the use of "judgment debts." Judgment debts are common when an incumbent party (Party A) loses power to an opposition party (Party B). The contracts that had been awarded to Party A's financiers typically get abrogated by the new government. Once back in power, however, Party A awards large settlements to the businesses whose contracts were abrogated under Party B's rule. There are a number of high-profile examples of judgment debts. When the NPP came to power in 2001, they canceled contracts that the NDC government had awarded to the Construction Pioneers due to their long-standing support of the NDC. When the NDC returned to power in 2009, the Construction Pioneers received a very large settlement, in the vicinity of 94 million Euros, for what Ghana's courts deemed an illegal abrogation of contracts by the NPP government.[57] The case illustrates not only the networks of business people that participate in extraction but also the role of judges and attorneys that make the judgment debts possible.

The Construction Pioneers are not the only business to have won a case like this. Indeed, such settlements are an increasingly common phenomenon.[58] In a widely publicized case, NDC financier Alfred Woyome won a sum of 51 million Ghanaian cedis (equivalent to approximately $25 million at the time) from the government for an abrogated contract to provide "financial engineering" services. According to widespread reporting, the services outlined in the contract were never actually rendered but the courts awarded the settlement anyway.[59] Though the Supreme Court of Ghana had at one point ordered Woyome to refund this sum of money to the Government, few believe that the government will actually compel him to do so, in part thanks to the party's networks within government. This shortage of meaningful oversight implies the continuing importance of these kinds of arrangements, which effectively allow party financiers to access greater amounts of money than procurement contracts alone would permit, helping them to recuperate money and contracts they do not gain as a result of having invested in the losing party. From the party's perspective, the judgment debts help them to assure financiers that, even in the event that the party loses an election, it will (eventually) be worth their while to contribute.

In addition to their links to individual business financiers, parties in Ghana also tend to have close relationships with civil society groups that

---

[57] Amoah et al. (2015: 134).

[58] Atta Mills (2018).

[59] There is abundant news coverage of this scandal. See, for example, "A-G Chases Woyome GHC 51 million," PeaceFM Online, August 12, 2014, or "Woyome challenges Judgement Debt Report," Daily Graphic Online, October 4, 2016.

assist in fundraising and extraction efforts. For the NDC, one noteworthy group is the 31st December Women's Movement (DWM). Founded
by Nana Konadu Agyeman Rawlings following the 1981 coup in which
her husband Jerry Rawlings came to power, the DWM served as a mix
between a mass organization and an organ of the revolution and, later,
a development NGO aimed at the advancement of women.[60] However, the DWM has been implicated in a number of financial deals
involving leading members of the NDC. For example, following Emma
Mitchell's departure as Minister of Trade and Industry in 1996 under
President Rawlings, it became clear that she had been involved in accepting $50,000 from a foreign inspection company "to pay the funds to
the DWM for 'party financing',"[61] In another case, it was alleged that a
French company paid the DWM over $500,000 in an attempt to influ-
ence its prospects to win the government's divestiture of the Ghana
Rubber Estates Limited, which members of the DWM had managed.[62]

In the NPP, the Young Executive Forum (YEF) has played a similar
role. Technically a wing of the NPP, the YEF engages up-and-coming
wealthy leaders from the business community to join the party from
a younger age. In so doing, they help to cultivate a donor base and
pool of potential political appointees. One regional party executive in the
Ashanti region explained that groups like the YEF "help [the party] to
get the most competent people, so in the future we can have a good cadre
of party leaders who support the party, and can bring their expertise to
government."[63] The YEF are known to be very active in soliciting donations from businesses for the financing of the party's campaigns.[64] For
example, in declaring his candidacy for president in 2007, NPP stalwart
Alan Kyerematen signaled his ability to take care of the party financially
by touting his leadership of the YEF and the influence it had gained in
the party.[65]

4.1.4   Agent Incentives and Party Control of Extraction

Why do the party's extraction agents not defect with the extracted
money? Why do they not use all or even most of it for their personal benefit? Ghana's durable, well-organized, internally democratic,
and value-infused parties produce a corps of party elites that, even when

---

[60] Whitfield (2018: 109).
[61] "Why Emma Mitchel Might Have Quit," The Ghana Chronicle, January 30, 1996.
[62] As reported by Nugent (2007: 265).
[63] Author interview, Kumasi, December 3, 2013.
[64] Agyeman-Duah (2003: 112).
[65] "Alan Kyerematen Launches Campaign," Daily Graphic, September 25, 2007.

placed in powerful positions, have strong incentives to remain loyal to the party. As such, incumbent political leaders can rely chiefly on party institutions (rather than their executive authorities) to ensure that extracted monies are used in service of the parties.

The two parties' longevity, organization, and values work in a synergistic manner to promote agent discipline. Agents can unquestionably profit personally from awarding government contracts to party financiers, but as one former NPP minister noted, "they don't take too much because it will hurt the party...The ministers, the chief executives [of public agencies], and the MMDCEs, they all want to help the party, that's why they get picked [for these positions]." These desires to help the party are indicative of party agents' commitment and values, but in many cases they are also in anticipation of future benefits given the longer time horizons associated with Ghana's institutionalized parties. One chief executive of a public commission said it this way:

I worked for the revolution [of 1981]. For many years after that we served, but had nothing. Sometimes no pay for months at a time. Only small pieces of bread to eat. We did it because we believed in the revolution. Today there are some party members who stay committed [to those ideals], but many members are looking for something else, for access and opportunities.[66]

Agents experience considerable top-down and bottom-up pressure from within the party. Top-down pressures emanate from either the presidency itself or from national and regional party chairs. Party agents who want to run for higher office or otherwise advance their position in the party, have strong incentives to act in the interest of these principals, who often serve as kingmakers in internal party contests. As just one of many examples, in September 2019, it was reported that the Deputy Minister of Energy, Dr. Mohammed Amin Adam, a leading contender to be elected as the NPP's parliamentary candidate for the Karaga constituency in Ghana's Northern Region, had constructed a new office complex for the party branch in Karaga. During an event in which Adam presented the office complex to local party members, a number of national, regional and local party officers encouraged NPP members in attendance to vote for Adam in the primaries, noting that delegates should "put the party first."[67]

---

[66] Author interview, Accra, November 7, 2013.

[67] This quote is attributed to Madam Rita Talata Asobayire, First National Vice Chairperson of NPP. See "Deputy Energy Minister constructs office complex for NPP," Ghana News Agency, September 23, 2019.

The 2007 primary election within the NPP provides another vivid example. With seventeen party members running to replace Kufuor at the top of the NDC ticket, candidates were eager to tout their past support of the party. In addition to touting his role in the NPP's YEF, Kyerematen declared that the chosen candidate "must have exhibited commitment, loyalty and leadership qualities within the NPP over the last 15 years." Another NPP candidate, Arthur Kennedy, described how the primary became intensely focused on who could raise money for the benefit of party executives:

The primary brought issues of money and personality differences into the ranks of [party] executives who were already divided...As money flowed from candidates to party functionaries based on who supported who, the party became more divided and interested in money. Party executives stopped building the party and took to trooping to Accra for contracts or hand-outs from big party men.[68]

Importantly, the party executives have ways to monitor the behavior of their extraction agents as it relates to procurement awards. In his account of local governments in Ghana, Joseph Luna explains that, although tendering committee meetings are not open to the public, there were frequently "contractors and party boys" present who "already knew the outcome."[69] An official at the PPA similarly noted that MPs "watch the tendering closely" to ensure that decisions benefit the party.[70]

Party agents also experience bottom-up pressures to award procurement contracts in ways that financially benefit the party. As noted earlier, politicians experience considerable pressure to serve the social and economic needs of their constituencies and to pay party activists, or "foot soldiers" for their work. Many of the party officials I interviewed cited strong pressures to keep the money flowing to party members and to the constituency, noting that "it is often the party-aligned businesses that provide jobs and materials that keep our members fed."[71] If those serving in extraction-rich positions do not fulfill these demands, they risk grassroots backlash, which can ricochet up the party chain and cause future problems related to party advancement.[72]

These examples convey how the parties' longevity, their internal organizations, and their values – often emphasizing mutual material benefit –

---

[68] Kennedy (2009: 6, 7).
[69] Luna (2019: 52).
[70] Author interview, Accra, June 24, 2017.
[71] Author interview, Takoradi, December 5, 2013.
[72] Driscoll (2015); Luna (2019).

shape the fundraising behavior of the party's extraction agents. Party leaders in Ghana regularly count on party agents to provide support to specific national, regional, or local party organizations. This system works in part because of party agents' own desires to move up the party ladder in the context of strong social pressures to share spoils with the party and, to a lesser extent, based on their nostalgic commitments to the party. It is also perpetuated by monitoring systems and grassroots pressures from within the party.

To summarize, Ghana's two main parties – the NDC and NPP – have, when in power, largely extracted money from the state by awarding procurement contracts to party-aligned businesses in return for financial or in-kind support to party chapters and election campaigns. This extraction system is primarily executed by the party elite who, as I explain in the next chapter, are placed into state positions where they can facilitate the extraction of state money through procurement processes. This system is enabled by dense party networks, including businesses and civil society groups, who help to channel extracted monies. The party institutions furthermore ensure that actors participating in this system have incentives to behave in the interest of the party.

4.2   Coercive Extraction in Benin

On the surface, the extraction of money from the state by incumbent politicians in Benin looks similar to that of Ghana. Wealthy individuals "sponsor" political candidates and/or run for office themselves. Political leaders – especially the president – are also known to award procurement contracts to party financiers in exchange for their support. As I detail in this section, however, the dynamics underlying these activities take on a much more contentious character, leading to practices of extraction that are more varied, more coercive, and ultimately more deeply reliant on state agents and structures.

One important difference between extraction in the two countries is that Benin's leaders are more reluctant to delegate extraction at all. They tend to maintain much tighter control over lucrative extraction opportunities, such as the award of procurement contracts, either by engaging in deals directly with financiers or limiting them all together. Another important difference is that, unlike in Ghana, Benin's political leaders have relied to a larger extent on the collection of rents and diversion of revenues from the state's bureaucratic organizations.

Even more fundamentally, the relationship between political principal and extraction agent in Benin takes on a much more coercive character than it does in Ghana. Whether the president is directly awarding contracts for financial support or co-opting bureaucrats to divert rents and revenues from their positions, they are compelled to use a range of tools – both rewards and punishments – to ensure that the spoils of extraction work in their favor and do not wind up in the hands of the opposition. As the following pages explain, Benin's weak party institutions contribute to this coercive system of extraction.

4.2.1   Political Financing in Benin: Costs and Sources

As in Ghana, electoral campaigns in Benin have become very costly in recent decades. Benin's 2013 Electoral Law, Article 110, forbade campaign expenses in excess of 2.5 billion CFA francs (around $4 million at 2016 exchange rates) for presidential candidates and 15 million CFA francs ($24,000) for legislative elections. One campaign official noted, however, that he had never seen the law enforced and estimated that expenditures for the top finishers in the 2016 election were "much, much more" than the amounts permitted.[73] An official working on the 2016 third-place finisher Sebastien Ajavon's campaign for president estimated the campaign's expenditures at around 3 billion CFA francs ($5 million).[74] One news report concluded that the 2016 election was "without doubt, the most expensive in the history of Benin: billions of CFA francs spent."[75] Dominika Koter has also documented rising electoral costs, noting that the sums given to voters during legislative elections have increased from around 500–1,000 CFA francs ($1–$2) per voter in 2007 to around 5,000 CFA francs ($10) per voter in the 2015 elections.[76]

Beninese law also mandates public funding for political parties.[77] Specifically, Article 40 of the 2003 Political Parties Act Number 2001-2 required the government to provide a financial grant to legally registered political parties holding at least one seat in the National Assembly. The law has more or less been followed regularly by Benin's presidents, though the timing of the disbursements has been unpredictable, causing some to speculate that the disbursements correspond to the President's

---

[73] Author interview, June 22, 2018. See also Koter (2017) on non-enforcement of spending limits.

[74] Author interview, June 29, 2018.

[75] "Présidentielle au Bénin: le bilan d'une campagne électorale à prix d'or," RFI Afrique, April 3, 2016.

[76] Koter (2017: 578). Both Koter and Ch et al. (2019) note that amounts vary considerably across urban and rural areas, with elections costing more in urban areas.

[77] The laws discussed here do not include new laws on parties and funding that were passed in advance of the 2019 and 2021 elections.

need or desire to exert control over party alignments and actual or potential opponents. Although the state funds provided have been substantial – 5 million CFA francs ($10,000) for each party – this amount is reportedly far from sufficient to make a difference in parties' abilities to compete and win.[78]

The combination of spending limits and insufficient public funds leads campaigns to use many "hidden" sources of funding, including "acts of plundering public resources" or "foreign interference."[79] A 2005 report by NDI makes a similar observation: "The party in power (and those that have ministers or support the government) get funds from state resources, foreign contributions, and by placing party members who then contribute."[80] At the local and legislative levels, a survey of candidates around the 2015 elections found that candidates were most likely to receive funding from their parties or coalitions or from unspecified "others."[81] Only around 6–10 percent reported having received funds from local or national businesses.

Historically, financing for Benin's parties and candidates has relied to a significant extent on the extraction of rents and revenues from the state's bureaucracy. In particular, there is considerable opportunity for rent-seeking in the public agencies responsible for regulating trade and transport, including the customs and port administrations, police, and gendarmes. Benin's economy is heavily reliant on informal re-export and transit trade with neighboring Nigeria, comprising upwards of 20 percent of GDP.[82] Agents at the Port of Cotonou, in particular, have served as "a principal source of [party] finance,"[83] where there is "a well-established relationship between the needs of political parties for extraordinary revenues in the run-up to elections and the level of informal payments collected from port users."[84] As Richard Banégas has written of the Port of Cotonou, "beyond its technical aspects, it always has an eminently political dimension."[85] Police and *gendarmes* are also important extractions agents. A 2006 study estimates that they collected anywhere from 200,000 to 300,000 CFA francs per day (equivalent to

---

[78] Saffu (2003: 25).
[79] Houndete, Eric. "Les sources de financement des partis politiques et des candidats au Bénin." Presentation to the *5ème séminaire international du Réseau des Compétences Electorales Francophones*, November 4, 2017.
[80] Bryan and Baer (2005: 33).
[81] Ch et al. (2019: 21).
[82] World Bank (2021).
[83] Bako-Arifari (2001: 42).
[84] Zinnes (2016: 33).
[85] Banégas (2014: 110).

$400–$600), significant portions of which would get funneled upwards to those in positions of authority.[86]

The prevalence of extraction from ports, customs, social welfare programs, taxes, and police functions was widely cited in interviews. As one NGO official explained, "Every chief of state has used rhetoric about reforming [the port's] operations. Some have succeeded in their programs to increase revenue collection, but none have succeeded in stopping the money to disappear...because they depend on it."[87] A former Port of Cotonou official added that "everyone knows that politicians depend on the port for more than just revenue for the state."[88] A former employee of the *Direction Générale des Impôts* (tax agency) further explained that "nearly all" of the employees in his unit were, at some point, approached by politicians with invitations to join political parties or movements "in recognition that [tax agents] had access to resources."[89]

Consistent with these accounts, surveys and public opinion polls conducted by entities such as the World Bank and Afrobarometer show consistently high levels of distrust of Benin's tax and customs agencies. In a 2007 survey on corruption in Benin conducted by the World Bank Institute, the respondents, all of whom were civil servants, rated political parties and the customs administration as the two most corrupt institutions.[90] Likewise, citizens have consistently reported high perceived levels of corruption among tax and customs agents relative to other state and political actors.[91] The distrust of these agencies is not surprising given the instrumental roles they have played in Benin's political financing systems.

While rents and revenues siphoned directly from the bureaucracy have formed an important source of political financing, domestic businesses have more recently become increasingly closely linked to politics by business elites running for office and self-financing their election campaigns.[92] The most obvious example is business magnate Patrice Talon's financial support of President Boni Yayi, through which he was able to secure privatization concessions, government contracts, influence in the cabinet, and widespread notoriety; all of which helped to propel him to presidency in 2016 without the support of an established party.

[86] Bako-Arifari (2006: 209).
[87] Author interview, Cotonou, November 18, 2013.
[88] Author interview, Cotonou, June 29, 2018.
[89] Author interview, Parakou, June 14, 2014.
[90] World Bank and Government of Benin (2007).
[91] Afrobarometer (2018).
[92] Koter (2017) and Pinkston (2016) demonstrate this empirically. Ch et al. (2019) also provide some evidence of this trend.

Despite the rising prominence of business people entering politics directly, the role of high-level officials extracting money through deals with businesses is by no means absent. Unlike in Ghana, however, presidents – rather than their agents – often preside directly over major extraction deals with both domestic and foreign businesses, a phenomenon I discuss in greater detail throughout this section.

4.2.2 Reluctant Delegation and Bureaucrats as Extraction Agents

The selection of extraction agents poses a difficult problem for Benin's presidents. The fluid and fragmented nature of Benin's party institutions, as well as the prevalence of independent candidacies for president (see Chapter 3), create a high likelihood of elite defection from Benin's loosely assembled ruling coalitions. As such, elite members of parties, coalitions, or governments are likely to have political interests that do not align with those of the president, and presidents find few political elites who can serve as reliable agents of extraction.

When it comes to extraction, Benin's political leaders have responded to this problem in two main ways. First, they have sought to limit the extent to which other political elites gain access to potentially lucrative extraction deals. Presidents have often managed lucrative procurement or privatization deals themselves. A former member of President Thomas Boni Yayi's staff explained,

Decisions about big public procurement contracts are almost always made inside the office of the president. It is very political. You can go to the procurement office (*Autorité de Régulation des Marchés Publics*) but they will not have information or they will not easily release. It's very political, especially now with the accusations and judicial processes against members of the previous regime.[93]

This insight is particularly instructive both for its revelation of the president's control over such decisions and the risks involved vis-à-vis future prosecution. One former minister further explained that it is "certain categories" of contracts that "finance the political parties," noting also that ministers "are not usually included in those affairs."[94] As the former presidential staff member explained, presidential oversight was especially prevalent in deals that involved larger "over the counter" contracts (*gré-à-gré* in French), in which there is no tendering process.

---

[93] Author interview, Cotonou, July 2, 2018.
[94] Author interview, Cotonou, June 22, 2018.

Several examples underscore the central roles of presidents – rather than their agents – in extractive procurement deals. In the run-up to his 2001 reelection, President Kérékou extracted around $2 million from a telecommunications deal with the U.S.-based Titan Corporation.[95] President Boni Yayi similarly maintained tight control over his relationship with key political financier (and now president) Talon, a relationship based largely on the award of contracts and privatization concessions in Benin's lucrative port and cotton sectors. Boni Yayi also involved himself directly in deals with Chinese contractors, for which ministers dubbed him "the first diplomat" in Benin-China relations.[96] Boni Yayi, around the time of his re-election in 2011, had developed a very close relationship with one particular Chinese state-owned enterprise, the China Railway 14th Construction Bureau. Thanks to their "presidential project" – the Godomey interchange on the outskirts of Cotonou – they went on to outpace other Chinese entities in winning construction contracts in Benin, despite having had less success in doing so in other countries.[97] Explaining why presidents often control these deals, one former minister said, "the challenge for the president is that he does not always know where the ministers stand politically."[98]

The second way that incumbents cope with uncertainties surrounding the political interests of elite agents is by relying more frequently on bureaucrats as extraction agents, much more so than their counterparts in Ghana. Politicians often seek out "wealthy employees of the state" to support them, especially "tax and customs agents."[99] In one detailed study of political parties competing in National Assembly elections in Parakou, the cotton capital and largest city in the Northern part of Benin, Agnes Badou documents how candidates court "rich and popular personalities" in the city who can provide resources and tap their networks for support.[100] These "sponsors" (*parrains* in French) often occupy posts in the regional or local governments.

Bureaucrats, particularly those who occupy positions in – or are placed into – "wet" posts collect rents and revenues that get funneled up to higher-level officials. For example, the 200,000–400,000 CFA francs collected as side payments at numerous points in the process of transporting goods from the Port of Cotonou northwards to Niger, as well

[95] United States District Court, Southern District of California. "Shurkin et al. vs. Titan Corp. et al.," File number: 04-CV-06-LAB LS, p. 43.
[96] Soulé-Kohndou (2019: 4).
[97] Lam (2016).
[98] Author interview, Cotonou, June 29, 2018.
[99] Author interview, Cotonou, June 20, 2014.
[100] Badou (2003: 18).

as eastwards into Nigeria by police and gendarmes well exceeds the monthly salary of most of the Beninese population.[101] The importation of second-hand vehicles alone is estimated to generate 6.5 billion CFA francs ($13 million) in informal (undeclared) profits.[102] Additionally, Arifari explains that the placement of individual customs officers is highly coordinated to allow movement from "dry" or "less lucrative posts" to "lucrative posts." In order to graduate to "wetter" posts, officers must deliver part of their earnings to those who place them in their "wet" positions.[103] These dynamics are most pronounced in state ministries that have greater access to rents and revenues, but they have been present to some extent in other sectors of the state apparatus as well.

4.2.3 Limited Party Networks and State-Concentrated Extraction

Lacking strong and stable roots in society, the business and civic networks of Benin's political parties are significantly more limited than those in Ghana (see Chapter 3). As such, leaders do not channel extraction broadly through non-state networks. Instability in politician–business relationships is particularly significant in this regard, demonstrating the severe challenges Benin's leaders have faced in cultivating networks of extraction.

The uncertain and highly transactional nature of political–business networks was particularly evident in the fragile (and highly visible) political financing arrangement between President Boni Yayi and then-businessman Patrice Talon. As mentioned earlier, Talon became a major financier for Boni Yayi's presidential campaigns in 2006 and 2011. In January 2011, just several months before Boni Yayi would face re-election, the government awarded one of Talon's companies – Benin Control – a large contract to operate a new import verification program at the Port of Cotonou.[104] One study suggests that this contract may have been the "biggest public procurement in Benin's history."[105] As a journalist described it to me, "the connection between the election and the contract were in the light of day."[106]

The tides quickly turned, however, when, after the 2011 election Boni Yayi sought additional financing from Talon to buy support from

---

[101] Bako-Arifari (2006: 209).
[102] Bako-Arifari (2006: 214).
[103] Bako-Arifari (2006: 210).
[104] "Arbitration tribunal rules against state in business dispute," Economist Intelligence Unit Politics Forecast, June 11, 2014.
[105] Ch et al. (2019).
[106] Author interview, Cotonou, November 18, 2013.

Deputies in the National Assembly for his efforts to amend constitutional term limits, which would have enabled Boni Yayi to run for a third term. When Talon refused to support Boni Yayi's efforts, for what are now obvious reasons (Talon won the presidential election in March 2016), Boni Yayi accused Talon and his associates of trying to assassinate him by poison, forcing Talon to flee the country.[107] The fallout from this event, as I describe later in Chapter 6, would color the remainder of Boni Yayi's time in office.

A similar pattern was apparent between then-President Mathieu Kérékou and real estate and construction mogul Sévérin Adjovi. Kérékou recruited Adjovi to run his 1996 campaign for president, despite the fact that Adjovi had strongly opposed Kérékou during the 1990–1991 transition. Former President Soglo, describing this surprising alliance between the two men, was alleged to say that "they engage in a sado-masochistic relationship with their former executioner."[108] Adjovi had himself run for President in 1991 but finished seventh with only a very small percentage of votes, but his political aspirations remained in tact.

After leading Kérékou's successful campaign for President in 1996, Adjovi served first as Minister of Defense, then later as Minister of Culture and Communications and, finally, as Minister of Commerce, Handicrafts and Tourism in Kérékou's government. During that time he became involved in the major extraction scandal with US firm Titan Corp, whose employees were accused of bribing the Beninese government to secure exemptions from customs duties and other favors to enable Titan's construction infrastructure in Benin's nascent telecommunications sector.[109] In the US Security and Exchange Commission's July 2005 filing for this case, they cite "numerous payments to Sévérin Adjovi's brother and his daughter, Chantal, to gain Sévérin Adjovi's influence with the Beninese government."[110]

Although Adjovi did not overtly challenge Kérékou with these funds, neither did the extracted rents help the president build a more coherent political coalition. Adjovi did go on to run for Mayor of Cotonou in the 2002 local elections, a position that could have propelled his chances on

---

[107] "Benin: Boni Yayi-Talon, une relation empoisonnée," Jeune Afrique, October 29, 2012.

[108] Adjovi (1998: 148).

[109] Tim Weiner, "Titan Corp. to Pay $28.5 Million in Fines for Foreign Bribery," New York Times, March 1, 2005.

[110] United States District Court, Southern District of California. "Shurkin et al. vs. Titan Corp. et al.," File number: 04-CV-06-LAB LS, p. 43. http://securities.stanford.edu/filings-documents/1030/TTN04-01/2005718_r01c_04676.pdf, accessed July 15, 2021.

the national political scene. The short-lived alliance between the two men underscores the unstable nature of these types of alliances and, importantly, the reasons why political leaders in Benin would find greater political security in diverting money more directly from the state apparatus or in administering deals with foreign entities that they can more easily control themselves.

4.2.4 Centralized and Coercive Control

Facing high risks of elite defection from the ruling coalition, feeble structures and norms within the party, and unstable partisan networks in society, incumbents in Benin rely to a greater extent on state authority and coercive means of control over their extraction efforts. As I have described above, one strategy used by leaders is the centralization of procurement decisions in the office of the president. The other, which I describe briefly here and in greater depth in the following chapters, is for leaders to assert authority over public personnel management decisions. These strategies enable incumbent leaders to retain as much control as possible over extracted resources amidst a highly fluid and uncertain political landscape.

Benin's presidents have sought to control extraction by using their powers to manage bureaucratic extraction agents. Benin's political leaders have been known to, among other things, cancel and/or interfere with civil service recruitment competitions, impose senior level staff on newly appointed ministers, dismiss personnel – sometimes highly capable bureaucrats – who do not serve the president's political needs, and interfere in the day-to-day workings of bureaucratic organizations.[111] Describing this general pattern of control, a high-ranking official at the Ministry of Public Service said: "Ministry chiefs may nominate for political posts and promotions. It then comes through [the Ministry of Public Service], but the Office of the President makes the final decision. This process has not changed very much over the years."[112] A former officer at the Port of Cotonou added that "You see a lot of leadership changes. If one tries to disrupt the system, their hands get cut."[113]

To the extent that incumbents exercise power over bureaucrats' jobs, bureaucrats are likely to have little choice as to whether to engage in extraction on behalf of incumbents. As one senior civil servant noted in reference to bureaucrats contributing to the extraction of money for

[111] These practices are described in depth in subsequent chapters.
[112] Author interview, Cotonou, July 4, 2018.
[113] Author interview, Cotonou, June 29, 2018.

incumbents' political operations "there are certainly offices where the pressure is very, very strong."[114] Such power imbalances imply that coercive dynamics are at work in the relationship between political leaders and their bureaucratic extraction agents – an issue I examine in depth in Chapter 7.

This overview of Benin's extraction system has emphasized how parties possess few, if any, of the institutional qualities that could help their leaders to manage the political risks and agency problems involved in extraction. As such, collusive forms of extraction are not available in Benin. Instead, Benin's political leadership has typically engaged in more coercive forms of extraction that centralize presidential control over extractive procurement deals, delegate direct extraction of state funds to bureaucrats, and use coercive instruments of control.

4.3   Analyzing Extraction in Survey Results

The preceding discussion has outlined key differences in how leaders in Ghana and Benin extract money from the state for political financing. The discussion highlights divergence in *to whom* incumbent leaders delegate extraction, *how* agents channel the extracted monies, and *which* instruments leaders use to maintain control over extraction. I now examine whether differences in extraction practices are evident in results of the two surveys of bureaucrats. I do so in two steps. First, I examine the results of the Classroom survey, which was administered in both countries, to compare the overall perceptions of bureaucrats across the two countries regarding the diversion of state resources from bureaucratic organizations.[115] I then look at results from both the Classroom and Workplace surveys to gain further insight into the dynamics surrounding procurement-based extraction in Ghana.

4.3.1   Diverting Resources to Parties

A principal difference between extraction in Benin and Ghana is that leaders in Benin rely to a much greater extent on bureaucrats to divert state rents and revenues to political coffers. This difference is strongly evident in the Classroom survey of bureaucrats. Figure 4.1 shows survey results reflecting bureaucrats' perceptions of diversion of their organization's resources to a political party. The survey asked respondents to

---

[114] Author interview, Ministry of Institutional and Administrative Reform, March 15, 2014.
[115] This part of the analysis also appears in Sigman (2022).

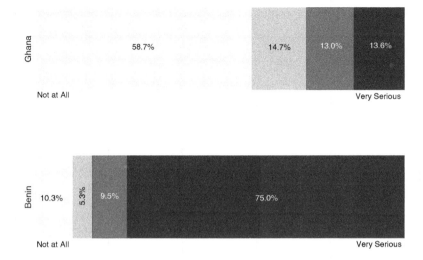

Figure 4.1 Diversion of resources to parties (Classroom survey)
Responses to questions asking to what extent "resources disappearing
for party use" is a problem in their organization. Benin: $n = 527$,
Ghana: $n = 484$. Source: Author's Classroom survey (2013–2014).

rate on a scale of 1–4, the extent to which they see "resources disappearing for party use" to be a problem in their organization.[116] Beninese
bureaucrats overwhelmingly saw resource diversion to parties as a serious problem (75.0 percent) in their organization, compared to only 13.6
percent of bureaucrats in Ghana – a statistically significant difference
($t = 25.4$).

To better understand the survey responses from Benin, I examine
whether certain types of bureaucrats report higher levels of concern
about resource diversion. Table 4.1, shows results from a series of
bivariate linear regressions investigating whether certain attributes of
bureaucrats are associated with higher levels of concern about resource
diversion. The independent variables include how many years an individual has worked in the public service, their gender, their age group,

---

[116] Whether or not the respondents see these issues as a problem is not necessarily akin
to the frequency of their occurrence, but they are likely to be related.

Table 4.1 *Bureaucrats' attributes and resource diversion in Benin (Classroom survey)*

	(1)	(2)	(3)	(4)	(5)	(6)
Years in Public Service	0.008					
	(1.11)					
Female		0.031				
		(0.34)				
Age			0.106**			
			(4.41)			
Employment Grade				0.109**		
				(3.37)		
Political Hire					0.154	
					(1.43)	
Party Member						−0.132
						(−1.48)
Observations	498	521	520	524	514	525
R-squared	0.002	0.000	0.036	0.021	0.004	0.004

Estimates based on bivariate OLS regression, ** $p < .05$, t-statistics in parentheses

their grade of employment,[117] whether they reported political links as the most important factor in their hiring, and whether they identified themself as a party member. The results indicate that older and higher-grade employees are more likely to express concerns about resource diversion than younger or lower-grade employees, perhaps because such practices have reportedly grown worse since the early 1990s. There is no statistically significant relationship between a respondent's political background and their expressed level of concern about resource diversion. Overall, concerns about resource diversion appear common among a wide range of public service employees.

In Table 4.2, I further assess whether the sector in which a bureaucrat works predicts their concern about resource diversion. The reference category used in the regression is the health sector, a sector that is recognized for its low levels of extraction and high levels of professionalism.[118] Those working in the infrastructure and welfare sectors were significantly more likely to report high levels of concern about resource diversion. These results are consistent with qualitative accounts of high levels of political extraction in port and road management as well as in

---

[117] Respondents were asked to select one of the following categories: junior staff, midlevel manager, deputy or assistant director, director, or other.

[118] This characterization of the health sector was noted by a number of interviewees.

Table 4.2 *Bureaucratic sector and resource diversion in Benin (Classroom survey)*

Local Government	0.263
	(1.35)
Education	0.118
	(0.73)
Welfare & Social Programs	0.368*
	(1.69)
Central Administration	0.022
	(0.13)
Trade & Industry	0.149
	(0.72)
Infrastructure	0.512**
	(2.73)
Justice & Human Rights	−0.067
	(−0.39)
Agriculture & Environment	0.093
	(0.55)
Observations	523
R-squared	0.028

Estimates based on OLS regression. Reference category = Health
$*p < .1$, $**p < .05$, t-statistics in parentheses

the state's social security program. I provide an additional discussion of these sectors in the next chapter.

The large magnitude of the difference in concerns about resource diversion between the two countries (Figure 4.1) suggests that these differences are not likely to be driven by social desirability bias (in Ghana) or by other survey-related factors. To further assess this possibility, I report results from the Workplace survey, which was conducted only in Ghana and included a greater diversity of questions, to see if we observe similarities in the reporting of relatively low levels of resource diversion in Ghana. In the Workplace survey, respondents were asked to rate how frequently "in my institution, public servants help divert government resources to a party or person with political links." Of 1,453 respondents, 85.4 percent reported resource diversion as occurring "rarely" or "never" and only 4.7 percent reported that it occurs "often" or "very often." Although the wording and response scale of this question are different from the question about resource diversion in the Classroom survey, the distributions of responses are similar in the sense that in neither case do bureaucrats report high levels of concern/frequency about resource diversion.

The Workplace survey also included a list experiment that indirectly asks Ghanaian respondents whether they have diverted resources to a politician or political party.[119] Participants were presented with the following question: "There are many activities that public servants undertake in the course of their jobs and daily lives. In regards to requests and opportunities in your job, how many of the following activities have you undertaken in the past two years?" Respondents were then randomly assigned to a control group, which received a list of either three innocuous (non-sensitive) items, or to a treatment group, which saw a list with the same three tasks plus an additional sensitive task: diverting government resources to a party or person with political links. The lists were presented as follows:

- You helped your manager with an important assignment for your organization
- You helped write a report for an international organization
- You helped a colleague with the completion of a task
- **Sensitive item**: You helped divert government resources to a party or person with political links

The results presented in Table 4.3 are estimated using the item count technique.[120] The analysis yields an estimate that 8.4 percent of those surveyed have engaged in diverting resources to a political party or politician. By comparison, the same experiment conducted in Uganda produced an estimate of 16.2 percent of respondents[121] and, in Malawi, the estimate was greater than 35 percent.[122] The experiment suggests the diversion of resources by this group of bureaucrats (central government, non-street level) is relatively rare in Ghana.

Looking across the results of the Classroom and Workplace surveys, the evidence suggests rather clearly that bureaucrats in Benin are widely concerned about the direct diversion of resources from their organizations to political parties. By contrast, Ghanaian bureaucrats report such practices as considerably less common and less concerning. These findings are largely consistent with the expectations of each country's extraction systems whereby leaders in Benin have relied to a much greater extent on bureaucrats to divert rents and revenues from their organizations to political coffers than have their counterparts in Ghana.

[119] The results of this experiment were first reported in Harris et al. (2020).
[120] Blair and Imai (2012).
[121] See Harris et al. (2020) for more information.
[122] See Chapter 8 for additional discussion.

Table 4.3 *Resource diversion list experiment*

Response	No	s.e.	Yes	s.e.
0	4.7	NA	NA	NA
1	22.7	.02	3.0	.02
2	50.1	.02	1.8	.02
3	17.4	.01	1.8	.00
4	NA	NA	1.8	NA
Total	94.9		8.4	

Estimated percentage answering affirmatively to the sensitive
item using item count estimation.

4.3.2 Extracting from Procurement

I also use the survey data to assess bureaucrats' perceptions of extraction
through procurement deals. First, in Figure 4.2, the results of the Classroom survey show that levels of concern among Beninese and Ghanaian
bureaucrats are similar, but that Ghanaians express slightly greater levels of concern about contracts being awarded to political supporters –
with 44.6 percent of respondents seeing this as a problem or serious
problem compared to 39.9 percent in Benin. That these results do not
vary as much across countries as they do for resource diversion is not
surprising given that extraction through procurement deals are common
in both countries but, as described above, are executed differently, with
more centralized presidential control in Benin. Nonetheless, in Ghana,
the percentage reporting politicized procurement in their organization
as a problem or serious problem (44.6 percent) is substantially larger
than the 26.6 percent of Ghanaians surveyed who express concerns
about resource diversion. The opposite is evident in Benin, where 84.5
percent of those surveyed saw resource diversion as a problem or serious problem, compared to only 39.9 percent reporting the same for
procurement.

Once again, the results of the Workplace survey provide additional
insight into patterns of collusive extraction in Ghana. In a series of questions about the importance of various factors in decisions about awarding procurement contracts in their organizations, Ghanaian bureaucrats
saw "financial support for the ruling party" as one of the most important factors. On an importance scale of 1–7, 32 percent of respondents
assessed an importance level of 5 or above. Respondents overall saw
financial support to the party as having a very similar level of importance
as the contractor's personal connections to decision makers and the contractor's party affiliation. Average ratings also placed financial support

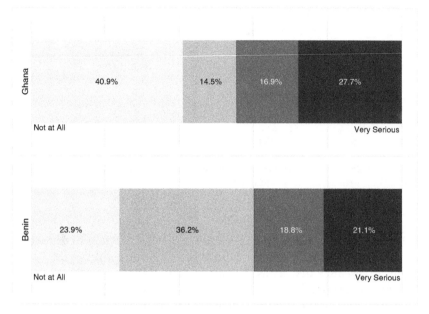

Figure 4.2 Procurement contracts (Classroom survey)
Responses to questions asking to what extent "contracts awarded for
political support and not to the firm that will get the job done" is a
problem in their organization. Benin: $n = 527$, Ghana: $n = 484$.
Source: Author's Classroom survey (2013–2014)

to the party as having greater importance than the contractor providing
gifts to those in decision-making positions or the ethnic/regional identity
of the contractor.

Finally, in the Workplace survey, Ghanaian bureaucrats were asked
who they saw as most influential in decisions about procurement contracts in their institution. Approximately 39 percent of respondents said
the procurement unit as a whole was most influential, followed closely by
a chief director or unit director in the ministry at 33 percent.[123] Ministers, agency chief executives, or other political appointees were the third

[123] Chief directors are the senior-most career position in a ministry. Although the survey
did not ask about this specifically, the politicization of chief directors in Ghana is
an issue that came up in a number of interviews and has been noted in research on
Ghana's public service by Ayee (2013) and Appiah and Abdulai (2017b), who explain
that politicization of the public service is felt more at the executive level (i.e., chief
executives, chief directors, and directors) than at the lower and middle levels. Thus,
although these individuals are career civil servants, it is increasingly common to see
them rotated when a new president takes office.

largest category comprising 17 percent of responses. As I show in the next chapter, ministers who are tightly connected to the party tend to oversee ministries with more abundant procurement opportunities.

4.4   Conclusion

This chapter has shown that incumbent political spending in Benin and Ghana is, to a significant extent, financed with money that politicians extract from the state. As the chapter's overview of extraction in Benin and Ghana demonstrates, however, the processes of extraction vary considerably across the two countries. Where parties are well-institutionalized, as in Ghana, incumbent leaders can, with relative ease, delegate extraction to the party elite, utilize networks to facilitate extraction, and rely on party rules, procedures, and norms to ensure that extraction agents act in the interest of the incumbent. This *collusive* system of extraction often involves the award of public procurement contracts in exchange for donations (kickbacks) to the party. The collusive system is, relatively speaking, efficient in terms of both raising money and serving key party constituencies.

By contrast, in Benin's highly unstable political party landscape, the delegation, network, and control problems involved in extraction are more difficult for political leaders to overcome. Due to a high risk of elite defection, incumbent leaders largely eschew fundraising through elite agents, opting instead to engage directly in deals with foreign or domestic businesses themselves or to co-opt bureaucrats who can extract rents and revenues from the state's "wet" agencies. Due to the prevalence of political risks, leaders often prefer to control and manage extraction themselves, even if it comes with greater legal risk.

As has begun to become evident in this chapter, and as I will expand upon in much greater detail in the following three chapters, the specific practices involved in Ghana's collusive system of extraction and Benin's coercive one imply different logics by which politicians use, manage and control the state's executive and bureaucratic institutions. Who they select as extraction agents, whether they engage partisan networks outside the state, and how they seek to control extraction processes shape both the scope and intensity of state politicization and the extent to which extraction efforts impair the state's ability to implement public policies.

5   Staffing the State for Extraction

When Nana Akufo-Addo took office as president of Ghana in January 2017, he drew worldwide attention for his "elephant-sized" cabinet of 110 ministers.[1] Many if not all were long-standing members of Akufo-Addo's party, the NPP. Sixty-seven were members of parliament. The finance minister, widely recognized as the most powerful minister, was Ken Ofori-Atta, an investment banker and long-time financier of the party. Well-known party faithful and financiers, particularly those with strong connections to the private sector, were allocated other high-profile portfolios such as trade and industry, roads and highways, and national security. Although Akufo-Addo claimed that 110 ministers were necessary "to make for the rapid transformation of [the] country," others quickly characterized these appointments as "jobs for the boys" of the NPP, who had not held power since 2000.[2]

Around the same time that Akufo-Addo was appointing members of his executive cabinet, the head of Ghana's Civil Service, Nana Kwesi Agyekum-Dwamena, described in a media interview the strong professional qualifications of Ghana's civil servants as follows: "if we bring you the CVs of Ghanaian civil servants, I tell you that it will be able to sink a ship."[3]

The quote underscores the largely merit-based system by which Ghana's public servants are recruited and hired – a system that stands in stark contrast to the politicized dynamics of executive minister selection exemplified by President Akufo-Addo's "elephant-sized" cabinet.[4]

---

[1] Forty of these appointees were senior ministers overseeing portfolios. The remaining seventy were deputy and regional ministers. Technically, the cabinet in Ghana can comprises only nineteen ministers, but there is no limit on the total number of ministers appointed. The use of the word "elephant" to describe Akufo-Addo's appointments relates to the NPP's mascot, which is an elephant.

[2] Chloe Farand, "Ghana's President defends appointing 'elephant-size' government of 110 ministers," The Independent, March 18, 2017.

[3] "CVs of Ghanaian civil servants can sink a ship," Joy Online News, May 18, 2017.

[4] Throughout this chapter and in the following chapters, when discussing bureaucrats in Ghana, I mostly use the terms "public servants" or "public service employees." The

136

In this chapter, I explain this unexpected pattern of recruitment – extensive politicization at the upper echelons of government combined with merit-based recruitment of career bureaucrats – as a logical implication of collusive extraction practices in Ghana. Leaders place trusted party elites into state positions where they can channel procurement contracts to party-aligned business financiers. Since Ghana's career bureaucrats are largely accessory to this extraction system, recruitment to Ghana's public service remains to a large extent apolitical – driven by merit, personal connections, or some combination of both.

The chapter also explains how patterns of state job distribution in Benin can be understood through the lens of its coercive system of extraction. Presidents fearing defections from their coalition seek to keep politically ambitious elites – many of whom cannot be trusted to remain loyal to the president – away from positions with access to resources. Although this appointment practice is itself clearly political, it results in the more frequent appointment of *apolitical* ministers – technocrats and personal loyalists – than we see in Ghana. In relying to a greater extent on bureaucrats to act as extraction agents, however, leaders in Benin are more likely to politicize recruitment to the public service – particularly to agencies with access to rents and revenues.

Thus, following from the simple insight that leaders seek to place trusted extraction agents in positions where they can access and control political money, and keep untrusted agents away from these positions, this chapter shows how different systems of extraction imply divergence in the recruitment and selection of state personnel across different levels of government. Unlike most studies of patronage jobs, this chapter looks holistically at patterns of politicized job distribution to both elite and rank-and-file clients. To investigate these patterns and linkages at the *executive* level, I use an original database containing detailed biographical data for all minister appointees ($n = 586$) spanning twelve different presidential terms across the two countries. I use these data to construct a novel measure of executive politicization with a Bayesian IRT model that measures the politicization of ministerial appointments as a latent variable. I pool this measure with ministry-level data on thousands of procurement contracts scraped from the website of Ghana's Public Procurement Authority as well as personnel and budgets to analyze how patterns of *executive* job distribution relate to the prevalence of extraction opportunities in ministries.

term "civil service" in Ghana technically refers only to individuals who work in the core set of government ministries, comprising about 1 percent of all state personnel. Public service, by contrast, refers to the entirety of public sector workers.

To investigate the relationship between extraction systems and *public service* recruitment, I draw, once again, on the two surveys of civil servants. The Classroom survey, fielded in 2013 and 2014 with a total of 1,096 public service employees from the two countries, enables me to compare patterns of recruitment across countries and investigate linkages between bureaucrats' perceptions of extraction in their organization and the prevalence of politicized recruitment. Once again, I use the Workplace survey, fielded in 2017 only in Ghana, to further investigate and reinforce findings from Ghana.

In connecting collusive and coercive extraction to patterns of state staffing, I offer two important contributions to the study of patronage and state politicization. First, the stark differences in recruitment across levels of government – the politicization of executive appointments combined with merit-based recruitment to the public service in Ghana, and the converse in Benin – challenge prevailing conceptions of state politicization in Africa and around the world. The most common of these views sees the staffing of state institutions as part and parcel of a broad and pervasive patronage system, often ethnically driven, in which political leaders distribute state jobs to attract and maintain political support. According to this perspective, powerful political patrons provide jobs to clients who, in return, are expected to provide, or have provided, some service of value to the patron. In such systems, the expectation is that politicization at high levels of government would trickle down to lower levels as high-ranking officials treat their offices more or less as their personal property. Professional and meritocratic norms and practices are thought to prevail only in isolated "pockets" of the state apparatus, while politicization and patronage prevail everywhere else. The analysis in this chapter challenges this perspective by showing the limits of these prevailing accounts of patronage job distribution.

Second, it is important to see the politicization of job distribution not only as a currency of clientelistic exchange but also as a reflection of leaders' desires to access and control state resources for extractive party finance. Whereas much of the literature on patronage emphasizes the distribution of state jobs as a means of political-ethnic brokerage,[5] voter mobilization,[6] and protection against violent threats to survival,[7] I instead emphasize job distribution as a means through which leaders control the resources of the state.[8] Importantly, the extraction-based

---

[5] Arriola and Johnson (2014).

[6] Wantchekon (2003).

[7] Arriola (2009); Roessler (2016).

[8] Similar arguments emphasizing control have been put forward by Grzymała-Busse (2007); Kopecký (2011); Gingerich (2013); Martínez-Gallardo and Schleiter (2015).

explanation I develop in this chapter can account for more nuanced patterns of politicization in state staffing, such as those I observe in Benin and Ghana and which have been documented in other African countries as well.[9]

The chapter is divided into three main parts. I begin with a brief discussion outlining the theoretical connection between extraction and the selection of state personnel at both executive and public service levels. Then, drawing on the biographical data of government ministers across the two countries, I show how concerns about extraction have produced divergent strategies of executive appointments in Benin and Ghana – and that these appointment strategies do not fully conform with prevailing accounts based on ethnic brokerage or vote mobilization. In the third section, I examine the links between extraction practices and public service recruitment. Using both qualitative accounts and survey data, I show that there is more frequent politicization of public service recruitment in Benin than in Ghana, and I provide further evidence that these patterns are consistent with the extraction-based argument.[10]

5.1 The Politicization of State Staffing

The politicized distribution of jobs in the state apparatus is often associated with weak and unresponsive government in Africa and throughout the world. By employing unqualified or politically motivated individuals, politicization undermines both the professionalism and the capacity of the state bureaucracy.[11] Though common in states throughout the world,[12] politicized recruitment is often depicted as the principal – or only – mechanism of recruitment to government jobs in African countries.[13]

Politicization of state staffing, as I use it in this chapter, involves the application of political criteria in the recruitment and selection of individuals occupying positions in the state apparatus. Politicization includes what is commonly called patronage – the distribution of jobs in exchange for electoral support,[14] and/or the discretionary selection of individuals based on their (perceived) political affiliations or loyalties.[15] All state

---

[9] For example, Francois et al. (2015); Johnson (2015); Simson (2018).

[10] Some of the material in the second and third parts of this chapter also appears in Sigman (2022).

[11] Weber (1978); Rauch and Evans (2000); Dahlström and Lapuente (2017).

[12] Piattoni (2001); Grindle (2012).

[13] See, for example, Jackson and Rosberg (1984: 424); Meredith (2005: 169, 201–202, 278–288, 490); de Sardan (2013).

[14] Kitschelt and Wilkinson (2007).

[15] Peters and Pierre (2004).

bureaucracies involve some formal level of political control over personnel matters, including recruitment and selection. The American system
is often cited as one that affords considerable powers to the chief executive in the appointment and management of state personnel, with some
4,000 political appointments under the president's control. However,
politicization of personnel selection can, and often does, go beyond what
is formally prescribed, meaning that the bounds of acceptable politicization are breached.[16] Moreover, the application of political criteria
can look different in different contexts. As Grindle writes, politicization is "an eminently flexible mechanism for achieving leadership goals,"
potentially serving multiple needs of incumbents simultaneously.[17]

There exist two common narratives about extensive politicization in
the selection of state personnel across African countries. The first narrative is that job politicization is pervasive within African government
institutions, including in appointments to high-level executive positions,
professional public servants, and street-level bureaucrats. This narrative
has historical roots in both colonial efforts to rule cheaply and despoti-
cally through local intermediaries as well as subsequent efforts by both
colonial and post-colonial leaders to "Africanize" the state administration.[18] As Martin Meredith describes, "the lines of patronage radiated
out from presidencies to regions, districts and villages. At each level, 'big
men' worked the system, providing followers and friends with jobs, contracts and favours in exchange for political support; in order to retain
support, they had to ensure the distribution of rewards."[19] Overall,
there has been little debate about the historical significance of African
state politicization generally – and politicized selection of state personnel
specifically – as a mechanism of political survival.[20]

The second common narrative about state job politicization in Africa
flows from the first: that politicized distribution of state jobs helps leaders
to manage a range of survival-related problems, from mitigating threats
of violent removal,[21] to servicing multiethnic coalition partners,[22] to
managing popular discontent,[23] and to mobilizing votes for electoral

---

[16] Peters and Pierre (2004: 2).

[17] Grindle (2012: 67).

[18] On the colonial origins of politicized selection of administrative personnel, see Migdal
(1988); Kohli (2004). On the post-colonial "Africanization" projects, see Kenny
(2015) and Chazan et al. (1999: 46–47).

[19] Meredith (2005: 169).

[20] For a critique of this perspective, see Mkandawire (2001).

[21] Arriola (2009); Roessler (2016).

[22] Buckles (2017); Ariotti and Golder (2018); Arriola et al. (2021b).

[23] Hassan (2020).

advantage.[24] According to this perspective, jobs constitute a flexible and attractive mechanism of clientelistic exchange. Jobs are appealing to political patrons because they are selective and attributable, rendering them "a perfect mechanism" for politicians to claim individual credit[25] and to cultivate political loyalty among clients.[26] For clients, jobs not only serve as a source of security but, in many cases, involve handsome benefits and "prebends" beyond the paycheck.[27] Throughout Africa and elsewhere, jobs are therefore widely seen as a durable means of political mobilization and cross-ethnic accommodation, even if their political use undermines state capacity.[28]

This perspective, however, tends to ignore considerable variation, documented in both historical and contemporary cases, in how and to what extent political parties manipulate the composition of executive and bureaucratic personnel. For example, James Coleman and Carl Rosberg described a spectrum of "party-states" that formed during the post-colonial period, in which parties' usage of the state varied.[29] According to Jennifer Widner, it was not until President Moi came to power in Kenya that widespread politicization of the state apparatus became part and parcel of the party's governing strategy.[30] Likewise, studies of the contemporary period reveal considerable variation in state staffing practices, for example in the extent to which privatization agencies are staffed by technocratic (or political) personnel,[31] in the high levels of education and diverse regional backgrounds of Ugandan bureaucrats,[32] and in the politicization of more menial jobs, but not professional ones, in Ghana's local governments.[33] In short, there are ample observations throughout Africa of merit-based recruitment to public office, high levels of technocracy and professionalism in public organizations, and cases of successful civil service reform, all of which imply that politicized recruitment practices vary considerably across both time and space. The existing emphases on ethnic brokerage, political threat management, and electoral mobilization as the principal drivers of politicization in staffing decisions, moreover, do not easily account for this variation. In short,

---

[24] Wantchekon (2003); Green (2010); Driscoll (2018).
[25] Golden (2003: 198).
[26] Grindle (2012: 67).
[27] Joseph (1987); Robinson and Verdier (2013).
[28] Geddes (1994); Dahlström and Lapuente (2017).
[29] Coleman and Rosberg (1966).
[30] Widner (1992).
[31] Teodoro and Pitcher (2017).
[32] Simson (2018).
[33] Driscoll (2018); Brierley (2021).

these observations raise questions about when and why leaders are more or less likely to politicize job distribution and whether existing theories can account for observed variation in these practices.

5.1.1   Staffing for Extraction

One important reason why political leaders may seek to apply political criteria in some cases but not others relates to their concerns about extracting money to finance their political operations: incumbent leaders might make staffing decisions that enhance their ability to access and control extraction. By using political criteria in the recruitment and selection of state personnel, incumbent leaders can place trusted agents into positions with access to extraction opportunities and keep potential opponents away from such positions. Different extraction strategies, however, imply variation in patterns of politicized state staffing.

The connection between extraction and politicized job distribution builds on two main strands of existing literature. First, it embraces the spirit of a large body of work on political control of the bureaucracy, concentrated primarily in studies of the United States and Europe. This literature focuses principally on how elected leaders, including presidents and legislators, as well as political appointees such as cabinet ministers, can and do exercise control over the behavior of bureaucratic personnel and organizations. Applying agency theories to the relationship between politicians and bureaucrats, research on political control of bureaucrats shows the varying ways that elected leaders use their appointment (or oversight) powers to exert and maintain control over the powers of the state.[34]

In its preoccupation with Western contexts, the "political control" literature has focused to a large extent on politicians' efforts to control the direction of policy planning and implementation. As Guy Peters and Jon Pierre explain, "if there are loyal party members administering public programs, so it has been argued, there will be less deflection of policy directions than in a system dominated by the career public service."[35] As I show in later chapters, this concern is not necessarily absent in African countries. However, where political mobilization and electoral success

---

[34] Moe (1989) provides the classic overview of this approach. Wood and Waterman (1991) demonstrate that, in the American system, political appointments represent the most important form of political control. Surveying European cabinet systems, Laver and Shepsle (1994) suggest that the extent to which appointments serve as a mechanism of control is likely to vary across countries and systems, particularly in light of variation in the formal and informal relationships between cabinet ministers and career public servants.

[35] Peters and Pierre (2004: 7).

depend to a large extent on clientelistic exchange, credibility, and/or distributive performance, political control of state *resources* is likely to be of primary concern to many elected leaders. As such, I adapt the conventional policy-focused approach to political control to the clientelistic context with an emphasis on control over resources rather than policy.[36]

Second, the extraction approach engages with an emerging literature that investigates the ways that bureaucrats provide political services to incumbent politicians. This body of work examines "patronage contracts" in which jobs (or promotions or salary increases) are provided to individuals who, in return, provide various types of political services once in office.[37] Agents may provide services because it advances their own interests[38] or because "contracts" are more coercive in nature, compelling civil servants to participate in order to retain their jobs or avoid undesirable transfers.[39] This perspective is important because it implies that politicians not only distribute jobs in exchange for electoral support but also to receive further extractive benefits from bureaucrats, once the politicians are in office. Daniel Gingerich emphasizes this point in his study of political corruption in Latin America, writing that "it makes little sense to think of government jobs as particularistic benefits used by parties to buy votes...The framework presented here advances a vision of such posts as instruments used by a party not to secure the votes of the job holders (which are taken for granted) but rather to secure a stream of resources flowing back to the party..."[40]

My approach bridges the political control and political services perspectives to articulate a simple argument: leaders seek to place politically loyal individuals into positions with greater opportunities for extraction and keep potential rivals away from those positions. In short, incumbents see the placement of reliable political allies as a way to control access to state money for political finance. Like the political services literature, this extraction lens assumes not only that incumbents distribute jobs in exchange for past political support but also (or alternatively) to

---

[36] Perhaps an alternative "control" perspective would emphasize constituency management, that is, politicians use their appointments for representational purposes such that the appointment of an individual from a particular group is important symbolically or in terms of their ability to advocate for their group's interest. I believe this representational control is implicit in either the policy or resource perspectives as, in either case, the appointed group member can represent either the policy or clientelistic/distributional interests of the group they represent.

[37] Oliveros (2016).

[38] Oliveros (2021).

[39] Iyer and Mani (2012).

[40] Gingerich (2013: 46).

leverage some political advantage from the individuals to whom jobs are distributed.

5.1.2   Empirical Expectations

Building on the idea that leaders distribute state jobs in ways that allow them to access and control extraction opportunities, I argue that the different extraction systems described in the previous chapter generate more nuanced expectations about patterns of politicization in state staffing decisions. More specifically, the idea that political leaders distribute jobs to gain control over extraction opportunities implies that the use of political criteria in the selection of state personnel is likely to vary at different levels of government as well as across institutions, depending on their available extraction opportunities.

To summarize the extraction methods outlined in the previous chapter, Ghana's highly institutionalized ruling parties extract collusively, while parties with lower levels of institutionalization, as in Benin, engage in more *coercive* forms of extraction. The key differences between these systems are (1) the types of agents involved; (2) the availability of extraction networks; and (3) the mechanisms of control. In collusive systems, leaders depend largely on elite party members working in partnership with business financiers or other outside actors. In coercive systems, distrust of many elite-level operatives leads the incumbent to centralize control over extraction and to seek out more coercible individuals: rank-and-file political supporters who are likely to depend on a state job for their livelihood. As I showed in Chapter 4, more collusive forms of extraction in Ghana take the form of providing public procurement contracts to partisan-affiliated businesses in exchange for financial support. Coercive extraction in Benin depends, to a larger extent, on civil servants who divert money from state coffers to party leaders.

Politicization Across Levels of Government
The first expectation is that collusive and coercive extraction systems generate divergence in the politicization of state jobs at different *levels* of government. Leaders in collusive systems, where party elite act as key extraction agents, are likely to apply criteria of political loyalty to higher-level executive appointments, since these positions are empowered to oversee lucrative extraction deals, such as the awarding of public procurement contracts in exchange for financial support. Thus, in collusive systems, executive-level politicization helps leaders to ensure that the most reliable extraction agents are placed into positions where they can carry out extraction activities. The prevalence of procurement-based

exchanges as a form of extraction in Ghana, and the power that ministers in particular have over the formation of tender committees, suggests that leaders should have an interest in appointing loyal party officials to ministerial posts, where they can act effectively as extraction agents.

Given the high probability of elite defection from their ruling parties and coalitions, leaders in coercive systems are likely to have a different approach to executive appointments. The high risk of elite defection means that placing individuals of questionable political loyalty into positions with control over extraction could empower opponents by granting them access to lucrative extraction deals. In such systems, therefore, the president is more likely to *eschew* the appointment of political individuals to executive posts. Faced with the prospect of empowering opponents, they opt to staff executive posts – especially those with extraction opportunities – with personal loyalists or technocrats, neither of whom are particularly likely to use the extracted state resources against the ruling party.

The anticipated patterns of politicization are different for public service hiring. Since public servants in the collusive system remain largely accessories to the extraction network, there is no clear extraction-related rationale for politicization of public service recruitment. It simply implies that politicization is likely to be more limited since it is not necessary for the practice of extraction.

Leaders in coercive systems, by contrast, are likely to rely to a greater extent on public servants as extraction agents. Incumbent leaders therefore seek to place those pre-disposed to support the incumbent into public service positions with access to rents and revenues, implying the placement of co-ethnics, party activists, or others with presumed loyalty into "wet" ministries or those with significant extraction opportunities.[41] The observable implication is that leaders in contexts of coercive extraction are more likely to interfere in, and exert control over, bureaucratic recruitment and hiring. A summary of the theorized variation in politicization of staffing at different levels of the state appears in Table 5.1.

Politicization Across Institutions
Not all government agencies are created equal in terms of their extraction potential. To pursue their extraction strategies, incumbent leaders look to place extraction agents in positions that contain more lucrative

---

[41] Although principals could, in theory, coerce any bureaucratic agent, coercion is less costly to monitor and implement if leaders enlist politically supportive agents such as co-partisans or co-ethnics (Hassan, 2020).

Table 5.1 *Extraction and state staffing empirical expectations*

Extraction Type	Who Extracts?	Staffing Across Levels of Government	Staffing Across Institutions
Collusive (Ghana)	Elite Party Officials	Party Agents Broadly Appointed to Executive Offices Limited Politicization of Public Service	Party Loyalists in Ministries with Greater Access to Extraction
Coercive (Benin)	President with Personal Loyalists	Limited Appointment of Political Elites in Executive	Political Elites Kept Away From Extraction-Rich Ministries
	Rank-and-File Bureaucrats	Politicization of Public Service Jobs	Supporters and Co-Ethnics in "Wet" Agencies

extraction opportunities. However, the institutions in which leaders seek to place potential extraction agents will vary depending on the different modes of extraction.

In collusive systems such as Ghana's, the potential for extraction depends on the availability of procurement contracts and party-affiliated businesses through which to funnel extracted monies. Extraction agents – those strongly embedded in the party – are therefore more likely to be placed in agencies that administer large volumes of procurement contracts or control the distribution of procurement opportunities. It is in these agencies that agents can facilitate the distribution of contracts or other benefits to party-affiliated actors in society who, in return, provide financial support to the party.

In coercive systems, such as Benin's, extraction by rank-and-file agents typically occurs in what are commonly called "wet" jobs or agencies – those where bureaucrats can gain access to rents or revenues, often in liquid form, for the benefit of their political principals or themselves. The extraction logic developed here suggests that politicization of hiring is most likely to occur for positions in these types of agencies, as well as the institutions responsible for hiring staff for those agencies. I summarize the expected patterns of politicization across institutions in Table 5.1.

5.2   Politicized Executive Staffing

As the discussion of Akufo-Addo's "elephant-sized" cabinet at the outset of this chapter illustrates, the politicization of executive offices in Ghana occurs very much in plain sight through the distribution of ministerial posts to key party operatives. This phenomenon of executive politicization is of course not unique to Ghana – it is institutionalized in places like the United States and occurs in many countries across the world. What is less clear, however, are the specific political motivations behind such appointment patterns and why they contrast with those of Benin.

To investigate the politicization of executive appointments, I draw on an original comprehensive database containing appointment and biographical data for all minister appointees from the two countries from the early 1990s through 2016.[42] In addition to including the dates of appointment and the portfolio allocated to each appointee, the database includes detailed information on each minister's educational, professional, and political backgrounds. Minister data come from a variety of sources including government communiqués, newspapers, legislative archives, and interviews with political historians.[43]

I use these data to estimate a *politicization* score for each appointee. The politicization score is designed to measure the salience of political criteria in the appointment decision. Of course, a major challenge in measuring politicized appointments is that it is not usually possible to observe the specific criteria on which appointments are based. To overcome this challenge, I conceptualize politicization as a latent variable, meaning that the value of the politicization score is inferred from observed variables that do not directly measure politicization. In this case, I estimate the latent politicization score using a set of nine binary variables listed in Table 5.2.

Two variables measure whether the individual has an educational background that is relevant to their assigned portfolio. An individual's educational background is coded as *generally* relevant if their degree relates, at a minimum, to their portfolio in a general way. For example, if a person appointed as minister of health has a degree in public policy or development, they would be coded 1 on the Education Match General variable. If an individual who is appointed as minister of health has a degree in medicine or public health, they would be coded as 1 for the Education Match Specific variable because their background has *specific* relevance to their assigned portfolio.

I apply the same coding for the appointee's stated profession. If, for example, an individual is a lawyer or an expert in constitutional law and

---

[42] The data begin with appointments made following the March 1991 elections in Benin and the December 1992 elections in Ghana. See Appendix C for a complete list of the data that were collected.

[43] In Benin, I consulted Pierre Métinhoué's (2005) historical records and I am grateful to him for providing additional data and insight.

Table 5.2 *Coded variables (items)*

Variable	Description
Education Match General	Does the individual have an educational background that is *generally* relevant to the assigned portfolio?
Education Match Specific	Does the individual have an educational background that is *specifically* relevant to the assigned portfolio?
Professional Match General	Is the individual's profession *generally* relevant to the assigned portfolio?
Professional Match Specific	Is the individual's profession *specifically* relevant to the assigned portfolio?
Experience Match	Does the individual have professional experience that is relevant to the assigned portfolio?
Party Affiliate	Is the individual publicly affiliated with, or a member of, a political party at the time of appointment?
Political Experience	Has the individual been politically active before the appointment?
Cadre/Officer	Has the individual held an office or recognizable position in the party (including founding member)?
MP	Has the individual served as a member of parliament?

they are appointed as minister of interior, they would be coded as having a professional background that is *generally* relevant to their assigned portfolio. If their stated profession is territorial administrator or police and they were appointed as minister of interior, they would be coded 1 for having a professional background that is *specifically* relevant to their portfolio.

For the Experience Match variable, I code whether any of the individual's previous three professional positions were relevant to their assigned portfolio. Since it was not always clear how to make a distinction between general and specific relevance in previous positions, any professional experience of relevance is coded as 1.

The remaining four variables are coded according to the appointee's political background. The Party Affiliate variable is coded 1 if the individual is publicly affiliated with, or a member of, a political party. The Political Experience variable is coded 1 if the individual has engaged in political activity beyond the affiliation/membership in a party. This includes having run for office, having worked on political campaigns, or having served as an advisor to a politician. The variable Cadre/Officer codes whether the individual has held a formal position in their political party, such as a founding member, a party chairperson, or a regional officer. The final political variable (MP) is coded 1 if the individual was a member of a parliament at or before the time of appointment.

Table 5.3 *Descriptive statistics for item variables*

Variable	Benin N	Benin (%)	Ghana N	Ghana (%)	Pooled N	Pooled (%)
Education not relevant	76	28.36	116	48.74	192	37.94
Education not specifically relevant	161	60.07	188	78.99	349	68.97
Profession not relevant	95	33.33	121	52.61	216	41.94
Profession not specifically relevant	166	58.25	164	71.30	330	64.08
Experience not relevant	169	58.68	114	46.15	283	52.90
Party Affiliate	216	70.82	264	96.00	480	82.76
Political Experience	193	62.26	230	83.33	423	72.18
Cadre/Officer	66	21.36	145	52.54	211	36.07
MP	82	26.45	181	65.85	263	44.88

Descriptive statistics for each of the nine variables are provided in Table 5.3. I reverse the coding of the technical variables for directional consistency across all variables (higher coding indicates less technical/more political). Although the two types of variables – technical and political – will not always relate to each other inversely, I do find using Cronbach's Alpha item-correlation test that the variables are internally consistent and can be reliably measured on a linear scale ($\alpha = 0.802$).[44] Looking across the nine variables, it is already evident from the summary statistics that individuals in Ghana have less relevant technical backgrounds and more robust political backgrounds. The one exception to this pattern is in the appointee's relevant job experience. Ministers in Ghana are more likely than those in Benin to have served previously in either government or in private sector positions that relate to their assigned portfolio. I discuss this phenomenon at greater length in Chapter 6.

I use a basic IRT model to estimate politicization scores. IRT models are used extensively in educational testing to estimate latent abilities of test-takers. They are, with greater frequency, finding application in the measurement of political science concepts including in public opinion polling, the aggregation of expert ratings, and measures of hard-to-observe or multi-dimensional concepts, such as democracy. The basic intuition behind the IRT approach is that the latent concept, in this case appointment politicization, predicts positive or negative values of the observed variables.

The model is designed such that an appointee with vast political experience but minimal relevant educational or professional background

---

[44] An alpha-statistic greater than 0.7 is generally considered acceptable for measurement.

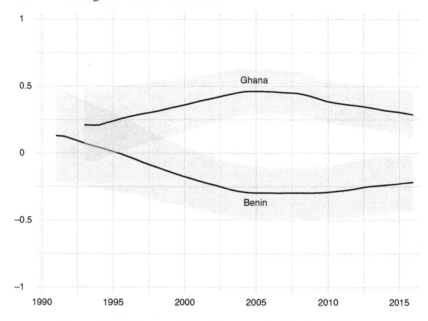

Figure 5.1 Minister politicization scores in Benin and Ghana
Politicization score estimates are depicted as local polynomial smooth
lines with 95% confidence intervals.

would receive a high politicization score. If, by contrast, the individual
has an educational or professional background that is highly relevant
to the assigned portfolio, but little or no political background, their
appointment would receive a low politicization score. The IRT model
estimates a politicization score for *each appointment*, allowing for the possibility that, even if an individual receives multiple appointments over
time, those appointments could have been based on different sets of
criteria.

The resulting politicization scores are scaled from -1.7 to 1.4.[45]
Overall, the average politicization score is considerably higher in Ghana
(0.31) than in Benin (-0.27), a statistically significant difference with
$t = 8.6$. Figure 5.1 graphs each country's average politicization scores
over time. From the late 1990s through 2016, Ghana's ministers
had significantly higher politicization scores than Benin's. The rise

[45] In Appendix C, I provide additional information about the model and conduct a
number of validation tests of the resulting politicization measure. I also present the
difficulty and discrimination parameters for each item, which show that both the
technical and political measures contribute to the variation in the politicization scores.

in politicization scores in Ghana in the late 1990s is consistent with accounts of President J. J. Rawlings' gradual acceptance of the (political) need to replace technocrats with "technopols" who were willing to serve the extractive interests of the NDC.[46] In Benin, the declining politicization scores in the 1990s and early 2000s coincide with significant episodes of ruling coalition fracture during the presidencies of Nicephore Soglo and Mathieu Kérékou.[47] As defections became more common, leaders increasingly turned to the appointment of technocrats and personal loyalists over political actors. By the time Boni Yayi assumed office in 2006, he saw that "political nominations [of ministers] come with a lot of [political] risk," preferring instead to "look closely at many CVs" to find those with better technical qualifications.[48] Since 2001, 40 percent of Beninese appointees have had no visible political background whatsoever.

As expected, Ghana's leaders frequently appoint those with political backgrounds to high-level executive posts, whereas Benin's leaders seek to keep potential elite political defectors away from such positions. In both countries, presidents have broad de facto discretion over minister appointments. They can appoint as many ministers as they see fit, determine their prerogatives, and dismiss them at will. There is, however, one important difference in the two countries' appointment rules: Ghana's constitution mandates that half of all Ministers of State should be MPs (Article 78), but no such provision exists in Benin's constitution. In practice, Ghanaian presidents can sidestep this requirement by appointing ministers who do not bear the formal title of Minister of State. Nonetheless, most Ghanaian presidents have far exceeded this requirement: MPs constitute 64 percent of minister appointments in Ghana. During President John Kufuor's second term in office (2005–2008), this percentage reached as high as 75 percent. Although the constitutional provision likely generates a norm that presidents allocate portfolios to MPs, there is also widespread acknowledgment of the extractive benefits associated with minister portfolios in Ghana.[49] The resources that are accessible from these positions benefit presidents, parties, as well as individual MPs in their efforts to raise funds for reelection and offer material support to their constituents.[50] In Benin, only 20 percent of ministers have been appointed from the National Assembly.

---

[46] Abdulai and Mohan (2019). See next section for further discussion.
[47] Banégas (2003).
[48] Author interview, Cotonou, November 14, 2013.
[49] Numerous interview respondents noted that MPs desire minister positions because of the benefits that accrue to them and their constituents.
[50] For example, Lindberg and Zhou (2009).

Apart from the constitutional requirement, there is no a priori reason to expect that Ghana's ministers would be more political than Benin's. Many accounts of government formation in Africa and elsewhere emphasize that presidents of weak parties and coalitions distribute minister posts to attract support from other elites or to neutralize threats from opponents.[51] Additionally, the low barrier to party entry in Benin means that elites could easily form their own parties and occupy leadership posts within them, implying that there should be a sufficient supply of political elites from which presidents could select more political ministers, if they choose.

Although informative, the politicization scores alone do not capture whether appointees are party loyalists, situational allies, or co-opted members of the opposition. To determine the political "type" of each appointee, I use available political information to code which of these categories best describes each appointee. Figure 5.2 shows the breakdown of this exercise using four categories: loyalist, new ally, opposition, and no political affiliation. Loyalists are either long-standing personal or political affiliates of the president or the ruling party, whose affiliation with them dates back to before the previous presidential election cycle. Individuals who have served as elected officials, candidates, or party officers prior to the most recent election would be coded as loyalists, as would the president's family members or individuals who worked with the president outside of politics. New allies are those who joined the ruling party or president during or after the previous presidential election cycle. The "Not Political" category refers to those who have no visible record of either political involvement or close personal affiliation to the president. The opposition category refers to those who are publicly affiliated with a party that is not the ruling party or part of the ruling coalition at the time of their appointment.

What is striking is the disproportionately large number of loyalists – 79.9 percent – among Ghana's appointees. By contrast, the very low percentage of new political allies and opposition members, around 3 percent each, suggests that the use of executive posts to buy support, build the party, or co-opt opposition members is comparatively rare in Ghana. Approximately 15 percent of appointees in Ghana have no apparent political background, suggesting the inclusion of at least some apolitical, technocratic ministers.

The political profiles of ministers look considerably different in Benin. According to Figure 5.2, ministerial posts are relatively evenly distributed among the four categories. Loyalists – many of whom are personal,

---

[51] For example, Widner (1992); Geddes (1994); Arriola (2009).

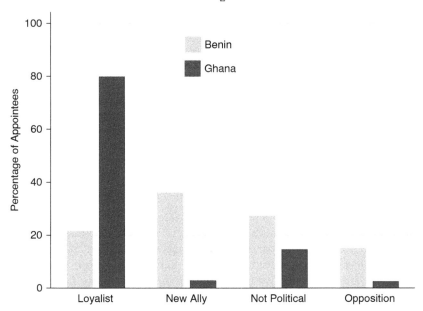

Figure 5.2 Political backgrounds of ministers in Benin and
Ghana
The graph depicts the proportion of minister appointees in each
country in each category.

rather than political acquaintances of presidents – comprise only 20.7
percent of appointees. Those with no apparent political background
comprise 29.1 percent. The largest category is that of new political allies,
those who joined the president's coalition no earlier than the most recent
election, making up 35.1 percent.[52] Finally, 14.8 percent are members
of an opposition party or coalition. Thus, whereas presidents in Benin
do appear to use minister posts to buy support or build coalitions, this
practice is more limited than most of the literature suggests.

The divergent patterns of politicization across the two countries are
generally consistent with the extraction-based expectations – and with
differences in party institutionalization more generally. The large proportion of party loyalists among Ghana's appointees conforms with the idea
of a collusive fundraising system in which party elite serve in positions
in which they can steer lucrative contract opportunities to party-aligned

[52] As I show in the next chapter, however, these individuals often have shorter tenures in
office.

businesses in exchange for the financial support from those businesses. By contrast, Benin's leaders have fewer elite loyalists on whom to rely as extraction agents, so they pursue an appointment strategy that engages a higher proportion of technocratic ministers and mixes in both new allies and opposition members. The cross-country comparisons, however, are merely suggestive. In the next section I analyze patterns of appointment within the two countries to better gauge whether the patterns of executive job distribution reflect the more specific expectations of the extraction-based theory.

5.2.1   Party Loyalty and Access to Extraction in Ghana

I gain further leverage by analyzing within-country patterns of portfolio distribution in Ghana, where ministers serve as key extraction agents. In delegating extraction to party agents, leaders in Ghana's collusive system should place their most trusted party elite into positions where they can facilitate the award of procurement contracts to party financiers. I investigate this claim by examining whether ministers with more robust experience within the ruling party are more likely to be placed into ministries with greater public procurement extraction opportunities.

To conduct this analysis, I first construct a measure of political loyalty that multiplies the politicization score used earlier in this section by a binary variable coding whether individuals are long-standing members of the president's party.[53] If an individual has extensive political experience as reflected by a high politicization score *and* a long-standing affiliation with the ruling party, they would receive a higher loyalty score. As expected, average loyalty scores are significantly higher in Ghana (0.72) than in Benin (0.29), with $t = 11.46$. The loyalty score serves as the key dependent variable in the analysis.

The independent variables measure the extractive potential of each ministry in each year using data on government contracts awarded by ministries between 2012 and 2016, the years for which complete contract data were available. The contract data were obtained from the website of Ghana's PPA along with in-person visits to their offices. In multiple discussions with employees at the PPA, they expressed confidence that nearly all central government MDA contracts awarded from 2012 to 2016 were contained in the database. Any unpublished contracts, they informed me, were likely to be small in number and withheld for reasons of either national security or parliamentary privilege. To

---

[53] I define "longstanding" as having become publicly affiliated with the party prior to the most recent presidential election cycle.

ensure that the withholding of national security contracts does not bias the sample, I remove the Ministry of Defence and Ministry of Foreign Affairs from the analysis presented in Table 2.[54] In total, I obtained data on 5,062 contracts, 2,298 of which were removed because they were awarded by entities other than central government MDAs, such as local governments, universities, healthcare facilities, and state-owned enterprises. Because contracts were at times denominated in various currencies, I converted all contract values to US dollars using the average exchange rate for the month in which the contract was signed. I then aggregate the total value and total number of contracts awarded for each ministry in each year.

I use time-series cross-sectional regression to test whether ministries with greater access to procurement are more likely to receive or retain a loyal ruling party agent as their minister. In years when a new appointment is made, I use the loyalty score of the new appointee. In years with no appointment, I use the loyalty score of the sitting minister, representing the leader's decision to retain that minister. I control for annual budget allocations, number of personnel,[55] and dummy variables coding (1) whether a new minister was appointed that year and (2) election years.

The results of the analysis are displayed in Table 5.4. In Models 1–4, I test the relationship using random effects models with robust standard errors clustered at the ministry level. All but one of the models (4) produces a positive and statistically significant relationship between ministry contracts and the appointment or retention of a loyal minister. In Models 5 and 6, I use fixed effects for ministries and years to test whether, as a ministry's contracting activity increases, its portfolio is more likely to be assigned to an individual with a higher political loyalty score. In all but one of the models (Model 4), the variables measuring contracting volume have, as expected, a positive and statistically significant effect on the political loyalty score of the appointee.

5.2.2   Executive Appointments in Benin

Compared to Ghana, Benin's ministers include more technocrats, more new political allies, and more opposition party members. Although this mixture may be to some extent expected in systems of proportional

---

[54] Author interviews at Public Procurement Authority, Accra, Ghana June 22, 2017; June 23, 2017; June 26, 2017.

[55] Personnel numbers are from the appendices of the Ministry of Finance's annual budget statements.

Table 5.4 *Procurement contracts and appointment of loyal ministers in Ghana*

	1	2	3	4	5	6
Value of Contracts (log)	0.022***		0.018*		0.021*	
	(2.65)		(1.96)		(1.83)	
Number of Contracts (log)		0.089**		0.077		0.105**
		(1.99)		(1.57)		(2.26)
Ministry Budget (% of total)			−0.443	−0.778	−1.780	−1.895
			(−0.50)	(−0.87)	(−0.92)	(−0.91)
Ministry Personnel (log)			0.022	0.028	0.063	0.079
			(0.61)	(0.79)	(1.08)	(1.41)
New Appointment			−0.035	−0.023	−0.048	−0.032
			(−0.40)	(−0.26)	(−0.58)	(−0.40)
Election Year			0.026	0.041	0.031	0.045
			(0.24)	(0.37)	(0.30)	(0.41)
Constant	0.044	0.152	−0.038	0.006	−0.354	−0.417
	(0.43)	(1.56)	(−0.15)	(0.02)	(−0.72)	(−0.93)
Fixed Effects	No	No	No	No	Yes	Yes
Observations	112	112	107	107	107	107
R-squared	0.08	0.04	0.04	0.03	0.06	0.08

$*p < 0.1$, $**p < 0.05$, $***p < 0.01$, t-statistics in parentheses
Panel regression with robust standard errors clustered by ministry. The dependent variable is the minister's loyalty score.

representation where the executive needs to assemble a multiparty governing coalition in parliament, as I show in this section, there is also considerable evidence of an extraction logic at play.

One sign of extraction-related concerns in ministerial appointments is the rarity with which new allies and opposition appointees receive portfolios that involve some level of control over principal extraction opportunities. Table 5.5 shows the political backgrounds of ministers to whom presidents have allocated four portfolios – finance, interior, public service, and public works/transportation – known for their extraction opportunities.[56] As is evident from the table, only two opposition figures (3.7 percent) have served at the head of these ministries.

---

[56] These specific portfolios were mentioned in a number of interviews. Aside from controlling the state's money, the finance ministry also oversees the customs and tax administrations. The interior ministry oversees the police and *gendarmes*, both of whom have abundant opportunities to extract rents. The public service ministry coordinates all hiring exams and competitions for entry into the public service. They also must approve all promotions. Finally, the public works/transportation ministry and the Ministry of Maritime Economy and Port Infrastructure have overseen the ports' administration.

Table 5.5 *Appointments to extraction-related posts in Benin*

	Not Political	Loyalist	New Ally	Opposition
Finance	7	4	1	0
	58.3%	33.3%	8.3%	0.0%
Interior	3	9	2	1
	20.0%	60.0%	13.3%	6.7%
Public Service	3	7	4	0
	21.4%	50.0%	28.6%	0.0%
Public Works/Transport	4	5	4	1
	28.6%	35.7%	28.6%	7.1%
Total	17	25	11	2
	41.2%	45.5%	20.0%	3.7%

The plurality of these positions – 45.5 percent – have gone to personal or, to the extent they exist, true and long-standing political loyalists of the president. Kérékou, for example, appointed "former barons" of his pre-1990 revolutionary government, the PRPB, to these posts, many of whom had become leaders in the main party supporting Kérékou, FARD-Alafia. These appointees included Ousmane Batoko and Boubacar Arouna at the Ministry of Public Service and Daniel Tawema at the Ministry of Interior and Public Security.[57] Among President Boni Yayi's loyalist appointees to these portfolios were personal affiliates, such as Pascal Irenee Koupaki, a technocrat who worked previously at *Banque Centrale des Etats de l'Afrique de l'Ouest* (BCEAO) and the International Monetary Fund (IMF), and a close associate of Patrice Talon who, at that time, was Boni Yayi's principal ally and financier, and Armand Zinzindouhoué, once described as the "right arm" of President Boni Yayi.[58]

Perhaps just as important as placing loyalists in control of these portfolios, presidents have clearly sought to keep those of questionable loyalty out of these positions. Indeed, as seen in Figure 5.2, a relatively large percentage (30.9 percent) of non-political individuals in Benin have been appointed as ministers, and an even higher percentage, 40.2 percent, were appointed to extraction-related posts listed in (Table 5.5).[59] While

---

[57] Banégas (2003: 47) discusses some of these "former barons."

[58] Zinzindouhoué was subsequently dismissed amidst mounting public and political pressure for Boni Yayi to address his alleged involvement in a Ponzi scheme scandal involving a nongovernmental entity called "ICC Services."

[59] Because of the nature of extraction in Ghana, where procurement opportunities often change from year to year, there is no straightforward comparison to make with Ghana. However, in difference-of-means tests, those with no political experience in Ghana

the intention behind the selection of technocrats may certainly have to do with bringing the desired technical skills and qualifications into government, it is also plausible that nonpolitical technocrats simply pose less of a threat than politically ambitious individuals at risk of defection.

Overall, it is difficult to identify any dominant logic underlying executive appointments in Benin. What is clear, however, is that there have been efforts to keep those of questionable loyalty – potential coalition defectors and opposition members – away from portfolios with access to extraction opportunities, favoring instead the placement of loyalists and technocrats into such positions.

5.2.3   Executive Appointments, Ethnic Brokerage, and Vote Mobilization

As noted earlier in this chapter, conventional accounts of job distribution in African countries suggest that political leaders distribute (or promise to distribute) jobs to mobilize votes. At the elite level, this practice involves the appointment of key brokers who mobilize entire voting blocs, often ethnic groups, on behalf of the winning candidate. In these scenarios, the president rewards the broker with a minister post, which grants them access to state resources and extraction opportunities. The theory set forth in this book, and specifically the foregoing analysis in this chapter, complicates this narrative by questioning the extent to which leaders would grant such access to vote brokers, particularly vote brokers in settings of weakly institutionalized parties that have incentives to defect from the incumbent's political coalition. Before concluding my analysis of executive appointments, I assess the extent to which these vote-mobilizing logics are evident in my minister data.

By combining data on a minister's regional origin (their birthplace or the area they represent in parliament) with subnational data on election results, I investigate the extent to which the electoral mobilization narrative holds in the two countries. Specifically, I analyze whether geographical areas that perform well for the incumbent are more likely to "receive" a minister appointment. The level of analysis is the *commune* level in Benin and the parliamentary constituency in Ghana.[60]

Table 5.6 provides a descriptive overview of distribution of ministerial portfolios to individuals from the ruling parties' stronghold, swing,

---

are significantly *less* likely to be placed atop ministries with more robust contracting opportunities ($t = 1.53$).

[60] These are the most granular levels for which election results data are available for both countries over a sufficient period of time. *Commune*-level election results are available for Benin's 1991, 2001, and 2006 elections. Constituency-level election results for Ghana are available for all elections that took place from 1996–2012. Hereafter I use the term "district" to generically refer to these territorial units.

Table 5.6 *Ministerial allocation to stronghold, swing, and opposition districts*

	Stronghold	Swing	Opposition
Benin	60%	11%	29%
Ghana	52%	35%	13%

Percent of minister appointees from each type of district based on election results.

and opposition districts. The districts are categorized using the incumbent president's vote percentages from the election directly preceding the minister's appointment. Districts that delivered 60 percent or more of their votes to the president are considered stronghold districts. Districts that delivered 40 percent to 60 percent of their votes to the president are considered swing districts. Districts that delivered less than 40 percent of their votes to the president are considered opposition districts.[61] The patterns of appointment in the two countries are quite different. In Benin, the majority of appointees are from opposition districts, making it unlikely that presidents are rewarding brokers for having mobilized voters.[62] In Ghana, a slim majority of appointees (52 percent) came from stronghold districts, followed by swing districts at 35 percent – results that are consistent with the idea that presidents may reward party brokers for their performance in turning out base supporters or performing well in contested areas.

To further analyze the potential electoral basis of minister selection, I test whether a district's vote performance predicts the appointment of a minister from that district. I use three different measures of vote performance: (1) the president's margin of victory (or defeat) in the district, (2) the change in the president's share of the vote between the first and second election rounds,[63] and (3) the change in the president's share of votes relative to the preceding presidential election cycle. The latter two measures capture potential improvements in vote performance, which are more plausibly linked to mobilization efforts than margin of victory. All tests use election data from the most recent presidential election before the appointment. The results are displayed in Table 5.7.

---

[61] In elections where there were two rounds of voting, I use results from the first round.

[62] Following recent work by Arriola et al. (2021), it is possible that Benin's presidents are appointing opposition representatives in order to induce fragmentation in the opposition.

[63] Benin had runoff rounds in all three elections included in the dataset. Ghana had runoffs only in 2000 and 2008.

Table 5.7 *District vote performance and likelihood of minister appointment*

	(1) Benin	(2) Benin	(3) Benin	(4) Ghana	(5) Ghana	(6) Ghana
President Vote Margin	−0.352			1.188***		
	(−0.95)			(4.78)		
Δ Vote Share 2nd Round		0.762			−1.082	
		(0.90)			(−0.80)	
Δ Vote Share Last Election			1.180			1.828
			(0.25)			(1.58)
District Size (log)	1.059***	0.967***	7.051**	0.314*	0.307	0.574*
	(3.40)	(3.12)	(2.44)	(1.66)	(1.00)	(2.18)
President Home Region	0.328	0.192	1.395	0.097	0.287	0.829**
	(0.51)	(0.32)	(0.33)	(0.32)	(0.73)	(2.29)
Capital	−0.783	−0.775	−5.428	0.161	−0.025	0.113
	(−1.10)	(−1.09)	(−0.85)	(0.52)	(−0.05)	(0.31)
Constant	−11.603***	−10.936***	−80.009***	−5.748***	−4.883	−8.374***
	(−3.66)	(−3.51)	(−2.62)	(−2.90)	(−1.54)	(−3.04)
Observations	231	230	77	1,417	424	1,021

Random effects logistic regression, z-statistics in parentheses. Dependent variable is whether or not an individual from the district was appointed minister in the succeeding presidential term.

$*p < .1, **p < .05, ***p < .01$

For Benin (Models 1, 2, and 3), there is no clear electoral logic at work. Specifically, there is no statistically significant relationship between the president's vote performance in the district and the likelihood that the district receives a minister portfolio. These results indicate that the preference for appointees from opposition districts in Benin, as depicted in Table 5.6, does not amount to a brokerage or vote mobilization strategy. In Ghana (Models 4, 5, and 6), districts that perform well for the president in terms of vote margin (Model 4) are more likely to receive a minister appointment. The predicted probability of a district receiving an appointment increases from 0.09 to 0.16 as a district moves from barely winning (a positive vote margin close to 0) to winning by a 50 percent margin. As in Benin, however, there is no appointment bonus for Ghanaian districts in which vote performance improves from one round or election to the next. Despite some apparent electoral logics at work in Ghana, these findings do not rule out the possibility that loyal party agents – those who help the party to win elections – are also seen as reliable extraction agents and placed as such.

At least two important takeaways emerge from this analysis. First, the extent to which leaders engage in the exchange of executive posts for electoral support varies considerably between the two countries. Only in Ghana do presidents regularly appoint ministers from high-performing districts. Second, there is little evidence that leaders use minister appointments to reward *improvements* in vote performance, rendering it unclear whether those appointed from stronghold areas receive appointments for their work as electoral brokers or for other reasons such as their extractive roles in the party. These findings leave considerable room for extraction-related motives to drive minister appointments.

5.3 Extraction and Public Service Staffing

Common accounts of state institutions in Africa often assume that politicization at one level of government is indicative of broader, systematic patronage throughout the state. With such strong evidence of pervasive politicization at the upper echelons of Ghana's executive apparatus, the expectation is that Ghana should also display a highly politicized system of recruitment and selection of public service personnel. Likewise, with the more mixed executive appointment strategies in Benin, we might assume the existence of a more professional public service that is divorced from politics. As I posit earlier in this chapter, however, different systems of extraction in the two countries are likely to produce divergent incentives for politicization and control at different *levels* of government. In particular, because Benin's parties rely to some extent on money extracted by rank-and-file agents, there is, as I demonstrate in this section, an elevated impetus for politicization of public service hiring practices.

In this section, I investigate politicization of recruitment to each country's public service institutions. I begin with a discussion of qualitative data from the two countries that suggest more limited politicization in Ghana and more extensive political interference in recruitment to Benin's public service. I then analyze data from the two surveys of bureaucrats to (1) assess whether these same patterns of recruitment are evident in survey responses; and (2) test the relationship between extraction methods and politicized public service recruitment.

5.3.1   The Limits of Politicized Recruitment in Ghana

Public service employees in Ghana tend to describe hiring processes as broadly merit-based in that anyone who is hired will have typically met the educational, skill-based, and experiential qualifications for the job. However, when decisions are made between equally qualified candidates, this is where political – and especially personal – affiliations sometimes enter the picture. One director-level employee in a health agency explained, "We almost always have well-qualified candidates at the interviews, but then someone high up in the institution might say that one of the candidates is better."[64] Recent studies of local governments similarly affirm that politicized hiring is relatively rare for professional and career public service positions, but may be more common for contract workers hired into more temporary and lower-level jobs such as drivers, security guards, or maintenance workers. Such practices may be especially common where there are strong pressures to hire the party's activists.[65]

There is, however, both evidence of, and concern for, greater political influence at the highest echelons of the public service. In particular, there is a widespread perception that senior-level administrative positions require political connections and support, with particular attention to political influences over the selection and movement of chief directors – the top career civil servant in each ministry. A manager at the Office of the Head of the Civil Service explained these higher-level hiring and promotion decisions, and their impacts further down the bureaucratic chain, as follows:

Most appointments are given to relatives, friends and at times applicants from the same religion/church as top officials and those recommended by top politi-

---

[64] Author interview, Accra, November 3, 2016.
[65] Driscoll (2018); Brierley (2021).

cians are considered....When most junior staff in the Public Service are due for promotion, they are delayed with the excuse that there are no funds to attend the scheme of service training which is required before promotion.[66]

Likewise, when a new party is elected into government, the effect of competitive politics on recruitment into the public service is "felt more at the executive level (i.e., chief executives, chief directors, and directors) than at the lower and middle levels."[67] This politicization at the upper echelons of the public service is also evident in Carola Lentz's ethnographic study of a number of long-standing employees of Ghana's civil service. Describing the processes through which the study's public service employees could (or could not) move into top positions, Lentz writes:

Of equal importance [to ethnicity] for arriving at, and remaining in, top positions in the public service were party-political alliances and the ability to "survive intrigues" by knowing "the ins and the outs of the office," having "informants" in the relevant ministries, and maintaining good contacts with the media.[68]

However, such decisions are not always overtly political in nature. One chief director – the highest career public servant in each ministry – who had come to occupy his position after the NPP government took office in early 2017 explained his placement as a chief director as follows: "I was very surprised to receive this position and I do not know why I was selected. I'm close to the end of my career and I have never been involved in any party."[69] Another chief director explained that changes that occur with new presidents or new ministers are usually because the new government wants a "fresh start."[70]

From the politicians' perspective, one former minister explained the reasons why he did not seek to influence the hiring decisions within his ministry as follows:

Me, I prefer to stay away from those decisions. If I get involved [in hiring processes], then I will have people lining up at my door asking for jobs. And if I try to intervene, the workers in the ministry will also be upset with me. It's better for [ministers] to sit on their hands, not let themselves get involved.[71]

[66] Survey follow-up questionnaire, April 7, 2017.
[67] Appiah and Abdulai (2017*b*: 15).
[68] Lentz (2014: 191,192).
[69] Author interview, Accra, February 24, 2017.
[70] Author interview, Accra, October 3, 2013.
[71] Author interview, Accra, October 8, 2013.

Although there is most certainly variation in the extent to which political appointees seek to influence the hiring decisions in their institutions, the modal assessment seems to suggest that such influence is, at most, limited in scope.

Limited political influence over public service recruitment in Ghana is perhaps even more surprising given that hiring decisions are largely concentrated within MDAs, rather than coordinated by a central body. In 2014, the Public Services Commission, which is the central coordinating body for Ghana's public service agencies, effectively removed themselves from all recruitment and hiring processes, granting complete control to the institutions under their purview. While Ghana's Office of the Head of the Civil Service retains a screening role in the recruitment of Ghana's *civil service* agents – comprising around 5,000 employees of the core public sector ministries – much of the formal and informal power over hiring decisions rests at the level of the ministries, departments, and agencies. Nearly all MDAs are headed by a presidential appointee, and many are also governed by a politically appointed board.

5.3.2   Politicized Recruitment in Benin

Such a move to relinquish central control over public service hiring decisions would seem unimaginable in Benin, where hiring processes are centralized and coordinated through the Ministry of Public Service, and, as one ministry employee noted, "guarded carefully by the president's office."[72] As I describe in the following paragraphs, there is a well-established pattern of political control over hiring processes, particularly in agencies that are commonly known to service politicians' extraction needs.

In a discussion with one unit director at the Ministry of Public Service in Benin, for example, he described, "a hierarchy of ministries" that control the apparatus of the state, including the distribution of state jobs. The higher up a ministry is in the hierarchy, the more resources they have, but also the more the President's office gets involved in their work, he explained. The Ministry of Economy and Finance, he noted, is at the top because it can allocate or withhold the funding necessary to hire new permanent agents of the state (civil servants). Next is the Ministry of Public Service, which, along with presidents themselves, can – and has – sought to interfere in the results of public service entrance contests and

---

[72] Author interview, Cotonou, April 2, 2014.

examinations. He explained specifically that control of this ministry is important because of the "riches" that are available.[73]

In one particularly illustrative example, upon taking office in April 2016, President Talon declared invalid the preceding government's recruitment competitions for the gendarmerie, the police, the customs service, the tax service, and the Ministry of Finance – all of which are widely known as "wet" agencies. The president convened a commission to investigate alleged irregularities to justify this decision. As stated in the commission's report, these competitions were riddled with irregularities and fraudulent results.[74] According to one official at the Ministry of Public Service, approximately one-third of the 1,700 or so selected customs agents came from the *commune* (municipal district) of Banté which, in the 2011 presidential election, delivered over 80 percent of its votes to President Boni Yayi in a field of fourteen candidates.[75] Whereas one employee at the Ministry of Public Service explained, "the cancellation was an important step to repair the fraudulent recruitment procedure,"[76] another noted that the Head of State and the Minister [of Public Service] were worried about "the fidelity" of some of those agents.[77]

Several years earlier, in a June 2012 recruitment competition for positions in the Ministry of Economy and Finance, then-Minister of Public Service, Kora Zaki, was accused of organizing parallel competitions, altering results in favor of her own family members and those of high-ranking members of her ministry, and elevating the level of qualification for some of the favored individuals.[78] On another occasion during Zaki's time as minister, the union representing customs agents claimed that one recruitment exercise yielded the same number of new employees as are typically hired over a three-year period, implying that those in power were seeking, even more than usual, to pack the customs service with friendly agents.[79]

While these scandals are not overtly political, politics is often intertwined with nepotistic hiring in Benin. Among the Classroom survey respondents, 44.4 percent of those in Benin who said they were hired

[73] Author interview, Ministry of Public Service, Cotonou, June 25, 2018.
[74] Cedric Amoussou, "Recrutements de 2015 au Bénin: Polémique et annulation des concours «frauduleux»," La Nouvelle Tribune, April 7, 2017.
[75] Author interview, Cotonou, July 3, 2018.
[76] Author interview, Ministry of Public Service, July 4, 2018.
[77] Author interview, Ministry of Public Service, June 25, 2018.
[78] Author interview, Ministry of Public Service, November 16, 2013. See, also, Charly Hessoun, "Concours frauduleux: Les contrevérités de Kora Zaki," La Nouvelle Tribune, April 29, 2014.
[79] "La Douane béninoise déclare pléthorique le nombre de 502 candidats déclarés douaniers admis à la Fonction publique," Agence Benin Presse, October 16, 2015.

with the help of family or friends also reported having participated in a political campaign during the most recent election. By comparison, only 7.4 percent of those in Ghana who reported being hired through friends or family said they had participated in a political campaign. Because parties in Benin are not typically organized at the grassroots level, connections through regional origins, family, and friends form the principal basis to identify and recruit political supporters. In other words, these disruptions and interventions in recruitment contests are a likely sign of efforts to exert some form of political control over who gets access to potentially lucrative positions.

5.3.3   Survey Analysis: Extraction and Public Service Staffing

The patterns of politicization in public service staffing described above are plainly visible in both the Classroom and Workplace surveys of public servants. Figure 5.3 shows the distribution of responses to two survey questions from the Classroom survey – conducted in both Benin and Ghana – asking bureaucrats about politicized recruitment to the public service. The first question asks respondents to choose the response that best describes how they came to be hired in their current organization: (1) through a family member or friend, (2) as a result of their political affiliation or involvement, or (3) through an exam, interview, or application process. Another question, using the same set of response categories, asks respondents to describe how others in their organization were hired. For both questions, there is a statistically and substantively significant difference between the two countries. Whereas 19 percent of the survey respondents in Benin reported that their political affiliation was the *principal* way that they obtained their job, less than 1 percent of respondents in Ghana answered in this way.[80] When asked about others in their organization, 15 percent of Beninese respondents said that political links were most important in hiring, whereas approximately 4 percent responded this way in Ghana.[81]

Although the surveys were conducted completely anonymously and there was no reason for respondents to believe otherwise, these responses

---

[80] The different proportions are statistically significant with $z = 9.87$.

[81] Once again, the differences in proportions between countries are statistically significant with $z = 5.96$. The difference-of-proportions tests collapse the data into two categories: those who say that political links are the most important and those who did not respond this way. For the question asking individuals if political links were important for them, the z-statistic is 9.87. For the question asking if political links were important for others in their organization, the z-statistic is 5.96.

How respondent was hired

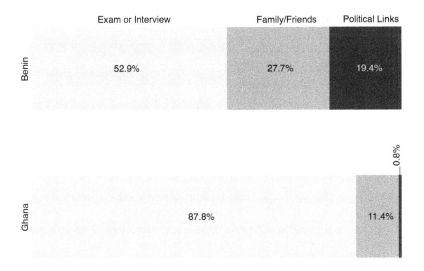

How others in organization are hired

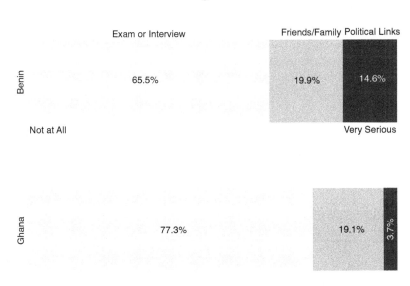

Figure 5.3 Public service job politicization in Benin and Ghana
The graphs depict responses to questions asking about the most
important factor in having obtained a job in the public sector.
Source: Author's Classroom survey (2013–2014).

do suggest the possibility of some social desirability bias, albeit in different directions in each country. Interestingly, more Beninese respondents reported that they themselves were hired based on political affiliation (20 percent) than their perception of political hiring among others in their organization (15 percent). One possible explanation for this pattern is that Beninese civil servants could benefit, in terms of promotion for example, from making their affiliation with a political party known.[82] In Ghana, however, respondents were more likely to say that *others* in their organization had been hired based on political criteria or personal relationships than was the case for themselves, suggesting the possibility of social desirability bias in that respondents do not want to admit that they were hired through political means.

To test whether social desirability bias is impacting the results in Ghana, I turn to another list experiment question that was included in the Workplace survey. In the experiment, respondents were shown a list of three to four possible factors that had helped them to obtain their first job in the public sector. Respondents were randomly assigned to a control group, which saw the following list *without* the sensitive item (political support), or a treatment group, which saw the list *with* the sensitive item included. This style of question is designed to minimize social desirability bias by making it unnecessary for respondents to have to explicitly identify the sensitive item – in this case support from politicians – as a contributing factor.

- Your job application did not contain any errors
- You had a recommendation letter from an international organization
- You benefited from previous work experience
- *Sensitive item*: You had support from a politician or someone with political links

In Table 5.8, I estimate the proportions of respondents in the treatment group (those whose list included the sensitive item) who answered affirmatively to the sensitive item.[83] The results of this estimation suggest that 7.1 percent of respondents indicated that they had support from a politician to obtain their first public sector job. Although this 7.1 percent is somewhat higher than 0.8 percent of Ghanaian respondents who admitted to political support in the Classroom survey, the different wording of the questions would lead us to anticipate this difference.

---

[82] Note that survey responses to questions about promotion are consistent with this interpretation.

[83] Following the analysis of the resource diversion list experiment presented in Chapter 4, I use the item count estimation technique.

Table 5.8 *Public service recruitment list experiment*

Response	No	s.e.	Yes	s.e
0	14.8	NA	NA	NA
1	50.9	.02	4.5	.02
2	26.4	.02	1.0	.01
3	2.5	.01	0.8	.00
4	NA	NA	0.8	NA
Total	94.6	7.1		

Estimated percentage answering affirmatively to the sensitive item using item count estimation.

Unlike the question about hiring in the Classroom survey, the design of the list experiment does not force respondents to say whether political support was *the most important factor* in their hiring.

The cross-country patterns in bureaucratic recruitment generally align with the extraction-based expectations. I find that politicized public service recruitment including the application of political criteria in hiring decisions and frequent political interventions in public service recruitment contests is quite common in Benin, where rank-and-file public servants are more likely to serve as extraction agents. Politicized recruitment is more limited in Ghana, where bureaucrats play a more marginal role in extraction. However, with only cross-country differences, it is difficult to confidently establish extraction as an explanation for these patterns. Thus, to further investigate the relationship between extraction practices and hiring, I analyze the survey data in more detail, examining how Beninese respondents' perceptions of extraction taking place within their organizations are (or are not) associated with politicized hiring practices.

I conduct regression analyses of Classroom survey responses from Benin to understand whether those who report higher levels of concern about resource diversion from their organizations are more likely to also see politicized hiring as a problem in their organization. Whereas past research has argued that politicized hiring is more likely to result in resource diversion than other forms of public service recruitment,[84] I argue that this relationship also works endogenously: that leaders politicize hiring to ensure their own benefit from the diversion of resources. I test this relationship using linear regression with perceptions of politicized hiring as the dependent variable. I control for bureaucrats' perceptions of other forms of political interference, including whether

---

[84] For example, Dahlström and Lapuente (2017); Oliveros and Schuster (2018).

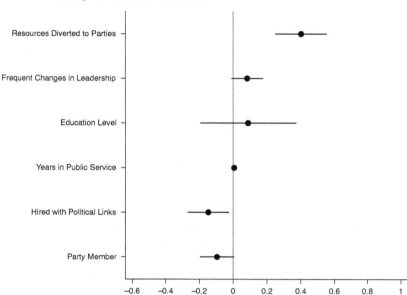

Figure 5.4 Extraction by bureaucrats and politicized hiring in Benin

Coefficients and 90% confidence intervals from OLS regression with robust standard errors clustered by organization type. The dependent variable is perceptions of "hiring of personnel because of their affiliation to the ruling party" as a problem in their organization. $N = 474$ and $r^2 = 0.29$. Analysis based on results of the Classroom survey (2013–2014).

they see political involvement in their day-to-day work and frequent changes in leadership as problems in their organization. I also control for individual-level attributes including years served in the public service, whether they were hired with political links, and whether they identify as a member of political party.

The results of these regressions, shown in Figure 5.4, demonstrate that there is a strong and significant relationship between bureaucrats reporting concern about resource diversion and politicized hiring in their organization. The relationship is robust to the inclusion of covariates measuring concerns about other forms of perceived political influence in one's organization, to attributes of individual respondents, and to different organization types. In Appendix D, I provide descriptive statistics for all variables and present full results along with those from robustness checks with alternative models.

5.4   Conclusion

This chapter has examined the connections between extraction strategies and the politicization of staffing decisions in both executive-level and public service positions. The observed patterns of politicization in Benin and Ghana not only question common conceptions of pervasive political patronage in African states but also demonstrate the ways that leaders' concerns about the extraction of money for political financing shape patterns of politicization in the staffing of the state apparatus.

The chapter documents in detail that executive appointments tend to be highly politicized in Ghana, where elite-level party agents collude in the award of procurement contracts to party-aligned businesses in exchange for their financial support. Party loyalists received approximately 218 of Ghana's 273 minister appointments from 1993 through 2016 (nearly 80 percent). Based on descriptive and regression analysis and resulting calculations, only around 17 percent of these appointments were plausibly rewards for improved vote performance in an electorally strategic district. Together, this evidence suggests that concerns *other than* voter mobilization are likely to be at play in these appointments.

Political leaders in Benin have pursued quite different executive appointment strategies than their counterparts in Ghana. Although the literature on elite political brokerage would expect that Benin's presidents widely reward individuals who mobilize voting blocs on behalf of the president, I find only very limited evidence of this phenomenon. Instead, because of the risks that brokers will defect from the ruling coalition, leaders tend to steer away from brokerage appointments when possible – keeping potential elite defectors away from positions that involve access to more lucrative extraction opportunities. This defensive approach to appointments is a product of the uncertainty of political alliances and the need to protect the financial resources of the state in a more coercive manner.

Moreover, the chapter shows that the patterns of politicized staffing at the executive level do not necessarily predict politicized recruitment of public service employees. Despite the high frequency with which party loyalists are appointed to ministerial posts in Ghana, these appointees do not typically interfere in recruitment processes in their ministries. Notwithstanding the difficulty of explaining why something *does not* occur, the lack of political interference makes sense given that public servants in Ghana do not typically serve as key extraction agents. In short, the collusive extraction methods described in the previous chapter help us to understand the unexpected patterns of politicized staffing decisions at different levels of the Ghanaian government.

By contrast, in Benin, where procurement-based financing is more tightly controlled by the president, he is more likely to appoint a mix of personal loyalists, technocrats with little political experience, new party supporters, and opposition members to ministerial posts. Despite higher levels of technocracy in Benin's executive, there is evidence of considerable politicization of bureaucratic recruitment, both in survey responses and well-known cases of political interventions in recruitment contests. Consistent with the extraction-based explanation, public service politicization appears to be more frequent in organizations characterized by high levels of party-directed resource diversion.

In addition to linking the different modes of extraction to practices of politicization in state staffing decisions, the patterns uncovered in this chapter challenge common assumptions about the systemic nature of the politicized selection of state officials in contexts of widespread clientelism. In particular, the extraction lens applied in this chapter shows why it is not always advantageous to distribute jobs in exchange for one-time political support. Unlike the provision of a school, hospital, electricity, agricultural supplies, or cash; jobs often come with the potential for ongoing access to state money. This means that incumbents must carefully decide which "boys" are appointed to particular jobs and where it may be less risky to let merit guide staffing decisions.

6   Extraction and the Executive

On August 9, 2013, Beninese President Boni Yayi, after seven years in office, dismissed all twenty-six members of his cabinet. At the time of this surprising action, there was no recent or upcoming legislative election that warranted modification of the governing coalition. There were no serious economic crises or social upheavals that the president was trying to resolve. There was no major change in the supply of patronage goods and services that would have prompted a change in coalition size. Instead, Boni Yayi's decision to dissolve the government reflected a major rupture in his relationship with businessman, financier, and eventual political opponent Patrice Talon. It also came amidst the rumored resignation of prime minister – and close Talon associate – Pascal Irenée Koupaki.

Although this particular reshuffle of executive personnel was one of the more dramatic in Benin's recent history,[1] it was not, and would not be, the only time that Benin's presidents uprooted their governments in ways that confound much of the prevailing wisdom on executive instability. In 1993, President Soglo made significant, but largely unexplained, changes to his government. In May 1998, President Kéréou, in a surprise move, elevated leaders of a number of small parties in government, effectively driving out a key member of his governing coalition, leader of the *Parti du renouveau démocratique* (PRD) and then-prime minister, Adrien Houngbedji. In addition to these headline-grabbing government changes, Benin's presidents have increasingly engaged in one-at-a-time individual replacements of ministers, often in ways that do not involve any obvious political or governing calculation.

In this chapter, I connect these increasingly frequent and seemingly erratic government reshuffles in Benin to both its system of coercive extraction and the executive appointment practices described in the previous chapter. In appointing a mix of personal loyalists, unknown

---

[1] As discussed in more detail later in the chapter, it was described as "shocking" and "without warning" in the news media.

technocrats, allies of newly formed coalitions, and opposition figures, Benin's presidents are more likely to encounter agency problems as they seek to protect extraction opportunities from elite defectors. To resolve these agency problems, leaders dismiss and shuffle ministers more frequently, even as such frequent changes produce an environment in which it is extremely challenging for leaders to advance their political and policy agendas.

As my theory foretells, these dynamics play out very differently in Ghana where, as described in the previous chapter, presidents staff executive positions primarily with party loyalists – many of whom participate in the party's extraction efforts. Ghana's leaders not only appoint party elite who they have come to know through internal party business and competition, but they can also count on these political appointees to act in the interest of the president and the party because the agents themselves have incentives to extract in service of the party. These dynamics lead to fewer ministerial dismissals and reshuffles in Ghana. When rotations do occur, they are actually likely to resolve, rather than exacerbate, agency problems and improve the political cohesion of the government. With more stable and cohesive executive institutions, Ghana's leaders have greater success simultaneously pursuing their political and policy agendas.

My principal empirical focus in this chapter is on the cabinets and the upper echelons of government ministries. In explaining how leaders' extraction strategies shape patterns of instability, cohesion, and, ultimately, performance in the state's executive institutions, this chapter illuminates two main pathways linking extraction to executive performance. First, the extraction and appointment dynamics described in the two preceding chapters produce more or less severe agency problems for leaders in their efforts to manage executive personnel. Variation in the nature and intensity of these problems leads incumbents to replace and rotate ministers with more or less frequency, generating divergent levels of executive instability. Second, the executive dynamics involved in coercive extraction undermine the cohesion of government actors, thereby impairing leaders' abilities to coordinate and sustain the implementation of their policy programs.

Throughout the chapter, I combine multiple sources of data to gain robust insight into patterns of political management of the executive. First, I use data on all minister appointments in Benin and Ghana from the early 1990s through 2016 – described in detail in the previous chapter – to compare and analyze patterns of stability and turnover. Second, I use qualitative data, primarily from interviews and journalistic accounts, to interpret the quantitative data and to provide illustrative examples of these dynamics. At the end of the chapter, I present data from the Classroom survey in both countries showing how bureaucrats perceive the executive dynamics explored in this chapter. Like the previous chapters, this multi-method approach combines cross-national comparison and within-country analyses to elucidate the interrelationships of party institutions, extraction practices, and executive performance.

Party institutionalization and extraction are not the *only* determinants of government performance, nor are they necessarily the most fundamental drivers of stability and cohesion in the executive. There is a large literature theorizing the constraints that leaders face in forming and retaining their political coalitions and allocating ministerial portfolios, which recent work has begun to analyze in African countries.[2] The goal of this chapter is more modest: to illustrate how different systems of extraction, and the appointment practices associated with each system, constitute an additional constraint on how leaders manage the state's governing institutions – and with what implications for policy performance.

The analysis presented in this chapter does, however, challenge the prevailing wisdom that widespread politicization of executive institutions necessarily undermines government performance. Although Benin's cabinets include more highly qualified technocrats, the high levels of instability and incohesion within the executive prove particularly detrimental to the pursuit, coordination, and sustained implementation of policy programs. Whereas in Ghana, major extraction scandals and intraparty conflict may squander government resources and temporarily impair governance, party leaders have the incentives and tools necessary to resolve these issues in ways that ultimately enable them to more successfully pursue their governing agendas.

The chapter begins by outlining the theoretical connections between extraction, executive politicization, and government stability. I then provide a comparative analysis of patterns of ministerial rotation in Benin and Ghana, illustrating several ways in which the levels of stability vary between the two countries. The third section delves into the dynamics behind increasing levels of government instability in Benin and their implications for the performance of executive institutions. In the fourth section, I analyze executive rotations in Ghana, showing how they tend to address performance issues and lead to longer-term resolution of intraparty conflicts. I conclude the analysis with bureaucrats' views of

---

[2] See, for example, a special issue of *The Journal of African Elections* on political coalitions (June 2014), as well as recent work by Ariotti and Golder (2018) and Kroeger (2018).

these dynamics, followed by a discussion of the implications for policy successes and failures in the two countries.

6.1   Extraction and Executive Performance

Previous chapters have established the problems leaders face in selecting and managing extraction agents as well as the party institutions that shape incentives for leaders and their agents to extract in collusive or coercive ways. Chapters 2 and 4, in particular, explained how the selection of *elite* extraction agents depends on the extent to which internal party structures reduce incentives for elites to defect from the ruling coalition and the extent to which they enable leaders to learn about the loyalties and competencies of party elites over time. Leaders of institutionalized political parties, such as those in Ghana, therefore select elite party loyalists to serve in ministerial positions where they can coordinate extraction deals. For less institutionalized ruling parties, such as in Benin where the risk of elite defection remains high, leaders are likely to *eschew* the placement of political elites into ministerial positions, opting instead to place personal loyalists and technocrats into executive positions with access to extraction opportunities. Thus, in contexts of low party institutionalization, like Benin, ministers tend to have more diverse professional and political backgrounds than in Ghana, where ministers are overwhelmingly selected from the ruling party elite.

I argue in this chapter that these divergent executive appointment practices, themselves driven by different extraction methods, hold important implications for the performance of the state's executive institutions. I focus on two key dynamics underlying this argument. First, different appointment practices imply differences in the frequency with which leaders dismiss or rotate ministers. Frequent rotations, particularly when they are politically driven, impair ministerial *stability*, making it difficult to develop and sustain policy-oriented action. Second, a more diverse corps of ministers combined with frequent rotations of those ministers undermines cohesion within the government. This incohesion, in turn, undermines elite commitment to the president's policy agendas and impairs inter-ministerial coordination. In this section, I review some of the key theoretical perspectives on executive stability, cohesion, and government performance.

6.1.1   Stability

A large body of scholarship from around the world links the stability of executive cabinets with government performance or even more broadly as a measure of "the health of the system."[3] Research has established that stable governments lead to credible policy commitments,[4] policy continuity,[5] the sustainability of reform processes,[6] informational advantages in policy administration,[7] and longer time horizons that allow for policy learning.[8] In short, frequent turnovers in the cabinet prevent ministers from developing the knowledge, experience, and credibility needed to manage complex policies and institutional dynamics.

To examine the relationship between extraction and executive stability, I focus on the frequency with which chief executives retain, replace, or rotate individual ministers, or what John Huber calls "portfolio volatility." Portfolio volatility reflects changes in the control of policy portfolios within the government.[9] The "portfolio volatility" approach is particularly useful for understanding stability and instability in presidential regimes[10] and permits comparison between single-party and multi-party governments such as those in Benin and Ghana. Given the prominence of strong chief executives and elite shuffling as a form of patronage politics in many African countries,[11] minister replacements and rotations are best seen as a "strategic resource" that go beyond conventional partisan logics of government formation.[12]

To understand the links between extraction and ministerial (in)stability, it is useful to briefly consider the main theoretical explanations for why leaders in Africa or similar contexts replace or rotate ministers more or less frequently. One common account emphasizes that leaders are more likely to exercise dismissal and rotation powers when their survival is threatened. Under threat, incumbents may seek to expand their cabinets,[13] share power more or less widely among ethnic

---

[3] Lijphart (1968: 72).

[4] Laver and Shepsle (1994).

[5] See Resnick (2013: 6), who explains how former Senegalese President Abdoulaye Wade cycled through seven different agriculture ministers thereby hindering policy continuity in that sector.

[6] Milio (2008).

[7] Huber (1998: 579–580) argues that ministers are more likely to obtain reliable information from career bureaucrats when they expect to be in a long run relationship with them. By contrast, if ministers are new to a particular post, they will need to form the relationships with bureaucrats necessary to gain information and coordinate policy (Huber, 1998: 579–580).

[8] Heclo (1977); Simmons (1997: 61).

[9] Huber (1998). Throughout this chapter I use the terms "portfolio volatility," "minister turnover" and "ministerial instability" interchangeably.

[10] See, for example, Martínez-Gallardo (2012).

[11] Bratton and van de Walle (1997); Arriola (2009).

[12] Martínez-Gallardo (2014: 4).

[13] Arriola (2009).

or social groupings,[14] or appoint more technocrats in order to improve their popular approval.[15] Institutions are likely to shape the extent to which leaders can pursue these strategies when seeking to shore up their political support.[16] Presidents who have less formal power,[17] who rely on personalistic bases of support (as opposed to party institutions),[18] or who can not easily monitor the actions of their ministers[19] will be more likely to exercise their appointment powers in times of political need.

At the microlevel, leaders are likely to replace or rotate ministers when they encounter agency problems. One type of agency problem, adverse selection, occurs when incumbent chief executives appoint ministers whose competencies or loyalties they do not know. Replacing or reshuffling ministers allows leaders to improve selection and weed out undesirable elements.[20] Problems related to interest alignment and information asymmetry produce similar dynamics: ministers (agents) can use information that is not available to the principal to pursue their own interests. When these problems pose a threat to a leader's agenda, replacements and rotations are likely to occur either as a way to dispose of the problematic ministers or to signal the consequences of "ministerial drift."[21]

Existing theory therefore expects that instability is most likely to occur under conditions of weaker institutional constraints and more severe agency problems. As previous chapters have established, these conditions map rather neatly onto the systems of low party institutionalization and coercive extraction, especially with respect to the high likelihood of elite defection in these contexts. Stronger party institutions – those that enable collusive modes of extraction – constrain leaders from frequently shuffling their ministers. As Alex Kroeger explains, leaders of institutionalized parties are unlikely to shuffle ministers frequently because, in doing so, they risk undermining the party as members realize "that they can no longer expect meaningful political promotion," dissuading them from engaging in further activity for the party. By contrast, leaders of more weakly institutionalized parties face comparatively little political risk in frequently shuffling their ministers because they maintain their political power through some combination of elite transactions, support

[14] Roessler (2016).
[15] Camerlo and Pérez-Liñán (2015).
[16] For an overview of institutional arguments related to minister tenure, see Fischer et al. (2012).
[17] Martínez-Gallardo (2012, 2014).
[18] Chaisty et al. (2018); Kroeger (2018).
[19] Indridason (2005).
[20] Huber and Martínez-Gallardo (2008).
[21] Indridason (2005); Hassan (2017).

from civil society, or direct (often-identity based) appeals to voters.[22] Lacking organized and rule-bound party structures, leaders in weakly institutionalized parties are therefore less constrained in their ability to shuffle ministers.

Not only do leaders in less institutionalized parties frequently shuffle ministers simply because they can, they also do so because they are likely to experience severe agency problems, particularly in terms of the selection and management of elite extraction agents. As Chapters 4 and 5 describe in the context of Benin, leaders of weaker parties seek to keep potential opponents away from "wet" ministerial posts where extraction opportunities are more abundant, opting instead to appoint personal loyalists and technocrats – those with little observed political ambition – to extraction-rich positions. Combined with the need to, at times, allocate portfolios to coalition partners and opposition figures, these appointment practices have considerable potential to generate frequent portfolio turnover because they are likely to involve problems related to both adverse selection and interest misalignment. Regarding adverse selection, personal loyalists and technocrats are unlikely to possess the political experience necessary to act as effective agents of the president, particularly when it comes to extraction, coalition maintenance, or other political tasks. Leaders in these contexts are also likely to encounter interest alignment problems when, once appointed, ministers work against the political interest of the incumbent. Technocrats, for example, may prefer to adhere to professional standards rather than engage in political tasks for the incumbent, and coalition partners or opposition members may prefer to serve alternative political principals or extract on their own behalf.

The main takeaway from this discussion is that contexts of coercive extraction are likely to be associated with more frequent shuffling of executive personnel. Empirically, I therefore expect more frequent minister dismissals and rotations in Benin than in Ghana. Conversely, the highly politicized corps of elite ministers in Ghana gives rise to greater stability in the executive, as it helps leaders to manage institutional constraints, mitigate agency problems, and, as I discuss next, promote cohesion and policy coordination.

6.1.2 Cohesion

Whereas executive stability helps to ensure that ministers have the knowledge and opportunities to pursue policy programs, the government's

---

[22] Kroeger (2018: 7).

ability to plan, coordinate, and implement public policy is ultimately limited if executive actors are unable to act in unison. A dearth of cohesion in the executive undermines commitment to the government's policy agenda and impairs coordination of policy action. Such conditions, I argue, are more likely to occur in contexts of coercive extraction.

The comparative literature identifies (at least) two types of government (in)cohesion that shape executive institutional performance. First, elite polarization, particularly when concentrated in the government, impairs leaders' ability to pursue their preferred policy programs. Ideological polarization, for example, weakens the ability of elites to resolve policy questions and debate within the existing political arrangements, leading to both inefficiency and inconsistency in policy implementation and reform.[23] Polarization, either in terms of identity or preferences about who should receive government patronage, also impairs collective action among elites, resulting most notably in the under-provision of public goods and resources.[24] Viewed from this perspective, cohesion helps to generate a set of clear and consistent policy goals and reinforces the commitment of key actors toward those goals.

A second type of cohesion relates not to polarization of interests, but rather to a corporate body or culture that binds ruling elites together and sets them apart from the social groups they govern. This view of cohesion is especially prevalent in studies of East Asian developmental states, such as Japan and South Korea, where the cohesion of political and business elites produced a synergy that enabled their governments to pursue the developmental policies that helped to grow and transform key industries.[25] Corporate cohesion at the apex of government may result from shared experience. For example, cohesive developmentalism in Brazil and South Korea has been viewed as the product of military-influenced cohesion and discipline, where "[developmental] priorities trickled down, molding the behavior of economic bureaucrats in a manner that contributed to the state's effectiveness."[26] This sense of cohesion among elites stands in stark contrast to the experience of Nigeria, where the military officers themselves lacked professionalism

---

[23] This argument is advanced, for example, by Waldner (1999: 151) in his study of developmental governance in the Middle East and East Asia. He explains that in the presence of such polarization, policy outcomes tend to be perceived as zero-sum. See also Frye (2010) on the effects of high polarization on state and market reform in postcommunist countries.

[24] There is a large literature linking ethnic diversity to uneven distribution of public goods. See, for example, Miguel and Gugerty (2005); Habyarimana et al. (2007).

[25] Johnson (1982); Evans (1995).

[26] Kohli (2004: 198).

and organizational discipline, which ultimately contributed to an inability of military rulers to effectively pursue developmental policies. As Peter Lewis explains, even after Nigeria transitioned from military to civilian rule, economic technocrats remained isolated in government, unable to penetrate political coalitions and forge an economic consensus.[27] An important takeaway from these studies is that technocrats must be integrated into a cohesive political structure, such as a mass party or a collegial military regime.

Collusive and coercive extraction produce different patterns of cohesion. To the extent that leaders in collusive systems of extraction select loyal, elite party officials as extraction agents, they are generally consistent with the types of elite cohesion that render executive institutions more effective. Party structures help to minimize adverse selection, reduce the frequency of elite rotation, and ensure that ministers work towards a common goal in support for the party. Well-organized parties have mechanisms through which to incorporate both political and technocratic personnel, or "technopols," capable of directing policy programs while simultaneously advancing the political and financial interests of the party.[28] Officials seeking to move up in the party or advance their particular faction may, at times, seek to undermine other party elites, but there are procedural mechanisms to resolve these issues. That executive personnel are more stable in these contexts helps to further cultivate cohesion, enabling ministers to learn over time how to work effectively with one another and without constant fear of dismissal.

Coercive extraction, however, is likely to involve a much less cohesive group of governing elites and, as such, a much more chaotic executive landscape. In coercive systems of extraction this dynamic is particularly evident in leaders' efforts to address agency problems. For leaders, the stakes of agency problems are particularly high if valuable political resources fall into the hands of present or future opponents, or those unable to manage them to the leaders' satisfaction. Under these conditions, ministers of questionable political loyalty remain isolated from key decisions and starved of the resources necessary for their ministries to contribute meaningfully to the government's policy programs. Technocrats are pressured to show loyalty to the incumbent or risk dismissal, thereby compromising their professional values and incentivizing politicized management of the bureaucracy.

The foregoing discussion implies that, despite high levels of executive politicization in collusive extraction systems like Ghana's, their

[27] Lewis (2007: 261).
[28] Abdulai and Mohan (2019).

governments are to a lesser extent impaired by the principal-agent problems and elite dynamics that commonly undermine stability and cohesion among ruling elites. In coercive systems of extraction, by contrast, the problems of delegating extraction, discussed at length in Chapters 2 and 4, undermine both stability and cohesion in the executive. Even if leaders in coercive systems seek to advance clear policy agendas, they are likely to encounter serious challenges in finding the right personnel and management practices to see those agendas through.

The remainder of the chapter investigates these dynamics in the context of Benin and Ghana. The analysis begins with a comparison of portfolio turnover rates in the two countries, showing that, as expected, they are significantly higher in Benin's coercive system than in Ghana's collusive one. The analysis then delves deeper into the internal executive dynamics within the two countries. It shows how Benin's leaders have, with increasing frequency, shuffled ministers in order to address a range of political and extraction-related problems, impairing cohesion and the successful pursuit of public policies. Then, turning to Ghana, I show that minister shuffles only very rarely occur in response to the types of loyalty concerns that are so prominent in Benin. Instead, Ghana's presidents shuffle ministers in ways that seek to defuse and resolve intraparty tensions, save face for the party, increase cohesion, and improve policy outcomes.

6.2   Comparing Executive Stability in Benin and Ghana

In the previous chapter I showed how concerns over control of extraction lead to the frequent appointment of high-ranking party officials to ministerial posts in Ghana. Benin's leaders, facing a less certain party landscape, tend to favor the appointment of non-political technocrats and personal loyalists, when possible. Ultimately, however, Benin's leaders pursue a more mixed appointment strategy to balance both coalitional and extraction concerns. These varied appointment strategies, as well as leaders' ongoing concerns about accessing and controlling state money for political finance, lead to divergent patterns of (in)stability in the executive.

A comparison of portfolio turnover rates in the two countries provides an overall sense of executive stability in the two countries. A measure of portfolio volatility developed by Arend Lijphart provides a simple way to compare executive stability across countries.[29] The measure adds together the total number of ministers who enter the cabinet, exit the

---

[29] Lijphart (1984).

cabinet, and are reshuffled in a given year, divided by the total number of ministers in the cabinet.[30] The annual volatility statistics are depicted alongside the number of ministers in Figure 6.1. The bars shaded in darker gray are years in which a new government was installed following an election.[31]

As expected, turnover rates are generally highest when a new president takes office: in Benin this occurs in 1991, 1996, 2006, and 2016; and in Ghana in 1993, 2001, 2009, and 2013.[32] Overall portfolio volatility tends to be significantly higher in Benin (.75) compared to Ghana (.48), and this relationship holds when excluding years in which new governments were formed following an election.[33] To put these figures in perspective, an average of 38.3 percent of ministerial portfolios turn over in intraterm years, compared to just 25.5 percent in Ghana.[34]

Intraterm portfolio turnover is also more erratic in Benin than in Ghana. In Benin, there will be years with very low turnover followed by years with very high turnover. In Ghana, with the exception of several years during the John Kufuor and John Atta Mills presidencies, there is a small but relatively consistent amount of reshuffling from year-to-year. These different patterns may not seem surprising given the multi-party coalitional composition of Benin's governments but, as I discuss in greater detail in the next section, many of the major reshuffles in Benin have actually *not* reflected a clear logic of attracting support in the National Assembly.

Volatility in Benin remained relatively low through the presidencies of Soglo and Kérékou – both of whom were established players in Benin's political landscape (see Table 6.1). With the election of Boni Yayi, however, intraterm volatility increased from an average of .66 from 1991

---

[30] Since the size of the cabinet can change from year to year, I use the average number of ministers serving at any given time throughout the year. In Ghana, only a maximum of nineteen ministers are technically members of the cabinet, but I include all "sector ministers" with portfolios, excluding deputy ministers and regional ministers since there are no equivalent positions in Benin. In other words, anyone with the title minister who is not minister of a region is included in the calculation.

[31] Presidential elections in Benin have typically taken place in March and new governments are typically installed in April. In Ghana, elections take place in December and new governments are installed in January the following year.

[32] Note that, in Ghana, John Mahama was not a new president in 2013 because he had assumed the presidency after the death of President John Atta Mills in August 2012. It was, however, his first time being elected as president and forming a government of his own making.

[33] See Table 6.1. This is a statistically significant difference with t-statistic equal to 1.72.

[34] In a calculation of portfolio turnover in thirty-five African countries from 2000 to 2010, an average of around 35 percent of ministers were replaced or reshuffled annually. I thank Leonardo Arriola for sharing this calculation.

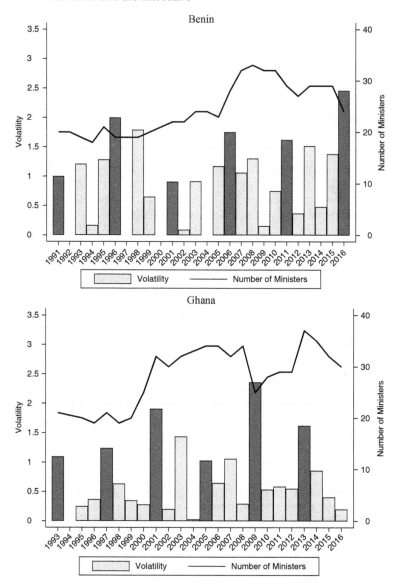

Figure 6.1 Annual portfolio volatility in Benin and Ghana
The graphs depict annual portfolio volatility in each country (bars)
and overall number of ministers (line). Bars shaded dark gray
represent years in which governments formed following an election.
Source: Author's data compilation.

Table 6.1 *Intraterm portfolio volatility*

Term	Benin Volatility	% Turnover	Term	Ghana Volatility	% Turnover
Soglo	0.67	33.7%	Rawlings 1	0.31	12.9%
Kérékou 1	0.61	31.1%	Rawlings 2	0.42	23.4%
Kérékou 2	0.55	27.8%	Kufuor 1	0.56	28.2%
Yayi 1	0.82	42.4%	Kufuor 2	0.67	33.3%
Yayi 2	0.94	46.8%	Mills	0.56	30.3%
			Mahama	0.49	20.8%
Average	0.72	36.4%		0.50	24.8%

Excludes years in which new or reelected presidents took office. The total differences are statistically significant, with $t = 1.72$ for volatility rates and 1.61 for annual percentage of portfolios that turn over.

through 2000, up to .88 for Yayi's two terms in office. In Ghana, portfolio volatility was highest during President Kufuor's second term in office from 2001 to 2008.

Viewed another way, the average number of days in office per minister is significantly lower in Benin than in Ghana. Given that presidential terms are five years long in Benin and only four years in Ghana, it would be reasonable to expect that ministers stay in their posts longer in Benin. This is not the case. Benin's ministers stay on average 707 days compared to 825 days in Ghana, generating a statistically significant difference with a high level of confidence $(t = 2.83)$.[35]

Additionally, ministers in Ghana are significantly more likely to receive multiple appointments than those in Benin, suggesting that, even when portfolios turn over in Ghana, the replacement appointees have experience in ministerial positions. There are forty-eight individuals in Benin who have received multiple appointments, meaning that 15 percent of all appointments have gone to someone who had already served in a ministerial post. In Ghana, seventy-three individuals have received multiple appointments, which translates into 26 percent of all appointments going to someone who has already served in a ministerial post. There are also approximately twice as many individuals in Ghana (thirteen) who have served multiple presidents as compared to Benin, where only seven have done so.

---

[35] The minimum and maximum days are similar in the two countries. The shortest tenure in Benin was eighteen days in office and the shortest in Ghana was twenty-four days. The longest stay in a ministerial post in Benin was 2,743 days and the longest in Ghana was 2,848.

In sum, Benin's executive, particularly since 2006, has experienced relatively high levels of instability in terms of the rate of portfolio turnover, the length of time each minister spends at their post, and the nonretention of experienced ministers. These patterns of instability stand in contrast to Ghana's executive which, despite substantial growth in the total number of ministers, has been considerably more stable and, importantly, has retained more experienced ministers.

6.3   Guarding Extraction: Executive Instability in Benin

In important ways, the relative instability in Benin's executive is traceable to both its coercive system of extraction and the staffing practices outlined in Chapter 5. Since party and coalition alignments became increasingly fluid throughout the 1990s and especially in the mid-2000s, political leaders have faced an increasingly uncertain political environment. Ministers, particularly those with political ambitions who stay in office longer are likely to have greater opportunities to command control of ministry personnel and extraction opportunities, thereby elevating the political threats posed to the incumbent.

This dynamic has produced instability in two important ways. First, it has led Benin's president to appoint, with some frequency, personal loyalists and technocrats, many of whom have subsequently struggled with the political tasks involved in portfolio management. These problems reflect a principal-agent logic of adverse selection. Second, presidents have engaged in more frequent dismissals of those they suspect of extracting resources or otherwise using their positions to build their own political movements. This latter dynamic reflects a problem of interest alignment and, as I explain later, is intensified when issues surrounding extraction arise.

The instability in Benin's executive has second-order implications as well. The frequent rotation of ministers, as well as the diversity of political and technical backgrounds that enter and exit the cabinet, generate an executive environment severely lacking in cohesion. This executive environment impairs policy planning, prevents interministerial coordination, and undermines government commitment to policy implementation.

6.3.1   The Dynamics of Executive Instability in Benin

As is evident from Figure 6.1, Benin's executive cabinets have become increasingly volatile since the adoption of a democratic constitution in the early 1990s. Growing levels of portfolio volatility in Benin reflect the increasing frequency of both government reshuffles and individual dismissals. A closer look at how Benin's presidents have sought to address these problems reveals that executive rotations are frequently related to leaders' concerns about controlling access to state resources.

Although the executive was generally more stable during the 1990s and early 2000s than since President Boni Yayi took office in 2006, incipient signs of executive instability were evident in ministerial shuffles during President Soglo's one term in office from 1991 through 1996. Following Soglo's first cabinet reshuffle in 1993, fifteen members of the Renewal coalition (*le Renouveau*) in the National Assembly renounced their support for Soglo, alleging that he was excluding the legislature from decision-making processes and engaging in "the solitary exercise of power."[36] It was around this time that Soglo's wife, Rosine Soglo, intensified her efforts to build the RB party into an organization where loyalty to the president, and to the Soglo family more generally, went without question.[37] Amidst an increasingly "hostile" National Assembly and a generally "unfavorable atmosphere,"[38] the Soglos became more "authoritarian" in their leadership styles both in government and in the party. This meant, among other things, "keeping the upper hand" over the party's finances, much of which were drawn from the Soglo's family wealth and foreign connections.[39] It also meant frequent rotations among party officers, often at the whim of Rosine Soglo:

From then on, these leaders [in the RB] became hostages, her clients. When she no longer needs them, she separates them or puts them in positions so uncomfortable that they have to resign. Her behavior and her political methods frustrate the ego of many politicians or educated party activists in a social logic that does not grant such a margin of maneuver.[40]

Initially, these loyalty-driven political machinations, although they did lead to proliferation and regionalization of Benin's parties,[41] did not translate directly into instability in the executive cabinet. Soglo refused to conduct politics through the division and distribution of the

---

[36] These claims were disputed since Soglo had apparently consulted the legislature prior to the September 1993 cabinet reshuffle. See Banks and Muller (1998: 93).

[37] For an in-depth account of Rosine Soglo's party-building efforts, see Tozzo (2004).

[38] Gazibo (2005: 178).

[39] At the outset of her party-building efforts, Rosine Soglo went to Ivorian President Felix Houpouet-Boigny, a close friend of her father's, to help with financing. See "Benin: les Soglo, histoire d'une dynastie énigmatique," Jeune Afrique, September 22, 2016.

[40] Tozzo (2004: 86).

[41] Banégas (2003).

"national pie" that many saw as necessary to maintain power.[42] This refusal to engage in patronage politics was evident in Soglo's second ministerial reshuffle, which came following the 1995 legislative elections.[43] During this reshuffle, Soglo maintained a significant technocratic and RB presence, with only five political ministers who were not members of the RB.

The first government appointed by President Kérékou upon his return to power in 1996 maintained the technocratic style established by Soglo in what Richard Banégas calls, "an overall trend towards the 'multiliateralization' of external assistance after the transition to multi-partyism."[44] Specifically, many of the ministers and their *directeurs du cabinet* (DC)[45] came from backgrounds in institutions such as the World Bank, the Food and Agriculture Organization (FAO), the International Fund for Agricultural Development (IFAD), and the African Development Bank (ADB). Leaders saw these individuals as most capable of rectifying Benin's economic problems. For both Soglo and Kérékou, however, their initial technocratic approaches were insufficient to manage the increasingly crowded political landscape. In short, to the extent that the selection of technocratic ministers undermined their ability to manage an increasingly fluid political landscape, both Soglo and Kérékou faced problems characteristic of adverse selection.

Although Soglo had his wife to manage the RB's politics somewhat separately from government, Kérékou was more inclined to use minister shuffles - "the line of action that had allowed him to establish his stability for seventeen years."[46] This response became apparent when, in 1998, Kérékou's supporting coalition from the 1996 election fell apart. Most notably, Prime Minister Adrien Houngbedji of the PRD resigned his post over dissatisfaction with his exclusion from the budget.[47] Kérékou proceeded to undertake the largest cabinet reshuffle of the multi-party era. He abolished the position of prime minister and placed one of the closest members of his inner circle from the PRPB period, Pierre Osho, in the senior-most role in government. He named thirteen new ministers representing seven parties, but with support of only about one-quarter of

---

[42] Banégas (2003: 224).

[43] In this election, the presidential coalition won thirty-two of eighty-three seats, twenty of which were won by RB candidates. No single opposition party or coalition won more than nineteen seats.

[44] Banégas (2003: 232). The term "multilateralization" refers to Benin's reliance on international donors, especially the IMF, to maintain fiscal and economic stability.

[45] Equivalent to chiefs of staff.

[46] Banégas (2003: 233).

[47] Maher (2004): 772.

the National Assembly. It was therefore not a desire for legislative votes that drove this reshuffle, but rather a concern with the preservation of the regional basis of the coalition and a concern that technocrats in government could become political rivals.[48] Kérékou was able to replace the support from Houngbedji and his PRD with millionaire Sefou Fagbohou from the *Mouvement africain pour la développement et le progrés* (MADEP) party. The cost of this political support, as Chaisty et al. (2018) explain, was the "outsourcing" of the foreign affairs portfolio to MADEP stalwart Kolawole Antoine Idji.

In March 2005, late in his second term, Kérékou again reshuffled his government, removing 2006 presidential contender and prime minister, Bruno Amoussou and foreign minister, Rogatien Biaou – both of whom appeared to have stood in the way of Kérékou's alleged efforts to delay the upcoming election in order to hold onto power. Kérékou also brought in a hardliner from the PRPB regime, Martin Azonhiho as defense minister, after Pierre Osho resigned over Kérékou's efforts to stall the 2006 election, which did not, in any case, ever come to fruition.[49]

Cabinet rotations escalated during President Boni Yayi's two terms in office from 2006 through 2016, when the rate of both government reshuffles and individual dismissals rose substantially. From 1991 through 2006 (when Boni Yayi took office) the average number of days a minister held office was 862, dropping to 591 during Boni Yayi's presidency. Ministerial rotations also became less predictable, with increasingly frequent dismissals of one or two ministers at a time, rather than periodic government reshuffles. Boni Yayi even replaced six ministers in March 2016, just three weeks before he would leave office at the end of his second term.

Like Kérékou, Boni Yayi used these rotations not only to attract political support but also to maintain some semblance of control in what, by many accounts, became an increasingly chaotic political scene. The need for control seemed especially pronounced with technocratic ministers, whom Boni Yayi often suspected of not acting in line with his interests. In one instance, he appointed Collette Houeto, a highly accomplished figure in education, as the minister of primary and secondary education. When Houeto sought to bring in a past colleague as her chief of staff in the ministry, also a highly respected expert in education, Boni Yayi expressed public disapproval of this choice and fired her after only four months as minister. According to one report, the dismissal was not

[48] Banégas (2003).
[49] "Twilight of the Chameleon," Africa Confidential, March 31, 2006.

for incompetence, but for "independence of mind and firmness." At the heart of the issue, according to one journalist, was that both Houeto and her chief of staff had been closely affiliated with educational programs of the Catholic Church which, in Boni Yayi's own words, "threatened the cohesion of the government,"[50] in what was likely a reference to his own evangelical background and that of several of his closest ministers. Indeed, throughout Boni Yayi's time in office, the Catholic Church became increasingly vocal in speaking out against Boni Yayi's "excesses of power."[51]

In another case, a former minister with a technocratic background explained that he was removed from his post when he declined to support Boni Yayi's bid for a third term, detailing how Boni Yayi had spent "twenty or thirty minutes in the weekly council of ministers meeting berating me to send a signal to others." While this individual noted that Boni Yayi's approach to management was somewhat different than preceding presidents, he explained that ministers have typically had some autonomy to do what they like with their ministries, but that this had sometimes "become a political problem for previous presidents."[52] Describing this agency problem, one political operative from Boni Yayi's FCBE party noted, "Nicephore [Soglo] lost the [1996] election because his government was too technocratic. The Chief of State wants competence, but he will not make the same errors."[53]

As these cases suggest, technocrats tend to be particularly vulnerable in their positions as they struggle to navigate the political environment. Those with no political experience average 632 days in their posts, compared to 740 among those with some kind of political experience. While this may, on its face, seem confusing, it is important to remember that Benin's presidents tend to place technocrats in positions with significant power over resources and extraction, whereas those with more overt political backgrounds are kept away from these positions. As an official at the Ministry of Foreign Affairs explained,

Presidents have wanted to surround themselves with knowledgeable people and to place them in important positions. That is their first concern. The technocrat[ic ministers] tend to promote more people with knowledge, so that is good. But there are political constraints for the technocrat[ic ministers] once they are in their posts. They need to legitimate themselves. They send men to the National Assembly [to build political connections]. The ministers are obliged to become

---

[50] Cotonou, March 18, 2014. See also, *Panapress*, July 16, 2006.
[51] Banégas (2014: 249).
[52] Author interview, Cotonou, June 22, 2018.
[53] Author interview, Cotonou, March 15, 2014.

more political, and then they start to profit politically from the ministry. But they also have to be very careful...in the ways they attract financial resources.[54]

The need for technocratic ministers to "be very careful" under the watchful eye of a politically insecure president underscores the problems leaders face in appointing technocrats and the reasons why they rotate them so frequently.

In addition to these issues surrounding the political inexperience of technocrats, President Boni Yayi also encountered significant problems with (apparent) political allies and financiers, particularly following his political and very public falling out in 2012 with Patrice Talon. The most visible of executive changes resulting from this frayed relationship was Boni Yayi's August 2013 dissolution of government, described briefly at the outset of this chapter. As has been recounted briefly in Chapter 4, cotton-magnate (and later president) Talon had been one of Boni Yayi's main political financiers in his 2006 and 2011 election victories. Boni Yayi had reportedly sought financial support from Talon in 2013 to help him mount an effort to amend the constitution and allow him to run for a third term. In Talon's words,

The president asked me to activate deputies to reform the Constitution to allow him to stand for re-election in 2016. I refused to dabble in this scheme. He then threatened to annihilate me by evoking the example of Mikhail Khodorkovski [former Russian oil tycoon, formerly close to the Kremlin and fallen into disgrace]...Here we are, he wants to eliminate me.[55]

The tension between the two deepened when, in October 2012, Boni Yayi accused Talon of having paid three of Boni Yayi's close associates, including his niece and bodyguard, to poison him in what Boni Yayi characterized as an attempted coup. Talon fled to France to avoid prosecution, but Boni Yayi continued to "hunt" potential accomplices throughout 2013 and early 2014.[56] The dismissal of the entire cabinet in 2013 was seen as a move to "reassert his authority over the government" and as "a pre-emptive move" against then-prime minister and a close associate of Talon, Pascal Irénée Koupaki, who was planning to resign his post in preparation to run for president in the 2015 elections.[57]

[54] Author interview, Cotonou, July 3, 2018.
[55] "Benin: Patrice Talon, itinéraire d'un ambitieux devenu paria," Jeune Afrique, November 20, 2012.
[56] "The Downward Slide of a Paranoid State," Africa Intelligence, March 6, 2013.
[57] "President Dismisses Cabinet," Economist Intelligence Unit, August 9, 2013.

The dismissal of the entire cabinet was even more disruptive to government than the many previous reshuffles. André Quenum, the publisher of Benin's main Catholic newspaper, *La Croix*, described the event as "a big shock" that was different from previous changes because "he suspended the whole government all of a sudden [and] nobody could see it coming, not even the ministers themselves. You woke up one day and then you just hear that you're not a minister anymore."[58] As another account noted, "the seemingly drastic measure of dismissing the cabinet [reinforced] the perception that the president is losing sight of his political agenda."[59]

Boni Yayi, however, "could not cut off all heads."[60] Those who survived were a small number of FCBE stalwarts or close personal associates of the president. For example, Marcel de Souza, the president's brother-in-law and former colleague from the BCEAO was retained. So too was one of Boni Yayi's "brothers in Christ," Martial Sounton, who was moved into the Ministry of Public Service. Komi Koutché, who had worked on Boni Yayi's election campaign in 2006, had become a particularly militant member of the FCBE, and was described as a "symbol of prevarication prevailing in [Boni Yayi's] system," was appointed Minister of Finance.[61]

These FCBE and personal loyalists were appointed alongside a number of unknown technocrats, who one journalist described as "those with whom Yayi did not need to worry himself."[62] According to Quénum, these appointees were "unknown" to Beninese people, causing consternation about their potential to act in their positions:

you wonder why this person is in this position. We wonder how good they will be at the position...you cannot call them senior politicians...we are going further and further toward collaborators, people around the president, who are not really influential people, who cannot really stand up to him, and then give their opinion and give a valuable contribution and that's not a good feeling to have.[63]

---

[58] Thomas Hubert, "President Yayi Boni dissolves his government - understanding the situation in Benin," interview with André Quenum, Radio France International, August 13, 2013.

[59] "President Dismisses Cabinet," Economist Intelligence Unit, August 9, 2013.

[60] "Bénin: les raisons d'un remaniement gouvernemental," Jeune Afrique, August 12, 2013.

[61] Raoul Mbog, "Bénin: pourquoi Lionel Zinsou a perdu," Le Monde, March 21, 2016.

[62] Author interview, "La Nation," November 18, 2013.

[63] Thomas Hubert, "President Yayi Boni dissolves his government - understanding the situation in Benin," interview with André Quenum, Radio France International, August 13, 2013.

A former minister echoed this sentiment: "[the president] appoints professional ministers but then, if they do not offer complete support to him, he wants them sacked urgently. That is what happened [with me]."[64] This commentary underscores the way that executive instability in Benin tends to intensify what might otherwise be routine agency problems, helping to explain why executive institutions in Benin have become increasingly unstable over time. As the political landscape has become less and less centered around the two big power players of Soglo and Kérékou, so too have the party networks and relationships that help to avert agency problems. The increasing fluidity of political coalitions and parties has effectively raised the stakes of granting access and control over extraction opportunities, personnel, and platforms to potential political opponents, hence the rising rate of portfolio turnover and shorter stays in office for many ministers.

More generally, presidents' concerns about controlling ministers have to do with, as one officer at the Ministry of Public Service put it, "ensuring that the ministry does not become the domain of another politician."[65] Ministers typically have the ability to recommend political appointees, hire contractual agents, and propose promotions, all of which grants them control of resources that could be used for political finance.[66] As one academic observer explained, depending on the budget and revenue-generating activities of the ministry, the ministers may or may not control significant resources. In addition, she noted, they also get the opportunity to be close to decision-making and to enjoy the large amount of prestige that comes with the post.[67]

6.3.2   Instability, Division, and Impaired Policy Performance

Both the frequency and nature of portfolio turnover in Benin impair government cohesion and undermine the ability of the government to plan, coordinate, and implement public policies. Two particular dynamics stand out in this regard. First, the mixture of loyalists, technocrats, new coalition allies, and opposition members generates a cabinet full of divergent preferences that lead not only to instability but also to interest polarization. Second, the frequent rotation of ministers creates an

---

[64] Author interview, Cotonou, June 24, 2018.

[65] Author interview, Cotonou, July 4, 2018.

[66] These areas of control over human resources in the ministry were cited by several interviewees. I am not, however, aware of any formal statutes that outline these powers of ministers.

[67] Author interview, Cotonou, July 3, 2018.

Table 6.2 *Political diversity in Benin's executive*

Term	Technocrat	Loyal Pol.	New Pol. Ally	Opposition	HHI
Soglo	0.26	0.30	0.030	0.13	0.27
Kérékou 1	0.17	0.15	0.32	0.37	0.29
Kérékou 2	0.36	0.17	0.36	0.11	0.30
Yayi 1	0.30	0.21	0.40	0.09	0.31
Yayi 2	0.36	0.30	0.28	0.06	0.30
Talon	0.43	0.19	0.38	0.0	0.37

Proportion of appointees with specified political background. The Herfindahl-Hirschman Index was calculated as the sum of squared proportions. Source: Author's data compilation.

environment in which competition and uncertainty among executive personnel undermine trust and coordination among ministers. Exploring these two dynamics in this section, I show how they are intensified under conditions of coercive extraction and illustrate their implications for the state's public policy performance.

Political Diversity and Division

As the previous chapter explains, Benin's cabinets tend to be comprised of a mix of personal loyalists, technocrats, new coalition allies, and opposition members. This diverse composition implies unaligned interests leading to the problems of instability described earlier. It also undermines cohesion as ministers' interests are unlikely to align with those of the president or with each other.

To measure the diversity of political interests across presidential terms (and for the purposes of comparing with Ghana later in the chapter), I calculate the Herfindahl–Hirschman Index (HHI) for the distribution of political backgrounds among ministers during each presidential term (Table 6.2).[68] Higher HHI scores indicate greater concentration of backgrounds and, presumably, interests. Although Benin's cabinets have become, overall, slightly more politically concentrated over time, the composition of the cabinets remains highly diverse in terms of backgrounds and interests. Opposition members comprise a small percentage across just about all presidential administrations. Comparable statistics for Ghana, provided later in the chapter, show considerably lower levels of political diversity among ministers compared to Benin.

This political diversity results in what one former presidential staff member described as the presence of several different "circles of power"

---

[68] HHI is commonly used to measure firm concentration in markets. It has also been used to measure party system fragmentation.

in the executive. During President Boni Yayi's time in office, for instance, these "circles" typically included, (1) associates of then-businessman Patrice Talon, (2) several "brothers in Christ" associated with Boni Yayi's evangelical church, and (3) a number of FCBE militants in charge of key sectors such as transportation. Technocrats, civil society members, and "regional representatives," many of whom are "brought in for political viability," tend not to be well connected with each other, or with the other groups present in the cabinet, making it "a challenge for them to work toward their objectives"[69]

The presence of these different circles of power often lead to the divergence of minister interests in ways that can make it especially difficult for the president to advance his or her objectives, whether those objectives are more distributive and political in nature or more public or technocratic. Philip Keefer, for example, has described the Beninese government's inability to make credible policy commitments as "extreme" for sub-Saharan Africa, noting that "every presidential initiative requires a fresh round of lobbying, including of members of [the president's] own coalition."[70]

Ministers themselves have also lamented a deficit of interest in, or commitment to, the president's agenda. According to one former minister of education under President Kérékou, Jijoho Padonou, divisions among the governing coalition quickly devolved in ways that undermined policy advancement. He explains,

for the 10 years in power by General Mathieu Kérékou in the era of democratic renewal, I would say that politicians did not help the man...We met around Mathieu Kérékou with other political parties to bring him to power. But very quickly, the leaders of these parties did not want to support the Head of State with their ideas for development...While some are trying to get closer to [the president] to help him better develop this country, others are trying to stop them.[71]

Similar problems were evident, or at least publicized as such, during President Boni Yayi's time in office. According to one former minister, Yayi would "spend time in each cabinet meeting talking about the agents he saw as menaces" to his agenda, often focusing specifically on "events that happened that he perceived as the fault of the minister."[72]

---

[69] Author interview, Cotonou, June 27, 2018.
[70] Keefer (2008: 11).
[71] Karim O. Anonrin, "Entretien avec un ancien ministre de l'éducation nationale," La Fraternité, November 6, 2015.
[72] Author interview, Cotonou, June 20, 2018.

Equally if not more debilitating to the executive is the competition that takes place among ministers in office. In this sense, executive cohesion suffers because of the "hierarchy of ministries" discussed in Chapter 5.[73] Ministries are highly unequal in their access to resources, both in terms of materials with which to fulfill official tasks, the salaries and allowances paid to public service employees, and the frequency with which one has "an occasion to eat." Ministers, particularly those with political ambitions, look to "move up" to higher-powered institutions. By many accounts, their ability to do so depends on the support – financial and political – that they provide to the president. In one particularly vivid example, in March 2016, just three weeks before his second and final term would come to an end, Boni Yayi "promoted" three ministers and terminated six others because they had "been weak in their support" for Boni Yayi's preferred successor, then-prime minister, Lionel Zinsou.[74] The "surprising" timing of the reshuffle underscores how political maneuvers largely overshadow governing concerns in the "game" of cabinet rotations.[75]

This discord among ministers is to some extent a product of the president's strong desire for loyalty and a willingness, that was increasingly apparent since 2001, to dismiss those they suspect of being disloyal. A former minister under President Boni Yayi explained that he was repeatedly prevented from advancing policy because of the difficulty of obtaining the necessary cooperation from other ministers, even for relatively simple tasks and transactions such as asking the Ministry of Environment to clear land before its sale as part of an international transaction to which the president and other ministers had already agreed.[76]

In another example, describing his efforts to reduce teacher absence by equipping teachers in remote areas with motorcycles, Jijoho Padonou explained that this effort had been undermined by other (unnamed) ministers who "branded the initiative as an effort to turn teachers into *zemidjans*" (motorcycle taxi drivers). One former minister noted, "loyalty was everything" to the president, and "to advance one's position, some ministers will accuse the other ministers of infidelity."[77] In other words, the need for ministers to demonstrate loyalty to the president generates incentives for others to undercut their fellow ministers, generating issues of both trust and coordination among executive actors.

---

[73] Author interview, Ministry of Transportation and Infrastructure, Cotonou, June 28, 2018.
[74] Africa Intelligence, March 17, 2016.
[75] "Présidentielle au Bénin: Ajavon y croit encore, Yayi remanie son gouvernement," Jeune Afrique, March 12, 2016.
[76] Author interview, Cotonou, July 2, 2018.
[77] Author interview, Cotonou, November 20, 2013.

Implications for state performance

That instability and division in Benin's cabinets undermine the performance of the state's executive institutions is evident in a number of different ways. The combination of low levels of political cohesion and high potential of dismissal (particularly during Boni Yayi's presidency), has created a governing environment in which ministers have struggled to move forward with policy initiatives in their sectors, to resolve problems related to strikes or other social upheavals, and to coordinate actions across ministries. Although these issues are not universal throughout government or over time, they are "perpetually visible" across a number of policy sectors, even those that tend to be regarded as relatively well-performing.[78]

One very apparent impact of executive fragmentation is the inability of Beninese ministers to gain prominence and attention for the country's programs on the global stage, where countries can attract greater levels of financing and donor support. This was the case with the minister of health who had served under both Kérékou and Yayi, Dorothée Kindé Gazard. Gazard, according to one former official in the Ministry of Health, is among the most competent and respected of any minister that has served in the government of Benin, with strong connections to the international community that empower her to accomplish goals even when the government does not provide support.[79] When Gazard sought to become the regional director for Africa of the World Health Organization, a position that could elevate Benin's health programs and financing, it was lack of support from Yayi that ultimately foiled her opportunity to be selected for the post. Citing her close connection to National Assembly President Malthurin Coffi Nago and the fact that she never became a *militant* (activist) for the ruling FCBE party, Yayi took a number of steps to undermine her efforts to occupy this strategic position.[80]

These unproductive dynamics are also evident in specific policy areas. In the health sector, for example, one account of a health technology program noted, "the unwillingness and self-interested attitudes of policy makers to engage in problems, and the high degree of politicization influencing public sector decision-making." The report noted specifically, "that power positions in [health technology management] are complex, and that a lack of political will had kept some previous policies

[78] Author interview, United States Agency for International Development, Cotonou, November 13, 2013.
[79] Author interview, Cotonou, November 13, 2013.
[80] La Nouvelle Tribune, November 6, 2014. The same article alleges that Yayi sabotaged chances for then-minister of foreign affairs, Jean-Marie Ehouzou, to become the head of the Economic Community of West African States.

from being implemented."[81] Likewise, a study of the telecommunications sector concluded that, despite significant investments of resources and external assistance, "very little progress has been made in terms of policy, legislation and regulation" and that "no lessons appear to have been learned" among executive actors.[82]

Of course, intra-executive dynamics are not the only reason for Benin's comparatively weak record of governance. Previous accounts have also emphasized the fragile nature of legislative-executive relations, the intensity of social tensions and protest, and the incoherence and uncertainty of donor involvement.[83] What this discussion highlights, however, is that the politics of extraction loom large behind the challenges elites face in pursuit of their policy goals. As Benin's political party landscape has become increasingly crowded and unstable since the democratic renewal, incumbent leaders have intensified their use of the executive cabinet both to manage their political support and defend politically valuable opportunities for extraction. Technocrats interested in policy advancement have remained in government in part because it is politically expedient and keeps valuable resources out of the hands of more politically ambitious individuals. But their presence also complicates executive dynamics in ways that are not always very productive for policy advancement.

Such issues are by no means unique to Benin's executives. As I describe in the next section, internal competition within Ghana's parties does, at times, spill over into government business in ways that undermine productivity. But Benin's highly fluid political landscape in which a minister's access to extraction poses existential political risks to the incumbent leads to an especially disruptive intensity of intra-executive competition in Benin.

6.4   Stability and Cohesion Among Internal Party Divisions in Ghana

Compared to their Beninese counterparts, leaders in Ghana encounter relatively few problems related to adverse selection and, only during isolated periods of intraparty tension, do they tend to encounter problems related to unaligned interests. In short, by appointing party loyalists – many of whom participate in the party's extraction efforts – Ghana's leaders effectively minimize agency problems that lead to instability. As

[81] Houngbo et al. (2017: 16).
[82] Sutherland (2011: 63).
[83] Magnusson (2001); Bierschenk (2009, 2014).

such, their executive bodies are more cohesive and, often, more effective in the pursuit of both political and policy goals.

As explained in the previous two chapters, by the time ministers in Ghana receive their appointments, they have often already proven themselves as party loyalists and effective fundraisers. Their reputations for party loyalty often come from their histories within the parties, particularly among those who served in Rawlings' PNDC regime (1981–1992) or those who stayed loyal to the predecessor-party movements of the NPP. In other cases, however, those without such long histories in the party demonstrate their loyalty by providing funds or other material support to the party's operations. If individuals have shown they have links to wealthy businesses or other sources of funds, they may be especially likely to receive a ministerial appointment. As such, the combination of well-organized parties and robust private sector networks that gives rise to Ghana's collusive fundraising system minimizes the chances that presidents encounter serious agency problems in the management of their executive personnel.

6.4.1 Understanding Minister Rotations in Ghana

Ghana's ministerial portfolios have generally turned over at lower rates than those of Benin (see Figure 6.1). The tendency of Ghana's presidents to appoint long-standing party leaders to ministerial posts means that rotations are only in rare cases driven by concerns about ministers' commitment or loyalty to the party. Instead, ministerial rotations in Ghana tend to reflect three underlying dynamics: (1) the need to raise funds or access resources for the party's future electoral contests; (2) a president's concern about delivering on campaign promises; or (3) intraparty competition, usually surrounding the succession of a second-term president.[84] In a few isolated cases, ministerial rotations have also occurred in the wake of extraction efforts gone awry, leading to the dismissal or rotation of ministers in order to save face for the party.

In a number of high-profile reshuffles, Ghana's presidents have rotated ministers to improve access to and use of state resources for the party's advantage. One of the first of these rotations was the resignation of Minister of Finance and Economic Planning Kwesi Botchwey in August 1995. Concerned about excessive borrowing and spending by the state oil company, the GNPC, Botchwey "stormed out" of Rawlings' government after he was "overruled on a plan for a spending splurge to win the

---

[84] This is not to say that these three types of motivations are not at times present in Benin. They are. But, in general, the concerns about political loyalty discussed in the previous section are far more common in Benin than in Ghana.

1996 elections."[85] Although Botchwey had helped Rawlings to manage and survive the severe fiscal crises of the 1980s and early 1990s, Rawlings reportedly grew frustrated with his inattention to the "political repercussions" of Ghana's structural adjustment programs.[86] Rawlings replaced Botchwey with Kwame Richard Peprah, an engineer with a degree in business from New York University, who was, like Botchwey, one of the architects of Ghana's liberalization program.[87] Unlike Botchwey, however, Peprah was accepting of the party's need to exceed spending limits specified by the reform programs, reflecting what Eboe Hutchful calls a transition from the technocratic approach of the PNDC regime to a greater reliance on party brokers in the administration of economic policy.[88] Lindsay Whitfield explains that, whereas the technocrats had been very focused on coordination with the World Bank and the IMF and the implementation of economic reforms, these new economic policymakers "lacked a strong vision for what policies were to achieve."[89] After the NPP took over in 2001, Peprah was prosecuted and eventually jailed (along with the former minister of food and agriculture) for his involvement in the so-called Quality Grain case in which officials in the NDC government established a fraudulent company to embezzle money from a state-run rice growing program.[90]

The case of Minister of Justice and Attorney General Martin Amidu, dismissed by President Mills in January 2012, is another instance in which a minister's insufficient attention to the financial needs of the party led to ministerial reshuffling. Amidu sought to vigorously investigate the circumstances surrounding NDC financier Alfred Woyome's fraudulent behavior relating to construction contracts and government payouts to build stadiums for the 2008 Africa Cup of Nations tournament hosted by Ghana. Concerned that Amidu's aggressive approach would expose the involvement of the NDC and key government operatives, Mills dismissed Amidu citing insubordination and "misconduct."[91] Indeed, shortly after Amidu's dismissal, Betty Mould Iddrisu, who had served as minister of justice and attorney general at the time that the questionable payments

---

[85] "It's the contract election," Africa Confidential, March 4, 2016.

[86] Green (1995: 583) and Abdulai and Mohan (2019).

[87] Moses Asaga quoted in Agyeman-Duah et al. (2008: 110). Asaga served as Deputy Minister of Finance from 1997 to 2000.

[88] Hutchful (2002).

[89] Whitfield (2018: 110).

[90] Reported widely in the Ghanaian and international media. The case docket was published as "The Quality Grain Case Docket 35878," Ghana General News, May 1, 2003.

[91] "Who Paid Whom for What?" Africa Confidential, February 17, 2012. In press interviews later on, Amidu claims that he amicably resigned from office.

were made to Woyome, resigned her post in government as then-minister of education. One report deemed the government's response to the Woyome affair as "defensive and cackhanded, if not outright dishonest" and "a nightmare" for Mills' 2012 reelection campaign.[92]

On the NPP side, President John Kufuor was highly reluctant to dismiss Minister of Roads and Transport Richard Anane after he was found guilty of corruption by Ghana's Commission on Human Rights and Administrative Justice (CHRAJ). One plausible reason for this reluctance is that, during his time as minister, he oversaw some seven large road contracts totaling over $120 million in value.[93] One particularly lucrative deal for the NPP involved a partnership with a US-based consortium to support Ghana International Airlines. Regional party chairmen held a stake in the airline through Anane's US-based consulting firm.[94] It was alleged in particular that Anane misled the Cabinet "into approving a partnership with Ghana International Airlines at a time when Ghana International Airlines did not exist."[95] Anane, described as "apparently unsackable,"[96] left his post after the Commission on Human Rights and Administrative Justice (CHRAJ) had recommended his dismissal, but Kufuor re-appointed him one year later after the Supreme Court effectively cleared him of any wrongdoing.[97]

As the cases of Anane and Mould Iddrisu suggest, dismissals or resignations sometimes occur when party or personal extraction efforts become exposed to the public. Such was the case in 1998 when President Rawlings fired minister of works and housing Kobina Fosu after a government inquiry found him responsible for paying out large sums of money to contractors who did not provide any services.[98] More recently, in 2015, minister of transport Dzifa Attivor resigned after having overseen the award of a contract to an NDC-affiliated business, Smarttys Productions, for a re-branding of the ministry's Metropolitan Mass

---

[92] "Who Paid Whom for What?" Africa Confidential, February 17, 2012.

[93] "Money Go Round," Africa Confidential, December 16, 2005.

[94] Whitfield (2018: 121) drawing on Africa Confidential 2006 Vol. 47, No. 9, p. 8 and *Democracy Watch* 2006 Vol. 7, No. 1, pp. 1–2.

[95] "Anane Others For Court Over Ghana International Airlines," Ghana General News, March 25, 2010.

[96] "Money Go Round," Africa Confidential, December 16, 2005.

[97] On the CHRAJ decision, see Commission on Human Rights and Administrative Justice, File No. 5177/2005: "In the Matter of Investigations into Allegations of Corruption, Conflict of Interest and Abuse of Power Against Hon. Dr. Richard Anane (MP) and Minister for Road Transport." On the Supreme Court decision, see Republic vs. High Court (Fast Track Division) Accra; Ex Parte Commission on Human Rights and Administrative Justice (Richard Anane Interested Party) [2007–2008] SCGLR 213.

[98] Oelbaum (2002: 310).

Transit buses. The rebranding campaign included printing large pho-
tos of Ghana's presidents (Rawlings, Kufuor, Mills, and Mahama) on
the side of 116 buses, with only Mahama's photo appearing in color.[99]

The rotation of ministers in Ghana is also driven by presidents' desires
to improve the performance of their governments, particularly when it
comes to delivering on campaign promises. In some cases this practice
reflects leaders encountering problems of adverse selection, but it is also
reflective of an effort to inject new energy into a stale administration.
In a study of minister reshuffles in Ghana, Joseph Ayee explains that it
is common in Ghana for under-performing ministers to be demoted or
dismissed and for high-performing ministers and deputy ministers to be
promoted. In these instances, presidents have sought to "correct error"
or to "deal with perceived ministerial incompetence."[100] A major government reshuffle in 2003, for example, helped to correct some "initial
slips" in the NPP's governing performance.[101] Among those reshuffled were Albert Kan-Dapaah, minister of energy, who had recently
announced a very unpopular 92 percent increase in fuel prices as well
as increases in electricity tariffs. Minister Felix Owusu-Agyepong, who
had served as minister of communications lost his portfolio while under
fire for having broken a contract with Telekom Malaysia.[102] In a press
release about the 2003 reshuffle, the president's spokesperson noted that
the president was "in a good position to assess the performance and
inputs of the various members of the team and re-position them to bring
more efficiency and increase the pace of his government."[103]

Government performance appeared as a major motivation for President Mahama's reshuffle in July 2014. The government was facing
falling currency values and rising inflation, impending debt problems,
and a series of labor protests popularly dubbed the "Occupy Ghana"
protests. Although President Mahama left the energy and finance ministers in place despite worrying trends in these sectors, he brought in
a number of individuals with strong track records in previous NDC
governments, including the "urbane" Ekwow Spio-Gabrah as minister
of trade and industry and Benjamin Kunbuor as minister of defence.
In 1998, Rawlings had also rotated Spio-Gabrah from the Ministry of

---

[99] This happened approximately one year before the 2016 election. Reported in the *Daily
      Graphic*, December 23, 2015.
[100] Ayee (2013: 12).
[101] Frempong (2007: 158).
[102] "Musical Chairs," Africa Confidential, May 16, 2003.
[103] "Government Names New Cabinet," Ghana News Agency, April 1, 2003.

Communications to the Ministry of Education to address mounting student unrest and widespread dissatisfaction with school quality.[104]

Presidents in Ghana have also been known to rotate ministers as a way to manage intraparty competition, especially competition surrounding who will become the party's next presidential candidate. The first of these episodes occurred in November 1998, approximately two years into Rawlings' second and final term in office. As George Bob-Milliar described, two main factions emerged amidst questions about who would run for president on the NDC ticket in the 2000 elections. One faction remained staunchly committed to the president while another, reformist, faction sought to build the party's future around individuals not closely associated with Rawlings. As these fault lines became increasingly apparent in 1998 and 1999, Rawlings not only unilaterally acted to declare that then-Vice President Mills would succeed Rawlings as the party's presidential nominee,[105] but he also "purged" reformist sympathizers from the cabinet and other government positions. Taking their places were long-standing allies of Rawlings from the PNDC regime such as J. H. Owusu Acheampong, Cletus Avoka and Samuel Nuama-Donkor.[106]

During his second term in office, President Kufuor took similar actions to manage internal party competition over the question of who would succeed him on the NPP ticket in the 2000 election. Not only did the familiar divides between the Busia (Kufuor) and Danquah (Akufo-Addo) factions resurface but, as early as 2003, Kufuor had been backing his close friend and political ally Alan Kyeremanten.[107] Kufuor moved another close factional ally, Papa Owusu Ankomah, from the parliamentary affairs portfolio to become minister of interior and, later, minister of trade and industry. As Arthur Kennedy explains, these moves reflected Kufuor's "covert" efforts to support Kyerematen over Akufo-Addo in particular.[108] As the primary race heated up in 2007, Kufuor forced the resignation of all candidates – seven in total – who held ministerial posts during that time.

To summarize, although problems related to adverse selection and unaligned interests are to some extent evident in the retention, dismissal, and rotation of ministers in Ghana, these are not the most important

[104] "Who Comes Next?" Africa Confidential, November 20, 1998.
[105] This event is commonly known as the infamous "Swedru Declaration" of June 1998.
[106] Bob-Milliar (2012a). Although these moves helped to settle the succession question, as I discuss below, they did not necessarily stifle party members' demands for reform and democratization of the party structures.
[107] Bob-Milliar (2012a: 582); Whitfield (2018: 113).
[108] Kennedy (2009: 16).

dynamics at play. Ghana's presidents often rotate ministers to improve extraction, inject new energy into government, and manage intraparty competition. These motivations have generally required less frequent and less disruptive portfolio changes than those observed in Benin.

6.4.2   Turnovers, Executive Cohesion, and Policy Performance

Not only has Ghana's executive experienced significantly lower levels of instability than Benin's, Ghana's portfolio turnovers are also less detrimental to government cohesion are those in Benin. As described in the previous sub-section, executive turnovers are frequently geared toward improving the government's ability to implement policy or campaign promises rather than managing potentially disloyal ministers. These types of reshuffles are more likely to *alleviate* concerns among ministers remaining in office than they are likely to *exacerbate* them. As such, the rotation and dismissal of ministers often play a stabilizing – rather than destabilizing – role in the state's executive institutions. As I describe in this section, one of the reasons why minister shuffles have this stabilizing effect is because of the high levels of cohesion among executive actors – a product of Ghana's collusive extraction system and the politicized selection of ministers described in the previous chapter.

As seen in Table 6.3, the concentration of long-standing party members in the executive, measured by the HHI in the far right column, is approximately double the comparable figures in Benin, which are presented earlier in Table 6.2. These high levels of political cohesion in Ghana's executive enable the government to pursue political and policy goals simultaneously. In other words, the appointment and rotation of political loyalists not only helps leaders to solve their delegation problems surrounding extraction but also facilitates coordinated action in pursuit of policy goals.

In Ghana, because the two parties have strong and distinct social roots, political cohesion implies a certain degree of social and professional cohesion. The NDC's traditional bases of support from lower-income and agricultural communities means that many of their leaders have professional roots in the public service, military, or academia, especially in left-leaning intellectual circles.[109] At various times over the course of the Rawlings, Mills, and Mahama presidencies, these groups became

---

[109] Nugent's (2007) detailed account of the workings of the People's National Democratic Congress (PNDC) government in the 1980s is particularly instructive for understanding the composition of the NDC's elite coalition. Nugent describes three main groups: "a confident coterie of technocrats...[with] a history of left-wing affiliations," "neo-traditionalists" consisting of "elite groupings that had been under-represented," and

Table 6.3 *Political diversity in Ghana's executive*

Term	Technocrat	Loyal Pol.	New Pol. Ally	Opposition	HHI
Rawlings 1	0.17	0.75	0.04	0.04	0.59
Rawlings 2	0.13	0.84	0.03	0.0	0.72
Kufuor 1	0.10	0.75	0.03	0.05	0.57
Kufuor 2	0.10	0.78	0.04	0.04	0.63
Mills	0.13	0.83	0.02	0.02	0.71
Mahama	0.26	0.72	0.02	0.00	0.59

Proportion of appointees with specified political background. The Hirschman-Herfindahl Index was calculated as the sum of squared proportions. Source: Author's data compilation.

resurgent in government. Whereas the technocrats had dominated policy decisions throughout much of the 1980s,[110] the revolutionary militants and those most faithful to the NDC's political project became more prominent in the mid-1990s. For example, at the outset of his presidential term in 2013, Mahama appointed three PNDC/NDC stalwarts – Alban Bagbin, Cletus Avoka, and E. T. Mensah – as ministers of state at the presidency to focus on the development and implementation of presidential priority projects.

As discussed in Chapter 3, the traditional social and elite bases of the parties are somewhat different from each other, with the NDC latching on to the Nkrumahist, leftist tradition and the NPP networked with the Danquah and Busia political traditions, as well as the wealthier, business-oriented segments of the Akan population. Kufuor, himself an Ashanti lawyer and businessman, elevated the Ashanti segments of this coalition in particular throughout his government, providing them with the "lion's share" of ministerial portfolios.[111]

These social bases of the NDC and NPP political coalitions are to some extent evident in the data on executive composition. Whereas NDC ministers have significant professional experience in the public, NPP's ministers are much more likely to have private sector backgrounds. The percentage of ministers who had previously served in government positions was particularly high in the Rawlings and Mahama governments at around 80–90 percent. The percentage of ministers with professional experience in the private sector was as high as 82 percent

the "cadres who staffed the 'revolutionary organs'" including members of the military, the DWM, and the what was known as the National Mobilization Program.

[110] Nugent (2007: 129).

[111] Bob-Milliar (2012a: 581).

in John Kufuor's NPP government, reflecting the business roots of the party.

The shared political and professional backgrounds within Ghana's governments help to facilitate policy coordination in ways that are not typically visible in Benin. In the development of Ghana's National Health Insurance Program (NHIP) in the early 2000s, for example, political cohesion proved important for both key policy design decisions and their expedient implementation. Design and planning for the program had begun immediately upon President Kufuor's assumption of office in January 2001, with the creation of a health insurance task force overseen by then-Minister of Health Dr. Richard Anane.[112] Major disagreements in policy design between Anane and the task force surfaced early on, leading to "total paralysis" of the task force.[113] Anane, who was both highly qualified as a medical doctor and public health expert and also a longtime member of the NPP, seemed the right person for the job. But as disagreements surrounding policy design were not getting resolved, President Kufuor, in his first major cabinet reshuffle in October 2001, moved Anane to the Ministry of Roads and Transport, while bringing in Dr. Kwaku Afriyie, who had previously been posted at the Ministry of Mines, Lands and Forestry. Afriyie was more tightly woven into Kufuor's inner circle, had made large fortunes in the cocoa industry, and had worked closely by Kufuor's side over the previous eight years.[114]

Over the next several years, Kufuor and Afriyie brought in more of their allies to the process, particularly as the 2004 election was approaching and there was greater and greater pressure to speed the implementation. The technical specialists who staffed the task force early on had been "slower to fully discern the political concerns, climate, influences and policy characteristics, their importance and how to create appropriate space to maneuver to steer policy in the desired technical direction within them."[115] The reorganization resulted in a team that was "cohesive [because] a majority of them knew each other prior to joining the team."[116] This cohesion facilitated the team's pursuit of "a common interest" and a commitment to an ambitious policy design that constituted a major break with the status quo. Despite international donors calling to halt the process due to a range of technical issues,[117] as political associates came to dominate the process of

[112] Agyepong and Adjei (2008) and Kusi-Ampofo et al. (2015) provide in-depth discussions of the task force.
[113] Wireko (2015: 167).
[114] Agyepong and Adjei (2008).
[115] Agyepong and Adjei (2008: 158).
[116] Wireko (2015: 169).
[117] Kusi-Ampofo et al. (2015).

Ghana's NHIP development, the implementation of the program prior to the 2004 elections became both increasingly pressing and increasingly attainable.[118]

One of the main reasons that the re-vamped team was able to more successfully develop the NHIP is that the team was more connected and more responsive to the political concerns of the presidency. The process of engaging key interests to avoid opposition involved significant coordination across Ghana's MDAs, including the Ghana Health Service, the Ministry of Local Government and Rural Development, among others. The task force members, led by Afriyie, briefed the cabinet and the president regularly to maintain high-level support for the direction of the policy. These briefings were "crucial for sustaining the agenda" because some of its members had been apathetic towards the reform.[119]

Of particular concern to political actors was the need to minimize opposition from key constituencies, especially concerning how the program was to be paid for. According to Wireko:

Although it seemed to be quite technical, much of the lesson drawing process had political undertones, involving conscious attempts to avoid opposition from key vested interests. For instance, in response to why the team deducted the workers' contributions to the NHIS from their pension (SSNIT) fund instead of their payroll, as observed in the social insurance nations they visited, Amoh (2013) noted, "we didn't want to stress them up."[120]

Another political concern was ideological in nature, particularly in decisions about whether health insurance would be provided publicly or privately. The NPP's private sector roots rendered a private insurance option important. "Thus, the strategy of accommodating private participation was also meant to deflate resistance from people on the far right, most of whom were believed to belong to the political party in power."[121]

This account of the politics behind the NHIP underscores the important role of the governing elite in pressing for progress in health reform and shaping the political prospects for its eventual success or failure. Kufuor's strategic placement and rotation of politically well-connected ministers actually facilitated, rather than hindered, the advancement of Ghana's landmark health insurance program. The governing elite, moreover, shared a common concern about getting the program off the ground in advance of the 2004 elections. They also came to share a

---

[118] Wireko (2015).
[119] Wireko (2015: 177).
[120] Wireko (2015: 172).
[121] Wireko (2015: 174).

socio-political interest in ensuring the program did not disadvantage certain stakeholder groups and remained ideologically consistent with their party and social principles. These interests were integral to the successful adoption and implementation of the program, which is now a well-cited case of successful healthcare policy development in sub-Saharan Africa.[122]

The importance of cohesive political and social interests is evident in other policy successes in Ghana as well. In designing and implementing decentralization reforms throughout the 1980s and 1990s, for example, former minister Kwamena Ahwoi, has explained how "a group of about thirty of us constituted a kind of political committee to put together the proposals for local government reforms." He continued, however, that they soon encountered difficulties in convincing some members of the committee, as well as bureaucrats and technocrats, to accept the devolution of power that was necessary for the reforms to be implemented.[123] Ahwoi touted the ways that his strength within the party helped him to overcome these challenges and drive the process forward:

Invariably there are a lot of turf wars between the ministries as to which sector should be decentralized, for example. I had a lot of problems, but not only was Rawlings committed to decentralization, I also had a close working relationship with him. So any time I had a problem with any of my colleague ministers on decentralization and the matter got to his desk he ruled in my favor, so much so that people thought that I had a lot of power. In fact, one of my colleagues summed it up by saying that I was building an empire.

Despite the importance of political coordination and negotiation for accomplishing goals like decentralization and the NHIP, Ghana's government also has appeared able and willing to engage technocrats when necessary without too much worry about compromising political goals. In the oil sector, for example, "technocrats have been central to all key negotiations, including contracting and identifying new partners and contentious discussions over the relative merits of the pipeline and refinery."[124] The frequent appointment of "technopols" to key positions in, for example, the Ministry of Finance further enables Ghana's presidents to simultaneously advance their policy and political goals.[125]

---

[122] See, for example, Carbone (2012).

[123] Itumeleng Makgetla, interview with Kwamena Ahwoi, Innovations for Successful Societies, Princeton University September 8, 2009.

[124] Hickey et al. (2015: 22).

[125] Abdulai and Mohan (2019).

6.4.3   Intraparty Competition and Long-Term Cohesion

Periods of internal party conflict in Ghana have had the potential to bring about the same types of incohesion, fear, and paralysis that have frequently undermined the functioning of executive institutions in Benin. However, even when Ghana's presidents have responded to such conflicts by dismissing or rotating ministers associated with a competing faction, the eventual resolution of these intraparty conflicts has typically led to longer-term processes of reform and learning within the parties.

Three periods of particularly tense intraparty competition merit specific attention in this regard. The first is the period in the lead-up to the 2000 elections. As described earlier in the chapter, shortly after Rawlings was re-elected in 1996, the NDC coalition, comprised of former PNDC leaders and an array of leaders from smaller Nkrumahist parties, fractured primarily along pro- and anti-Rawlings fault lines. The pro-Rawlings faction supported the president's plan for Mills to succeed him as the party's presidential candidate. The anti-Rawlings contingent was eager to see a shift in the center of gravity of the party away from the Rawlings-Mills alliance. Between November 1998 and January 1999, after the infamous "Swedru decalaration" in June 1998, Rawlings reshuffled eight ministers – largely elevating those who remained loyal and dismissing those (along with others serving in the government at the time) who sympathized with the reformist faction.

Following their defeat in the 2000 election, the NDC adopted a number of reforms. One of the most important of these reforms was the adoption of an official policy document, "A social democratic agenda for Ghana," to guide the party's goals and programs.[126] Although it's not immediately clear that the adoption of this document has had any meaningful effect on policy or governance in the eight years that the NDC held office from 2009 to 2016, it did provide, as one regional NDC official put it, "a united identity" based on "helping the poor, the farmers, the fishermen."[127]

Another important reform within the NDC during this time was the separation of the role of "party founder" (Rawlings) from that of "party leader." Formally adopted on April 27, 2002, this change in the party constitution meant that Rawlings was no longer the *de facto* head of the party. The reform also created the post of national chairman, which

---

[126] Bob-Milliar (2012*a*: 588). At the time, according to Abbey (2018: 18), NDC officials were considering a number of traditional ideologies including communism, socialism, social democracy, liberalism, and capitalism, but ultimately selected social democracy as most compatible with the NDC's PNDC roots.

[127] Author interview, Takoradi, December 5, 2013.

Obed Asamoah, a staunch internal rival of Rawlings, won narrowly in 2002.[128] Even though Asamoah lost the chairmanship in 2006 and later branched off to form his own party, the Democratic Freedom Party (DFP), he brought the DFP back into the NDC in 2011, citing its growing internal democracy.[129]

Although new cracks in the party became visible during Mills' presidency from 2013 to 2016, these new divisions were primarily resolved institutionally *within* the party rather than through the distribution and withholding of ministerial posts or through the fracturing of the NDC coalition. Dissatisfied with Mills' performance in office, especially his apparent tolerance of corruption within his own government as well as his lack of interest in prosecuting officials from the previous NPP government, both former President Rawlings and his wife, Nana Konadu Agyeman Rawlings, became increasingly critical of Mills. Tensions around Mills' handling of government business came to a head in 2011 when Agyeman Rawlings challenged Mills in the NDC's presidential primary contest.[130] The post-2000 reforms within the NDC meant that approximately 3,000 party delegates would vote to choose the NDC's presidential nominee that year. Despite the intense criticism of Mills from members of the pro-Rawlings faction, Mills prevailed with over 96 percent of the delegates' votes.

Under the surface of Rawlings' criticism of Mills was his apparent resentment that many members of Mills' cabinet came from the Nkrumahist tradition, which Rawlings saw as a threat to his own legacy.[131] Despite this criticism, there was no obvious effort on Mills' part to use cabinet appointments to buy support from the pro-Rawlings faction. His January 2011 reshuffle, which occurred before Agyeman Rawlings formally declared her intention to contest Mills for the presidential nomination, was, according to Mills, "to introduce fresh and new ideas, and tap into different kinds of expertise." It did not seem to imply that any outgoing ministers had committed "any crime or misconduct themselves."[132] Moreover, after the NDC primary contest was resolved, there was no immediate reshuffling geared towards Mills' consolidation of power within the party – a sign of maturing party institutions that need not necessarily rely on state power to manage internal party strife.

---

[128] Bob-Milliar (2012*a*: 589).
[129] Specifically, he said that "the raison d'être of our departure from the NDC has evaporated." Daily Graphic, October 9, 2011.
[130] "NDC and Nana Konadu Rawlings – Showdown in Suyani," The Africa Report, July 6, 2011.
[131] Bob-Milliar (2012*a*: 595).
[132] "Reshuffle Not for Misconduct," Ghana News Agency, February 14, 2011.

Similar events have been visible within the NPP. The ruptures within the NPP, particularly those pitting the traditional Busia faction against the Danquah faction, continue to color the NPP's internal party contests. After Kufuor won the presidency in 2001, the Busia/Kufuor faction consolidated its power base by monopolizing ministerial posts in key sectors of the state apparatus and Kufuor-faction members continued to receive the lion's share of ministerial portfolios through the course of his presidency.[133] Nonetheless, at the height of intraparty tensions following the NPP's loss in the 2008 election, the party further democratized its internal rules and procedures. Specifically, the party increased the size of its internal selectorate from 2,340 to 115,000 delegates in what George Bob-Milliar calls "cooperative factionalism."[134] Although the power inequity between the two factions may have escalated tensions between them, these tensions were at least temporarily resolved when Nana Akufo-Addo, a Danquah-ist, was elected the next party leader over Kufuor's "hand-picked" successor, Alan Kyerematen by NPP delegates at their 2007 party meeting.

In Ghana, these periods of tense intraparty competition have at times distracted governments from their policy agendas, but their resolutions have actually advanced and expanded democratic rules and procedures within the two parties. The internal party rules have subsequently provided mechanisms to resolve intraparty elite conflict such that leaders can largely avoid both agency and cohesion problems in their selection and rotation of ministers. In short, these cycles of division, reconciliation, and reform that animate Ghana's internal party dynamics help to consolidate the ruling elite into cohesive political units.

6.5   Downstream Impacts: How Bureaucrats Perceive the Executive

To what extent are these different executive dynamics related to stability and cohesion perceived by bureaucrats? In the Classroom survey, Beninese and Ghanaian public servants were asked about the extent to which they felt that (1) frequent changes in leadership and (2) disputes among ministers or politicians posed problems in their organizations. In Figure 6.2, I show the proportions of bureaucrats surveyed in each country who responded that they saw these issues as either problems or serious problems.[135] Respondents in Benin overwhelmingly saw these issues as

---

[133] Bob-Milliar (2012a: 581).
[134] Bob-Milliar (2012a: 583).
[135] For ease of visualization, the responses are collapsed from four categories into two.

problems – upward of 70 percent on both questions – whereas fewer than 40 percent in Ghana rated these issues as problems in their organizations.

The survey results are generally consistent with the cross-country differences in executive institutions described throughout this chapter. They also suggest that the observed instability and incohesion in Benin's executive have widely felt impacts on the day-to-day work of bureaucrats. Political dynamics in Ghana's executive also appear to be felt by the bureaucrats surveyed, but their reverberations throughout the bureaucracy appear less severe. In the next chapter, I further investigate the impacts of political extraction on the bureaucrats' work environments, showing once again that coercive methods of extraction are considerably more detrimental to institutional performance.

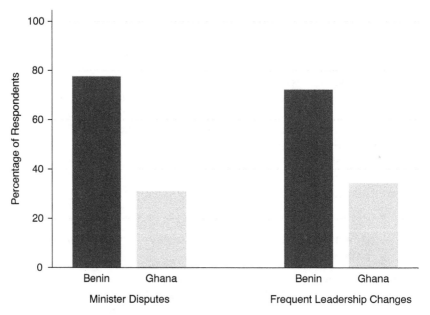

Figure 6.2 Bureaucratic perceptions of the executive (Classroom survey)
The graph depicts the proportion of survey respondents that rated disputes between ministers and frequent changes in leadership as problems or serious problems in their organizations. Source: Author's Classroom survey (2013–2014).

6.6   Conclusion

This chapter has shown how the different strategies of extraction in Benin and Ghana produce more or less stability and cohesion in their respective executive institutions. Despite the highly politicized appointment of government ministers discussed in Chapter 5, Ghana's executive institutions are more stable and managed by a more cohesive group of ministers. This, I argue, is because Ghana's presidents, in pursuing a strategy of collusive extraction, face fewer agency problems in the selection of ministers. As such, portfolios are shuffled less frequently and the party elites who comprise the executive are able to act more collectively. In short, one byproduct of Ghana's system of collusive extraction is relative stability and cohesion in the country's government, which clearly produces an environment that is more conducive to the pursuit of developmental policies, both in terms of social programs such as the NHIP and sector-specific economic growth. While some in Ghana lament the lack of professionalism among ministers that comes with the appointment of party elite, the stability, experience, and cohesion in Ghana's cabinets generate a clear advantage in terms of the ability of presidents to see their policy and political agendas through.

This is not to say that Ghana's executive is free from afflictions such as financial mismanagement and the politicized distribution of public goods and services. Indeed, the collusive system does achieve its goals of extracting large sums of money from the state, inevitably limiting the potential for governing success. At the time of this writing, the state had yet to recover money from NDC financier Alfred Woyome, who neither delivered on his contracting agreements nor returned the money, despite his having lost court cases in a number of venues. Nearly one-third of development projects remain uncompleted,[136] an issue that many Ghanaians attribute to deep problems in contracting processes.

Notwithstanding these widely recognized issues, there is little question that, once in office, Ghana's party leaders can and do often achieve their political and policy agendas, regardless of the content of those agendas. Whether it's the implementation of the NHIP, the successful (if at times tumultuous) development of Ghana's oil and gas sector, or the implementation of a major public sector pay reform (the "Single Spine Salary Program"), Ghana's executives have shown considerable capacity to make good on campaign promises while at the same time servicing the extraction and distribution systems that satiate the party's political needs.

---

[136] Williams (2017).

This level of executive capacity is rarely on display in Benin. With the notable exception of significant expansions in access to basic education – supported over decades by large volumes of donor support – it is difficult to cite one major public policy success that is attributable, even in part, to executive action. Repeated efforts to privatize state enterprises, enforce customs regulations, reform the civil service, expand access to healthcare, and develop an oil and gas industry have remained largely stagnant or have progressed only in fits and starts despite stated intentions. In other words, the issues of executive instability and division documented in this chapter have real implications in terms of governing outcomes.

Overall, the analysis in this chapter further suggests that the different modes of extraction, and especially the divergent executive appointment and rotation practices they engender, help to explain variation in cabinet volatility, cohesion, and, ultimately, the effectiveness of state executive institutions. Importantly, the accounts of these two countries suggest that a strategy based on politicization of elite appointments, perhaps counter-intuitively, has the potential to produce higher-performing executives.

7   Extraction and the Bureaucracy

The impacts of extraction on government institutions are not limited to the executive. This chapter examines how extraction practices shape the day-to-day work environments for the state's bureaucratic employees. Whereas previous chapters established that different modes of extraction shape leaders' decisions about, first, the staffing of state institutions and, second, their management of executive-level personnel, this chapter moves further "downstream" in the state apparatus to investigate how the different extraction practices shape the state's bureaucratic organizations and personnel. Although *any* extraction of resources from the state is likely to disrupt the workings of bureaucratic organizations, I argue that the practices associated with coercive extraction are particularly detrimental to organizational productivity for public service employees. Bureaucrats working in contexts of coercive extraction are, simply put, less likely to have the autonomy, resources, and motivations necessary to fulfill organizational missions and execute their tasks. These findings further illuminate why state institutions in Benin – and in contexts of low party institutionalization and coercive extraction more generally – have been far less effective than those in Ghana in implementing programs of high priority on their development agendas.

This chapter addresses three mechanisms linking extraction strategies to bureaucratic institutional performance. First, in their efforts to access and control opportunities for extraction, political leaders in Benin's coercive extraction system are more likely to interfere in the day-to-day workings of bureaucratic organizations. As a result, bureaucrats in such environments tend to feel more worried about gaining the approval of politicians, which in turn creates an environment characterized by overly rigid adherence to rules and bureaucratic paralysis. Second, because leaders in coercive systems of extraction are more likely to rely on bureaucrats to collect rents and siphon revenues for political finance, the disappearance of resources will be both more acute and more visible to bureaucrats, resulting in bureaucrats feeling more resource-constrained in their jobs. Third, many of the dynamics described in this chapter and previous ones – higher levels of politicized staffing of the bureaucracy (Chapter 5), the lack of clear policy vision emanating from the executive apparatus (Chapter 6), the lower levels of autonomy for bureaucrats (present chapter), and deficiencies in resources (present chapter) – work together to create a highly demotivating environment for bureaucrats. In sum, a range of practices associated with coercive extraction generates the types of organizational environments that undermine bureaucratic performance.

The chapter draws extensively from the Classroom (2013–2014) and Workplace (2017) surveys that I conducted with public service employees in Benin and Ghana, most of whom occupy managerial, technical/professional, or administrative positions in central government MDAs.[1] Following previous chapters, I present results of the Classroom survey to illustrate major differences across the two countries. I also exploit the more wide-ranging set of questions in the Workplace survey, especially on issues of political interference, resource sufficiency, and public service motivation, to conduct individual-level analyses using regression analysis.[2] Specifically, I examine how and to what extent the specific extraction practices associated with collusive and coercive systems – awarding contracts to party financiers and diverting rents and revenues to political parties – shape bureaucrats' perceptions and motivations surrounding their work.

The analyses show rather clearly that practices associated with coercive extraction generate perceptions among bureaucrats of more frequent interference by politicians and more serious resource deficiencies. They are also robustly associated with lower levels of personnel motivation. Although some of these problems are also prevalent where politicians collude in extraction, both their scope and intensity are consistently more severe where bureaucrats participate centrally in extraction, as they have in Benin's coercive extraction system.

The results of the analyses that I conduct in this chapter speak to broader questions about when and why political leaders interfere in the day-to-day workings of the state's bureaucratic institutions – and how their actions may purposely or inadvertently shape bureaucrats' ability to do their jobs. The findings underscore the importance of political financing generally, and extraction of money from the state

---

[1] As discussed in Chapter 1, the Classroom survey sample includes a small number of local government and street-level bureaucrats. The Workplace survey sample completely comprises central government bureaucrats who do not occupy street-level positions.

[2] Descriptive statistics for all variables used in the regression models are provided in Appendix E.

in particular, as key coordinates of bureaucratic performance. Despite increasing attention to variation in bureaucratic behavior and performance both within and across African countries, there remain major gaps in understanding when and why political leaders motivate, permit, or hinder public servants in the successful performance of their duties. Although extraction methods comprise just one of many possible factors that shape politician–bureaucrat relationships, the evidence presented in this chapter suggests that political financing motivations and practices ought to occupy a more central place in this genre of work.

The chapter begins with a theoretical discussion of three main channels through which the extraction of state money shapes bureaucratic organizational environments, including bureaucrats' autonomy from political interference, the sufficiency (or deficiency) of organizational resources, and the motivations of bureaucrats. I then analyze how and to what extent collusive and coercive extraction practices shape these three facets of bureaucracies in Benin and Ghana. The chapter concludes with a discussion of the broader implications for state performance.

7.1   Extraction Politics and Bureaucratic Performance

A large literature spanning the fields of political science, public administration, sociology, and economics links attributes of bureaucratic institutions to major governing outcomes such as economic growth,[3] the delivery of public goods and services,[4] and the survival of democracy.[5] Why and how bureaucratic institutions perform more or less effectively, however, is less clear. Explanatory perspectives range from deep historical processes of state institutional development,[6] to the structures and incentives of political principals,[7] to the presence or absence of particular organizational rules, management, and oversight structures,[8] to the *esprit de corps* or the culture of the organization.[9]

Without denying the potential importance of any of these explanations, the discussion that follows focuses more specifically on how the extraction-related motivations of politicians can shape the organizational environments in which bureaucrats operate on a day-to-day basis. It links, in particular, variation in extraction practices to (1) the

---

[3] Evans and Rauch (1999).
[4] See Pepinsky et al. (2017) for an overview.
[5] Linz and Stepan (1996); Acemoglu and Robinson (2006).
[6] Kohli (2004); Besley and Persson (2011).
[7] Moe (1989); Lewis (2010); Gulzar and Pasquale (2017).
[8] Rauch and Evans (2000); Olken (2007).
[9] Grindle (1997); McDonnell (2020).

incentives of political principals to interfere in the administrative work of bureaucrats (autonomy and political interference); (2) the availability of material resources for bureaucrats to use in pursuit of their missions (resource sufficiency); and (3) the motivations of bureaucrats to perform their jobs well (personnel motivation). Across these three categories, I argue that practices associated with coercive extraction undermine the conditions necessary for effective bureaucratic performance.

7.1.1   Bureaucratic Autonomy and Political Interference

There is a growing body of theory and evidence from around the world demonstrating that the insulation of bureaucrats from political pressures improves their performance. This argument is prevalent in studies of East Asian developmental states, where successful state-led economic transformations are often attributed to the autonomy granted to professional bureaucrats, particularly those charged with the implementation of economic policies.[10] Applying these principles to the African context, Lindsay Whitfield and coauthors explain that to effectively implement industrial policies, state bureaucrats "must have political backing from the ruling elites and a significant degree of autonomy from political pressures stemming from within the coalition...they must be trusted by the ruling elites but also knowledgeable of the targeted industry."[11] Across an array of policy areas and countries, research on African bureaucracies has found that personnel and organizations tend to perform better when they are insulated from political pressures[12] and have more autonomy in their day-to-day work.[13] High levels of political and managerial control tend to produce excessive formalism, where concern about adherence to the rules overrides concerns about the attainment of official goals.[14] As Jean-Paul Olivier de Sardan notes, the large discrepancy between "the formal and the real" in West African bureaucracies, means that over-subscription to formal rules is likely to be synonymous with under-performance in the "real" work of the bureaucracy.[15] This condition contributes to the existence of what Thomas Bierschenk calls a "double bind," in which bureaucrats find it difficult to perform their functions without fear of some kind of reprisal.[16]

[10] Johnson (1982); Evans (1995).
[11] Whitfield et al. (2015: 20).
[12] Harris et al. (2019); McDonnell (2020).
[13] Rasul and Rogger (2018); Rasul et al. (2021).
[14] Price (1975).
[15] de Sardan (2013: 45).
[16] Bierschenk (2014).

There are (at least) two important reasons to believe that political officials engaging in more coercive forms of extraction would generate greater levels of political interference in the day-to-day work of bureaucrats. First, extraction conducted by bureaucrats seeking rents and diverting revenues, as occurs more frequently in Benin's coercive system, depends on the participation of bureaucrats. From the perspective of the political principal pursuing a coercive extraction strategy, it is important to tightly watch and control bureaucrats' behavior because of the roles they play – either as facilitators or potential spoilers – in the ruling party's extraction. This concern is less salient in collusive systems where party elites conspire with businesses to extract money through procurement processes. If participation from career bureaucrats is required at all in such arrangements, it is only a select few who sit on tendering or procurement committees. In short, coercive extraction is likely to produce more extensive forms of political interference that can complicate bureaucrats' efforts to work towards organizational missions and goals and impair institutional performance.

Second, as discussed extensively in Chapter 6, incumbent presidents in more coercive systems are likely to remove and rotate ministers more frequently than their counterparts in collusive systems. In such environments, ministers fearing for their survival in office will face greater pressure to either ensure that bureaucratic actions conform with the interests or directives of the president or the ruling party, or extract in their own interests before they are dismissed from their positions. In either scenario, ministers will themselves interfere more frequently in the day-to-day work of bureaucrats. By contrast, in collusive systems of extraction, the alignment of interests among political leaders and ministers generally implies a more permissive arrangement whereby ministers are not operating under the watchful eye of an insecure party leader. Although ministers in this context are likely to have incentives to interfere in specific decisions about procurement contracts,[17] they are less likely to closely monitor other types of tasks.

7.1.2   Resource Sufficiency

Bureaucratic organizations must possess the resources necessary to conduct their policy, administrative, regulatory, or service delivery functions. Even where bureaucracies have well-established rule-bound, meritocratic structures; deficiencies or skewed allocations in resources can seriously impair performance.[18] Here, I focus on the ways that different modes of extraction shape the availability of resources within

[17] Luna (2019).
[18] Chibber (2002); Dasgupta and Kapur (2020).

the bureaucracy, as well as bureaucrats' perceptions about whether the resources in their organizations are sufficient to execute their jobs well.

I argue that coercive methods of extraction are especially likely to exacerbate problems related to resource sufficiency. Their adverse impact works through two possible channels. First, as described in previous chapters, one strategy used by presidents in coercive systems is to delegate extraction to bureaucrats, particularly those who depend on state employment for their sustenance. Where this practice is prevalent, resource shortfalls felt within the organization are likely to be more common – and more visible – as bureaucrats actively participate in siphoning state funds for political use. This practice not only depletes the organizational resource base but does so in a way that is likely to be visible to other employees in the organization. In other words, by delegating extraction to bureaucrats, leaders in coercive systems magnify resource issues for public organizations.

Second, resource insufficiencies may be exacerbated by the selection of ministers with interests that are not aligned with those of the president. As described in Chapters 5 and 6, an important feature of the coercive system of extraction involves the appointment of non-loyal ministers to executive posts. Not knowing how long they will remain at their posts, or if they will remain allied with the incumbent for long, these co-opted ministers have incentives to extract as much as possible in whatever ways possible, as long as it does not go so far as to raise the possibility of prosecution or imprisonment. Ministers of this type may therefore manage their ministries in ways that are more extractive, leading once again to the greater and more visible depletion of organizational resources.

It is important to note that collusive systems are no less vulnerable to financial loss. However, one important difference between collusive and coercive systems is that financial losses in collusive systems are likely to be executed in budgetary and planning phases, such as in the allocation of funds for procurement. This system does not as *visibly* deplete the supply of resources available to public service employees to carry out their day-to-day work.

7.1.3 Personnel Motivation

Across both public and private sector organizations, motivated employees are more likely to perform their jobs well.[19] Higher levels of personnel motivation are associated with productivity, improved management practices, responsiveness to performance incentives, accountability, and

---

[19] For a general elaboration of the relationship between personnel motivation and organizational behavior, see Pinder (2014).

trust in government.[20] Such findings underscore why efforts to understand different types and determinants of personnel motivation are of growing interest to both scholars and practitioners in public administration[21] and constitute an important frontier in the study of state organizations.[22]

Studies of the motivations of bureaucratic personnel, however, have produced less clarity about the ways that political institutions shape personnel motivation. In one model, for example, policy-motivated bureaucrats self-select into the public service when political arrangements allow for bureaucratic discretion in decision-making.[23] Alternatively, a bureaucrat's political ideology can predict their level of Public Service Motivation (PSM): individuals who hold more left-wing ideological views are likely to have higher levels of PSM.[24] Still other studies focus on the importance of leadership in shaping personnel motivation, but they tend not to make a clear distinction between the leadership practices of politicians versus public managers.[25]

How do the behaviors and incentives of political leaders shape the day-to-day motivations of public service personnel? Political and policy environments are likely to constitute important "background conditions" that affect whether public servants "see themselves as working for an institution that advances prosocial ends."[26] Such dynamics will undoubtedly shape whether bureaucrats maintain the motivations that draw them to work in the public service in the first place, as well as the organizational commitment and job satisfaction that sustain these motivations among personnel.

I focus on two types of personnel motivation that are potentially shaped by the political extraction environment. The first – public service motivation – relates to an individual's "altruistic motivation to serve the interests of a community of people, a state, a nation or humankind."[27] This type of motivation is other-regarding in the sense that it focuses on a motivation to help others for no private reward.[28] Public service motivation is what attracts individuals to work in public, rather than private organizations, and is found to contribute to public service

---

[20] Bellé (2013); Ashraf et al. (2014); Callen et al. (2015).
[21] Brewer (2008); Ritz et al. (2016).
[22] See, for example, Esteve and Schuster (2019).
[23] Gailmard and Patty (2007).
[24] Perry (1997).
[25] See Esteve and Schuster (2019: 50) for an overview of these leadership-focused studies.
[26] Moynihan and Soss (2014: 329).
[27] Rainey and Steinbauer (1999: 20).
[28] Le Grand (2003); Perry (2010).

employees' broader attitudes towards their jobs.[29] In simplest terms, public service motivation reflects a set of attitudes and values related to one's concern for others.

A second type of motivation, which I call "work motivation," relates to the intensity of an individual's desire to complete the tasks associated with one's work. Work motivation may be derived extrinsically through, for example, the employee's desire for a salary increase, performance bonus, or promotion. However, work motivation may also relate to the individual's intrinsic and individual desire to succeed in their work. There is a motivation that inheres in the relationship between individuals and tasks that is not necessarily attributable to either public service motivation or the potential of future rewards or sanctions.[30] Unlike public service motivation, work motivation is not specific to certain types of jobs or organizational missions. Thus, whereas public service motivation reflects attitudes toward serving others, work motivation reflects some measure of effort that an individual puts into his or her work.

I propose two paths linking extraction to the public service and work motivations of bureaucratic personnel. First, if public servants work in organizations where political leaders regularly coerce employees to participate in extraction, their concerns and motivations surrounding service to the public and completion of work tasks will diminish in the face of pressure to serve political principals. As politicians engage in coercive extraction and seek to exert greater control in how the organization's personnel are managed, bureaucrats become further demotivated as their professional qualifications and expertise are discarded and political loyalty and compliance rewarded. Moreover, in that coercive systems of extraction result in more severe and more visible diversions of organizational resources, bureaucrats will be further demotivated to perform their day-to-day work.

Second, the elite discord that is common in coercive systems of extraction, described at length in Chapter 6, is likely to have a detrimental impact on the motivations of public service employees. Diverse and unaligned political and policy interests among the governing elite impair the formation and articulation of clear policy objectives as well as clear public service missions and goals. Lacking a coherent sense of the larger policy and public service objectives of their work, bureaucrats lose faith in the idea that public service employment actually involves public service, or that working hard in their positions will make a difference in the pursuit of larger goals. Arbitrary and unpredictable shifts in political

---

[29] Lyons et al. (2006); Bozeman (2007).
[30] Esteve and Schuster (2019: 10).

mandates create confusing environments for bureaucrats, draining them of momentum and motivation to perform.[31] To the extent that coercive systems of extraction are characterized by elite instability and low levels of cohesion, they are likely to have demotivating impacts on bureaucratic personnel.

The broader hypothesis that emerges from this discussion is that the partisan interactions and elite practices involved in coercive extraction are likely to generate conditions that are commonly associated with low-performing bureaucratic organizations. Leaders employing more coercive modes of extraction will interfere more frequently in bureaucratic decisions, facilitate more severe and visible resource shortages, and act in ways that demotivate public service personnel. In such environments, even if incumbent leaders have clear policy agendas that they hope to pursue during their terms in office, their need to extract money from the state – or prevent potential opponents from doing so – generates working conditions that militate against the successful implementation of their policy agendas.

7.2 Extraction, Autonomy, and Political Interference

The preceding discussion implies that Benin's coercive system of extraction is likely to produce bureaucratic environments characterized by low levels of autonomy for public servants and politicians interfering in the day-to-day work of the organization. These management patterns result in part from efforts by presidents and ministers in Benin to seek continual control over who gains access to extraction opportunities and how extracted resources are used. Thanks to their more reliable agents, leaders in Ghana's collusive system, by contrast, are less concerned about protecting extraction opportunities, especially in a coercive manner. They are, therefore, less likely to interfere in day-to-day bureaucratic affairs, allowing greater autonomy for bureaucrats.

Differences in overall levels of bureaucratic autonomy and political interference across the two countries are evident from the results of the Classroom survey. In Figure 7.1, I show the percentage of respondents from each country who express concerns related to autonomy and political interference in their organization. Specifically the questions asked respondents to rate, on a scale of 1-4, the extent to which they see "political interference," an "inability to voice an opinion or act because it might damage the ruling party," and "qualified personnel getting sacked because of their political affiliation" as a problem in their

---

[31] Moore (1995: 33).

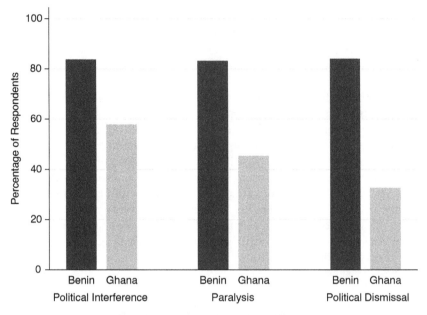

Figure 7.1 Autonomy, interference, and dismissals
(Classroom survey)
The graph depicts the percentage of respondents that see each issue as
a problem or serious problem in their organization. Source: Author's
Classroom survey (2013-2014).

organization. Across all three questions, upwards of 80 percent of Beninese respondents saw these issues as a problem or serious problem in
their organization. The responses are far more mixed in Ghana. While
more than half (58 percent) saw political interference as a problem,
smaller groups of respondents – 42 percent and 33 percent respectively – reported an inability to act due to political reprisal and political
dismissals as problems in their organizations.

The cross-country differences alone do not necessarily imply that
extraction practices contribute to these divergent response patterns. In
regression analyses using the Workplace survey results, which allow me
to include a broader range of variables and exploit variation within
Ghana, I test whether different types of extraction are associated with
limited autonomy and political interference.[32] To measure bureaucratic

───────────────

[32] Although party-directed resource diversion is comparatively low in Ghana, there
is enough variation in the data to estimate the relationship between its perceived
frequency in an organization and other organizational attributes.

autonomy (lefthand panel), I use a survey question asking how frequently, on a five-point scale, the respondent "feels worried that someone from the ruling party will not approve of my work." To measure political interference (righthand panel) I average together responses to two survey questions about political interference. The questions ask respondents to rate how frequently, on a five-point scale, (1) "Someone from the ruling party guides a particular decision in my institution," and (2) "Someone from the ruling party influences who is designated as beneficiaries or recipients for a particular program." The independent variables – those measuring extraction – are the same as those used in Chapter 4, asking respondents: (1) how frequently individuals in their organization divert resources to a political party and (2) the importance of providing financial support to the ruling party to win a procurement contract. Whereas the former is indicative of more coercive modes of extraction, the latter is central to collusive extraction. The correlation between the resource diversion and procurement measures is 0.20, suggesting that these different forms of extraction do not frequently co-occur. The regressions include fixed effects for the MDA in which an individual works, which controls for unobserved variation across different public service institutions. I also control for a number of respondent demographic variables, suggesting that the results are not driven by other features of the organizational environment, nor by specific demographic attributes that may affect bureaucrats' perceptions of such practices.

The results, displayed in Figure 7.2, show that those who report working in organizations where bureaucrats more frequently engage in party-directed diversion of organizational resources report significantly greater levels of (1) concern about their autonomy (left-hand panel) and (2) political interference in their organization (right-hand panel). Procurement-based extraction in one's organization is also associated with elevated levels of concern about autonomy and higher reported frequency of political interference, but to a significantly lesser extent than in contexts of direct resource diversion by bureaucrats. In short, the results indicate, with a quite high level of confidence, that practices associated with coercive extraction generate greater concerns among bureaucrats about their ability to act without fear of political reprisal and greater perceived frequency of political interference in their day-to-day work environments.

7.2.1   *Qualitative Accounts of Political Interference in the Bureaucracy*

The regression results are consistent with the argument that coercive extraction impedes bureaucratic autonomy and creates a more

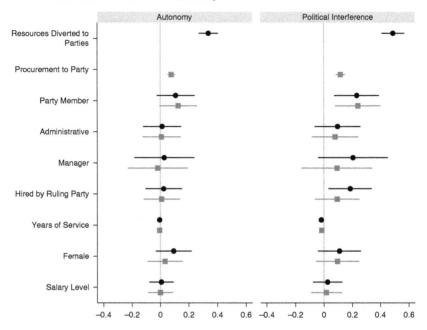

Figure 7.2 Extraction, autonomy, and political interference
(Workplace survey)
Estimates based on OLS Regression with institution-fixed effects, 95%
confidence intervals. Lefthand panel: Model 1 (dark gray circles),
$N = 1,072$ and R-squared $= 0.19$. Model 2 (light gray squares),
$N = 1,146$ and R-squared $= 0.12$. Righthand panel: Model 1 (dark
gray circles), $N = 1,009$ and R-squared $= 0.29$. Model 2 (light gray
squares), $N = 1,055$ and R-squared $= 0.21$.

politicized environment in which bureaucrats fear the consequences
of acting in ways that upset ministers, who themselves are monitored
closely by the president. These findings are also supported by qualitative data gleaned from interviews and secondary sources on the political
management of the bureaucracy in Benin. Illustrating this perspective,
one long-time employee at Benin's Ministry of Foreign Affairs explained
that he has seen this trend intensify since President Boni Yayi's election
to office in 2006:

Since Yayi was elected, the chiefs of state have used the Council of Ministers and
the *service de controle et audit* to know what is going on in ministries. Ministers'
work is followed and the president is apprised of what's happening in ministries.

The ministers who are close to the president have more freedom and resources, but the other ministers and their employees are closely watched."[33]

He went on to describe how this intensified level of political control has "changed the ways state agents conduct policy," noting that, in some cases, technical experts are now more likely to be "pushed aside."

A close observer of Benin's public sector echoed this assessment, explaining that she saw two important "logics" developing. The first is that there are fewer and fewer "technical decisions and actions," noting, "the technicians now have much less influence" because the "logic of promotion and access to budgets is such that it is necessary to be close to political power." The second "logic" is a reaction to the first, whereby the "*cadre administratif*" has adapted to "develop strategies to benefit from the inaction by politicians" to act on their private interests rather than on their technical or professional ones.[34] In other words, in the face of politicians' efforts to exert greater control over the state's bureaucratic functions, bureaucrats cope in ways that are likely to erode public service motivation (more on that below) and, ultimately, erode bureaucratic performance.

These dynamics are considerably more varied in Ghana, where 58.9 percent of respondents in the Workplace survey said they "never" feel worried that someone from the ruling party will disapprove of their work and another 22.3 percent said that they "rarely" feel this way. Even where bureaucrats feel controlled or threatened by political leaders, the dynamics seem, in many cases, limited to the upper echelons of staff. As one employee of the Ghana Education Trust Fund explained, "political influences often affect staffing at the agency head level but there is also the perception that exposing your political affiliation is a danger to remaining at post."[35] An employee at Ghana's Nursing and Midwifery Council further noted, "some public servants are more motivated just on favouritism...those at the top are more susceptible to it because they either handle the money and other government property or exercise authority over them."[36]

When politicians do seek to control the work of bureaucrats, they tend to do so in a way that appears less about "sidelining" and more

---

[33] Author interview, Cotonou, June 29, 2018.
[34] Author interview, Cotonou, July 3, 2018. See, also, Bierschenk (2008) on the "privatization" of Benin's justice system.
[35] Online follow-up survey, April 7, 2017. Following the Workplace survey, respondents were invited to participate in an online follow-up survey where they could provide additional commentary on the topics included in the survey.
[36] Ghana online follow-up survey, April 7, 2017.

about negotiating tensions that inevitably arise from unaligned interests between politicians and bureaucrats. In her ethnographic study of senior public servants in Ghana, Carola Lentz describes how bureaucrats, in discussing "conflict-ridden relations" with political appointees, maintain a strong sense of their moral and professional duties to behave in the public interest:

> They did not express any feeling that the state to whom they had pledged their loyal service had not honoured its side of this contract and failed them, and that they could therefore legitimately withdraw from their obligations. On the contrary, the sense of a moral contract which both sides needed to respect, and indeed did respect, was dominant...Most interviewees insisted that their moral contract was with the state and the constitution to which they pledged an oath, not the government.[37]

Although any generalizations about an entire state bureaucracy should be treated with serious caution, both quantitative survey results and qualitative inquiries point to meaningful differences in politician-bureaucrat relations across the two countries, as well as across organizations where bureaucrats participate more or less frequently in extracting money for political finance. Not only do bureaucrats in Ghana's collusive system of extraction report higher levels of autonomy and lower levels of political interference, but I also find evidence that political pressures that do occur may have more limited influence on the bureaucrats' behavior. As further analysis of Benin's bureaucratic-intensive coercive system of extraction shows, low levels of autonomy for public servants appear to pose serious problems for professional behavior, motivations, and, ultimately for bureaucratic performance.

7.3   Extraction and Resource (In)Sufficiency

Both collusive and coercive extraction can result in serious financial loss to the state, but how politicians go about extracting money in these different systems has divergent implications for how these losses are felt by bureaucrats in their jobs. As theorized earlier in this chapter, the involvement of bureaucrats in coercive extraction is likely to deplete the organizational resources in more serious and visible ways. When bureaucrats widely serve as key extraction agents, problems related to resource deficiencies are more acute.

Figure 7.3 shows overall differences in bureaucrats' perceptions about resource sufficiency across the two countries. Bureaucrats in both countries widely report insufficient resources as problems or serious problems

---

[37] Lentz (2014: 196).

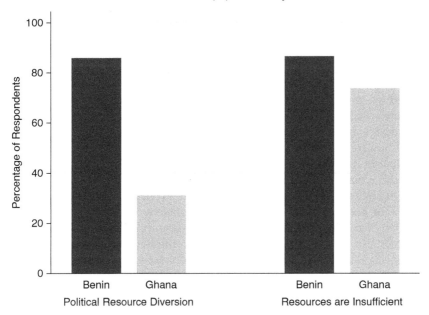

Figure 7.3 Resource sufficiency and political diversion (Classroom survey)
The graph depicts the percentage of respondents that see each issue as a problem or serious problem in their organization. Source: Author's Classroom Survey (2013–2014).

in their organizations: 87 percent in Benin and 75 percent in Ghana see insufficient resources as a problem or serious problem in their organization. Compared to the fifteen other potential organizational problems that appeared in the survey questions, resource deficiency ranked as the fourth most serious in Benin and the second most serious problem in Ghana.[38] Clearly, public servants in both countries feel their organizations are constrained because they lack the necessary material resources, though the levels of concern are somewhat higher among those surveyed in Benin.

[38] Results not shown. Rankings based on calculations of mean rating for each category of problem. The remaining fifteen include (not exact wording): lack of competent leadership, personnel have low level of motivation, political interference, rules are too strict, personnel lack qualifications or technical skills, missions/goals change frequently, labor disputes/strikes, corruption, appointment of unqualified directors, hiring of unqualified junior personnel due to party affiliation, qualified personnel sacked for party affiliation, disputes among politicians, contracts awarded for political support, inability to voice opinion due to political concerns, frequent changes in leadership.

Despite similar overall views on the severity of resource deficiencies, those reporting high levels of "resources disappearing for party use" are more likely (in both countries) to report resource deficiencies. As I first explained in Chapter 4, and shown again for convenience in Figure 7.3, responses from the two countries diverge considerably when asked whether resources disappearing for political party use is a problem in one's organization. Those surveyed in Benin are much more likely to see resources disappearing from their organizations for party use, with upwards of 85 percent seeing this as a problem or serious problem compared to only around 31 percent in Ghana.

Respondents in Benin were significantly more likely to rate *both* insufficient resources and diversion of resources to party as serious problems. Over 80 percent of those who said insufficient resources were a serious problem also said that party-directed resource diversion is a serious problem. In Ghana, however, only 19 percent rated both as serious problems, suggesting that the co-occurrence of these issues, while present, is not reflective of the main resource insufficiency dynamics in Ghana.

Once again, the Workplace survey provides an opportunity to further explore the connection between extraction and perceptions of resource insufficiency. Using linear regression, I examine whether those who report working in organizations with higher levels of resource diversion are more likely to agree with the statement: "I have sufficient resources to get my job done."[39] I also test whether politicized procurement affects views of resource insufficiency. Once again, I use institution fixed effects to control for unobserved variation across institutions and I include a number of respondent attribute controls.

The results, displayed in Figure 7.4, confirm that those who report more frequent diversion of resources to parties in their organizations are also more likely to report *not* having sufficient resources to get their jobs done. I find that procurement-based extraction also has a negative relationship with perceptions of resource sufficiency, but the relationship is significantly weaker than with party-directed resource diversion.

Taken together, the findings suggest that when bureaucrats engage in activities that result in leakage of organizational resources – as occurs frequently in Benin's coercive system of extraction – they are more likely to see lacking resources as a barrier to getting their jobs done. While the analysis of bureaucratic perceptions may or may not match actual resource deprivations, a number of officials interviewed made clear that

---

[39] The question asks respondents to rate their level of agreement on a 5-point scale where 1 is "strongly disagree" and 5 represents "strongly agree." The mean response for 1,639 respondents is 2.36 with standard deviation of 1.15.

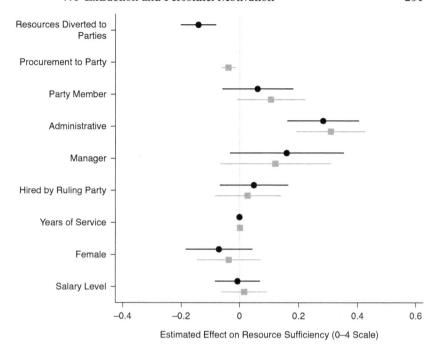

Figure 7.4 Extraction practices and resource sufficiency (Workplace survey)
Estimates based on OLS Regression with institution fixed effects and 95% confidence intervals. Model 1 (dark gray circles), $N = 1,103$ and R-squared $= 0.22$. Model 2 (light gray squares), $N = 1,272$ and R-squared $= 0.21$.

such perceptions constrain productivity. As one employee at the Ministry of Public Service in Benin noted, "under the previous government, if you were with [the ruling party] you could take anything. You could take this sofa [from the office]...yes, it was for the profit of the person, but especially for the politicians. How can one work in an office where the furniture is disappearing?"[40]

7.4   Extraction and Personnel Motivation

As outlined earlier in the chapter, I also expect extraction practices to differentially shape the motivational environment for public service personnel. To assess personnel motivations I examine both individual

---

[40] Author interview, Cotonou, June 28, 2018.

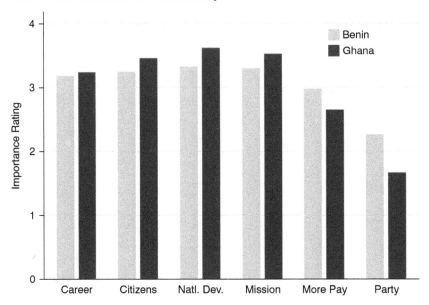

Figure 7.5 Reasons for working hard in current position (Classroom survey)
The graph depicts respondents' average levels of agreement (1 = not at all, 4 = strongly agree) with each factor as a reason to work hard in their organization. Source: Author's Classroom survey (2013–2014).

attitudes of public servants as well as their perceptions of organization-level motivations. Figure 7.5 shows the mean level of agreement with statements about the survey respondents' motivations for working hard. Specifically, the series of questions asks survey respondents to rate their level of agreement with statements about an array of potential consequences of working hard in their organizations.[41] When it comes to believing that their work will contribute to national development, advance their careers, help to achieve the goals of their organization and benefit other citizens, average responses in Ghana are slightly higher than those in Benin, but overall levels of agreement are very high across

[41] The statements all begin with "If I work hard in my current job" and are listed here in the order in which they appear (from left to right) in Figure 7.5. (1) I will have a better chance of advancing my career; (2) it will help the people/clients that our organization serves; (3) it will help Ghana's (Benin's) development; (4) it will help advance the goals and mission of the organization; (5) I will be likely to get a higher-paying job; (6) it will help the ruling party win the next election. Responses are on a scale from 1 to 4 where 1 represents "strongly disagree" and 4 represents "strongly agree."

the two countries. With respect to their hard work benefiting the party's electoral prospects and pay rises, however, average level of agreement drops off in both countries but considerably more so in Ghana, where the average responses were firmly in the "disagree" range.

While the cross-country differences are illuminating, they, once again, do not on their own provide information about whether modes of extraction are linked to different types or intensity of personnel motivation. I further investigate the relationship between extraction and motivation by, again, analyzing data from the Workplace survey. Specifically, I examine whether bureaucrats' reported levels of public service and work motivation are related to their perceptions of personnel diverting resources to political parties.

I construct two indices to measure motivation. The first is a standard measure of public service motivation.[42] Public service motivation in this context consists of an array of principles and values, such as the willingness to sacrifice for the common good or beliefs that all people should be treated equally. As discussed earlier, such values are theorized to make public service employees more committed to serving their community, their organization, or working on behalf of all individuals in society. The index of public service motivation is constructed using a basic principal components model to aggregate responses to sixteen attitudinal questions commonly used to measure public service motivation, such as one's commitment to public values and compassion and willingness to sacrifice for others.[43]

The second index is a measure of work motivation. This measure captures the extent to which individuals report working hard in their positions. It aggregates together respondents' levels of agreement with the following three statements:

- I start work early or stay late to finish my job
- I am willing to do extra work for my job that isn't really expected of me
- I put forth my best effort to get my job done regardless of any difficulties

Figure 7.6 shows the results of regressions testing the relationship between organizational extraction practices and the survey respondent's

---

[42] Kim et al. (2012).

[43] The full list of questions is provided in Appendix F. All indicators are measured on a 5-point scale from strongly disagree (1) to strongly agree (5). For more in-depth analysis of these motivation measures, see Sigman et al. (2018) for Ghana-specific results and Meyer-Sahling et al. (2018) for cross-country results.

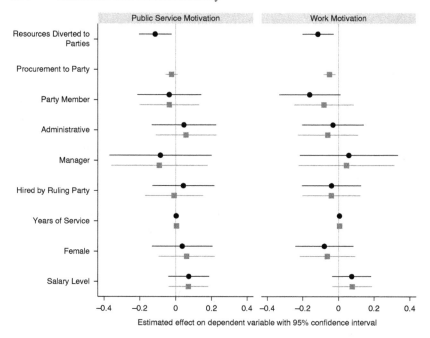

Figure 7.6 Extraction and personnel motivation (Workplace survey)
Estimates based on OLS Regression with institution fixed effects and 95% confidence intervals. Lefthand panel: Model 1 (dark gray circles), $N = 1,096$ and R-squared = 0.02. Model 2 (light gray squares), $N = 1,179$ and R-squared = 0.05. Righthand panel: Model 1 (dark gray circles), $N = 1,103$ and R-squared = 0.10. Model 2 (light gray squares), $N = 1,103$ and R-squared = 0.06.

motivation levels. As in previous tests, I include one model (dark gray circles) in which the main independent variable is the perceived frequency of employees diverting organizational resources to political parties and a second model (light gray squares) in which the main independent variable is the frequency of awarding contracts to party financiers. The results are generally consistent with previous tests in that higher frequency of diversion of resources to parties is associated with lower levels of motivation. In the tests of public service motivation, these coefficients are noticeably lower than among respondents reporting high levels of procurement-based extraction in their organizations.

Although the results fit with expectations outlined previously in the chapter, they do not adequately address the possibility of selection bias that may result from the different patterns of recruitment associated with the different systems of extraction (Chapter 5). The potential bias emerges from the idea that those who were hired through political links are more likely to be employed in organizations where resource diversion is common and, because of their hiring process, are more likely to have lower levels of public-service and work motivation. I therefore conduct one additional set of tests using a sample restricted only to respondents who reported that they did *not* obtain their jobs with the help of politicians.[44] The results, presented in Appendix G, show that the relationship between resource diversion and motivation levels remains negative and statistically significant. Overall, there appears to be a robust pattern in which individuals who work in organizations where diversion of resources to parties is common display, on average, lower levels of motivation, especially public service motivation. This result speaks to the likelihood that coercive extraction in particular may act as a demotivating force for the state's bureaucratic personnel.

I now turn briefly to qualitative accounts of bureaucratic employees' motivation. In both countries, interviewees expressed serious concerns about the motivational environments of the state's bureaucratic organizations. In fact, after Ghana's Head of Civil Service made the public statement about the robust C.V.'s of Ghanaian civil servants that would be able to "sink a ship" (discussed at the outset of Chapter 4), he went on to say that he is "concerned much more about attitude."[45] Interviewees in Benin and Ghana, however, spoke somewhat differently about problems related to employee motivation. In Ghana, for instance, several interview respondents emphasized the role of ministers or other high-ranking ministry officials in cultivating motivation among employees. One former minister explained, "since it's not really possible to change the personnel in the ministry, you have to just find a way to motivate them with your own goals and own vision for the ministry."[46] This kind of comment stands in contrast to a former minister in Benin who noted, "Ministers cannot appoint their *Secrétaire Général* [of the ministry]. The Head of State chooses them. This really ties the hands of the ministers to develop their own programs and manage the agents of the state."[47] This comment speaks in particular to the way that presidents' concerns

[44] As described in Chapter 5, the list experiments included in the Workplace survey suggest limited (if any) social desirability bias in these results.
[45] " 'CVs of Ghanaian civil servants can sink a ship' – Head of Civil Service demands positive work attitude," *Joy Online News*, May 17, 2018.
[46] Author interview, Accra, July 14, 2014.
[47] Author interview, Cotonou, June 21, 2018.

about controlling ministers, detailed at length in the previous chapter, shape the ministry's professional and motivational environments.

Another difference that emerged in interviews across the two countries had to do with the motivational problems that resulted from hiring processes of rank-and-file bureaucratic personnel. One manager in Ghana's Ministry of Gender explained, "public servants who are hired on merit basis are officers who have the passion and commitment to serve the nation and therefore accepted the appointment and so are self-motivated. As a result they do not condone corrupt practices."[48] In Benin, however, there was a sense that even if one is hired through meritocratic processes, they are unlikely to be very motivated to work in a highly politicized environment where, as discussed above, bureaucrats often get "pushed aside" in the midst of politicized management of the ministry. Additionally, while multiple managers I spoke with asserted the strong qualifications of many Beninese public servants, some noted that, often, qualified individuals were placed into agencies and positions where they could not effectively apply their skills. As one division director in an infrastructure-sector ministry noted, "we have many very capable engineers in Benin...but it can be difficult to hire them."[49] In a study of these kinds of "mismatches" in employee qualifications and work positions in Benin's local governments, Lazare Kovo argues this problem is particularly detrimental to performance.[50]

7.5   Conclusion

The evidence presented in this chapter supports the broad hypothesis that the practices associated with coercive extraction are especially prone to undermine the productivity of the state's bureaucratic organizations. In raising the stakes of political control over the bureaucracy and engaging bureaucrats more centrally in extractive political financing, coercive extraction reaches more deeply into the day-to-day work environments of the state's bureaucracy. This can be particularly disruptive to bureaucratic function in terms of political interference in decision-making, the perceived or actual availability of resources, and the motivations of bureaucratic personnel.

I also find that, when elite politicians collude in extraction, the combination of well-aligned elite interests and less extensive participation of bureaucrats proves considerably less disruptive to the work

---

[48] Online follow-up survey, April 7, 2017.
[49] Author interview, Cotonou, June 25, 2018.
[50] Kovo (2018).

environments in bureaucratic organizations. These patterns are evident in comparing and contrasting politician–bureaucrat relationships in Benin and Ghana, as well as in individual-level analyses within Ghana.

The analysis conducted in this chapter also implies that the staffing and executive dynamics, described in Chapters 5 and 6, respectively, shape the broader institutional environment in which bureaucrats operate. It illustrates how both politicized staffing decisions at various levels of government and elite (in)stability in the executive – both themselves shaped by party institutions and their associated extraction dynamics – interact to shape the pressures, motivations, and materials that form the day-to-day working environments for many of the state's bureaucratic personnel. When incumbent leaders hire and rely on partisan bureaucrats to help facilitate their extraction strategies, it raises the stakes of political control, depletes the resources of the organization, and acts as a demotivating force for public service-oriented bureaucrats. Moreover, if incumbent leaders distrust and frequently rotate the elites who sit atop government ministries, bureaucrats are more likely to struggle with competing directives, policy disruptions, and uncertainty around personnel changes. In short, a broader picture that considers together patterns of staffing at different levels of government, executive stability, and bureaucratic structures, illuminates the important ways in which leaders' extraction efforts shape the overall performance of the state apparatus.

Thus, we can now return to one of the puzzles motivating this research: how different systems of extraction in Benin and Ghana relate to their divergent records of success in implementing their signature public policy goals.[51] As I have shown in this and preceding chapters, Ghana's collusive system of extraction avoids major disruptions to the state's governing institutions. It avoids the types of instability, incohesion, and bureaucratic work environments that are widely associated with weak governments around the world. As such, Ghana's leaders, despite causing serious financial loss to the state in the course of their collusive practice of extraction, have managed to establish more clearly-articulated governing agendas, to elevate a relatively unified set of elites to serve both political and policy agendas, and to sustain a public service that is both more professional and more empowered to contribute to policy processes.

---

[51] As discussed in Chapters 1 and 6, the Ghanaian government has managed to implement ambitious programs and improve performance in key areas such as health insurance, tax collection, energy sector development, tertiary education, and transportation.

In Benin's coercive system, by contrast, politicians' efforts to coerce and control bureaucrats as agents of extraction impair the potential effectiveness of the broader governing apparatus. The coercive methods of extraction pursued by leaders produce highly politicized executive institutions infused with instability and mistrust, resulting in unproductive, bureaucratic environments. Together, these institutional environments minimize the chances for policy success. Even amidst genuine interest in advancing their governing agendas, Benin's leaders struggle to make meaningful progress in policy implementation.

8   Reflections on Parties, Extraction, and State Performance

I have shown in this book that it is both necessary and fruitful to interrogate *how* leaders extract money from the state. Of particular importance are questions about how leaders, faced with pressures to extract, confront choices about delegation, networks, and control. These choices are important because they determine the extent to which leaders must rely on the power and authorities of the state itself in the course of their extractive pursuits. I demonstrate that when extraction is regularized and concentrated among party and business elite, it is considerably less likely to undermine the work environments of state institutions. By contrast, when incumbents extract money in ways that are less predictable and more reliant on rank-and-file public service employees, it is more likely to disrupt the productivity of the state's executive and bureaucratic institutions. Thus, where leaders can rely principally on the party's agents, networks, and mechanisms of control, they are less likely to impede the productivity and effectiveness of the state. Absent these party structures, leaders extract in ways that require greater political intrusion into the state's governing apparatus.

Through in-depth examinations of two competitive democracies in Africa, the book has advanced two main arguments. First, political party institutions condition *how* leaders extract from the state. Party institutions are key to understanding who leaders enlist as extraction agents, how they channel money through political networks, and which instruments of control leaders use to ensure that the extracted monies benefit the ruling party. In Ghana's collusive system of extraction, where leaders are embedded in highly institutionalized political parties, leaders delegate extraction to elite party agents who coordinate with partisan networks to channel extracted monies. Strong internal mechanisms of control – including rules and procedures for party advancement and strong partisan norms and values – ensure that extracted monies benefit the party. Lacking strong and stable party institutions and fearing elite defection, leaders in Benin have resorted to more coercive methods of extraction. These methods have included both the president's efforts to tightly control lucrative extraction deals and/or threats to more vulnerable actors, namely rank-and-file bureaucrats, to compel their participation in the collection of rents or diversion of state revenues.

Second, I have argued that, as observed in Benin, low party institutionalization and coercive extraction result in more intrusive forms of state politicization that impair the day-to-day functioning of the state's executive and bureaucratic institutions. In their efforts to guard extraction opportunities from potential opponents, leaders in Benin rotate and dismiss ministers – or threaten to do so – in ways that breed division and instability in the executive. These dynamics undermine commitment to the president's governing agenda and hamper inter-ministerial coordination. In coercing rank-and-file supporters to participate in their extraction projects, leaders in coercive systems not only politicize the recruitment of career bureaucrats, but they are considerably more likely to interfere in the day-to-day work of bureaucratic agencies, leading to a de-motivating and unproductive work environment.

The implications of these different patterns of extraction and state politicization are evident in policy successes and shortcomings across the two countries. Ghana has outpaced many African countries in the implementation of a healthcare program, in expansions of access to tertiary education, in the development of its oil and gas industry, and so on. Although very messy at times, its governments have sustained these programs despite disruptions from intense election campaigns and turnovers of power, and despite major financial losses resulting from political extraction. Benin's governing record is considerably less distinguished. There has been little progress on key priorities such as cotton sector reform, national health insurance, and energy sector development.

In the pages that follow, I extend and reflect on these arguments. I begin with a brief investigation into the question of generalizability: can the argument travel to other countries? I then discuss how future research and policy approaches might better incorporate party institutions, which, as the book shows, act as key drivers of governance. In the final words of the book, I reflect on how emerging political developments in Benin, Ghana, and across the continent are likely to shape the contours of extraction in the future and what these developments mean for the advancement of effective democratic states.

8.1   Beyond Benin and Ghana

The two systems of extraction described in the preceding chapters are not specific to Benin and Ghana. Extraction has taken more collusive forms in other countries where institutionalized ruling parties hold power such as in Botswana, Rwanda, South Africa, and Tanzania. Likewise, the contours of coercive extraction are evident in countries in Africa where ruling parties lack strong institutions. The extraction framework presented in Chapter 2 can also be adapted to contexts of intermediate party institutionalization, for example where elite coalitions are unstable but voter attachments to parties are strong, or vice versa. To establish the potential generalizability of the theory, I briefly investigate four additional countries. First, I examine two "shadow" cases – Botswana and Malawi – that mirror the collusive and coercive systems observed in Ghana and Benin respectively. I then turn attention to two countries where party institutionalization is of a more ambiguous nature – Uganda and Senegal – to demonstrate how the collusive and coercive frameworks may be adapted to other contexts.

8.1.1   Collusive Extraction in the Botswana Democratic Party

I have detailed in the preceding chapters how incumbent leaders of Ghana's highly institutionalized political parties pursue more collusive methods of extraction whereby elite party agents work collectively to channel state money through supporter networks, often in the form of state procurement contracts to party-affiliated businesses. Longer party time horizons, internal party rules and procedures for member advancement, and shared values of mutual material benefit among party members incentivize agents to extract in service of the party and help leaders to overcome problems related to delegation and control. Collusive extraction is relatively efficient in terms of fundraising and requires less-intrusive forms of state politicization.

Much has been written about Botswana as an exemplar of strong state performance in Africa, some going so far as to view Botswana as one of the few developmental states outside of East Asia. Equal if not more notable about Botswana is that its strong economic performance is largely dependent on natural resources, namely diamonds.[1] There are indeed a multitude of explanations for Botswana's high level of state performance and it is not my intention to either review or compete with them here. Instead, my more modest intention is to show, first, that Botswana's well-institutionalized ruling party, the BDP, extracts political money from the state in a collusive manner that is reflective of the system in Ghana, albeit one that is more concentrated within Botswana's

---

[1] For example, Leftwich (2000) has classified Botswana as a developmental state and Dunning (2008) explains how Botswana has overcome challenges commonly associated with the resource curse.

unique public-private partnership in the diamond sector. Second, I demonstrate the ways that this system helps to sustain cohesion at the apex of government and a high level of professionalism among the bureaucratic ranks.

In Botswana, the ruling BDP has, for much of its history, colluded closely with the De Beers diamond company through Debswana, the long-running public-private diamond venture.[2] The unique partnership between the two entities has, by several accounts, allowed for a rather liberal flow of money between the BDP and De Beers. As one study describes it, "De Beers and the BDP have knit the political and corporate structures together" in a system defined by the "blurring of corporation, state, and party."[3]

De Beers' support to the BDP has come in multiple forms. It is now widely known, for example, that De Beers provided funds to former President Ketumile Masire, who served from 1980 through 1998, in the form of bailouts for Masire's personal agricultural companies, the most well known of which was G. M. Five. Specifically, De Beers provided both funding and managerial services to Masire's private ventures "during their time of need," which happened to occur in the lead-up to the 1984 and 1989 elections.[4] The payments were facilitated by the long-time managing director of Debswana, Louis Nchindo. The financial relationship between De Beers and the BDP leadership, however, extended well beyond President Masire and his close associates like Nchindo. In the course of investigations surrounding these deals, one account explains that the chief executive officer of De Beers Botswana offered an additional explanation that "we have made donations to the BDP over the years and most recently in the late 1990s."[5] De Beers' support to the BDP did not cease when Masire left power in 1998. In 1999, donations to the BDP from "undisclosed foreign sources" via Swiss bank accounts were subsequently traced to De Beers.[6] There is also evidence to suggest that De Beers was paying for the BDP's political consultants and other party expenses.[7] Although the network is more concentrated, this stable, ongoing financial relationship facilitated by

---

[2] In order to operate in the country, De Beers partnered with Botswana's government in the late 1960s to create Debswana, originally called the De Beers Botswana Mining Company. De Beers and the Government of Botswana hold equal 50 percent shares in the company.

[3] Sharife (2016: 78).

[4] Good (2010: 91). See, also, Sharife (2016).

[5] Good (2010: 91).

[6] This donation is described by both Molomo (2000: 78) and Good (2010: 90).

[7] Sharife (2016: 79).

the committed party elite is consistent with the contours of collusive extraction described in Ghana.

Since the 1990s, moreover, the BDP's sources of financing appear to have become more diverse and less centered around the president. In the run-up to the 1999 election, De Beers continued to contribute, albeit anonymously from an "undisclosed foreign source" via a Swiss bank account. In addition to these foreign sources, however, other senior, rich, and ambitious party members such as Satar Dada, the country's car magnate, and the BDP's treasurer, have come to play an important role in financing the party.[8] In exchange for his financing, Dada "enjoys millions from government contracts through his various businesses" including as a major supplier of vehicles to government institutions.[9] These senior party members and financiers from the private sector either serve as ministers themselves, as in the case of Charles Tibone and Robert Masitara,[10] or, as in the case of Nchindo, key appointees facilitate these exchanges.

Although there is "a near fusion" of the BDP with the senior ranks of the state's bureaucracy and many senior bureaucrats eventually become involved in politics, there is little if any evidence to suggest that rank-and-file bureaucrats play a role in political financing. Botswana is consistently rated among the most professional and impartial bureaucracies in Africa, and its level of public sector corruption is among the lowest on the continent.[11] The appointment of bureaucratic personnel is largely conducted on the basis of qualification and experience,[12] and the political elite have "fairly consistently sought expert advice from leading bureaucrats," displaying a "closeness and mutuality of interest built upon their common involvement in cattle and commerce, and the not uncommon tendency for cabinet ministers to arise from the ranks of the senior bureaucracy."[13]

To summarize, extraction practices in Botswana's institutionalized BDP do not give rise to the types of intrusive politicization in governing dynamics that can seriously impair the state's ability to pursue public policy goals. The party elite, consisting primarily of a fused set of ministers and business leaders, collude to extract money through procurement

---

[8] Good (2008: 90).
[9] See, for example, "Nobody Funds You for Nothing," Botswana Gazette, June 14, 2019.
[10] Good (2008: 90).
[11] According to V-Dem data, for instance, Botswana is far above the African average on measures of "rigorous and impartial public administration" and on the absence of corruption in public sector organizations.
[12] Thovoethin (2014: 260).
[13] Good (1994: 499).

or through links between the government, Debswana, and De Beers. Although senior bureaucrats may eventually become part of this political elite, the elite themselves do not have extraction-related motivations to politicize or interfere in the day-to-day work of bureaucratic organizations. Although factional disputes within the party are a persistent issue, such as in the 2019 election when former President Ian Khama did not fully support the BDP nominee (and eventual winner) Mokgweetsi Masisi; these issues tend to get resolved in ways that perpetuate the party's hegemony in Botswana's politics.

8.1.2   Coercive Extraction in Malawi

Much like in Benin, political parties in Malawi tend to have low levels of institutionalization. One of the defining features of Malawi's party landscape is frequent and high-profile defections and divisions that generate new parties.[14] The first high-profile split occurred in 2005 when President Bingu wa Mutharika left the ruling United Democratic Front (UDF) to form the Democratic Progress Party (DPP). The second occurred in 2012 when, following Mutharika's death, his chosen successor and brother, Peter Mutharika, expelled then vice president Joyce Banda from the party. She went on to create the Progress Party (PP) and subsequently served as president of Malawi until 2014. Whereas Malawi's parties are arguably more durable than Benin's, there are few rules and procedures vis-á-vis leadership structures and succession. The UDF, for example, never held a convention after 1993, and members "had few opportunities to voice or advance themselves through the party convention.[15] Their roots in society remain either highly regionalized or lacking all together, and the parties are largely devoid of collective values or ideals. One manifestation of these weak institutions is that leaders may join coalition governments as ministers even if their own parliamentary group has not decided to support the government. Parties may therefore occupy both government and opposition roles at the same time.[16]

Party leaders in Malawi, like those in Benin, rely on a range of more controlled and coercive fundraising strategies. Presidents themselves have maintained tight control over party finances. The first president of the current democratic era, Bakili Muluzi, reportedly served as principal financier of the ruling party UDF.[17] An "enormously wealthy" man,

---

[14] VonDoepp (2005).

[15] VonDoepp (2005: 77). Note that some parties in Malawi do hold internal elections, especially for the selection of parliamentary candidates.

[16] Svåsand (2013).

[17] VonDoepp (2005: 77).

Muluzi personally oversaw major party purchases such as the "scores of UDF vehicles, bought duty-free in Muluzi's name," which later served as the basis for a corruption investigation pursued by the successor DPP government.[18] President Bingu wa Mutharika was also known for keeping tight control over extraction and party financing operations, holding several ministerial portfolios himself. At one point, the party's former treasurer general under Mutharika was reported to have said that "party finances were the preserve of the party president," meaning Mutharika.[19]

This trend appears to have continued. Although he was not the main financier of the DPP, President Peter Mutharika had reportedly personally overseen the party's finances, at least some of which came from the business sector or wealthy individuals looking for preferential treatment for their businesses. Describing this arrangement, Boniface Dulani writes that this level of control:

was illustrated in mid-2018 when the Secretary General of DPP denied knowledge of the party's bank account, whose sole signatory was President Peter Mutharika (The Nation 2018). Chikoko (2015) describes the treasurers of Malawi's political parties as "mere figure heads who hold the titles without actually executing responsibilities expected of their office. Instead, it is party presidents that keep the money, and only the presidents know sources of the funds." As noted by Svasånd (2014:285), this has contributed to the centralization of power in the parties' especially since "the funding is paid out to the bank account managed by the party leader."[20]

There is also evidence, however, that presidents have at times delegated extraction practices to public servants. This delegation is not surprising given the frequent occurrence and high visibility of politically motivated anti-corruption prosecutions. The most visible example of bureaucratic participation in party extraction activities was during the "cashgate" scandal of 2013 when bureaucrats were caught with trunks full of embezzled state money in their vehicles. Sometime after the scandal came to light, it became clear that "some of the main culprits were connected to the then ruling People's Party of President Joyce Banda" and that "many implicated in the scandal were either members of the then-ruling People's Party or its sympathisers."[21]

---

[18] "Queuing for Court," Africa Confidential, November 19, 2004.
[19] "Party Financing in Malawi: The Best Kept Secret?" The Nyasa Times, July 11, 2013.
[20] Dulani (2019: 140).
[21] Dulani (2019: 142–143).

The prevalence of civil servant participation in political extraction in Malawi is borne out in the results of a 2017 civil servant survey conducted in Malawi, which that mirrors the Workplace survey from Ghana that is referenced throughout the previous chapters of this book.[22] In a list experiment question designed to detect whether bureaucrats have, in the course of their jobs, diverted resources to a political party, an estimated 35 percent of Malawian civil servants surveyed admitted to having done so. The comparable estimate in Ghana was around 8 percent.

The implications of these extraction practices are evident in Malawi's executive and bureaucratic institutions. The executive is rife with highly politicized cabinet reshuffles, very often accompanied by allegations of corruption against outgoing ministers who have extracted money but not remained sufficiently loyal to the president. Muluzi, for example, placed "men (and a few women) that he could trust and/or manipulate to head ministries, run parastatals, convene advisory boards and manage departments...technical specialists with evidence-based policy experience, were among those not making policy."[23] After the elections in May 2004 in which Bingu wa Mutharika prevailed, he "fell out with the UDF top brass and Muluzi" then subsequently "ordered the arrest of a high-ranking UDF functionary on corruption charges...and several high-ranking officials were charged for their alleged role in the illegal sale of the strategic grain reserve in 2001 that had triggered a devastating famine."[24]

Within the civil service, World Bank staff have reported high levels of politicization, explaining that civil servants' careers often "depend on their loyalty."[25] Another study of Malawi's civil service describes "asymmetric power relations" and widespread practices associated with "maintenance of indebtedness" whereby junior civil servants pay "commissions" to more senior officials, many of whom are politically connected.[26] The impacts of these dynamics are visible in terms of performance, as explained by Booth and coauthors:

failure to delegate significant powers has not only helped to de-motivate the bureaucracy, but also increased inefficiency...Within bureaucracies such as the civil service (and to a lesser extent in private businesses) vital decisions get

[22] As described earlier, the Workplace survey was part of a larger cross-national project that, in Africa, included Malawi and Uganda. The cross-country results discussed here are presented by Meyer-Sahling et al. (2018).

[23] Booth et al. (2006: 25).

[24] Anders (2009: 126).

[25] World Bank Group Malawi Country Team (2018: 24).

[26] Anders (2002).

delayed if people are afraid to take action in the absence of authority from above, to question irrational instructions, to bypass obsolete rules whose origins and function are obscure, or to tackle problems in a proactive manner. It is observed that this constantly stalls project planning and implementation in Malawi. When, in addition to these general cultural issues, the politicians who run governments make it clear that they do not trust their senior officials to take even the smallest initiatives, the effect on efficiency has to be extremely damaging.[27]

These accounts of party extraction, executive instability, and a de-motivating bureaucratic environment in Malawi resonate strongly with the patterns observed in Benin. Fearing elite defection, leaders seek to control, at times coercively, the flow of resources to potential opponents. These control efforts have implications for the day-to-day functioning of executive and bureaucratic institutions and generate a highly politicized environment that prioritizes loyalty and obedience over policy performance.

8.1.3   Intermediate Institutionalization: The NRM in Uganda

The countries considered thus far are cases where party institutionalization is unequivocally high or low, with Ghana and Botswana in the former category and Benin and Malawi in the latter. How does extraction work in countries with more intermediate levels of party institutionalization? To reflect on this question, I briefly consider the case of Uganda's ruling NRM. The NRM under President Yoweri Museveni has held power since 1986. Although multiparty presidential elections are permitted, the NRM uses a range of coercive and co-optation strategies to ensure their victory. Nonetheless, elections are to some extent competitive with Museveni garnering around 60 percent of the (not free and fair) vote and the NRM often struggling to gain a comfortable majority of seats in Parliament.[28] The NRM lacks internal coherence, a defined network of political actors, or a clear and "binding ideology."[29] It serves largely as "an unruly catch-all for aspiring political elites"[30] that is "highly disorganised, personalised, and even a chaotic mess at times." What the NRM lacks in organizational coherence, however, it makes up for in its mobilization capacity. The organizational chaos at the upper echelons of the party, Vokes and Wilkins argue, has not undone

---

[27] Booth et al. (2006: 25).
[28] Based on the election results from the three past multiparty presidential elections held in 2006, 2011, and 2016.
[29] Vokes and Wilkins (2016: 583).
[30] Collord (2016).

its "machine-like mobilisation network that connects Museveni to his rural base: outreach programmes, call centres, and a national grass-roots mobilisation network that is unparalleled in Uganda."[31]

This semi-institutionalized party arrangement poses an interesting challenge to the theory of collusive and coercive extraction laid out in Chapter 2. The "chaos" among party elites reflects to some extent the conditions of noninstitutionalized parties and more coercive forms of extraction. The grassroots mobilization machine, however, implies that there are strong roots in society, collective norms, and potential mechanisms of control built into the party, at least at the lower levels where local members may want to move up in the machine. Overall, this configuration suggests that extraction is likely to look more coercive than collusive, with extraction concentrated in and around the party leader, as well as some delegation to lower-level party operatives.

Accounts of the NRM's extraction activities do suggest that it is Museveni himself who oversees the NRM's principal extraction activities. Such activities have, since the late 1990s, taken a wide variety of forms including NRM-owned businesses that profited from various fraudulent activities, direct embezzlement from ministries and the military, the use of "ghost soldiers" and secretive procurement deals in the military, as well as typical privatization and public procurement deals with businesses.[32] In many cases Museveni oversaw these operations himself or "under the control of individuals close to the presidency and members of the very inner circle of the ruling coalition."[33] The president and his inner circle of leaders maintain control over these extracted funds in part through arrests, dismissals, and other coercive tools against those who may be wielding too much power with extracted resources.[34]

On another level, however, the NRM has used the proliferation of state organizations to broaden patronage opportunities – and extraction – to service its grassroots-level machine.[35] The NRM has created "an elastic and ever-expanding ruling coalition," but this coalition exists "more so at the local level than at the top."[36] To accommodate this "ever-expanding coalition," Museveni grew the state apparatus – serving not only as a

---

[31] Vokes and Wilkins (2016: 584).

[32] For overviews, see Khisa (2019) and Tangri and Mwenda (2013).

[33] Khisa (2019: 99) provides an overview of these activities.

[34] For example, Khisa (2019: 104–105) describes forced resignations, formal accusations of abuse of office, and embezzlement. They also note, however, that these allegations are rarely seriously prosecuted in court.

[35] Vokes and Wilkins (2016) note that this machine exists primarily in the south of the country where Museveni enjoys the most support.

[36] Khisa (2019: 98).

source of patronage jobs but also to enable his supporters to extract for political purposes. As Tangri and Mwenda (2013) describe:

> Many new specialized institutions were created (such as the Uganda Revenue Authority and the Uganda Investment Authority) to enable the state to implement specific structural adjustment reforms. In 2002 Uganda had over seventy semi-autonomous government agencies, employing over 40,000 persons. By 2012, their number had grown to 171 with around 145,000 employees. Even the size of the civil service had grown: by 2005 it numbered nearly 230 000 employees, and by 2010 it had reached 320,000. Thus, contrary to the neoliberal prescriptions of the IFIs, the size of Uganda's public administration was greatly expanded. A large public sector was to provide political leaders and state officials with manifold opportunities for serving their private and political interests.

In sum, the extraction landscape in Uganda appears to reflect both the coercive nature of the NRM's hegemonic power in Uganda as well as its rather benevolent relationship with the grassroots. Thus, among elites, extraction reflects the coercive system that is typical of ruling parties with low levels of institutionalization. At the apex of the party, Museveni tightly controls major extraction opportunities, even going so far as to situate them within the military where they can be concealed under the auspices of national security. Its engagement with lower-level extraction agents, however, is more reflective of a collusive system in which there exists a sense of linked collective interest, albeit an interest that is heavily shaped by the long-standing hegemonic position of the NRM. As Michaela Collord describes, there is considerably less control at the local level where individual employees of state agencies can extract for their political needs.[37] What makes this "unruly" system nonthreatening is both the tight control at the top and the hegemonic grassroots position of the NRM, not to mention the frequent use of coercive tactics to intimidate elite opponents.

8.1.4 Party De-Institutionalization in Senegal

Finally, I consider the case of Senegal, where each of the three ruling parties that have held power since independence have shown successive weakness in terms of their party institutions. The mass-based Parti Socialiste (PS), which held power in Senegal from independence in 1960 through 2000, was among one of Africa's more institutionalized political parties.[38] In opposition for many years, the PDS also possessed many of the features of well-institutionalized political party organizations.[39]

---

[37] Collord (2016).
[38] Riedl (2014).
[39] Kelly (2020).

Since the PDS won power in 2000, however, it became increasingly per-sonalistic,[40] and the party system generally has become more highly fluid and candidate-centered.[41] Focusing in particular on the PDS, which held power under President Abdoulaye Wade from 2000 through 2012, I briefly discuss how these processes of de-institutionalization have brought about more concentrated and coercive extraction practices.

The PDS was the main opposition party in Senegal from 1974 through 2000. Its leader, Abdoulaye Wade, held an academic background and espoused largely liberal economic principles. During the 1980s and 1990s, Wade and other members of the PDS served at various times in the PS government. He eventually prevailed in the 2000 presidential elections in what became Senegal's first inter-party transfer of power. By then, however, internal institutions had already started to weaken as the internal elections – a key mechanism of advancement for party members – that had been scheduled for 1996 had experienced con-tinued delays. Following Wade's successful election to office in 2000, Catherine Kelly describes how the party atrophied in both its mobi-lization potential and in its institutional coherence. She explains how Wade informally changed the composition of executive boards (the Directing Committee), dis-empowering the "old guard" and undermin-ing opportunities for meaningful coordination and deliberation.[42] These changes bled into government. Whereas, during Wade's first term, Prime Ministers Idrissa Seck (2002–2004) and Macky Sall (2004–2006) were "both able to propose their ideal ministerial cabinet" and maneuver as they liked, both men soon fell out of favor with Wade and defected from the party to start their own. The vacuum was filled by Wade's son, Karim and a group of his followers known as the *Génération du Con-cret*.[43] Dubbed the "Minister of the Sky and the Earth," Karim Wade was granted control over a growing number of powerful government portfolios – many of which had very large procurement contracts with international companies, thus serving as major extraction opportuni-ties. During this period, Wade deposited upwards of $200 million in banks in Monaco.[44] These developments, according to Kelly, "exac-erbated popular suspicion that President Wade was preparing his son for succession within the PDS," and drove further defections from the

---

[40] Osei (2013).

[41] Resnick (2013).

[42] Kelly (2020: 179).

[43] Generation of Concrete in English. This is in reference to efforts to embark on major land and infrastructure developments, especially in and around Dakar.

[44] This was reported widely in the Senegalese and international media.

party.[45] Thus, as the PDS's institutions deteriorated and elite defections from the party became more frequent, access to extraction opportunities became increasingly concentrated around Wade and his family. This, in turn, precipitated further atrophy in the party – a development that ultimately aided PDS-defector Macky Sall in his rapid rise to power.

There is some suggestive evidence that, in the face of these defections, Wade moved to politicize and exert greater control over the bureaucracy and its hiring processes. One senior leader at Senegal's elite school for public servants (*Ecole Nationale d'Administration et Magistrature* (ENAM)) explained that, during Wade's second term, the government stopped engaging in the regular process for recruitment whereby the Prime Minister's office formally requests a specified number of ENAM graduates for positions in the civil service. For a period of at least two years, the official reported, the government made no requests at all to ENAM, suggesting that they were using "other means" to staff the bureaucracy.[46] In her study of several of Senegal's key ministries, Martha Johnson notes that, during this time, the government used its national health plan to elevate patronage opportunities and political control by hiring contractual workers and increasing the volume of construction procurement contracts.[47] Whether these efforts were aimed at controlling extraction from bureaucratic organizations remains unclear but, overall, these anecdotes suggest the possibility of a connection between the de-institutionalization of the ruling party, the evolution of extraction activities, and the politicization of the civil service.

These brief forays into the political extraction dynamics in Botswana, Malawi, Uganda, and Senegal convey linkages between party institutions, extraction, and state politicization across different contexts. Botswana's ethnically homogeneous population, resource-dependent economic structure, and dominant-party political landscape differ in important ways from Ghana's.[48] Yet, in both countries, highly institutionalized ruling parties produce more collusive systems of extraction. Likewise, Malawi's British colonial heritage and first-past-the-post electoral system are dissimilar from Benin, yet its weak parties appear to drive leaders to adopt more coercive methods of extraction, just

---

[45] Kelly (2020: 180). When Karim Wade did not succeed in his bid to become Mayor of Dakar in 2009 it became clear that he would not have the political support necessary to win a presidential election. Some time later, Abdoulaye Wade decided to pursue a third term of office in the 2012 election.

[46] Author interview, Dakar, April 19, 2012.

[47] Johnson also explains that these efforts were ultimately limited by donor involvement.

[48] Ghana does have significant natural resource revenue from gold and, more recently, from oil, but it is not considered a resource-dependent country.

as they do in Benin. Additionally, the more authoritarian setting in Uganda, where elite coalitions are unstable but voter attachments to the dominant NRM are strong, shows how the framework linking party institutions, extraction, and state politicization can be adapted to a more intermediate case of party institutionalization.[49] The case of party de-institutionalization in Senegal provides further evidence that party institutions shape leaders' extraction practices in a variety of settings. The cases also help to highlight the different ways that political leaders manage their state institutions for extraction.

8.2   Rethinking Governance through the Lens of Party Institutions

In one way or another, much of political science is concerned with how leaders manage state resources to advance their own political interests. In traditional democratic theory, politicians invest state resources in policies and programs designed to gain or maintain support from the median voter. In pork-barrel and clientelistic models of politics, politicians use state power to redistribute resources to specific constituencies that support them politically. In Marxist approaches, the state represents a tool of the dominant classes to advance their own material interests. Just as scholars have rigorously analyzed median-voter dynamics, targeted distribution, and Marxist superstructures, so too should we more intently analyze variation in how leaders extract financial resources from the state for their political projects. Viewed this way, extraction is not an exception or pathology to "normal" governing behavior, it is a response – albeit sometimes a very destructive one – to a set of political conditions and incentives. And just like any government decision, it may be carried out in more productive or more destructive ways.

The argument set forth in this book, that party institutions shape whether leaders extract in ways that are more or less disruptive to the state's institutional environment, conveys the importance of studying institutional variation in Africa, even when considering illicit or covert behavior. Scholarship on African politics has rightly recognized the centrality of extraction for understanding patterns of political competition

---

[49] I have not yet applied the framework to a case where elite coalitions are durable but partisan attachments among voters are relatively weak. One possible case might be Ethiopia's EPRDF. The EPRDF involved a relatively stable (ethnic) elite alliance, which led the party's elite to form a network of for-profit entities serving the party's financial needs (Abegaz, 2013). The EPRDF's weak internal structure, however, characterized by frequently "changing strategies of political mobilization and organization," has meant that party leaders use more coercive forms of control over coalition members (Vaughan, 2011).

and governance across the continent. By and large, however, these per-spectives have assumed a large degree of uniformity in leaders' extraction practices and, consequently, in the ways that extraction undermines both democracy and state institutional performance. The dominant narrative has been that, as long as leaders continue to extract large volumes of resources from the state at their discretion, advancements in government effectiveness will be limited. This narrative tends to equate extraction generally with low levels of state performance, driving questions that focus primarily on the conditions under which leaders may be more or less constrained in their efforts to extract from the state.

Although it is not my intention to dispute the idea that extraction – and state exploitation more generally – pose major governance challenges, I have shown in this book that it is both necessary and fruitful to investi-gate not only *if* leaders extract money from the state, but *how* they do it. The focus of future inquiries on political extraction should turn to questions about the extent to which leaders carry out their exploitation strategies *within* or *outside of* the state apparatus. For leaders with strong parties surrounding them, or other strong linkage mechanisms to society, they may pursue their extraction goals with minimal interference in the day-to-day workings of the state. Thus, parties are important not only, as Samuel Huntington famously argued, because they channel participa-tion of the potentially rancorous masses, but also because they provide the structures through which elites can pursue their political projects with less (or more) disruption to the state.[50]

This perspective on the virtues of well-institutionalized parties calls for continued attention to variation in party institutions in Africa and across the world. Recent scholarship has made considerable progress in documenting variation (or lack thereof) in party institutions,[51] under-standing parties' historical institutional origins,[52] and connecting party institutions to policy and reform outcomes.[53] The preceding chapters, however, illustrate how party institutions condition the choices lead-ers make about when and how to strategically use the state for their political advantage, and the successes or failures they are likely to expe-rience in doing so. These choices, particularly when they concern how to extract the resources of the state, have significant implications not only for incumbents' political survival, but for broader patterns of gov-ernance. They impact, among other things, the types of state personnel

---

[50] Huntington (1968).
[51] Elischer (2013); Hicken and Kuhonta (2015); Mainwaring (2018); Meng (2021).
[52] LeBas (2011); Riedl (2014); Morse (2018).
[53] Pitcher (2012); Cruz and Keefer (2015).

recruited, the quality of leadership and coordination at the apex of government, and the bureaucratic work environments in which the state's public servants operate.

The book points to some specific ways to incorporate parties and party institutionalization into studies of political management of the state. In Chapter 5, I show how the strength of party institutions combines with leaders' concerns about party financing to shape decisions about the distribution of state jobs. The chapter argues that leaders not only distribute jobs to mobilize political support – the preoccupation of much of the literature on clientelism – but also to gain and protect access to the state's pecuniary resources. These findings convey the importance of moving beyond simple accounts of parties, especially clientelistic parties, as vote mobilizers. Parties involve significant internal administrative dimensions that, as this book has shown, are often contentious and constrained. How parties confront these administrative tasks is critical for understanding their behaviors as vote mobilizers and governing entities.

In Chapter 6, I show that within Ghana's well-organized and internally democratic parties, repeated interactions over time enable party members to learn about each others' loyalties and competencies. These learning processes generate trust among the party elite in ways that spillover into executive cabinets. As my analysis of Ghana's executive suggests, this trust can exist even in the presence of internal party factions as well as in the absence of strong programmatic agendas. These findings challenge the conventional wisdom that parties' (or coalitions') ideological and programmatic compositions (or lack thereof) drive governing outcomes. Instead, I show how the strength and durability of parties' organizations and the existence of shared brands or identities have equal or greater relevance for understanding how parties govern. By providing opportunities for repeated interactions among party members, these particular dimensions of party institutionalization can generate trust and familiarity that allows party actors to act as more efficacious governing agents. For scholars, this insight implies that it is equally (if not more) important to study party organizations and party brands than it is ideological positions or programmatic agendas. For practitioners, it implies that investments in intra-party institution building may be just as important as programs that enhance party-voter linkages.

The book also develops new empirical tools that can be used to advance these areas of inquiry. Throughout Chapters 2 and 3, I draw on a wider-than-usual range of indicators to describe variation in party institutionalization. Combining data from sources such as the Database of Political Institutions and V-Dem, as well as from a number of individual authors,[54] depicts variation in party institutionalization in a new light and offers considerable promise for improvements in cross-national analysis of the different dimensions of party institutionalization. My use of detailed background data on government ministers along with IRT models for data aggregation in Chapters 5 and 6 demonstrates the utility of biographical data for understanding varieties of party-government linkages. Future research on party institutions can use these methods to better understand both the extent to which and the ways in which parties penetrate government. Moreover, the book conveys the potential utility of the perspectives of bureaucrats, who often occupy front row seats to parties' governing behaviors, for gauging hard-to-observe phenomena.

Finally, the book calls for greater attention to the nexus of party institutions and party fundraising strategies. The literature on clientelistic parties in particular has only begun to theorize why and how parties raise and manage funds in the ways that they do.[55] There is much more to understand about how parties' internal organizations and linkages with society shape fundraising and, importantly, impact downstream actors such as public servants, business communities, and citizens. In this book, for example, I have barely scratched the surface of how these downstream actors response to leaders' extraction strategies, whether they engage in efforts to resist or modify extraction, and how they perceive their roles in party extraction. A more robust understanding of the varied dynamics involved in parties' fundraising efforts will most certainly yield important new insights about the ways that party institutions shape the formal and informal relationships on which governance outcomes depend.

8.3   Money, Parties, and Politics: The Present and Future of Democratic States in Africa

On a more practical level, the book raises a number of important questions about pressing global issues surrounding money in politics. Can democracy survive if politicians continue to extract large volumes of money from the state to bolster their political advantage? What, if any, institutional protections will guard against these trends?

Recent developments in Benin and Ghana help to shed light on the sustainability of extraction-based democracy. In Benin, recent

[54] Specifically, I use data from Bleck and Van de Walle (2018); Sanches (2018); Meng (2021).
[55] See especially Arriola (2012); Bussell (2012).

constitutional changes advanced by President Talon have sought to deal with the country's fluid party landscape. One key amendment, which effectively guaranteed Talon a victory in Benin's February 2021 presidential election, requires candidates for president to hold a certain number of endorsements from elected officials before they are eligible to run. Whether this requirement would rein in elite defection and build more stable coalitions remains highly uncertain, particularly as Talon has stepped up repressive measures against his opponents. These developments come on the heels of contentious party-related laws that were passed in advance of the 2019 parliamentary elections. These laws effectively guaranteed that only ruling party affiliates could afford to pay the state's filing fees. In the wake of these changes, Talon also moved to arrest former prime minister and 2016 election opponent Lionel Zinsou on charges of corruption and he forced former President Boni Yayi into exile in Togo after Boni Yayi led protests over Talon's moves surrounding the parliamentary elections. Rather than playing the elite loyalty and rotation games on display from Benin's previous presidents, Talon appeared to be pursuing an even more coercive approach to managing elite defection. This approach may ultimately prove less intrusive into the state's executive and bureaucratic institutions, but it has already posed serious threats to the continuation of free and fair political competition as major democracy ratings such as Freedom House and V-Dem have now downgraded Benin's democratic status. Talon's approach is also likely to undermine the professionalism and neutrality of law enforcement and judiciary institutions.

Although extensive coercive repression of opponents seems somewhat less likely in Ghana, there are also reasons for concern about the sustainability of Ghana's collusive system of extraction. In recent years, procurement-based extraction practices have grown in both intensity and complexity. Not only have efforts by contractors to obtain judgment debts continued with each successive transfer of power but there is also a growing trend in which contractors sell their contracts to third parties, enabling the original awardee to profit without having to complete the work or otherwise fulfill the terms of the contract.[56] The most high profile of these cases, exposed by investigative reporter Manasseh Azure Awuni in 2019, involved businesses owned and operated by A. B. Adjei, the head of Ghana's Public Procurement Agency who was effectively awarding contracts to himself, then selling them to third parties. This practice not only generates more income for the initial contract awardee and, presumably, for the party, but it also helps the party to grow its

---

[56] I am grateful to George Bob-Milliar for bringing this practice to my attention.

network of partisan-aligned businesses. These developments speak to the broader paradox of the book: that stronger party institutions help leaders to *both* extract more efficiently and improve governing performance. However beneficial for party members this may be, the trend could easily backfire as unqualified businesses gain access to contracts and as a ruling party loss in a subsequent election brings this proliferating yet hollow network to its knees. In May 2021, President Akufo-Addo dismissed a zealous auditor general who sought to stymie the governing party's extraction efforts. Ultimately, the extent to which such events will threaten democratic competition in Ghana remains uncertain, as periodic pushback against this system from courts, civil society, and frustrated voters could help to keep it somewhat in check.

It is rather more difficult to speculate on the broader question of whether and how state money will continue to serve as a chief source of political finance for politicians in Africa and elsewhere. Ultimately, the conditions and pressures that give rise to extraction politics are magnified in many African countries where politics has, over the past several decades, become intensely competitive, more participatory, and extremely expensive. It is difficult to see how, if at all, these trends would abate in the coming years as incumbents by and large maintain control over the formal and informal powers of the state, and as more and more foreign investment flows to African governments. That said, to the extent that increasing capital flows to and within Africa distribute economic resources to regime opponents and undermine political control over the economy, it is possible that new and less state-centric forms of political finance may emerge.

For now, however, extraction of state money for political finance remains the rule rather than the exception. With this reality, an important question is how states might improve their governing performance in the presence of widespread extraction. The answer I offer in this book is that building stronger party institutions may enable leaders to simultaneously pursue both their policy and political goals. If ruling parties can minimize their elite agency problems and execute their political extraction projects with minimal involvement of state organizations, there is a greater likelihood that they will serve their citizens with some success.

Appendix A Surveys of Bureaucrats

This section provides additional information about the two surveys of bureaucrats introduced in Chapter 1 and referenced throughout the book. As noted in Chapter 1, the Classroom survey was conducted in both Benin and Ghana from October 2013 through June 2014. It was a written survey of 1,096 public sector employees, 581 in Benin and 515 in Ghana. The survey was conducted in a variety of public administration education and training programs that enroll public sector employees such as executive MPA programs, night classes in public administration, and trainings arranged by the governments. All surveys were administered in class visits by either myself or trained research assistants.

The Workplace survey was conducted only in Ghana in March/April 2017 and was part of a broader cross-national study.[1] The survey was conducted face-to-face in central government offices in the capital city of Accra. A total of 1,641 public service employees participated in the survey.

Both surveys were completely anonymous. The questionnaire used in the Classroom survey did not ask respondents for their names, organizations, or titles. The Workplace survey did capture the specific organizations in which respondents worked, but did not collect participants' names or titles.

A.1   Organizations Included in the Survey

The Classroom survey did not collect the data on the name of the organization in which each participant worked, but it did include questions about the type of organization. Table A.1 shows the distribution of these responses. In the Workplace survey, we did track the organization names for each respondent. The distribution of participants by organization is shown in Table A.2.

---

[1] Meyer-Sahling et al. (2018).

Table A.1 *Classroom survey organization type*

Organization Sector	Benin	Ghana
Agriculture/Fisheries	6.56%	0.20%
Central Management	15.54%	30.72%
Commerce & Industry	6.39%	3.91%
Education	16.41%	32.49%
Environment	6.74%	0.00%
Health	11.40%	16.83%
Justice	12.95%	2.94%
Other	1.04%	1.57%
Public Works	9.33%	2.94%
Social Advocacy	5.53%	2.15%
Territorial Admin/Local Govt	8.12%	6.26%

Table A.2 *Organizations included in the Workplace survey*

Organization	N	Percent
Bank of Ghana	7	0.4
Controller and Accountant General	37	2.3
CSIR Food Research Institute	23	1.4
Copyright Office	7	0.4
Department of Feeder Roads	41	2.5
Driver Vehicle Licensing Authority	27	1.6
Energy Commission	44	2.7
Environmental Protection Agency	28	1.7
Fair Wages and Salaries Commission	19	1.2
Forestry Commission	31	1.9
Ghana AIDS Control Program	8	0.5
Ghana Audit Service	42	2.6
Ghana Cocoa Board	20	1.2
Ghana Educational Trust Fund	24	1.5
Ghana Health Service	26	1.6
Ghana Investment Fund for Electronic Communication	28	1.7
Ghana Investment Promotion Center	30	1.8
Ghana Medical and Dental Council	16	1.0
Ghana National Service Secretariat	30	1.8
Ghana Pharmacy Council	25	1.5
Ghana Revenue Authority	12	0.7
Ghana Standards Authority	71	4.3
Ghana Statistical Service	32	2.0
Information Services Department	39	2.4

(cont.)

Table A.2 *(cont.)*

Organization	N	Percent
Lands Commission	112	6.8
Ministry of Communications	23	1.4
Ministry of Defence	48	2.9
Ministry of Education	67	4.1
Ministry of Employment and Labour Relations	42	2.6
Ministry of Energy	37	2.3
Ministry of Finance and Economic Planning	70	4.3
Ministry of Food and Agriculture	29	1.8
Ministry of Foreign Affairs and Regional Integration	66	4.0
Ministry of Gender, Children and Social Protection	41	2.5
Ministry of Health	77	4.7
Ministry of Information	14	0.9
Ministry of Trade and Industry	62	3.8
Ministry of Works and Housing	24	1.5
Ministry of Youth and Sports	32	2.0
National Identification Authority	60	3.7
National Information Technology Agency	39	2.4
National Board for Small Scale Industries	5	0.3
Petroleum Commission	5	0.3
Nursing and Midwifery Council	55	3.4
Office of the Head of the Civil Service	29	1.8
Registrar General's Department	32	2.0
Other/Not Specified	5	0.3
Total	1,641	100

A.2   Sample Demographics and Populations

Both survey samples are based primarily on access and convenience, with efforts to stratify the sample in a general sense across public service institutions and levels of employment. The tasks of defining the sample frame and obtaining a representative sample are extremely difficult in these environments. Even if it is possible to obtain complete lists of employees, the lists are not always up to date with transfers, retirements, and detail assignments, complicating efforts to locate individual employees.

In Benin, some population statistics were available from the Ministry of Public Service's *"Tableau de bord des agents de l'etat."*[2] The total number of state employees in 2014 (the year I conducted the survey) was 57,502, which does not include "Category A" employees whose jobs correspond to teaching and research functions in universities and research

---

[2] In Table A.3, I draw on statistics provided in the 2017 and 2018 versions.

Table A.3 *Benin survey sample demographics*

	Classroom	Official[a]
Sample/population size	581	57,502
Proportion female	36%	26%
Proportion with bachelors degree	36%	NA
Average age	36–40[a]	41
Proportion in senior position	18%	NA
Average years in current position	9	5–10

[a]The Classroom survey asked respondents to select their age category.

laboratories. The ministry provides basic demographic statistics for this population, which are shown in Table A.3

In Ghana, there is considerable fragmentation of the public sector into different administrative categories: public service agencies, civil service agencies, semi-autonomous organizations, independent commissions, and so on. This fragmentation complicates estimates of the population of public sector employees. An economic census conducted by the Ghana Statistical Service in 2014 finds that 434,784 individuals work in government organizations, with an additional 109,562 personnel in quasi-government and parastatal organizations or public limited companies.[3] This total estimate of 544,346 is somewhat higher than the Ministry of Finance and Economic Planning's 2014 budget statement, which lists the total number of personnel as of December 2013 – approximately the same timing as the IBES survey – as 509,783 total employees.

Of the 509,783 employees listed in Ghana's budget statement, an estimated 410,000 work in MDAs whose functions are primarily to deliver street-level services such as the Ghana Education Service, health service facilities, and certain security and law enforcement organizations such as the Ghana Prisons Service and the Ghana Customs Service. Thus, an estimated 100,000 employees work in MDAs whose functions are primarily administrative rather than street-level service delivery.[4]

Table A.4 shows sample demographics for the surveys in Ghana. I also include demographics from a survey by Rasul et al. (2021) that included all Civil Service employees at professional grades of technical

---

[3] Ghana Statistical Service, Integrated Business Establishment Survey: National Employment Report, September 2015. Statistics drawn from Table 3.7 on p. 19.

[4] Around 5,000 employees who work at the main ministries are formally classified as "civil servants."

Table A.4 *Ghana survey sample demographics*

	Classroom	Workplace	Rasul et al.
Sample size	515	1,641	2,986
Proportion female	44%	47%	45%
Average age	31–35[a]	38	42
Years of service	7	11	14
Proportion with undergraduate degree	67%	67%	70%
Proportion in senior position	25%	NA[b]	21%
Average years in current position	8	NA	9

[a]The Classroom survey asked respondents to select their age category.
[b]The Workplace survey did not include a question about grade of employment.

and administrative officers ($n = 2,986$).[5] While the gender distributions of the three surveys are very similar, the Rasul et al. sample skews somewhat older than the samples in the other two surveys, which is expected based on their efforts to target professional-grade employees. The Workplace survey also appeared to capture a more highly educated group than the other two surveys.

Overall, the survey samples used in the paper are in most ways similar to what we know about the population (Benin) or to other survey samples (Ghana). There are, however, several areas of divergence. In both countries, the Classroom survey samples appear to skew young, likely due to the survey having been administered in schools and training programs. Additionally, in Benin, the survey sample contains a larger share of female employees than is present in the population. In Ghana, the Workplace survey appears to capture a more highly educated group of employees than the other two surveys.

[5] I am grateful to Martin Williams, Imran Rasul, and Daniel Rogger for sharing these data.

Appendix B Investigating Bias Using Survey Weights

To investigate potential bias in the survey samples, I apply iterative proportional fitting (Kolenikov, 2014) to weight the obtained survey samples to better align with what is known about the population demographics. Specifically, I apply weights to calibrate gender proportions in the Classroom survey for Benin. I do not apply weights to the responses in Ghana because the demographics of this sample align with what is known about the population. I compare the weighted responses from Benin to (1) the unweighted responses from Benin, and (2) the unweighted responses in Ghana. Table B.1 shows the distributions of responses to key survey questions that are used to gauge differences between Benin in Ghana. As is clear from this table, the application of weights produces only very minor changes in the response distributions, and in no way alters the main findings described in Chapters 4–7. Given that the weights do not produce any major differences, it is not necessary to repeat regression analyses with weighted responses.

Table B.1 *Survey responses with weighted samples*

Table or Figure	Survey Question	Response Category[a]	Benin Classroom Unweighted	Benin Classroom Weighted	Ghana Classroom Unweighted
4.1	Resource Diversion	1	10.3	10.5	58.7
4.1	Resource Diversion	2	5.3	5.5	14.7
4.1	Resource Diversion	3	9.5	9.1	13
4.1	Resource Diversion	4	75	74.9	13.6
4.2	Procurement Politicization	1	23.9	23.3	41
4.2	Procurement Politicization	2	36.2	37	14.5
4.2	Procurement Politicization	3	18.8	18.8	16.8
4.2	Procurement Politicization	4	21.1	20.9	27.7

(cont.)

Table B.1 (cont.)

Table or Figure	Survey Question	Response Category[a]	Benin Classroom Unweighted	Benin Classroom Weighted	Ghana Classroom Unweighted
5.7	Recruitment Self	Exam/Interview	52.9	52.8	84.6
5.7	Recruitment Self	Friends/Family	27.7	28.3	14.4
5.7	Recruitment Self	Political Links	19.4	18.9	1
5.7	Recruitment Other	Exam/Interview	65.5	65.7	73.7
5.7	Recruitment Other	Friends/Family	19.9	20.3	22
5.7	Recruitment Other	Political Links	14.6	13.9	4.3
7.1	Political Interference	1	8	7.8	27.6
7.1	Political Interference	2	9.7	9.7	14.6
7.1	Political Interference	3	57	56.1	19.1
7.1	Political Interference	4	25.4	26.4	34.4
7.1	Political Paralysis	1	7.7	7.6	38.5
7.1	Political Paralysis	2	10.8	10.7	16.2
7.1	Political Paralysis	3	61.5	61.2	15.6
7.1	Political Paralysis	4	20	20.5	23.9
7.1	Political Dismissal	1	7	7	57.7
7.1	Political Dismissal	2	10.5	10.9	13.6
7.1	Political Dismissal	3	44.7	44.1	14.2
7.1	Political Dismissal	4	37.8	38	14.6
7.3	Resource Sufficiency	1	5.3	5.3	12.1
7.3	Resource Sufficiency	2	9	9.3	14.2
7.3	Resource Sufficiency	3	37.9	37.9	25.9
7.3	Resource Sufficiency	4	47.9	47.5	43.2
7.5	Work Motivation	1	35.8	36	52.3
7.5	Work Motivation	2	15.9	16.4	26.7
7.5	Work Motivation	3	34.1	33.3	10.1
7.5	Work Motivation	4	14.2	14.3	5.6

[a]Higher values represent ratings of more serious problem, more frequency, or importance.

Appendix C Measuring Politicization of Minister Appointments

In Chapter 5, I analyze biographical and appointment data for all government minister appointees in Benin and Ghana from the early 1990s through 2016. The dataset covers 1991–2016 for Benin and 1993–2016 for Ghana. It excludes deputy and regional ministers in Ghana, who are generally classified as "junior ministers" and for whom there are no comparable ministerial appointments in Benin.

Each appointment or rotation is a separate observation in the dataset. An individual who is rotated from one portfolio to another, or is re-appointed after having left office, will have multiple observations in the dataset. For example, if an individual is first appointed as minister of agriculture and is later appointed as minister of finance, these appointments will appear as separate observations. The data collected for each appointment are listed and described in Table C.1.

Table C.1 *Appointment data collected*

Variable	Description
Appointee Name	The full name of the appointee
Portfolio(s) Assigned	The portfolios to which this appointee is assigned at the time of appointment
Appointment Date	The date that the appointed individual took office
End Date	The date the appointed individual left their appointed position
Birthplace/Hometown	The appointee's place of birth or the location they identify as their hometown
Constituency/*Commune*	The electoral district of the individual's birthplace or hometown, or the district they represent as an MP
Highest Degree	The highest educational degree obtained by the appointee before the appointment
Year of Highest Degree	The year the appointee obtained their highest educational degree

(cont.)

Table C.1 *(cont.)*

Variable	Description
School	The school at which the appointee received their highest degree
Field	The field of the appointee's highest degree
Stated Profession	The appointee's stated profession at the time of their appointment
Previous Position 1	The appointee's professional position at or immediately preceding the time of their appointment
Previous Position 2	The appointee's second most recent professional position
Previous Position 3	The appointee's third most recent professional position
Current Party Affiliation	The appointee's party at the time of appointment
Previous Party Affiliation(s)	The appointee's previous party affiliations (if different from current affiliation)
Party Officer/Cadre	Party offices or positions held by the appointee prior to appointment
Member of Parliament	Was the appointee an elected member of parliament at the time of their appointment?
Political Experience	A short qualitative description of the appointee's political experience including whether they have ever run for office, whether they have served as an advisor to the president or another politician, whether they have financed the party or candidate, etc.

Missing data were an issue with the education and professional variables in particular (see Table C.2 for the number of observations for each coded variable/item). Generally, however, missingness is distributed more or less evenly over time, across countries, and among both more political and more technocratic types of ministers.

C.1   Bayesian IRT Estimation

Using the data on minister appointments, I estimate a latent *Politicization* score for each appointee using a Bayesian Item-Response Theory (IRT) model. The *Politicization* score measures the extent to which each appointment is likely to have been motivated by a political logic. The basic intuition behind this approach is that individuals with *less* relevant technical backgrounds and *more* political experience are more likely to have been appointed with some political motivation in mind. The IRT model allows for measurement of the politicization of each appointment as a continuous variable, thus capturing varying degrees to which political logics may have been at play.

Table C.2 *Item-test correlation of observed indicators for politi-cization estimation*

Variable	N	Sign	Item-test Corr	Item-test Corr	AVE Inter-item covariance	α
Education not relevant	506	+	0.646	0.514	0.067	0.779
Education not specifically relevant	506	+	0.676	0.559	0.066	0.774
Profession not relevant	515	+	0.732	0.619	0.063	0.764
Profession not specifically relevant	515	+	0.714	0.599	0.064	0.767
Experience not relevant	535	+	0.586	0.426	0.070	0.790
Party Affiliate	580	+	0.587	0.468	0.073	0.786
Political Experience	586	+	0.610	0.472	0.070	0.786
Cadre/Officer	585	+	0.505	0.332	0.075	0.805
MP	586	+	0.594	0.428	0.070	0.790
Test Scale					0.070	0.802

The table displays results of a Cronbach's alpha test indicating the extent to which items can be measured on a single scale. $\alpha > 0.7$ is usually considered reliable.

The model uses nine dichotomous variables (items) that I coded from the data listed in Table 5.2. The nine items are summarized in Tables 5.1 and 5.2 and the coding is described in the accompanying text in Chapter 5.

I estimate the latent politicization score for each appointment by fitting an IRT model with Bayesian MCMC estimation. The basic function of an IRT model is to measure the relationship between an estimated latent trait and a set of observed outcomes or characteristics, called items (they also appear in Table C.2 above). The model estimates a latent level of politicization for each appointment that predicts that individual's "scores" (values) on each of the nine observed items.

For ease of computation and interpretation, I reverse the coding of the educational, professional, and experience match variables such that appointments of individuals with relevant backgrounds are coded as 0 and those without relevant, or specifically relevant backgrounds are coded as 1. While this reversal complicates the interpretation of parameters (explained below), it permits a unidirectional estimation of latent politicization scores.

I show that the nine items are conducive to measurement on a single scale using Cronbach's alpha, which correlates the score for each scale item with the total score for each observation, and then compares that to the variance for all individual item scores. The resulting α ranges from 0 to 1 where 0 means that all of the scale items are entirely independent from one another and scores closer to 1 mean that the items have high covariances. As seen in Table C.2, $\alpha = 0.802$, which is well within the accepted range of consistency.

For the IRT estimation, I use a 2-parameter logistic model that estimates both difficulty and discrimination parameters for each of the nine items (presented in Table C.3). Implemented using Stata's bayesmh command, the model uses normal priors and 50,000 MCMC iterations.

In addition to estimating a politicization score for each appointment, the model produces difficulty and discrimination parameters. Difficulty parameters represent the item location on the latent space, measuring how much political motivations must be "present" in the appointment in order for the appointee to reach a particular value on each item. Items with negative difficulties are relatively "easy" for appointees to obtain, meaning, in this case, that they do not require high levels of politicization. Items with positive difficulties are considered to be relatively hard to obtain, thereby requiring higher levels of politicization.

Table C.3 *IRT model difficulty and discrimination parameters*

Item	Mean	SD	HPD Low	HPD High
Difficulty				
Education not relevant	0.382	0.07	0.246	0.521
Education not specifically relevant	−0.578	0.07	−0.719	−0.436
Profession not relevant	0.222	0.06	0.109	0.337
Profession not specifically relevant	−0.391	0.06	−0.516	−0.273
Experience not relevant	0.111	0.09	−0.057	0.279
Party Affiliate	−1.391	0.14	−1.669	−1.139
Political Experience	−0.943	0.12	−1.169	−0.716
Cadre/Officer	0.753	0.14	0.494	1.031
MP	0.226	0.09	0.040	0.412
Discrimination				
Education not relevant	2.402	0.30	1.828	2.978
Education not specifically relevant	2.760	0.36	2.078	3.488
Profession not relevant	4.571	0.92	2.998	6.319
Profession not specifically relevant	3.915	0.69	2.709	5.284
Experience not relevant	1.346	0.16	1.023	1.663
Party Affiliate	1.518	0.19	1.144	1.895
Political Experience	1.294	0.16	0.994	1.624
Cadre/Officer	0.836	0.12	0.609	1.060
MP	1.129	0.14	0.850	1.401

As seen in Table C.3, the items that require the most politicization are the variables coded for individuals who hold official positions in their political party and who possess educational backgrounds that are not even *generally* relevant to their portfolio.

Discrimination parameters measure how well items identify subjects at different levels of the latent trait. In other words, it measures the extent to which each item distinguishes between subjects with lower and higher levels of the latent trait. A high discrimination parameter value suggests that an item differentiates the latent trait between subjects. In this case, the high discrimination parameters associated with the professional match variables mean that appointees *without* relevant professional experience are likely to have different politicization scores than those with relevant professional experience. Discrimination parameters resulting from the model are displayed in the lower panel of Table C.3. For both the difficulty and discrimination parameters, it is clear that both types of variables – technical and political – are driving variation in the estimated politicization scores.

The IRT model produces estimates of politicization for every appointee in the dataset ($N = 586$) and includes the highest posterior density (HPD) intervals, which are used as confidence intervals for each estimate. The resulting politicization variable is scaled from -1.74 to 1.44 with a mean of 0.

C.2   Validating the Politicization Measure

I assess the validity of the politicization measure in two steps. First, I compare the estimates obtained from the IRT model to other aggregation methods, showing that the IRT model produces similar scores but has two distinct advantages over other methods: (1) it estimates a score for every appointment in the dataset regardless of missing information; and (2) it produces confidence intervals in the form of HPDs. Second, I examine the face validity of the measure using biographical information for minister appointees with scores at each quartile boundary.

Comparison with Alternative Aggregation Techniques

Table C.4 shows correlation coefficients for politicization with alternative latent variable aggregation techniques including frequentist IRT, principal components analysis, factor analysis, and latent class analysis. The Bayesian IRT model produces scores that are very similar to other techniques, but has two distinct advantages over other methods: (1) it

Table C.4 *Politicization score correlations*

Aggregation Technique	r	N
IRT (not Bayes)	1.00	445
Principal Components Analysis	0.99	445
Factor Analysis	0.99	445
Latent Class Analysis	0.89	586

The table displays correlation coefficients between
Politicization scores and similar measures constructed with
alternative aggregation techniques.

estimates a score for every appointment in the dataset regardless of missing information; and (2) it produces confidence intervals in the form of HPDs.

Face Validity

I provide brief vignettes of individuals with politicization scores at each quartile boundary. Individuals at both poles of the politicization scale have backgrounds that provide an unequivocal sense that their appointments were based on political and technical qualifications respectively. Those at the 25th, 50th, and 75th percentile boundaries have more mixed backgrounds.

- **Minimum**: Minister of Health with a PhD (*Doctorat Agregat*) in Parasitology and Microbiology. Stated profession is university professor in faculty of public health. Previous positions include professor of microbiology and minister of public health. This individual has no apparent political experience, is not affiliated with a political party or part of any party leadership, and has never served in parliament.
- **25th Percentile**: Minister of Industry and Commerce with a degree in environmental management and water quality. Stated profession is environmental management consultant and previous professional positions include Minister of Energy, municipal councilor for a political party, and director of a center for university workers at a major university. A party member who has held official positions locally.
- **50th Percentile**: Minister of Rural Development with a doctorate in veterinary medicine and stated profession is a veterinarian. Previously served as the head of the restructuring unit for the Ministry of Rural Development and a national coordinator for a Food and Agriculture Organization (FAO) program. Was a member of parliament associated with a national party at the time of appointment but had not served in any party leadership roles.

- **75th Percentile**: Minister of Tourism with degrees in French and education. Stated profession is educationist. Previously served as Deputy Minister of Education and Head Mistress of a school for girls. Served in Parliament and as a national party officer.
- **Maximum**: Minister of Works and Housing with a degree in national defense from The Ghana Military. Stated profession is Squadron Leader (ret) and past positions include regional minister (appointed), an administrator at the National Development and Productive Institute, and a soldier in the Ghana Army. Was a founding member of a political party and was a member of parliament at the time of appointment.

Appendix D   Resource Diversion and Politicized Hiring

In Chapter 5, I investigate whether bureaucratic perceptions of the diversion of resources to political parties in Benin are associated with higher levels of concern about politicization of hiring in their organizations (Figure 5.4). Table D.1 provides descriptive statistics for all variables used in these regressions.

The first variable, Politicized Hiring, is the dependent variable in Figure 5.4. It asks respondents to rate the seriousness of "hiring of unqualified or unmotivated personnel because of their affiliation to the ruling party" as a problem in their organizations on a scale of 1–4, where 4 represents a serious problem. Resources Diverted to Parties is the main independent variable in Figure 5.4, and asks respondents to rate the seriousness of "resources disappearing for party use" as a problem in their organization. Political Interference, Frequent Changes in Leadership, and Frequent Labor Strikes represent other types of perceived political influence on the organization. These questions also ask participants to rate the seriousness of each of these problems in their organizations on a scale of 1–4. The remaining variables: Education Level, Female,

Table D.1 *Descriptive statistics for figure 5.4 (Classroom survey, Benin only)*

Variable	Mean	SD	Min	Max	N
Politicized hiring	3.45	0.92	1	4	529
Resources diverted to parties	3.49	0.99	1	4	527
Political interference	3.00	0.82	1	4	539
Frequent changes in leadership	2.89	0.99	1	4	530
Frequent labor strikes	3.13	0.88	1	4	540
Education level	1.48	0.71	1	3	581
Female	0.36	0.48	0	1	560
Years in public service	7.92	6.06	0	25	538
Hired with political links	0.19	0.40	0	1	563
Party member	0.37	0.48	0	1	564

Years in Public Service, Hired with Political Links and Party Member. Education Level is measured in three groups, 1 = no bachelors degree, 2 = bachelors degree, 3 = advanced degree. Years in service is the number of years the individual has been employed in the public service. I also include dummy variables for different organization types, including local government (baseline), central management agencies (such as Ministries of Finance and Public Service), sector ministries (health, education, agriculture, interior, etc.), and semi-autonomous or autonomous agencies (i.e., state-owned enterprises). See Table D.1 for detailed breakdowns.

In Table D.2, I show results for four different models that regress bureaucrats' perceptions of politicized hiring in their organization (measured on a 1–4 scale) on perceived diversion of resources to political parties. Model 1 provides the results of a basic bivariate OLS regression with standard errors clustered by organization type. Model 2 adds a range of covariates and reflects full results of the analysis depicted in

Table D.2 *Extraction by bureaucrats and political hiring*

	(1)	(2)	(3)	(4)
Resources Diverted to Parties	0.429***	0.401***	0.905***	0.882***
	(9.03)	(5.60)	(7.78)	(4.83)
Political Interference		0.132		0.378
		(1.67)		(1.47)
Frequent Changes in Leadership		0.083		0.245**
		(1.90)		(2.09)
Frequent Labor Strikes		0.111*		0.308***
		(2.54)		(2.61)
Education Level		0.088		0.539
		(0.66)		(0.90)
Female		−0.018		−0.056
		(−0.12)		(−0.12)
Years in Public Service		0.006		0.024
		(0.84)		(1.21)
Hired with Political Links		−0.147*		−0.407**
		(−2.55)		(−2.51)
Party Member		−0.095		−0.407***
		(−2.02)		(−3.52)
Local Govt (baseline org. type)		0.000		0.000
		(.)		(.)
Central Management Agency		−0.070**		−0.270***
		(−3.95)		(−8.32)

(cont.)

Table D.2 *(cont.)*

	(1)	(2)	(3)	(4)
Sector Ministry		0.175*		0.406
		(2.49)		(1.38)
Autonomous/Semi-Autonomous		0.017		−0.047
		(0.51)		(−0.34)
Other		−0.081		0.030
		(−1.56)		(0.16)
Observations	523	474	523	474
(Pseudo) R-squared	0.210	0.292	0.101	0.165

$^*p < 0.1$, $^{**}p < 0.05$, $^{***}p < 0.01$, t-statistics, and z-statistics in parentheses
Dependent variable is bureaucrats' perceptions of politicized recruitment. Models 1 & 2: OLS regression, SE clustered by organization type. Models 3 & 4: Ordered logistic regression, SE clustered by organization type.

Figure 5.4. Models 3 and 4 use the same sets of variables as the first two models, but employ maximum-likelihood ordered logistic regression. In all models, the independent variable – resource diversion to parties – has a large and statistically significant relationship to the dependent variable.

Appendix E Variables Used in Chapter 7 Regressions

Table E.1 shows descriptive statistics for all Workplace survey variables used in the regression analyses conducted in Chapter 7 (Figures 7.2, 7.4, 7.6).

Table E.1 *Chapter 7 survey regressions descriptive statistics (Workplace survey)*

Variable	Mean	SD	Min	Max	N
Bureaucratic Autonomy	1.70	1.03	1.00	5.00	1,508
Political Interference	0.00	1.27	−1.54	2.99	1,370
Resource Sufficiency	2.33	1.15	0.00	4.00	1,639
Public Service Motivation	0.00	1.48	−12.81	0.63	1,618
Work Motivation	0.00	1.28	−5.44	1.36	1,639
Political Resource Diversion	1.53	0.91	1.00	5.00	1,348
Procurement for Party	3.04	2.35	1.00	7.00	1,453
Party Member	0.31	0.46	0.00	1.00	1,342
Administrative Position	0.47	0.50	0.00	1.00	1,639
Managerial Position	0.12	0.32	0.00	1.00	1,639
Hired by Ruling Party	0.31	0.46	0.00	1.00	1,616
Years of Service	10.94	8.94	0.00	45.00	1,616
Female	0.47	0.50	0.00	1.00	1,627
Salary Level	2.55	0.95	1.00	6.00	1,609

Appendix F Indicators of Public Service Motivation

The following indicators are used to construct an index of public service motivation in Chapter 7. The questions ask respondents to rate their level of agreement with the following statements on a scale of Strongly Disagree (1) to Strongly Agree (5).

- I admire people who initiate or are involved in activities to aid my community
- It is important to contribute to activities that tackle social problems
- Meaningful public service is very important to me
- It is important for me to contribute to the common good
- I think equal opportunities for citizens are very important
- It is important that citizens can rely on the continuous provision of public services
- It is fundamental that the interests of future generations are taken into account when developing public policies
- To act ethically is essential for public servants
- I feel sympathetic to the plight of the underprivileged
- I empathize with other people who face difficulties
- I get very upset when I see other people being treated unfairly
- Considering the welfare of others is very important
- I am prepared to make sacrifices for the good of society
- I believe in putting civic duty before self
- I am willing to risk personal loss to help society
- I would agree to a good plan to make a better life for the poor, even if it costs me money.

Appendix G Extraction and Personnel Motivation Supplemental Tests

In Chapter 7, Section 7.4, I warned that the relationship between extraction through bureaucratic resource diversion and low levels of work and public service motivation could be driven by selection bias. Specifically, because bureaucrats who engage in resource diversion are more likely to have been recruited politically to their jobs (Chapter 5), it is possible that low levels of motivation are reflective of the recruitment process rather than the prevalence of resource diversion. To assess whether this kind of selection bias might be at work, I replicate the tests on a restricted sample including only respondents who reported that they did *not* obtain their jobs with the help of politicians. The results, displayed in Table G.1, remain consistent with those depicted in Figure 7.6: resource diversion has a stronger negative relationship to motivation than does procurement-based extraction.

Table G.1 *Extraction and personnel motivation (restricted sample)*

	(1)	(2)	(3)	(4)
Resources Diverted to Parties	−0.137**		−0.092*	
	(−2.33)		(−1.68)	
Politicized Procurement		−0.039*		−0.039*
		(−1.87)		(−1.91)
Party Member	−0.038	−0.043	−0.186*	−0.109
	(−0.35)	(−0.43)	(−1.81)	(−1.11)
Administrative Position	0.007	0.047	0.098	0.066
	(0.06)	(0.45)	(0.95)	(0.66)
Managerial Position	−0.161	−0.169	0.040	0.028
	(−0.98)	(−1.07)	(0.26)	(0.18)

(cont.)

Table G.1 *(cont.)*

	(1)	(2)	(3)	(4)
Years of Service	0.001	0.004	0.006	0.008
	(0.20)	(0.72)	(1.21)	(1.58)
Female	0.117	0.119	−0.115	−0.118
	(1.14)	(1.24)	(−1.19)	(−1.28)
Salary	0.031	0.035	0.133**	0.127**
	(0.47)	(0.54)	(2.13)	(2.06)
Hired by Ruling Party	0.029	0.018	0.013	0.008
	(0.28)	(0.18)	(0.14)	(0.09)
Observations	792	851	798	857
R-squared	0.06	0.07	0.1	0.09

*$p < 0.1$, **$p < 0.05$, ***$p < 0.01$, *t*-statistics in parentheses
In Models 1 & 2, the dependent variable is Public Service Motivation. In Models 3 & 4, the dependent variable is Work Motivation.

Bibliography

Abbey, Michael. 2018. "Social Democracy; the AFRC & PNDC Ideals: The Ideo-logical Identity of the National Democratic Congress (NDC)." Friedrich Ebert Stiftung, Ghana.

Abdulai, Abdul-Gafaru. 2017. "Rethinking Spatial Inequality in Development: The Primacy of Power Relations." *Journal of International Development* 29(3):386–403.

Abdulai, Abdul-Gafaru and Gordon Crawford. 2010. "Consolidating Democracy in Ghana: Progress and Prospects?" *Democratization* 17(1):26–67.

Abdulai, Abdul-Gafaru and Giles Mohan. 2019. "The Politics of Bureaucratic 'Pockets of Effectivenes': Insights from Ghana's Ministry of Finance." ESID Working Paper, University of Manchester.

Abegaz, Berhanu. 2013. "Political Parties in Business: Rent Seekers, Developmentalists, or Both?" *Journal of Development Studies* 49(11):1467–1483.

Acemoglu, Daron and James A. Robinson. 2006. *Economic Origins of Dictatorship and Democracy*. New York: Cambridge University Press.

Adams, Samuel, Kingsley S. Agomor and Wilfried Youmbi. 2017. "What Influences Swing Voters' Choices? Reflection on Ghana's Elections." *The Journal of Social, Political, and Economic Studies* 43(3/4):246–271.

Adebanwi, Wale and Ebenezer Obadare. 2011. "When Corruption Fights Back: Democracy and Elite Interest in Nigeria's Anti-Corruption War." *Journal of Modern African Studies* 49(2):185–213.

Adida, Claire, Jessica Gottlieb, Eric Kramon and Gwyneth McClendon 2017. "Reducing or Reinforcing In-Group Preferences? An Experiment on Information and Ethnic Voting." *Quarterly Journal of Political Science* 12(4):437–477.

Adjovi, Emmanuel. 1998. *Une élection libre en Afrique: la présidentielle du Bénin, 1996*. Paris: Karthala Editions.

Afrobarometer. 2018. Afrobarometer Data Round 7. https://www.afrobarometer.org/data/

Agyeman-Duah, Ivor. 2003. *Between Faith and History: A Biography of J.A. Kufuor*. Trenton: Africa World Press.

Agyeman-Duah, Ivor, Christine Kelly and Wole Soyinka. 2008. *Economic History of Ghana: Reflections on a Half-Century of Challenges and Progress*. Oxfordshire: Ayebia Clarke.

Agyepong, Irene Akua and Sam Adjei. 2008. "Public Social Policy Development and Implementation: A Case Study of the Ghana National Health Insurance Scheme." *Health Policy and Planning* 23(2):150–160.

Aivo, Frédéric Joël. 2008. "La Perception des Partis Politiques au sein de L'opinion Publique." In *Le Fonctionnement des Partis PoLitiques au Bénin*, eds. Jan Niklas Engels, Alexander Stroh, and Léonard Wantchékon. Cotonou: Freidrich Ebert Stiftung (FES-Benin).

Akindes, Simon. 2015. "Civil-Military Relations in Benin: Out of the Barracks and Back–Now What?" In *The New African Civil-Military Relations*, eds. Martin Rupiya, Gorden Moyo and Henrik Laugesen. Pretoria: APPRI, 38–63.

Allen, Chris. 1992. "Restructuring an Authoritarian State: 'Democratic Renewal' in Benin." *Review of African Political Economy* 19(54):42–58.

Amoah, Michael, Kwesi Aning, Nancy Annan and Paul Nugent. 2015. *A Decade of Ghana: Politics, Economy and Society: 2004-2013*. Leiden: Brill.

Anders, Gerhard. 2002. "Like Chameleons. Civil Servants and Corruption in Malawi." *Bulletin de l'APAD*. 23 -24: 1 -22

Anders, Gerhard. 2009. *In the Shadow of Good Governance: An Ethnography of Civil Service Reform in Africa*. Leiden: Brill.

Anders, Gerhard. 2017. "Malawi Faces Toughest, Most High-Profile Trial Yet in Massive Cashgate Scandal." African Arguments. February 8, 2017.

Andrews, Sarah and Lauren Honig. 2019. "Elite Defection and Grassroots Democracy under Competitive Authoritarianism: Evidence from Burkina Faso." *Democratization* 26(4):626–644.

Ang, Yuen Yuen. 2020. *China's Gilded Age: The Paradox of Economic Boom & Vast Corruption*. New York: Cambridge University Press.

Appiah, Daniel and Abdul-Gafaru Abdulai. 2017a. "Competitive Clientelism and the Politics of Core Public Sector Reform in Ghana." ESID Working Paper, Manchester University.

Appiah, Daniel and Abdul-Gafaru Abdulai. 2017b. Politicization of Bureaucracy. In *Global Encyclopedia of Public Administration, Public Policy, and Governance*, ed. Ali Farazmand. Cham: Springer, pp. 1–8.

Apter, David. 1966. "Ghana." In *Political Parties and National Integration in Africa*, ed. James Coleman and Carl Rosberg. Princeton: Princeton University Press, pp. 259–317.

Ariotti, Margaret H. and Sona N. Golder. 2018. "Partisan Portfolio Allocation in African Democracies." *Comparative Political Studies* 51(3):341–379.

Arriola, Leonardo R. 2009. "Patronage and Political Stability in Africa." *Comparative Political Studies* 42(10):1339–1362.

Arriola, Leonardo R. 2012. *Multi-Ethnic Coalitions in Africa: Business Financing of Opposition Election Campaigns*. Cambridge: Cambridge University Press.

Arriola, Leonardo R., Donghyun Danny Choi, Justine M. Davis, Melanie L. Phillips and Lise Rakner. 2021a. "Paying to Party: Candidate Resources and Party Switching in New Democracies." *Party Politics* 28(3): 507–520.

Arriola, Leonardo R., Jed DeVaro and Anne Meng. 2021b. "Democratic Subversion: Elite Cooptation and Opposition Fragmentation." *American Political Science Review* 115(4):1358–1372.

Arriola, Leonardo R. and Martha C. Johnson. 2014. "Ethnic Politics and Women's Empowerment in Africa: Ministerial Appointments to Executive Cabinets." *American Journal of Political Science* 58(2):495–510.

Arthur, Peter. 2010. "Democratic Consolidation in Ghana: The Role and Contribution of the Media, Civil Society and State Institutions." *Commonwealth
& Comparative Politics* 48(2):203–226.

Asante, Kojo and George Kunnath. 2017. "The Cost of Politics in Ghana."
Westminster Foundation for Democracy.

Ashraf, Nava, Oriana Bandiera and B. Kelsey Jack. 2014. "No Margin, No
Mission? A Field Experiment on Incentives for Public Service Delivery."
Journal of Public Economics 120:1–17.

Asunka, Joseph. 2016. "Partisanship and Political Accountability in New
Democracies: Explaining Compliance with Formal Rules and Procedures
in Ghana." *Research & Politics* 3(1):2053168016633907.

Asunka, Joseph. 2017. "Non-Discretionary Resource Allocation as Political
Investment: Evidence from Ghana." *The Journal of Modern African Studies*
55(1):29.

Atta Mills, Cadman. 2018. "Politics, Policy, and Implementation: The 'Ghanaian Paradox'." Brookings, Africa in Focus.

Austin, Dennis. 1964. *Politics in Ghana, 1946–1960*. Vol. 242, London: Oxford
University Press.

Avis, Eric, Claudio Ferraz and Frederico Finan. 2018. "Do Government
Audits Reduce Corruption? Estimating the Impacts of Exposing Corrupt
Politicians." *Journal of Political Economy* 126(5):1912–1964.

Ayee, Joseph. 2013. "Public Administrators under Democratic Governance in Ghana." *International Journal of Public Administration* 36(6):
440–452.

Ayee, Joseph, Felix K. G. Anebo and Emmanuel Debrah. 2007. "Financing
Political Parties in Ghana." Codesria.

Ayee, Joseph R. A. 2001. "Civil Service Reform in Ghana: A Case Study of
Contemporary Reform Problems in Africa." *African Journal of Political
Science/Revue Africaine de Science Politique* 6(1):1–41.

Ayee, Joseph R. A. 2011. "Manifestos and Elections in Ghana's Fourth Republic." *South African Journal of International Affairs* 18(3):367–384.

Badou, Agnès Oladoun. 2003. "Partis politiques et strategies electorales à
Parakou." Institut für Ethnologie und Afrikastudien.

Bagbin, Alban S. K. and Albert Ahenkan. 2017. "Political Party Financing and
Reporting in Ghana: Practitioner Perspectives." In *Political Marketing and
Management in Ghana: A New Architecture*, ed. Kobby Mensah. Cham:
Palgrave Macmillan.

Bako-Arifari, Nassirou. 2001. *La corruption au port de Cotonou: douaniers et
intermédiaires*. Vol. 83, Paris: Karthala Editions.

Bako-Arifari, Nassirou. 2006. " 'We Don't Eat the Papers:' Corruption in
Transport, Customs and the Civil Forces." In *Everyday Corruption and
the State: Citizens and Public Officials in Africa*, ed. Giorgio Blundo and
Jean-Pierre Olivier de Sardan. London: Zed Books, pp. 177–225.

Baldwin, Kate. 2013. "Why Vote with the Chief? Political Connections and
Public Goods Provision in Zambia." *American Journal of Political Science*
57(4):794–809.

Banégas, Richard. 1998*a*. "« Bouffer l'argent. » Politique du ventre, démocraties et clientélisme au Bénin." In *Le clientélisme politique dans les sociétés contemporaines*, ed. Briquet Jean-Louis and Sawicki Frédéric. Paris: Presses Universitaires de France, pp. 75–109.

Banégas, Richard. 1998*b*. "Marchandisation du vote, citoyenneté et consolidation démocratique au Bénin." *Politique Africaine* 69:75–88.

Banégas, Richard. 2003. *La démocratie à pas de caméléon: transition et imaginaires politiques au Bénin*. Paris: Karthala Editions.

Banégas, Richard. 2014. "L'autoritarisme à pas de caméléon?" *Afrique Contemporaine* 1:99–118.

Banégas, Richard. 1995. "Action collective et transition politique en Afrique. La conférence nationale du Bénin," *Cultures & Conflits* 17(1):1–12.

Banks, Arthur S. and Thomas C. Muller, eds. 1998. *Political Handbook of the World: 1998*. Binghamton: CSA Publications and Binghamton University, State University of New York.

Barkan, Joel D. 1995. "Debate: PR and Southern Africa: Elections in Agrarian Societies." *Journal of Democracy* 6(4):106–116.

Barma, Naazneen H., Kai Kaiser, Tuan Minh Le and Lorena Vinuela. 2012. *Rents to Riches: The Political Economy of Natural Resource-Led Development*. Washington, DC: The World Bank.

Bates, Robert. 1981. *Markets and States in Tropical Africa*. Berkeley: University of California Press.

Bauhr, Monika and Nicholas Charron. 2018. "Insider or Outsider? Grand Corruption and Electoral Accountability." *Comparative Political Studies* 51(4):415–446.

Bayart, Jean Francois. 1993. *The State in Africa: The Politics of the Belly*. London: Longman.

Beck, Linda. 2008. *Brokering Democracy in Africa: The Rise of Clientelist Democracy in Senegal*. Cham: Palgrave Macmillan.

Bellé, Nicola. 2013. "Experimental Evidence on the Relationship Between Public Service Motivation and Job Performance." *Public Administration Review* 73(1):143–153.

Berman, Bruce J. 1998. "Ethnicity, Patronage and the African State: The Politics of Uncivil Nationalism." *African Affairs* 97(388):305–341.

Bernhard, Michael, Allen Hicken, Christopher Reenock and Staffan I. Lindberg. 2020. "Parties, Civil Society, and the Deterrence of Democratic Defection." *Studies in Comparative International Development* 55(1): 1–26.

Bersch, Katherine, Sérgio Praça and Matthew M. Taylor. 2017. "State Capacity, Bureaucratic Politicization, and Corruption in the Brazilian State." *Governance* 30(1):105–124.

Bértoa, Fernando Casal and Edalina Sanches. 2019. "Political Party Finance Regulation in 13 African Countries." The Conservative Party and Westminster Foundation for Democracy, London.

Besley, Timothy and Torsten Persson. 2009. "The Origins of State Capacity: Property Rights, Taxation, and Politics." *American Economic Review* 99(4):1218–1244.

Besley, Timothy and Torsten Persson. 2011. *Pillars of Prosperity: The Political Economics of Development Clusters*. Princeton: Princeton University Press.

Bierschenk, Thomas. 2008. "The Everyday Functioning of an African Public Service: Informalization, Privatization and Corruption in Benin's Legal System." *The Journal of Legal Pluralism and Unofficial Law* 40(57):101–139.

Bierschenk, Thomas. 2009. "Democratization without Development: Benin 1989–2009." *International Journal of Politics, Culture, and Society* 22(3):337–357.

Bierschenk, Thomas. 2014. "Sedimentation, Fragmentation and Normative Double-Binds in (West) African Public Services." In *States at Work*, ed. Thomas Bierschenk and Jean-Pierre Olivier de Sardan. Leiden: Brill, pp. 221–245.

Bierschenk, Thomas and Jean-Pierre Olivier de Sardan. 2003. "Powers in the Village: Rural Benin Between Democratisation and Decentralisation." *Africa* 73(2):145–173.

Bizzarro, Fernando, John Gerring, Carl Henrik Knutsen et al. 2018. "Party Strength and Economic Growth." *World Politics* 70(2):275–320.

Bjarnesen, Mariam. 2020. "The Foot Soldiers of Accra." *African Affairs* 119(475):296–307.

Blair, Graeme and Kosuke Imai. 2012. "Statistical Analysis of List Experiments." *Political Analysis* 20:47–77.

Bleck, Jaimie and Nicolas Van de Walle. 2013. "Valence Issues in African Elections Navigating Uncertainty and the Weight of the Past." *Comparative Political Studies* 46(11):1394–1421.

Bleck, Jaimie and Nicolas Van de Walle. 2018. *Electoral Politics in Africa since 1990: Continuity in Change*. Cambridge: Cambridge University Press.

Bob-Milliar, George. 2012*a*. "Party Factions and Power Blocs in Ghana: A Case Study of Power Politics in the National Democratic Congress." *Journal of Modern African Studies* 50(4):573–601.

Bob-Milliar, George. 2012*b*. "Political Party Activism in Ghana: Factors Influencing the Decision of the Politically Active to Join a Political Party." *Democratization* 19(4): 668–689.

Bob-Milliar, George M. 2014. "Party Youth Activists and Low-Intensity Electoral Violence in Ghana: A Qualitative Study of Party Foot Soldiers' Activism." *African Studies Quarterly* 15:1–25.

Bob-Milliar, George M. 2019. " 'We Run for the Crumbs and Not for Office': The Nkrumahist Minor Parties and Party Patronage in Ghana." *Commonwealth & Comparative Politics* 57(4):445–465.

Bob-Milliar, George M. and Jeffrey W. Paller. 2018. "Democratic Ruptures and Electoral Outcomes in Africa: Ghana's 2016 Election." *Africa Spectrum* 53(1):5–35.

Boone, Catherine. 2003. *Political Topographies of the African State*. Cambridge: Cambridge University Press.

Booth, David, Diana Cammack, Jane Harrigan, Edge Kanyongolo, Mike Mataure and Naomi Ngwira. 2006. "Drivers of Change and Development in Malawi." Overseas Development Institute, London.

Bozeman, Barry. 2007. *Public Values and Public Interest: Counterbalancing Economic Individualism*. Washington, DC: Georgetown University Press.

Brass, Jennifer N., Justin Schon, Elizabeth Baldwin and Lauren M. MacLean. 2020. "Spatial Analysis of Bureaucrats' Attempts to Resist Political Capture in a Developing Democracy: The Distribution of Solar Panels in Ghana." *Political Geography* 76:102087.

Bratton, Michael and Nicolas van de Walle. 1997. *Democratic Experiments in Africa: Regime Transitions in Comparative Perspective*. Cambridge: Cambridge University Press.

Brenya, Edward, Samuel Adu-Gyamfi, I. Afful et al. 2015. "The Rawlings' Factor in Ghana's Politics: An Appraisal of Some Secondary and Primary Data." *Journal of Political Sciences & Public Affairs* S1: 1–14.

Brewer, Gene A. 2008. "Employee and Organizational Performance." In *Motivation in Public Management: The Call of Public Service*, eds. James L. Perry and Annie Hondhegem. Oxford: Oxford University Press, pp. 136–156.

Brierley, Sarah. 2020. "Unprincipled Principals: Co-opted Bureaucrats and Corruption in Ghana." *American Journal of Political Science* 64(2):209–222.

Brierley, Sarah. 2021. "Combining Patronage and Merit in Public Sector Recruitment." *The Journal of Politics* 83(1):182–197.

Brierley, Sarah and Eric Kramon. 2020. "Party Campaign Strategies in Ghana: Rallies, Canvassing and Handouts." *African Affairs* 119(477):587–603.

Briggs, Ryan C. 2021. "Power to Which People? Explaining How Electrification Targets Voters Across Party Rotations in Ghana." *World Development* 141:105391.

Bryan, Shari and Denise Baer. 2003. "Money in Politics: A Study of Party Financing Practices in 22 Countries." National Democratic Institute.

Buckles, Grant T. 2017. "Internal Opposition Dynamics and Restraints on Authoritarian Control." *British Journal of Political Science* 49(3):883–900.

Bussell, Jennifer. 2012. *Corruption and Reform in India: Public Services in the Digital Age*. Cambridge: Cambridge University Press.

Bussell, Jennifer. 2019. *Clients and Constituents: Political Responsiveness in Patronage Democracies*. Oxford: Oxford University Press.

Bwalya, John and Owen Sichone. 2016. " 'I Will Crawl Before You': Political Endorsements, Defections and Patronage in Zambian Elections." *Africa Insight* 46(3):118–130.

Callaghy, Thomas Myde. 1987. "The State as Lame Leviathan: The Patrimonial Administrative State in Africa." In *The African State in Transition*, ed. Zaki Ergas. Cham: Palgrave Macmillan, pp. 87–116.

Callen, Michael, Saad Gulzar, Ali Hasanain, Yasir Khan and Arman Rezaee. 2015. "Personalities and Public Sector Performance: Evidence from a Health Experiment in Pakistan." Working Paper #21180. National Bureau of Economic Research.

Camerlo, Marcelo and Aníbal Pérez-Liñán. 2015. "The Politics of Minister Retention in Presidential Systems: Technocrats, Partisans, and Government Approval." *Comparative Politics* 47(3):315–333.

Carbone, Giovanni. 2012. "Do New Democracies Deliver Social Welfare? Political Regimes and Health Policy in Ghana and Cameroon." *Democratization* 19(2):157–183.

Caselli, Francesco and Tom Cunningham. 2009. "Leader Behaviour and the Natural Resource Curse." *Oxford Economic Papers* 61(4):628–650.

Centeno, Miguel. 2002. *Blood and Debt : War and the Nation-State in Latin America.* University Park, PA: Pennsylvania State University Press.

Ch, Rafael, Mathias Hounkpe and Léonard Wantchekon. 2019. "Chapter 4: Campaign Finance and State Capture." In *Economic Development and Institutions (EDI): Benin Institutional Diagnostic.* Paper #: WP19/BID05.

Chabal, Patrick and Jean-Pascal Daloz. 1999. *Africa Works: Disorder as a Political Instrument.* Bloomington: Indiana University Press.

Chaisty, Paul, Nic Cheeseman and Timothy J. Power. 2018. *Coalitional Presidentialism in Comparative Perspective: Minority Presidents in Multiparty Systems.* Oxford: Oxford University Press.

Chang, Eric C. C. and Miriam A. Golden. 2007. "Electoral Systems, District Magnitude and Corruption." *British Journal of Political Science* 37(1): 115–137.

Chazan, Naomi. 1991. "The Political Transformation of Ghana Under the PNDC." In *Ghana: The Political Economy of Recovery,* ed. Donald Rothchild. Boulder, CO: Lynne Reinner, pp. 21–47.

Chazan, Naomi, Peter Lewis, Robert Mortimer, Donald Rothchild and Stephen John Stedman. 1999. *Politics and Society in Contemporary Africa.* Boulder, CO: Lynne Rienner.

Check, Nicasius Achu, Tsholofelo Madise, Nkululeko Majozi and Yukihiko Hamada. 2019. "The Integrity of Political Finance Systems in Africa: Tackling Political Corruption." International IDEA Policy Paper Number 20.

Cheeseman, Nic. 2018. *Institutions and Democracy in Africa.* Cambridge: Cambridge University Press.

Chhibber, Pradeep and Ken Kollman. 2009. *The Formation of National Party Systems: Federalism and Party Competition in Canada, Great Britain, India, and the United States.* Princeton: Princeton University Press.

Chibber, Vivek. 2002. "Bureaucratic Rationality and the Developmental State." *American Journal of Sociology* 107(4):951–989.

Coleman, James and Carl Rosberg. 1966. *Political Parties and National Integration in Tropical Africa.* Berkeley: University of California Press.

Collord, Michaela. 2016. "From the Electoral Battleground to the Parliamentary Arena: Understanding Intra-Elite Bargaining in Uganda's National Resistance Movement." *Journal of Eastern African Studies* 10(4):639–659.

Coppedge, Michael, John Gerring, Carl Henrik Knutsen et al. 2019. "V-Dem Dataset v9." www.v-dem.net.

Cox, Gary W. and Mathew D. McCubbins. 1994. "Bonding, Structure, and the Stability of Political Parties: Party Government in the House." *Legislative Studies Quarterly* 19(2):215–231.

Croese, Sylvia. 2017. "State-Led Housing Delivery as an Instrument of Developmental Patrimonialism: The Case of Post-War Angola." *African Affairs* 116(462):80–100.

Cruz, Cesi and Philip Keefer. 2015. "Political Parties, Clientelism, and Bureaucratic Reform." *Comparative Political Studies* 48(14):1942–1973.

Cruz, Cesi, Philip Keefer and Carlos Scartascini. 2020. "Database of Political Institutions." https://datacatalog.worldbank.org/search/dataset/0039819.

Daddieh, Cyril K. and George M. Bob-Milliar. 2012. "In Search of 'Honorable' Membership: Parliamentary Primaries and Candidate Selection in Ghana." *Journal of Asian and African Studies* 47(2):204–220.

Dahlström, Carl and Victor Lapuente. 2017. *Organizing Leviathan: Politicians, Bureaucrats, and the Making of Good Government.* Cambridge: Cambridge University Press.

Dasgupta, Aditya and Devesh Kapur. 2020. "The Political Economy of Bureaucratic Overload Evidence from Rural Development Officials in India." *American Political Science Review* 114(4):1316–1334.

De Mesquita, Bruce Bueno, Alastair Smith, Randolph M. Siverson and James D. Morrow. 2005. *The Logic of Political Survival.* Cambridge, MA: MIT Press.

De Oliveira, Ricardo Soares. 2015. *Magnificent and Beggar Land: Angola Since the Civil War.* Oxford: Oxford University Press.

Decalo, Samuel. 1973. "Regionalism, Politics, and the Military in Dahomey." *The Journal of Developing Areas* 7(3):449–478.

Dendere, Chipo. 2021. "Financing Political Parties in Africa: The Case of Zimbabwe." *The Journal of Modern African Studies* 59(3):295–317.

Dickovick, J. Tyler. 2008. "Legacies of Leftism: Ideology, Ethnicity and Democracy in Benin, Ghana and Mali." *Third World Quarterly* 29(6):1119–1137.

Driscoll, Barry. 2015. The Perverse Effects of Political Competition: Building Capacity for Patronage in Ghana. PhD thesis, University of Wisconsin.

Driscoll, Barry. 2018. "Why Political Competition Can Increase Patronage." *Studies in Comparative International Development* 53(4):404–427.

Driscoll, Barry. 2020. "Democratization, Party Systems, and the Endogenous Roots of Ghanaian Clientelism." *Democratization* 27(1):119–136.

Dulani, Boniface. 2019. "Political Parties, Campaign Financing and Political Corruption in Malawi." In *Political Corruption in Africa*, ed. Inge Amundsen. Cheltenham: Edward Elgar, pp. 135–154.

Dunning, Thad. 2008. *Crude Democracy: Natural Resource Wealth and Political Regimes.* Vol. 7, Cambridge: Cambridge University Press.

Duverger, Maurice. 1959. *Political Parties, Their Organization and Activity in the Modern State.* London: Methuen.

Elischer, Sebastian. 2013. *Political Parties in Africa: Ethnicity and Party Formation.* Cambridge: Cambridge University Press.

Eme, Okechukwu Innocent and Nkechi Anyadike. 2014. "Political Financing in Africa: A Comparative Study of Kenya and Nigeria: Proposal for Reform." *Mediterranean Journal of Social Sciences* 5(27 P1):22.

Erdmann, Gero and Ulf Engel. 2007. "Neopatrimonialism Reconsidered: Critical Review and Elaboration of an Elusive Concept." *Commonwealth & Comparative Politics* 45(1):95–119.

Esteve, Marc and Christian Schuster. 2019. *Motivating Public Employees*. Cambridge: Cambridge University Press.

Evans, Peter. 1995. *Embedded Autonomy: States and Industrial Transformation*. Princeton: Princeton University Press.

Evans, Peter and James E. Rauch. 1999. "Bureaucracy and Growth: A Cross-National Analysis of the Effect of 'Weberian' State Structures and Economic Growth." *American Sociological Review* 64(5):748–765.

Ewald, Jonas. 2013. *Challenges for the Democratisation Process in Tanzania: Moving Towards Consolidation 50 Years After Independence?* Dar es Salaam: African Books Collective.

Falodi, F. 2016. *Counting Issues from $2.1bn Arms Fund Diversion*. Lagos: Lagos State Federal Ministry of Information and Culture.

Ferree, Karen. 2010. *Framing the Race in South Africa: The Political Origins of Racial Census Elections*. Cambridge: Cambridge University Press.

Ferree, Karen E., G. Bingham Powell and Ethan Scheiner. 2014. "Context, Electoral Rules, and Party Systems." *Annual Review of Political Science* 17:421–439.

Figueroa, Valentin. 2021. "Political Corruption Cycles: High-Frequency Evidence from Argentina's Notebooks Scandal." *Comparative Political Studies* 54(3–4):482–517.

Fischer, Jörn, Keith Dowding and Patrick Dumont. 2012. "The Duration and Durability of Cabinet Ministers." *International Political Science Review* 33(5):505–519.

Fomunyoh, Christopher. 2001. "Democratization in Fits and Starts." *Journal of Democracy* 12(3):37–50.

Francois, Patrick, Ilia Rainer and Francesco Trebbi. 2015. "How is Power Shared in Africa?" *Econometrica* 83(2):465–503.

Frempong, Alexander K. D. 2007. "Political Conflict and Elite Consensus in the Liberal State." In *Ghana: One Decade of the Liberal State*, ed. Kwame Boafo-Arthur. Dakar: Codesria Books, pp. 128–164.

Friedman, Steven. 2010. "Government Buy The People? Democracy and the Private Funding of Politics in South Africa." In *Paying for Politics: Party Funding and Political Change in South Africa and the Global South*, ed. Anthony Butler. Auckland Park, South Africa: Jacana Media (Pty) Ltd, pp. 155–169.

Frye, Timothy. 2010. *Building States and Markets After Communism*. Cambridge: Cambridge University Press.

Gailmard, Sean and John W. Patty. 2007. "Slackers and Zealots: Civil Service, Policy Discretion, and Bureaucratic Expertise." *American Journal of Political Science* 51(4):873–889.

Gazibo, Mamoudou. 2005. "Foreign Aid and Democratization: Benin and Niger Compared." *African Studies Review* 48(3):67–87.

Geddes, Barbara. 1994. *Politician's Dilemma: Building State Capacity in Latin America*. Berkeley: University of California Press.

Geddes, Barbara, Joseph Wright and Erica Frantz. 2018. *How Dictatorships Work: Power, Personalization, and Collapse.* Cambridge: Cambridge University Press.

George, Alexander L. and Andrew Bennett. 2005. *Case Studies and Theory Development in the Social Sciences.* Cambridge, MA: MIT Press.

Gingerich, Daniel W. 2013. *Political Institutions and Party-Directed Corruption in South America: Stealing for the Team.* Cambridge: Cambridge University Press.

Gisselquist, Rachel M. 2008. "Democratic Transition and Democratic Survival in Benin." *Democratization* 15(4):789–814.

Golden, Miriam A. 2003. "Electoral Connections: The Effects of the Personal Vote on Political Patronage, Bureaucracy and Legislation in Postwar Italy." *British Journal of Political Science* 33(02):189–212.

Golden, Miriam A. and Paasha Mahdavi. 2015. The Institutional Components of Political Corruption. In *Routledge Handbook of Comparative Political Institutions*, eds. Jennifer Gandhi and Rubén Ruiz-Rufino. New York: Routledge, pp. 404–420.

Golooba-Mutebi, Frederick. 2016. "The Cost of Politics in Uganda." Westminster Foundation for Democracy Background Paper, London.

Good, Kenneth. 1994. "Corruption and Mismanagement in Botswana: A Best-Case Example?" *The Journal of Modern African Studies* 32(3):499–521.

Good, Kenneth. 2008. *Diamonds, Dispossession & Democracy in Botswana.* Suffolk: James Currey and Boydell & Brewer.

Good, Kenneth. 2010. "Predominance and Private Party Funding in Botswana." In *Paying for Politics: Party Funding and Political Change in South Africa and the Global South*, ed. Anthony Butler. Auckland Park, South Africa: Jacana Media (Pty) Ltd, pp. 81–95.

Green, Daniel. 1995. "Ghana's 'Adjusted' Democracy." *African Studies Review* 22:577–585.

Green, Elliott. 2010. "Patronage, District Creation, and Reform in Uganda." *Studies in Comparative International Development* 45(1):83–103.

Greene, Kenneth F. 2007. *Why Dominant Parties Lose: Mexico's Democratization in Comparative Perspective.* Cambridge: Cambridge University Press.

Grindle, Merilee S. 1997. "Divergent Cultures? When Public Organizations Perform Well in Developing Countries." *World Development* 25(4):481–495.

Grindle, Merilee S. 2012. *Jobs For the Boys: Patronage and the State in Comparative Perspective.* Cambridge, MA: Harvard University Press.

Grzymała-Busse, Anna. 2007. *Rebuilding Leviathan: Party Competition and State Exploitation in Post-Communist Democracies.* Cambridge: Cambridge University Press.

Grzymała-Busse, Anna. 2008. "Beyond Clientelism: Incumbent State Capture and State Formation." *Comparative Political Studies* 41(4–5):638–673.

Guardado, Jenny 2018. "Office-Selling, Corruption, and Long-Term Development in Peru." *American Political Science Review* 112(4):971–995.

Gueye, Babacar, Abdoul Wahab Cissé and Abdoul Aziz Mbodji. 2017. "Pathways to Senegal's National Assembly: The Costs of Securing A Seat." Westminster Foundation for Democracy, London.

Gulzar, Saad and Benjamin J. Pasquale. 2017. "Politicians, Bureaucrats, and Development: Evidence from India." *American Political Science Review* 111(1):162–183.

Gyimah-Boadi, Emmanuel. 1994. "Ghana's Uncertain Political Opening." *Journal of Democracy* 5(2):75–86.

Gyimah-Boadi, Emmanuel. 2009. "State Funding for Political Parties in Ghana." Center for Democratic Development Critical Perspectives No. 24.

Gyimah-Boadi, Emmanuel and Donald Rothchild. 1990. Ghana. In *Public Administration in the Third World: An International Handbook*, ed. Venkateswarier Subramaniam. Westport, CT: Greenwood.

Habyarimana, James, Macartan Humphreys, Daniel N. Posner and Jeremy M. Weinstein. 2007. "Why Does Ethnic Diversity Undermine Public Goods Provision?" *American Political Science Review* 101(4):709–725.

Handley, Antoinette. 2008. *Business and the State in Africa*. Cambridge: Cambridge University Press.

Hanson, Jonathan K. and Rachel Sigman. 2021. "Leviathan's Latent Dimensions: Measuring State Capacity for Comparative Political Research." *Journal of Politics* 83(4):1495–1510.

Harding, Robin. 2015. "Attribution and Accountability: Voting for Roads in Ghana." *World Politics* 67(4):656–689.

Harris, Adam, Brigitte Seim and Rachel Sigman. 2019. "Information, Accountability and Perceptions of Public Sector Programme Success: A Conjoint Experiment Among Bureaucrats in Africa." *Development Policy Review* 38(5):594–612.

Harris, Adam S. 2020. "At the Borders of Identity: Identity Construction and Racial Bloc Voting." *Journal of Race, Ethnicity and Politics* 5(2):326–355.

Harris, Adam S., Rachel Sigman, Jan-Hinrik Meyer-Sahling, Kim Sass Mikkelsen and Christian Schuster. 2020. "Oiling the Bureaucracy? Political Spending, Bureaucrats and the Resource Curse." *World Development* 127:104745.

Hassan, Mai. 2017. "The Strategic Shuffle: Ethnic Geography, the Internal Security Apparatus, and Elections in Kenya." *American Journal of Political Science* 61(2):382–395.

Hassan, Mai. 2020. *Regime Threats and State Solutions: Bureaucratic Loyalty and Embeddedness in Kenya*. Cambridge: Cambridge University Press.

Hassan, Mai and Thomas O'Mealia. 2018. "Uneven Accountability in the Wake of Political Violence: Evidence from Kenya's Ashes and Archives." *Journal of Peace Research* 55(2):161–174.

Heclo, Hugh. 1977. *A Government of Strangers: Executive Politics in Washington*. Washington, DC: Brookings Institution Press.

Heilbrunn, John R. 1993. "Social Origins of National Conferences in Benin and Togo." *The Journal of Modern African Studies* 31(2):277–299.

Herbst, Jeffrey. 2000. *States and Power in Africa: Comparative Lessons in Authority and Control*. Princeton NJ: Princeton University Press.

Hicken, Allen. 2011. "Clientelism." *Annual Review of Political Science* 14:289–310.

Hicken, Allen and Erik Martinez Kuhonta. 2015. *Party System Institutionalization in Asia: Democracies, Autocracies, and the Shadows of the Past*. Cambridge: Cambridge University Press.

Hickey, Sam, Abdul-Gafaru Abdulai, Angelo Izama and Giles Mohan. 2015. "The Politics of Governing Oil Effectively: A Comparative Study of Two New Oil-Rich States in Africa." Effective States and Inclusive Development (ESID) Working Paper No. 54.

Holland, Alisha C. 2017. *Forbearance as Redistribution: The Politics of Informal Welfare in Latin America*. Cambridge: Cambridge University Press.

Horowitz, Donald L. 1985. *Ethnic Groups in Conflict*. Berkeley: University of California Press.

Houngbo, P. Th., H. L. S. Coleman, M. Zweekhorst, Tj De Cock Buning, D. Medenou and J. F. G. Bunders. 2017. "A Model for Good Governance of Healthcare Technology Management in the Public Sector: Learning from Evidence-Informed Policy Development and Implementation in Benin." *PLOS ONE* 12(1):e0168842.

Houngnikpo, Mathurin C. and Samuel Decalo. 2013. *Historical Dictionary of Benin*. New York: Rowman & Littlefield.

Hounkpe, Julien Coomlan. 2018. "Présentation de la Charte des partis politiques et du Code électoral au Bénin." Unpublished manuscript.

Huber, John D. 1998. "How Does Cabinet Instability Affect Political Performance? Portfolio Volatility and Health Care Cost Containment in Parliamentary Democracies." *American Political Science Review* 92(03):577–591.

Huber, John D. and Cecilia Martínez-Gallardo. 2008. "Replacing Cabinet Ministers: Patterns of Ministerial Stability in Parliamentary Democracies." *American Political Science Review* 102(02):169–180.

Huber, John D. and Charles R. Shipan. 2002. *Deliberate Discretion?: The Institutional Foundations of Bureaucratic Autonomy*. New York: Cambridge University Press.

Huntington, Samuel P. 1968. *Political Order in Changing Societies*. New Haven: Yale University Press.

Hutchful, Eboe. 2002. *Ghana's Adjustment Experience: The Paradox of Reform*. Geneva: UNRISD.

Hyden, Göran. 1983. *No Shortcuts to Progress: African Development Management in Perspective*. Berkeley: University of California Press.

Hyden, Göran. 2010. "Where Administrative Traditions are Alien: Implications for Reform in Africa." In *Tradition and Public Administration*, eds. Martin Painter and B. Guy Peters. Cham: Palgrave Macmillan, pp. 69–83.

Ichino, Nahomi and Noah L. Nathan. 2013. "Crossing the Line: Local Ethnic Geography and Voting in Ghana." *American Political Science Review* 107(2):344–361.

Ichino, Nahomi and Noah L. Nathan. 2018. "The Evolution of Candidate Selection Methods in Ghana." In *Routledge Handbook of Primary Elections*, ed. Robert G. Boatright. Abingdon: Routledge, pp. 369–383.

Ichino, Nahomi and Noah L. Nathan. 2021. "Democratizing the Party: The Effects of Primary Election Reforms in Ghana." *British Journal of Political Science* 53(3):1168–1185.

Indridason, Indridi H. 2005. "A Theory of Coalitions and Clientelism: Coalition Politics in Iceland, 1945–2000." *European Journal of Political Research* 44(3):439–464.

International IDEA. 2019. "Political Finance Database." www.idea.int/data-tools/data/political-finance-database.

International IDEA and Center for Democratic Development. 2004. "Ghana: Country Report Based on Research and Dialogue with Political Parties."

International Labor Organization. 2021. "ILO Statistics." https://ilostat.ilo.org.

Iyer, Lakshmi and Anandi Mani. 2012. "Traveling Agents: Political Change and Bureaucratic Turnover in India." *Review of Economics and Statistics* 94(3):723–739.

Jackson, Robert H. and Carl G. Rosberg. 1982. "Why Africa's Weak States Persist: The Empirical and the Juridical in Statehood." *World Politics* 35(1):1–24.

Jackson, Robert H. and Carl G. Rosberg. 1984. "Personal Rule: Theory and Practice in Africa." *Comparative Politics* 16(4):421–442.

Johnson, Chalmers. 1982. *MITI and the Japanese Miracle*. Stanford: Stanford University Press.

Johnson, Martha C. 2015. "Donor Requirements and Pockets of Effectiveness in Senegal's Bureaucracy." *Development Policy Review* (33):783–804.

Johnson, Martha Claire. 2009. Democracy and the Emergence of Meritocratic Bureaucracies: Explaining Variation in the Senegalese State. PhD thesis, University of California, Berkeley.

Joseph, Richard. 1987. *Democracy and Prebendal Politics in Nigeria: The Rise and Fall of the Second Republic*. Cambridge: Cambridge University Press.

Kang, David C. 2002. *Crony Capitalism: Corruption and Development in South Korea and the Philippines*. Cambridge: Cambridge University Press.

Kapur, Devesh and Milan Vaishnav. 2018. *Costs of Democracy: Political Finance in India*. Oxford: Oxford University Press.

Keefer, Philip. 2008. "Political Market Imperfections, Clientelism and the Quality of Democracy." Center for the Study of Imperfections in Democracy (DISC), Central European University. Working Paper 2008/3.

Keefer, Philip and Stephen Knack. 2007. "Boondoggles, Rent-Seeking, and Political Checks and Balances: Public Investment Under Unaccountable Governments." *The Review of Economics and Statistics* 89(3): 566–572.

Kelly, Catherine Lena. 2018. "Party Proliferation and Trajectories of Opposition: Comparative Analysis from Senegal." *Comparative Politics* 50(2): 209–229.

Kelly, Catherine Lena. 2020. *Party Proliferation and Political Contestation in Africa: Senegal in Comparative Perspective*. New York: Palgrave Macmillan.

Kennedy, Arthur. 2009. *Chasing the Elephant into the Bush: The Politics of Complacency*. Bloomington: Authorhouse.

Kenny, Paul D. 2015. "The Origins of Patronage Politics: State Building, Centrifugalism, and Decolonization." *British Journal of Political Science* 45(1):141–171.

Khisa, Moses. 2019. "Inclusive Co-optation and Political Corruption in Museveni's Uganda." In *Political Corruption in Africa: Extraction and Power Preservation*, ed. Inge Amundsen. Cheltenham: Edward Elger, pp. 95–115.

Kim, Eun Kyung. 2018. "Sector-Based Vote Choice: A New Approach to Explaining Core and Swing Voters in Africa." *International Area Studies Review* 21(1):28–50.

Kim, Eun Kyung. 2020. "Economic Signals of Ethnicity and Voting in Africa: Analysis of the Correlation Between Agricultural Subsectors and Ethnicity in Kenya." *The Journal of Modern African Studies* 58(3):361–395.

Kim, Sangmook, Wouter Vandenabeele, Bradley E. Wright et al. 2012. "Investigating the Structure and Meaning of Public Service Motivation Across Populations: Developing an International Instrument and Addressing Issues of Measurement Invariance." *Journal of Public Administration Research and Theory* 23(1):79–102.

Kitschelt, Herbert and Steven Wilkinson. 2007. *Patrons, Clients and Policies: Patterns of Democratic Accountability and Political Competition*. Cambridge: Cambridge University Press.

Klaus, Kathleen and Jeffrey W. Paller. 2017. "Defending the City, Defending Votes: Campaign Strategies in Urban Ghana." *The Journal of Modern African Studies* 55(4):681–708.

Klitgaard, Robert. 1988. *Controlling Corruption*. Berkeley: University of California Press.

Kohli, Atul. 2004. *State-Directed Development: Political Power and Industrialization in the Global Periphery*. Cambridge: Cambridge University Press.

Kolenikov, Stanislav. 2014. "Calibrating Survey Data Using Iterative Proportional Fitting (Raking)." *The Stata Journal* 14(1):22–59.

Kopecký, Petr. 2011. "Political Competition and Party Patronage: Public Appointments in Ghana and South Africa." *Political Studies* 59(3):713–732.

Koter, Dominika. 2016. *Beyond Ethnic Politics in Africa*. Cambridge: Cambridge University Press.

Koter, Dominika. 2017. "Costly Electoral Campaigns and the Changing Composition and Quality of Parliament: Evidence from Benin." *African Affairs* 116(465):573–596.

Kovo, Lazare. 2018. "Local Governance and Bureaucrats' Performance: What Really Matters?" Unpublished Manuscript.

Kpundeh, Sahr John. 1994. "Limiting Administrative Corruption in Sierra Leone." *The Journal of Modern African Studies* 32(1):139–157.

Kramon, Eric. 2018. *Money for Votes: The Causes and Consequences of Electoral Clientelism in Africa*. Cambridge: Cambridge University Press.

Kramon, Eric and Daniel N. Posner. 2016. "Ethnic Favoritism in Education in Kenya." *Quarterly Journal of Political Science* 11(1):1–58.

Kroeger, Alex M. 2018. "Dominant Party Rule, Elections, and Cabinet Instability in African Autocracies." *British Journal of Political Science* 50(1):79–101.

Krueger, Anne O. 1974. "The Political Economy of the Rent-Seeking Society." *The American Economic Review* 64(3):291–303.

Kunicová, Jana and Susan Rose-Ackerman. 2005. "Electoral Rules and Constitutional Structures as Constraints on Corruption." *British Journal of Political Science* 35(4):573–606.

Kura, Sulaiman Balarabe. 2014. "Clientele Democracy: Political Party Funding and Candidate Selection in Nigeria." *African Journal of Political Science and International Relations* 8(5):124–137.

Kurer, Oskar. 2014. "Definitions of Corruption." In *Routledge Handbook of Political Corruption*, ed. Paul Heywood. Abingdon: Routledge pp. 44–55.

Kusi-Ampofo, Owuraku, John Church, Charles Conteh and B. Timothy Heinmiller. 2015. "Resistance and Change: A Multiple Streams Approach to Understanding Health Policy Making in Ghana." *Journal of Health Politics, Policy and Law* 40(1):195–219.

Laebens, Melis G and Anna Lührmann. 2021. "What Halts Democratic Erosion? The Changing Role of Accountability." *Democratization* 28(5):908–928.

Lam, Katy Ngan Ting. 2016. *Chinese State Owned Enterprises in West Africa: Triple-Embedded Globalization*. Abingdon: Routledge.

Laver, Michael and Kenneth A Shepsle, eds. 1994. *Cabinet Ministers and Parliamentary Government*. Cambridge: Cambridge University Press.

Lawson, Letitia. 2009. "The Politics of Anti-Corruption Reform in Africa." *The Journal of Modern African Studies* 47(01):73–100.

Le Grand, Julian. 2003. *Motivation, Agency, and Public Policy: Of Knights and Knaves, Pawns and Queens*. Oxford: Oxford University Press.

LeBas, Adrienne. 2011. *From Protest to Parties: Party-Building and Democratization in Africa*. Oxford: Oxford University Press.

Leftwich, Adrian. 2000. *States of Development: On the Primacy of Politics in Development*. Cambridge: Polity Press.

Lentz, Carola. 2014. "I take an Oath to the State, not the Government: Career Trajectories and Professional Ethics of Ghanaian Public Servants." In *States at Work*, eds. Thomas Bierschenk and Jean-Pierre Olivier de Sardan. Leiden: Brill, pp. 175–203.

Levitsky, Steven. 2003. *Transforming Labor-Based Parties in Latin America: Argentine Peronism in Comparative Perspective*. Cambridge: Cambridge University Press.

Levitsky, Steven and Lucan A. Way. 2002. "The Rise of Competitive Authoritarianism." *Journal of Democracy* 13(2):51–65.

Levitsky, Steven and Daniel Ziblatt. 2018. *How Democracies Die*. New York: Penguin Random House LLC.

Lewis, David E. 2010. *The Politics of Presidential Appointments: Political Control and Bureaucratic Performance*. Princeton: Princeton University Press.

Lewis, Peter. 2007. *Growing Apart: Oil, Politics, and Economic Change in Indonesia and Nigeria*. Ann Arbor: The University of Michigan Press.

Lijphart, Arend. 1968. "Typologies of Democratic Systems." *Comparative Political Studies* 1(1):3–44.

Lijphart, Arend. 1984. *Democracies: Patterns of Majoritarian and Consensus Government in Twenty-One Countries*. New Haven: Yale University Press.

Lindberg, Staffan I. 2005. "Consequences of Electoral Systems in Africa: A Preliminary Inquiry." *Electoral Studies* 24:41–64.

Lindberg, Staffan I. 2006. *Democracy and Elections in Africa*. Baltimore: John Hopkins University Press.

Lindberg, Staffan I. 2007. "Institutionalization of Party Systems? Stability and Fluidity Among Legislative Parties in Africa's Democracies." *Government and Opposition* 42(2):215–241.

Lindberg, Staffan I. 2010. "What Accountability Pressures do MPs in Africa face and How do They Respond? Evidence from Ghana." *The Journal of Modern African Studies* 48(01):117–142.

Lindberg, Staffan I. and Yongmei Zhou. 2009. "Co-optation Despite Democratization in Ghana." In *Legislative Power in Emerging African Democracies*, ed. Joel D Barkan. Boulder, CO: Lynne Rienner, pp. 147–176.

Linz, Juan J. and Alfred Stepan. 1996. *Problems of Democratic Transition and Consolidation: Southern Europe, South America, and Post-Communist Europe*. Baltimore: Johns Hopkins University Press.

Lockwood, Sarah J., Matthias Krönke and Robert Mattes. 2022. "Party Structures and Organization Building in Africa." *Party Politics* 28(2):203–207.

Lodge, Tom. 1998. "Political Corruption in South Africa." *African Affairs* 97(387):157–187.

Luna, Joseph. 2019. *Political Financing in Developing Countries: A Case from Ghana*. Abingdon: Routledge.

Lupu, Noam. 2016. *Party Brands in Crisis: Partisanship, Brand Dilution, and the Breakdown of Political Parties in Latin America*. New York: Cambridge University Press.

Lyons, Sean T., Linda E. Duxbury and Christopher A. Higgins. 2006. "A Comparison of the Values and Commitment of Private Sector, Public Sector, and Parapublic Sector Employees." *Public Administration Review* 66(4):605–618.

Magaloni, Beatriz. 2006. *Voting for Autocracy: Hegemonic Party Survival and its Demise in Mexico*. Vol. 296, Cambridge: University Press Cambridge.

Magnusson, Bruce. 1996. "Benin: Legitimating Democracy: New Institutions and the Historical Problem of Economic Crisis." *L'Afrique Politique* 33–54. https://www.karthala.com/612-afrique-politique-1996-democratisation-arret-sur-image-9782865376605.html

Magnusson, Bruce A. 2001. "Democratization and Domestic Insecurity: Navigating the Transition in Benin." *Comparative Politics* 33(2): 211–230.

Magnusson, Bruce A. and John F. Clark. 2005. "Understanding Democratic Survival and Democratic Failure in Africa: Insights from Divergent Democratic Experiments in Benin and Congo (Brazzaville)." *Comparative Studies in Society and History* 47(3):552–582.

Maher, Joanne, ed. 2004. Europa World Yearbook Volume 1, 1st Edition. London: Europa Publications.

Mainwaring, Scott. 2018. *Party Systems in Latin America: Institutionalization, Decay, and Collapse*. Cambridge: Cambridge University Press.

Mainwaring, Scott and Fernando Bizzarro. 2019. "The Fates of Third-Wave Democracies." *Journal of Democracy* 30(1):99–113.

Mainwaring, Scott and Timothy R. Scully. 1995. *Building Democratic Institutions: Party Systems in Latin America*. Stanford: Stanford University Press.

Mamdani, Mahmood. 1996. *Citizen and Subject: Contemporary Africa and the Legacy of Colonialism*. Princeton: Princeton Univeristy Press.

Manning, Carrie. 2005. "Assessing African Party Systems after the Third Wave." *Party Politics* 11(6):707–727.

Martin, Lucy and Pia J. Raffler. 2021. "Fault Lines: The Effects of Bureaucratic Power on Electoral Accountability." *American Journal of Political Science* 65(1):210–224.

Martínez-Gallardo, Cecilia. 2012. "Cabinet Stability and Policymaking in Latin America." In *The Oxford Handbook of Latin American Political Economy*, eds. Javier Santiso and Jeff Dayton-Johnson. Oxford: Oxford University Press, 310–335.

Martínez-Gallardo, Cecilia. 2014. "Designing Cabinets: Presidential Politics and Ministerial Instability." *Journal of Politics in Latin America* 6(2): 3–38.

Martínez-Gallardo, Cecilia and Petra Schleiter. 2015. "Choosing Whom to Trust: Agency Risks and Cabinet Partisanship in Presidential Democracies." *Comparative Political Studies* 48(2):231–264.

Mbaku, John Mukum. 1994. "Bureaucratic Corruption and Policy Reform in Africa." *The Journal of Social, Political, and Economic Studies* 19(2):149.

Mbaku, John Mukum. 2000. *Bureaucratic and Political Corruption in Africa: The Public Choice Perspective*. Malabar, FL: Krieger.

McDonnell, Erin Metz. 2020. *Patchwork Leviathan: Pockets of Bureaucratic Effectiveness in Developing States*. Princeton: Princeton University Press.

Meng, Anne. 2021. "Ruling Parties in Authoritarian Regimes: Rethinking Institutional Strength." *British Journal of Political Science* 51(2): 526–540.

Mensah, Kobby, ed. 2017. *Political Marketing and Management in Ghana: A New Architecture*. Cham: Palgrave Macmillan.

Meredith, Martin. 2005. *The Fate of Africa: A History of Fifty Years of Independence*. New York: Public Affairs.

Métinhoué, Pierre Goudjinou. 2005. *Les gouvernements du Dahomey et du Bénin: mai 1957–février 2005*. Porto Novo: Centre National de Production de Manuels Scolaires.

Meyer-Sahling, Jan, Christian Schuster and Kim Sass Mikkelsen. 2018. "Civil Service Management in Developing Countries: What Works?". Report for the UK Department for International Development (DFID).

Mietzner, Marcus. 2007. "Party Financing in Post-Soeharto Indonesia: Between State Subsidies and Political Corruption." *Contemporary Southeast Asia* 29(2):238–263.

Migdal, Joel S. 1988. *Strong Societies and Weak States: State-Society Relations and State Capabilities in the Third World*. Princeton: Princeton University Press.

Miguel, Edward and Mary Kay Gugerty. 2005. "Ethnic Diversity, Social Sanctions, and Public Goods in Kenya." *Journal of Public Economics* 89(11–12):2325–2368.

Milio, Simona. 2008. "How Political Stability Shapes Administrative Performance: The Italian Case." *West European Politics* 31(5):915–936.

Mill, John Stuart. 1872. *A System of Logic 8th ed., Vol. 2.* London: Longmans, Green, Reader and Dyer.

Mkandawire, Thandika. 2001. "Thinking About Developmental States in Africa." *Cambridge Journal of Economics* 25(3):289–314.

Mkandawire, Thandika. 2015. "Neopatrimonialism and the Political Economy of Economic Performance in Africa: Critical Reflections." *World Politics* 67:563–612.

Moe, Terry M. 1989. The Politics of Bureaucratic Structure. In *Can the Government Govern?* eds. John E. Chubb and Paul E. Peterson. Vol. 267, Washington: The Brookings Institution, pp. 285–323.

Molomo, Mpho G. 2000. "Understanding Government and Opposition Parties in Botswana." *Journal of Commonwealth & Comparative Politics* 38(1): 65–92.

Montgomery, John D. 1987. "Probing Managerial Behavior: Image and Reality in Southern Africa." *World Development* 15(7):911–929.

Moore, Mark Harrison. 1995. *Creating Public Value: Strategic Management in Government.* Cambridge, MA: Harvard University Press.

Morrison, Minion K. C. 2004. "Political Parties in Ghana through Four Republics: A Path to Democratic Consolidation." *Comparative Politics* 36(4):421–442.

Morse, Yonatan L. 2018. *How Autocrats Compete: Parties, Patrons, and Unfair Elections in Africa.* Cambridge: Cambridge University Press.

Moynihan, Donald P. and Joe Soss. 2014. "Policy Feedback and the Politics of Administration." *Public Administration Review* 74(3):320–332.

Mozaffar, Shaheen. 1997. "Electoral Systems and Their Political Effects in Africa: A Preliminary Analysis." *Representation* 34(3–4):148–156.

Mwakikagile, Godfrey. 2014. *Statecraft and Nation Building in Africa: A Post-Colonial Study.* Dar es Salaam: New Africa Press.

Mwangi, Oscar Gakuo. 2008. "Political Corruption, Party Financing and Democracy in Kenya." *The Journal of Modern African Studies* 46(2):267–285.

Nathan, Noah L. 2019. *Electoral Politics and Africa's Urban Transition: Class and Ethnicity in Ghana.* Cambridge: Cambridge University Press.

Ndulo, Muna. 2000. "Political Parties and Democracy in Zambia." International IDEA.

Ninsin, Kwame A. 2006. "Political Parties and Political Participation in Ghana." Konrad Adenauer Stiftung Foundation, Berlin.

Norris, Pippa and Andrea Abel Van Es. 2016. *Checkbook Elections?: Political Finance in Comparative Perspective.* Oxford: Oxford University Press.

Nugent, Paul. 1995. *Big Men, Small Boys and Politics in Ghana: Power, Ideology and the Burden of History.* Accra: Asempa Publishers.

Nugent, Paul. 2007. "Banknotes and Symbolic Capital." In *Votes, Money and Violence,* eds. Matthias Basedau, Gero Erdmann and Andreas Mehler. Uppsala and Pietermaritzburg: Nordic Africa Institute and University of Kwazulu-Natal Press, pp. 252–275.

Nwajiaku, Kathryn. 1994. "The National Conferences in Benin and Togo Revisited." *The Journal of Modern African Studies* 32(3):429–447.

Nwankwor, Chiedo. 2021. "Women Cabinet Ministers' Substantive Representation in Africa." *Social Politics: International Studies in Gender, State & Society* 28(1):241–264.

O'Dwyer, Conor. 2006. *Runaway State-Building: Patronage Politics and Democratic Development.* Baltimore: Johns Hopkins University Press.

Oelbaum, Jay. 2002. "Populist Reform Coalitions in Sub-Saharan Africa: Ghana's Triple Alliance." *Canadian Journal of African Studies/La Revue canadienne des études africaines* 36(2):281–328.

Olarinmoye, Omobolaji Ololade. 2008. "Godfathers, Political Parties and Electoral Corruption in Nigeria." *African Journal of Political Science and International Relations* 2(4):66.

Oliveros, Virginia. 2016. "Making it Personal: Clientelism, Favors, and the Personalization of Public Administration in Argentina." *Comparative Politics* 48(3):373–391.

Oliveros, Virginia. 2021. "Working for the Machine: Patronage Jobs and Political Services in Argentina." *Comparative Politics* 53(3):381–427.

Oliveros, Virginia and Christian Schuster. 2018. "Merit, Tenure, and Bureaucratic Behavior: Evidence from a Conjoint Experiment in the Dominican Republic." *Comparative Political Studies* 51(6):759–792.

Olivier de Sardan, Jean-Pierre. 1999. "A Moral Economy of Corruption in Africa?" *Journal of Modern African Studies* 37(1):25–52.

Olivier de Sardan, Jean-Pierre. 2013. "The Bureaucratic Mode of Governance and Practical Norms in West Africa and Beyond." In *Local Politics and Contemporary Transformations in the Arab World*, eds. Malika Bouziane, Cilja Harders and Anja Hoffman. London: Palgrave Macmillan, pp. 43–64.

Olken, Benjamin A. 2007. "Monitoring Corruption: Evidence from a Field Experiment in Indonesia." *Journal of Political Economy* 115(2):200–249.

Olorunmola, Adebowale. 2016. "The Cost of Politics in Nigeria." Westminster Foundation for Democracy, London.

Olowu, Bamidele. 2001. "Pride and Performance in African Public Services: Analysis of Institutional Breakdown and Rebuilding Efforts in Nigeria and Uganda." *International Review of Administrative Sciences* 67(1):117–134.

Olson, Mancur. 1993. "Dictatorship, Democracy, and Development." *American Political Science Review* 87(3):567–576.

Opalo, Ken Ochieng. 2019. *Legislative Development in Africa: Politics and Postcolonial Legacies.* Cambridge: Cambridge University Press.

Opoku, Darko Kwabena. 2010. *The Politics of Government-Business Relations in Ghana, 1982-2008.* Cham: Palgrave Macmillan.

Organisation for Economic Co-operation and Development. 2021. "OECD iLibrary." www.oecd-ilibrary.org

Osei, Anja. 2013. "Party-Voter Linkage in Senegal: The Rise and Fall of Abdoulaye Wade and the Parti Démocratique Sénégalais." *Journal of African Elections* 12(1):84–108.

Osei, Anja. 2016. "Formal Party Organisation and Informal Relations in African Parties: Evidence from Ghana." *The Journal of Modern African Studies* 54(1):37–66.

Osei, Anja. 2018. "Elite Theory and Political Transitions: Networks of Power in Ghana and Togo." *Comparative Politics* 51(1):21–42.

Paget, Dan. 2019. "The Rally-Intensive Campaign: A Distinct Form of Electioneering in Sub-Saharan Africa and Beyond." *The International Journal of Press/Politics* 24(4):444–464.

Painter, Martin and B. Guy Peters. 2010. Administrative Traditions in Comparative Perspective: Families, Groups and Hybrids. In *Tradition and Public Administration*, eds. Martin Painter and B. Guy Peters. New York: Palgrave Macmillan, pp. 19–30.

Paller, Jeffrey W. 2019. *Democracy in Ghana: Everyday Politics in Urban Africa.* Cambridge: Cambridge University Press.

Pavão, Nara. 2018. "Corruption as the Only Option: The Limits to Electoral Accountability." *The Journal of Politics* 80(3):996–1010.

Pepinsky, Thomas B., Jan H. Pierskalla and Audrey Sacks. 2017. "Bureaucracy and Service Delivery." *Annual Review of Political Science* 20:249–268.

Perry, James L. 1997. "Antecedents of Public Service Motivation." *Journal of Public Administration Research and Theory* 7(2):181–197.

Perry, James L. 2010. "Introduction to the Symposium on Public Service Motivation Research." *Public Administration Review* 70(5):679–680.

Peters, B. Guy and Jon Pierre, eds. 2004. *The Politicization of the Civil Service in Comparative Perspective: A Quest for Control.* London: Routledge.

Piattoni, Simona. 2001. *Clientelism, Interests, and Democratic Representation: The European Experience in Historical and Comparative Perspective.* Cambridge: Cambridge University Press.

Piccolino, Giulia. 2015. "Making Democracy Legible? Voter Registration and the Permanent Electronic Electoral List in Benin." *Development and Change* 46(2):269–292.

Pierskalla, Jan H. and Audrey Sacks. 2020. "Personnel Politics: Elections, Clientelistic Competition and Teacher Hiring in Indonesia." *British Journal of Political Science* 50(4):1283–1305.

Pinder, Craig C. 2014. *Work Motivation in Organizational Behavior.* New York: Psychology Press.

Pinkney, Robert. 1972. *Ghana Under Military Rule, 1966-1969.* London: Methuen.

Pinkney, Robert. 1997. *Democracy and Dictatorship in Ghana and Tanzania.* London: Macmillan Press.

Pinkston, Amanda Leigh. 2016. Insider Democracy: Private Sector Weakness and the Closed Political Class in Democratic Africa. PhD thesis, Harvard University.

Pitcher, Anne. 2012. *Party Politics and Economic Reform in Africa's Democracies.* Cambridge: Cambridge University Press.

Pitcher, Anne, Mary H. Moran and Michael Johnston. 2009. "Rethinking Patrimonialism and Neopatrimonialism in Africa." *African Studies Review* 52(1):125–156.

Pitcher, M. Anne. 2017. "Party System Competition and Private Sector Development in Africa." *The Journal of Development Studies* 53(1):1–17.

Posner, Daniel N. 2005. *Institutions and Ethnic Politics in Africa*. Cambridge: Cambridge University Press.

Posner, Daniel N. and Daniel J. Young. 2018. "Term Limits: Leadership, Political Competition and the Transfer of Power." In *Institutions and Democracy in Africa: How Rules of the Game Shape Political Developments*, ed. Nic Cheeseman. Cambridge: Cambridge University Press, pp. 260–278.

Pottie, David. 2003. "Party Finance and the Politics of Money in Southern Africa." *Journal of Contemporary African Studies* 21(1):5–26.

Price, Robert M. 1975. *Society and Bureaucracy in Contemporary Ghana*. Berkeley: University of California Press.

Rabinowitz, Beth. 2018. *Coups, Rivals, and the Modern State*. Cambridge: Cambridge University Press.

Raffler, Pia. 2020. "Does Political Oversight of the Bureaucracy Increase Accountability? Field Experimental Evidence from a Dominant Party Regime." *American Political Science Review*, forthcoming.

Rainey, Hal G. and Paula Steinbauer. 1999. "Galloping Elephants: Developing Elements of a Theory of Effective Government Organizations." *Journal of Public Administration Research and Theory* 9(1):1–32.

Rakner, Lise and Nicolas van de Walle. 2009. "Opposition Weakness in Africa." *Journal of Democracy* 20(3):108–121.

Randall, Vicky and Lars Svåsand. 2002. "Party Institutionalization in New Democracies." *Party Politics* 8(1):5–29.

Rasul, Imran and Daniel Rogger. 2018. "Management of Bureaucrats and Public Service Delivery: Evidence from the Nigerian Civil Service." *The Economic Journal* 128(608):413–446.

Rasul, Imran, Daniel Rogger and Martin J. Williams. 2021. "Management, Organizational Performance, and Task Clarity: Evidence from Ghana's Civil Service." *Journal of Public Administration Research and Theory* 31(2):259–277.

Rauch, James and Peter Evans. 2000. "Bureaucratic Structure and Bureaucratic Performance in Less Developed Countries." *Journal of Public Economics* 75(1):49–71.

Rauschenbach, Mascha. 2017. "Mobilizing Party Supporters: The Allocation of Campaign Rallies in Ghana's 2012 Elections." Working Paper, March 10.

Reno, William. 1999. *Warlord Politics and African States*. Boulder, CO: Lynne Rienner Publishers.

Resnick, Danielle. 2013. "Personalistic Policy-Making in a Vibrant Democracy: Senegal's Fragmented Response to the 2007/08 Food Price Crisis." UNU WIDER Working Paper 15/2013.

Resnick, Danielle. 2014. *Urban Poverty and Party Populism in African Democracies*. Cambridge: Cambridge University Press.

Reuter, Ora John and Jennifer Gandhi. 2011. "Economic Performance and Elite Defection from Hegemonic Parties." *British Journal of Political Science* 41(1):83–110.

Reynolds, Andrew. 1995. "Debate: PR and Southern Africa: The Case for Proportionality." *Journal of Democracy* 6(4):117–124.

Ricart-Huguet, Joan. 2020. "Colonial Education, Political Elites, and Regional Political Inequality in Africa." *Comparative Political Studies* 54(14): 2546–2580. 0010414021997176.

Riedl, Rachel Beatty. 2014. *Authoritarian Origins of Democratic Party Systems in Africa*. Cambridge: Cambridge University Press.

Ritz, Adrian, Gene A. Brewer and Oliver Neumann. 2016. "Public Service Motivation: A Systematic Literature Review and Outlook." *Public Administration Review* 76(3):414–426.

Roberts, Tyson. 2019. "Why Did Many Voters Boycott Benin's April 28 Elections?" Washington Post Monkey Cage Blog, May 10, 2019. https://www.washingtonpost.com/politics/2019/05/10/why-did-many-voters-boycott-benins-april-elections/

Robinson, James A. and Ragnar Torvik. 2016. "Endogenous Presidentialism." *Journal of the European Economic Association* 14(4):907–942.

Robinson, James A. and Thierry Verdier. 2013. "The Political Economy of Clientelism." *The Scandinavian Journal of Economics* 115(2):260–291.

Roessler, Philip. 2016. *Ethnic Politics and State Power in Africa: The Logic of the Coup-Civil War Trap*. Cambridge: Cambridge University Press.

Roll, Michael, ed. 2014. *The Politics of Public Sector Performance: Pockets of Effectiveness in Developing Countries*. Abingdon: Routledge.

Ronen, Dov. 1975. *Dahomey: Between Tradition and Modernity*. Ithaca: Cornell University Press.

Rose-Ackerman, Susan. 1978. *Corruption: A Study in Political Economy*. New York: Academic Press.

Rose-Ackerman, Susan. 1999. *Corruption and Government: Causes, Consequences and Reform*. Cambridge: Cambridge University Press.

Ross, Michael L. 2012. *The Oil Curse: How Petroleum Wealth Shapes the Development of Nations*. Princeton: Princeton University Press.

Rouban, Luc. 2007. "Public Management and Politics: Senior Bureaucrats in France." *Public Administration* 85(2):473–501.

Saffu, Yaw. 2003. "The Funding of Political Parties and Election Campaigns in Africa." In *Funding of Political Parties and Election Campaigns Handbook Series*, eds. Reginald Austin and Maja Tjernström. Stockholm: International Institute for Democracy and Electoral Assistance, pp. 21–30.

Sakyi, E. K., K. S. Agomor and Daniel Appiah. 2015. "Funding Political Parties in Ghana: Nature, Challenges and Implications." International Growth Centre Working Paper.

Sanches, Edalina Rodrigues. 2018. *Party Systems in Young Democracies: Varieties of Institutionalization in Sub-Saharan Africa*. London: Routledge.

Saylor, Ryan. 2014. *State Building in Boom Times: Commodities and Coalitions in Latin America and Africa*. Oxford: Oxford University Press.

Scartascini, Carlos, Cesi Cruz, and Philip Keefer. 2021. Database of Political Institutions 2020. http://dx/doi.org/10.18235/0003049

Schuster, Christian, Lauren Weitzman, Kim Sass Mikkelsen et al. 2020. "Responding to COVID-19 through Surveys of Public Servants." *Public Administration Review* 80(5):792–796.

Scott, James C. 1969. "Corruption, Machine Politics, and Political Change." *American Political Science Review* 63(4):1142–1158.

Scott, James C. 1972. "Patron-Client Politics and Political Change in Southeast Asia." *American Political Science Review* 66(01):91–113.

Seawright, Jason and John Gerring. 2008. "Case Selection Techniques in Case Study Research." *Political Research Quarterly* 61(2):294–308.

Seely, Jennifer C. 2009. *The Legacies of Transition Governments in Africa: The Cases of Benin and Togo.* New York: Palgrave Macmillan.

Sharife, Khadija. 2016. "Flaws in Botswana's Diamond Industry." *World Policy Journal* 33(2):77–81.

Shefter, Martin. 1977. "Party and Patronage: Germany, England, and Italy." *Politics and Society* 7:403–451.

Shleifer, Andrei and Robert W. Vishny. 1993. "Corruption." *The Quarterly Journal of Economics* 108(3):599–617.

Shugart, Matthew Soberg and Rein Taagepera. 1989. *Seats and Votes.* New Haven: Yale University Press.

Sigman, Rachel. 2022. "Which Jobs for Which Boys? Party Finance and the Politics of State Job Distribution in Africa." *Comparative Political Studies* 55(3):351–385.

Sigman, Rachel, Valeriya Mechkova, Jan Meyer-Sahling, Christian Schuster and Kim Sass Mikkelsen. 2018. "Civil Service Management Practices for a More Motivated, Committed and Ethical Public Service in Ghana." Report Prepared for the Ghana Public Services Commission.

Simmons, Beth A. 1997. *Who Adjusts?: Domestic Sources of Foreign Economic Policy During the Interwar Years.* Princeton: Princeton University Press.

Simson, Rebecca. 2018. "Ethnic (In)Equality in the Public Services of Kenya and Uganda." *African Affairs* 118(470):75–100.

Skowronek, Stephen. 1982. *Building a New American State: The Expansion of National Administrative Capacities, 1877-1920.* Cambridge: Cambridge University Press.

Slater, Dan. 2010. *Ordering Power: Contentious Politics and Authoritarian Leviathans in Southeast Asia.* New York: Cambridge University Press.

Sokomani, Andile. 2005. "Money in Southern African Politics: The Party Funding Challenge in Southern Africa." *African Security Studies* 14(4):81–90.

Soulé-Kohndou, Folashadé. 2019. "Bureaucratic Agency and Power Asymmetry in Benin–China Relations." In *New Directions in Africa–China Studies*, eds. Chris Alden and Daniel Large. Abingdon: Routledge, pp. 209–224.

Stampini, Marco, Ron Leung, Setou Diarra and Laureline Pla. 2011. "How Large is the Private Sector in Africa? Evidence from National Accounts and Labor Markets." Institute for the Study of Labor, Discussion Paper No. 6267.

Stokes, Susan C., Thad Dunning, Marcelo Nazareno and Valeria Brusco. N.d. *Brokers, Voters, and Clientelism: The Puzzle of Distributive Politics.* Cambridge: Cambridge University Press.

Sutherland, Ewan. 2011. "Republic of Benin – Chaos, Corruption and Development in Telecommunications." *Info* 13(5):63–85.

Svåsand, Lars. 2013. "The Concept of Opposition and the Structure of Opposition in Malawi." *Commonwealth & Comparative Politics* 51(3):306–325.

Tangri, Roger. 1999. *The Politics of Patronage in Africa: Parastatals, Privatization and Private Enterprise*. Trenton: Africa World Press.

Tangri, Roger and Andrew M. Mwenda. 2006. "Politics, Donors and the Ineffectiveness of Anti-Corruption Institutions in Uganda." *The Journal of Modern African Studies* 44(1):101–124.

Tangri, Roger and Andrew M. Mwenda. 2013. *The Politics of Elite Corruption in Africa: Uganda in Comparative African Perspective*. Abingdon: Routledge.

Teodoro, Manuel P. and M. Anne Pitcher. 2017. "Contingent Technocracy: Bureaucratic Independence in Developing Countries." *Journal of Public Policy* 37(4):401–429.

Thovoethin, Paul-Sewa. 2014. "Techno-Bureaucratic Governance and Developmental State in Africa: Botswana and Nigeria in Comparative Perspective." Proceedings of the 1st International Conference on Social Sciences and Humanities, Gaborone, Botswana.

Tilly, Charles. 1985. War-Making and State-Making as Organized Crime. In *Bringing the State Back In*, eds. Peter Evans, Dietrich Rueschemeyer and Theda Skocpol. Cambridge: Cambridge University Press.

Tilly, Charles. 1990. *Coercion, Capital, and European States, AD 990-1990*. Cambridge, MA: Blackwell.

Tozzo, Émile A. 2004. "Rosine Soglo, Famille et Entreprise Politique." *Politique Africaine* (3):71–90.

van de Walle, Nicolas. 2001. *African Economies and the Politics of Permanent Crisis: 1979-1999*. Cambridge: Cambridge University Press.

van de Walle, Nicolas. 2003. "Presidentialism and Clientelism in Africa's Emerging Party Systems." *The Journal of Modern African Studies* 41(2):297–321.

van de Walle, Nicolas. 2007. Meet the New Boss, Same as the Old Boss? The Evolution of Political Clientelism in Africa. In *Patrons, Clients and Policies: Patterns of Democratic Accountability and Political Competition*, eds. Herbert Kitschelt and Steven I. Wilkinson. Cambridge University Press, pp. 50–67.

Vaughan, Sarah. 2011. "Revolutionary Democratic State-Building: Party, State and People in the EPRDF's Ethiopia." *Journal of Eastern African Studies* 5(4):619–640.

Vokes, Richard and Sam Wilkins. 2016. "Party, Patronage and Coercion in the NRM'S 2016 Re-Election in Uganda: Imposed or Embedded?" *Journal of Eastern African Studies* 10(4):581–600.

VonDoepp, Peter. 2005. "Party Cohesion and Fractionalization in New African Democracies: Lessons from Struggles Over Third-Term Amendments." *Studies in Comparative International Development* 40(3):65–87.

Wahman, Michael. 2017. "Nationalized Incumbents and Regional Challengers: Opposition- and Incumbent-Party Nationalization in Africa." *Party Politics* 23(3):309–322.

Wahman, Michael. 2019. "The Cost of Politics in Malawi." Westminster Foundation for Democracy, London.

Waldner, David. 1999. *State Building and Late Development*. Ithaca: Cornell University Press.

Wantchekon, Leonard. 2003. "Clientelism and Voting Behavior: Evidence from a Field Experiment in Benin." *World Politics* 55(03):399–422.

Wardle, Peter. 2017. *Cost of Politics: Synthesis Report*. Westminster Foundation for Democracy, London.

Weber, Max. 1978. *Economy and Society: An Outline of Interpretive Sociology*. Berkeley: University of California Press.

Weghorst, Keith R. and Michael Bernhard. 2014. "From Formlessness to Structure? The Institutionalization of Competitive Party Systems in Africa." *Comparative Political Studies* 47(12):1707–1737.

Weghorst, Keith R. and Staffan I. Lindberg. 2013. "What Drives the Swing Voter in Africa?" *American Journal of Political Science* 57(3):717–734.

Weyland, Kurt Gerhard. 1998. "The Politics of Corruption in Latin America." *Journal of Democracy* 9(2):108–121.

Whitfield, Lindsay. 2009. " 'Change for a Better Ghana': Party Competition, Institutionalization and Alternation in Ghana's 2008 Elections." *African Affairs* 108(433):621–641.

Whitfield, Lindsay. 2018. *Economies After Colonialism: Ghana and the Struggle for Power*. Cambridge: Cambridge University Press.

Whitfield, Lindsay, Ole Therkildsen, Lars Buur and Anne Mette Kjær. 2015. *The Politics of African Industrial Policy: A Comparative Perspective*. Cambridge: Cambridge University Press.

Widner, Jennifer A. 1992. *The Rise of a Party-State in Kenya: From "Harambee" To "Nyayo"*. Berkeley: University of California Press.

Widner, Jennifer A. 1997. Political Parties and Civil Societies in Sub-Saharan Africa. In *Democracy in Africa: The Hard Road Ahead*. Boulder, CO: Lynne Rienner, pp. 65–81.

Williams, Martin J. 2017. "The Political Economy of Unfinished Development Projects: Corruption, Clientelism, or Collective Choice?" *American Political Science Review* 111(4):705–723.

Wireko, Ishmael. 2015. Explaining Radical Change in Ghanaian Health Care Policy. PhD thesis, University of Saskatchewan.

Woldense, Josef. 2018. "The Ruler's Game of Musical Chairs: Shuffling During the Reign of Ethiopia's Last Emperor." *Social Networks* 52:154–166.

Wood, B. Dan and Richard W. Waterman. 1991. "The Dynamics of Political Control of the Bureaucracy." *American Political Science Review* 85(3):801–828.

World Bank. 2021. "World Development Indicators." https://databank.world bank.org/source/world-development-indicators

World Bank and Government of Benin. 2007. "Benin: La corruption et la gouvernance: Rapport des resultats de l'enquete diagnostique."

World Bank Group Malawi Country Team. 2018. "Malawi Systematic Country Diagnostic: Breaking the Cycle of Low Growth and Slow Poverty Reduction." World Bank Report No. 132785.

Xiao, Shiyang and Xufeng Zhu. 2022. "Bureaucratic Control and Strategic Compliance: How do Subnational Governments Implement Central Guidelines in China?" *Journal of Public Administration Research and Theory* 32(2):342–359.

Young, Crawford. 1994. *The African Colonial State in Comparative Perspective.* New Haven: Yale University Press.

Zinnes, Clifford. 2016. "Evaluation Design and Implementation of Benin Port Project." NORC at the University of Chicago, Performance Evaluation Design Report (Final).

Zolberg, Aristide. 1966. *Creating Political Order: The Party States of West Africa.* Chicago: Rand McNally.

Index

31st December Women's Movement, 116, 204

Adjavon, Sebastien, 78
Adjei, A.B., 256
adverse selection, 111, 178, 179, 181, 186, 188, 198, 202, 203
African National Congress (ANC), 29, 35, 38, 41
Africanization, 99, 140
Afriyie, Kwaku, 206
agency problems, 9, 128, 174, 178, 179, 181, 182, 190, 193, 198, 199, 211, 213, 257
Agyeman-Duah, Ivor, 103
Ahidjo, Ahmadou, 92
Ahwoi, Kwamena, 208
Akufo-Addo, Nana, 82, 108, 136, 146, 203, 211, 257
al-Bashir, Omar, 11
alternative explanations, 11–18, 95–102
Amematekpor, Tommy, 103
Amidu, Martin, 200, 201
Amin Adam, Mohammed, 117
Amoussou, Bruno, 75, 189
Anane, Richard, 112, 201, 206
Angola, 11–13, 36, 44
Ankomah, Papa Owusu, 203
Appiagyei, Patricia, 112
Appiah-Menkah, Akenten, 114
Argentina, 2
Arouna, Boubacar, 157
Atta Mills, John, 74, 78, 82, 112, 183, 200–205, 209, 210
Attivor, Dzifa, 201
Avoka, Cletus, 203, 205
Azonhiho, Martin, 189

Bagbin, Alban, 105, 107, 108, 110, 205
Bank of Central African States, 13
Batoko, Ousmane, 157

Benin, 20
  backgrounds of politicians in, 38
  bureaucracy in, 97–100, 164–166, 226, 227, 231, 236, 256
  case selection of, 18, 19, 71, 95, 102
  civil society in, 75, 78, 90
  colonial history of, 98, 99
  democracy in, 71
  economy of, 19, 95–97, 121, 188
  electoral institutions in, 100, 101
  elite cohesion in, 193–197
  elite defection in, 256
  ethnic politics in, 76, 89, 95
  executive institutions in, 149–153, 156, 158–161, 171, 173, 174, 182–198, 212, 214, 238, 256
  extraction environment in, 77–80, 102
  extraction in, 70, 119–128
  party institutionalization in, 18, 49, 52, 70, 80–82, 87–91, 104, 120, 123, 125, 127, 128
  political financing in, 120–123, 125, 191, 193, 215
  public financing of campaigns in, 33
  regime trajectory in, 72–76
  regime trajectory of, 102
  state performance in, 19, 20
Benin Control, 125
Biaou, Rogatien, 189
Black Economic Empowerment program, 40, 61
Bongo family (of Gabon), 13
Boni Yayi, Thomas, 73, 75, 78, 88, 90, 122–126, 151, 157, 165, 173, 183, 185, 187, 189–192, 195–197, 226, 227, 256
Botchwey, Kwesi, 199, 200
Botswana, 28, 34, 51, 241–244
Botswana Democratic Party (BDP), 34, 241–244
bureaucratic institutions, 2, 9, 10, 13–15, 18, 27, 69, 71, 97–100, 128, 135, 215

305

Printed in the USA
CPSIA information can be obtained
at www.ICGtesting.com
CBHW072237201124
17775CB00008B/495